The Crisis of the
Roman Catholic Church
in America

A PEOPLE ADRIFT

PETER STEINFELS

SIMON & SCHUSTER

New York London Toronto Sydney Singapore

SIMON & SCHUSTER
Rockefeller Center
1230 Avenue of the Americas
New York, NY 10020

For information about special discounts for bulk purchases,
please contact Simon & Schuster Special Sales:
1-800-456-6798 or business@simonandschuster.com

Book design by Ellen R. Sasahara

Manufactured in the United States of America

2   4   6   8   10   9   7   5   3   1

Library of Congress Cataloging-in-Publication Data
is available.

ISBN 0-684-83663-7

To Peggy,
friend, spouse, lover,
with whom I have been thrashing out these matters
since we were seventeen.

Contents

He got into a boat and his disciples followed him. Suddenly a violent storm came up on the sea, so that the boat was being swamped by waves; but he was asleep. They came and woke him, saying, "Lord, save us! We are perishing!" He said to them, "Why are you terrified, O you of little faith?" Then he got up, rebuked the winds and the sea, and there was great calm.

Matthew 8: 23–27
(New American Bible)

Author's Note

A T six-fifteen on the morning of November 20, 1996, I left the hotel by the Chicago River and walked to Holy Name Cathedral. The dawn sky was cloudy and pale blue. The air was cold but still, as though the Windy City were holding its breath for the day's events: the funeral Mass and burial of Cardinal Joseph Bernardin, Roman Catholic archbishop of Chicago.

Zigzagging north and west from the hotel, I quickly reached the familiar streets named for the Great Lakes: Ontario, Erie, and finally Superior. Every intersection brought me closer to my earliest memories. Here was the block where I rode my tricycle at the age of three. And here, beyond the archdiocesan offices where I would later pick up my press credentials to attend the cardinal's funeral, was the busy corner where, at more or less the same age, I had dashed across the broad sweep of Michigan Avenue. I recalled my still-shaken mother describing this transgression over the telephone to her mother, while I worried that my title of "Grandma's little darling" was in serious jeopardy.

Anyone needing evidence of Catholicism's place in the life of the United States should have witnessed Chicago's mourning for Cardinal Bernardin. For a week, the event overshadowed everything else in the news media. Mourners lined up around the clock for three days and nights to pay their respects. With Chicago temperatures hovering just below and above freezing, people waited five hours to enter the yellow stone Holy Name Cathedral, where they prayed, wept, and signed the books of condolence. Old women layered themselves with sweaters. Families bundled children in parkas and drove in from the suburbs. A fourteen-year-old Baptist boy who planned to be a missionary came on crutches. At times the lines stretched for six blocks.

Now, however, less than two hours before the cathedral would be closed and readied for the midday Mass of Christian Burial, the line of mourners extended only a few ranks beyond the cathedral doors. I joined the people moving briskly through the doors and up the central aisle. At the head of the aisle, the body of Cardinal Bernardin lay in white vestments, his bishop's miter on his head, his crozier and other symbols of authority on a table closer to the altar.

I stayed only a moment. The vested body lay there in the frozen manner of a thousand stone bishops atop their tombs in the world's cathedrals. This properly honored corpse was only a reminder of the churchman I had come to admire more and more since the early 1980s, when he chaired the committee that drafted "The Challenge of Peace," a landmark 1983 pastoral statement by the American hierarchy on the morality of nuclear armaments. He had already played a key role in the American hierarchy as the general secretary of the National Conference of Catholic Bishops from 1968 to 1972 and then, while archbishop of Cincinnati, as elected president of the conference. In 1982, Bernardin was named by Pope John Paul II to head the church in Chicago, for many decades the nation's largest archdiocese.

I covered some of his major talks on religion and politics, developed friendships with several of his advisers, and joined them and him on occasions when he could relax and chat off the record. More such opportunities arose when my wife worked on a project the cardinal sponsored in his last year, a project he had put on hold while undergoing, with apparent success, surgery and treatment for pancreatic cancer. At the end of August 1996 she had been with me in Chicago for a meeting of the Religion Newswriters Association when we got a call to come to the archdiocesan office. At the press conference, Cardinal Bernardin announced that the cancer had returned and was incurable. "We can look on death as an enemy, or we can look on it as a friend," he said. "As a person of faith, I see death as a friend, as a transition from earthly life to the eternal." Over the next two months, we had several more brief opportunities to be with him before he died.

So it was more than just another assignment as a reporter that brought me to the line of mourners. But it was not the man alone. For me, the deceased cardinal was part of a vast tangle of associations and memories and hopes. There were his friends who were also my friends. The city that had become his city and that had once been my city. This church that had shaped me. The Roman Catholic Church. The American Catholic Church. The Chicago Catholic Church. Holy Name Cathedral itself. As an infant, I had been baptized in this building. The old baptistery and baptismal font were gone now. Inside the cathedral only the wooden latticework of the vaulting seemed to have survived the renovations undertaken in 1968 and 1969. (Many Catholics might have taken that as an image of the church as a whole after Vatican II.) My memory, however, needed no more. In 1950, as a fourth-grader, I had come here to see my father's painting of the Assumption of the Blessed Virgin into heaven stretched from altar to ceiling. He disparagingly called it a "poster," commissioned and quickly painted for the celebration of Pope Pius XII's solemn definition of that dogma. Later he would take us from our suburban parish to solemn high pontifical Masses here; I learned how Palestrina can stand your nerves on end and transport your spirit to that very latticework and beyond. The summer after high school, I worked nearby, sweeping the floor and filing clippings from the *Congressional Record* for the monthly publication of the Catholic Council on Working Life. A product of Catholic involvement in the labor movement and one of many change-minded groups that gave Chicago Catholicism a special character, the Council on Working Life tried to inject Christian principles into labor relations, business practices, and economic policy. After work, I would meet Peggy O'Brien at the cathedral. Only a few feet from this corner where reporters covering the Bernardin funeral were now jammed, the two of us would kneel together for evening Mass before finding a cheap movie or walking along the lake.

All that morning I went about my assignment, getting my press credentials, finding a spot in the gaggle of reporters from which, with sufficient stretching, I could observe the ceremony and fill a notebook with scribbles. The tears that now and then welled in my eyes were not only tears of sorrow but of acknowledgment and gratitude for all these influences. Sacrament, edifice, art, doctrine, parental example, youthful devotion, adolescent romance, a teacher here, a mentor there—all part of passing on the faith from person to person, generation to generation. For millions of people in Chicago and elsewhere in the nation, the cardinal had done his part. Some he touched deeply and decisively, particularly in his last years' struggle with cancer, but for many others it was a nudge, a fleeting word on television, a phrase or concept like "seamless garment" or "consistent ethic of life," a message delivered indirectly through parish pulpits or parochial schools, or even through his management and consolidation (of which most Chicago Catholics would never be aware) of the institutions that helped their faith survive or flourish.

A longtime aide to the cardinal, Monsignor Kenneth Velo, delivered the funeral homily. Velo reached beyond the mourners in the cathedral and explicitly addressed himself to people listening on car radios or in their kitchens, in nursing homes or classrooms. "You are all dignitaries," he reminded them, "and I greet you as family and friends." He was personal, heartfelt, lovingly humorous at times. He also managed to evoke matters that appealed strongly to different groups within the church and the city, from concern about abortion and assisted suicide to compassion for those on death row, including even an old-fashioned appeal to young people to consider a life of service, like the cardinal's, as priests or sisters.

For the seventeen miles that the funeral cortege carried Cardinal Bernardin's body to Mount Carmel Cemetery in the western suburb of Hillside, people lined the streets, waving, weeping, praying. Construction workers doffed their hard hats. A purple-clad Rollerblader paused, bowed, and folded his hands in prayer. A man in a blood-smeared apron came out from his job at a meatpacker's. Sometimes the praise was simultaneously sincere and stereotyped. The cardinal was "a good man," Chicagoans told reporters. He was "like a father," a friend to all. And so on. (Four years later, New Yorkers would also talk that way about the deceased Cardinal John O'Connor.) In no small measure, people were projecting their own pains and struggles onto a religious leader whose losing battle with cancer and open and honest confrontation with death had stirred waves of identification and affection. Many people had been brought to touch again the roots of their own faith, whatever it might be, and to realize that they drew the same kind of strength from those roots as the cardinal had. For the Catholics those roots were not only personal and internal but communal and institutional—that whole network of parishes, schools, clubs, agencies, ethnic links, core beliefs, shared rites, and embedded practices that knit the church together.

The mourning and the funeral displayed the full reach of American Catholicism. Jewish leaders had conducted an unprecedented service in the cathedral the day before. The funeral itself was marked by prayers in a half dozen languages, by polyphony as well as gospel music and full-voiced congregational hymns; and the cortege to the cemetery passed elderly women sprinkling themselves with holy water as well as kids holding up signs saying, BYE JOE. The cardinal was laid to rest amidst solemn and ancient blessings, folk religiosity, and spontaneous farewells.

In a hotel room high above the Chicago River, I tried to squeeze the day's events—and even more, their meaning for the city and the church—into a story for the *Times.* The television was still following the funeral procession through Chicago's streets. Of my own bottled-up feelings, I could let out just enough to fuel the sentences and keep me hunched over my laptop. It was later, when the phone calls to the copy desk and the second edition revisions were finished, that I could sink into my emotions, soaking in them as in a hot bath. The snow was falling steadily now. I thought of James Joyce's closing to "The

Dead" in *Dubliners*—the snow covering Ireland and the lonely churchyard—and as I drifted off to sleep, like Gabriel Conroy in Joyce's story I could imagine snow falling: falling on the Chicago River, on Holy Name Cathedral, on the cemetery where Bernardin had been laid to rest, snow indeed falling throughout the whole universe, as Joyce wrote, "upon all the living and the dead."

I woke at dawn. There was yet no sun, no pink streaks in the southeast. The ground was white with the night's snow. The sky, the lake, and the river flowing like a broad, straight road beneath the hotel window were all different shades of gray. The buildings were black-and-white grids. A few tiny black figures moved, silhouetted against the snow or standing out from the wet, shiny sidewalks. A gull soared by my window.

I LIKE TO IMAGINE that this book was conceived that night. Not because I wanted to write about Cardinal Bernardin, although he plays a prominent role at points in the story, as he necessarily must in any account of recent American Catholicism. Indeed, his pioneering efforts to confront the problem of sexual abuse of minors by Catholic priests (as well as the dramatic episode of being falsely accused of abuse himself) have proved far more relevant to the church's current situation than I realized in 1996 or even when I finally began writing several years later. Yet what was visible in Chicago's cathedral and streets that day was the furthest thing from the church in crisis so often portrayed in the media, especially since the beginning of January 2002. This was a Catholicism alive and rooted, public in its service to the city and the city's poor and suffering, united in mourning with Baptist and Jewish neighbors, and speaking to the most traditional and personal of mysteries: death and the apparent unfairness of life. It was the way that the day's events wove together for me the personal and the public, the past and the present, and focused my mind on the whole fabric of American Catholicism that may have planted the seed for this project.

As senior religion correspondent for the *New York Times* since 1988, I had, of course, covered American Catholicism extensively, from papal visits to abortion politics. I had come to the paper from the editorship of *Commonweal*, a liberal journal published by Catholic laypeople, where I had toiled in the 1960s while pursuing graduate studies in history at Columbia University and before moving on to the field of bioethics and then political journalism. In 1978, I returned to *Commonweal*, serving first as executive editor, then as editor in chief. My parents were *Commonweal* readers, a species of Vatican II Catholics before their time, so distinctive in the 1930s, 1940s, and 1950s that they were typically, sometimes derisively, called "*Commonweal* Catholics." My parents were also intellectuals and artists. My father was a muralist; the offspring of a Jewish-Irish marriage, he had been raised a Catholic and had consciously chosen to devote himself to church art. In our home, the heritage of Catholic Christianity, its liturgy, theology, and history, was the stuff of everyday life, translated into fresco, mosaic, oil on wood panels, and the painted and glazed ceramic tiles that were fired in the basement kiln. This faith was obviously serious but never beyond critical examination and discussion.

Acknowledgments

M Y CONCLUSIONS about Catholicism have been influenced by the marvelous opportunity, afforded by nearly a decade of reporting religion for the *Times*, to encounter the experiences of other religious groups in the United States, primarily of evangelical and mainline Protestant Christianity, of Eastern Orthodoxy, and of Judaism in its several varieties, but also of the world faiths newly implanted here, like Islam and Hinduism, and of indigenous American faiths like Mormonism and Christian Science. I have drawn freely on my reporting for the *Times* in this book as well as on articles, reviews, and talks published in *Commonweal* and elsewhere. Where it seemed relevant, I have actually quoted these articles; more often I have simply noted the original version; but always, when I felt I said something right the first time around, I have not tried to alter my words. Two stints as a visiting professor, at the University of Notre Dame and at Georgetown, have given me a chance to reintroduce myself to scholarly work on the history and sociology of religion in Europe and the United States and to work within two Catholic institutions struggling to define and maintain their religious identity while upholding freedom of inquiry and honoring the values of diversity and pluralism.

Participation in the Lilly Seminar on Religion and Higher Education from 1997 to 2000 and in several related projects funded by the Lilly Endowment provided encounters with major scholars and educators from different religious perspectives (and none) who have grappled with issues of faith, pluralism, and intellectual life. Similarly, issues of faith, pluralism, and political, cultural, and economic activity were the meat and potatoes of a three-year study, American Catholics in the Public Square, that I codirected between 2000 and 2003, one of a family of projects supported by the Pew Charitable Trusts examining the role of major religious traditions in civic life.

This book reflects a lifetime of influences—people, publications, and events. Only a small fraction have made their way into the text or notes. Even to begin listing the others—theologians, historians, social scientists, activists, editors, writers, teachers, and just friends, as well as important books and conferences—would be impossible, and in the case of some very thoughtful, devoted, and helpful church officials, might associate them with conclusions for which they are in no way responsible. I would like to acknowledge them all collectively while thanking, in particular, two individuals whose capacity for intellectual analysis, concern for justice, responsiveness to pastoral needs, and commitment to the gospel have inspired me over many years.

The Reverend J. Bryan Hehir, student and teacher of ethics and international affairs, explicator of papal texts and church-state theory, has served at different times as an adviser to the bishops, professor at Georgetown and Harvard, pastor of Saint Paul's Church in Cambridge, Massachusetts, consultant to Catholic Relief Services, head of the Harvard Divinity School, and most recently of Catholic Charities USA. The Reverend Monsignor Philip J. Murnion was one of the remarkable priests my wife and I met decades ago at Saint Gregory the Great Parish in Manhattan, where he presided at the First Communion of our children. I am convinced that through his work as director of the National Pastoral Life Center and related endeavors he knows more than any other one person about what is happening at every level and in every region of the Catholic Church in the United States. He should have written this book, if he didn't have better things to do. Although I discussed this book with both Bryan and Phil at various points in its writing, neither of them has read a word of it, let alone endorsed its framework or conclusions. There is not a chapter, however, that is not marked by their ideas or written without thought to their potential criticism.

Finally, my deep gratitude to Alice Mayhew. Her guidance, patience, and persistence as an editor made this book possible. Her friendship made it, amazingly enough for such a drawn-out and sometimes painful project, fun.

Introduction

T ODAY the Roman Catholic Church in the United States is on the verge of either an irreversible decline or a thoroughgoing transformation.

A few years ago, that proposition might have seemed melodramatic, typical journalistic sensationalism. Then, in the first half of 2002, the church was hit with a gale of revelations about sexual molestation of minors by priests, and as the winds of scandal continued to howl and howl, it seemed that no statement about the Catholic Church was too melodramatic or exaggerated to get a serious hearing. My own analysis of the sex scandal, somewhat different from the standard versions, will come later. But the important point is that the church faced these rather stark alternatives of decline or transformation before the revelations and would do so today even if this shocking sexual misconduct had never occurred. The reasons the church faces major choices about its future, while not unrelated to aspects of the scandal, go even deeper, to two intersecting transitions in American Catholic life. How the church responds (or fails to respond) to those transitions will determine its course for much of this century.

That future is obviously of great interest to devout Catholics. It should be of interest, in fact, to other thoughtful Americans, and to non-Americans who recognize the place that the American church occupies in both the world's most powerful nation and the world's largest single religious body. The fate of American Catholicism will have a significant impact on the nation's fabric, its political atmosphere, its intellectual life, and its social resilience. It will have a significant impact on worldwide Catholicism; in short, on the world.

1

The American Catholic Church is a unique institution. In ways obvious or mysterious, profound or trivial, the Catholic Church provides a spiritual identity for between 60 and 65 million Americans, approximately one-fourth of the population. These millions are Catholic in amazingly diverse ways. For some, their faith is the governing force of their lives. For others, it is a childhood memory with little impact (so they think) on their adult existence, something casually evoked by a poll taker's question, for want of any other religious label. There are Catholics for whom the church is the source of peace and joy, and Catholics for whom it is the cause of fierce anger and outrage. Not infrequently, these are the same Catholics. In recent years, if the Gallup poll is believed, approximately 30 million Catholics go to Mass at least once a week, although this total appears to have at least temporarily dropped by several million because of the sex scandal. Other measures put the number at Sunday Mass on an ordinary weekend at somewhat under 20 million. Another 15 to 17 million go to Mass regularly, some at least monthly, many of them "almost" every week. Even in the year of the sex scandal, half of the nation's Catholics say that their religion is "very important" in their lives, and another third say it is "fairly important."

The church spans the nation with its parishes, elementary and secondary schools, colleges and universities, hospitals and clinics, and a social service system second only to the government's. Despite the impact of the sex scandals, Catholicism remains a powerful moral force in a society with fewer and fewer moral authorities of any sort.

Like virtually no other American institution, the Catholic church is a bridge. Unlike the nation's second largest religious body, the Southern Baptist Convention, or many other geographically concentrated faith groups, the Catholic church links regions: Catholic New England with Catholic New Mexico, by way of the urban Midwest— Cleveland, Chicago, Milwaukee, Saint Louis. What is more crucial, the church bridges races and classes, suburban neighborhoods and inner-city ghettoes. It links power brokers on Wall Street or Capitol

Hill, whose grandparents were immigrants from Europe, with newly arrived immigrants from Latin American, Haiti, the Philippines, and Southeast Asia.

In Los Angeles, for example, the cardinal archbishop, Roger Mahony, has mixed easily with the city's newspaper editors and Hollywood executives, but he is also viewed as an advocate for struggling Hispanics and other outsiders. In his archdiocese's 287 parishes, Mass is said in thirty-eight languages. More than half of the Brooklyn diocese's parishioners are said to speak English as their second language. In Holland, Michigan, the home of the tulip festivals and a daunting number of denominations descended from Dutch Calvinism, Saint Francis de Sales Catholic Church often greets callers with a phone message in both Spanish and English—and has a special monthly Mass in Vietnamese.

A church that embraces so many different groups inevitably becomes not only a bridge but also a battleground for the culture wars dividing American society. Many of the issues facing Catholicism mirror those of the larger society: anxieties over rapid change, sexuality, gender roles, and the family; a heightening of individualism and distrust of institutions; the tension between inclusiveness and a need for boundaries; a groping for spiritual meaning and identity; doubts about the quality of leadership.

THE SIZE AND STRETCH of American Catholicism would have been unthinkable, probably even appalling, to most of the leading citizens of the young United States two centuries ago. At the time of the American Revolution, the twenty-five thousand Catholics in the former colonies constituted but one-tenth of 1 percent of the population, and their church, in the eyes of many of their countrymen, embodied everything that the brash new nation was striving to escape. Catholicism was the hereditary foe of the liberty in whose name the Revolution had been fought. It was the seedbed of superstition and the sworn enemy of Protestant conscience, enlightened reason, and scientific advancement. Worldly, corrupt, and cynical, the Church of Rome was viewed as a stronghold of priestcraft, moral corruption, medieval obscurantism, and monarchical tyranny. New England piety and Enlightenment rationalism, however divided in other respects, could unite on this.

Those Revolutionary-era forebears could scarcely have imagined, certainly not with equanimity, that in a little more than a century, the Catholic Church would become the nation's single largest religious body. On the eve of the nation's bicentennial, Catholicism would be implanted in 18,500 parishes; the church had created a skein of flourishing institutions, with 8,500 elementary schools and 1,600 high schools, 245 colleges and universities, 750 hospitals and health clinics that, along with a network of social services, treated or assisted over 35 million people each year. In many a Northern and Midwestern city, Catholic spires defined neighborhoods the way that Congregational, Presbyterian, Methodist, and Baptist steeples had anchored rural villages and small towns.

What would have assuredly baffled those first generations of Americans even more is the fact that by the middle of the twentieth century, Roman Catholicism, the once alien creed, had become virtually identified with Americanism. In the 1940s and 1950s, there was scarcely a more reliable indicator of being patriotic, it seemed, than being Catholic. It would not be long before the last barrier fell: in 1960, John F. Kennedy was elected president.

Having confounded the assumptions and expectations of early Americans about Catholicism's American destiny, history now did the same to Catholics. The church had won its vaunted place in the American mainstream by standing apart, by celebrating and inculcating democratic and conventional middle class values, but in its own way—at arm's length and within its own all-embracing institutions. Now the defensiveness could be relaxed; the permeable membrane with which the church had guarded its members could be officially dissolved. But barely had the American Catholic Church sunk back for a few moments of comfort into the soft upholstery of acceptance than it was thrown into turmoil.

The sources of that turmoil were both internal and external. First and foremost, the Second Vatican Council upended Catholicism's theological and liturgical certainties. But it was the church's fate that such an unprecedented effort at self-scrutiny and renewal coincided with all that was summed up in the shorthand phrase "the sixties." In the United States that meant the civil rights struggle, the rise of a youthful counterculture, and the conflict over Vietnam. The civil rights struggle, although it began in the South, where Catholics were lightly represented, posed painful questions about widespread attitudes and practices to which Catholics had individually and in-stitutionally often accommodated. Eventually the campaign against racial discrimination sent tremors through the urban neighborhoods that had long been Catholic ethnic strongholds. Likewise, the coun-tercultural revolt that dumped the gray flannel suit, "I like Ike," and *Leave It to Beaver* for drugs, sex, and rock 'n' roll struck hard at the moral restraint and respectability that the church had taught to waves of immigrants and their suburban children, sometimes as though equivalent to the gospel itself. Finally, America's engage-ment in Vietnam, denounced by Catholic priests and church-bred antiwar activists, tore at American Catholics' confidence that their faith and their enthusiastic Americanism coincided.

American Catholicism, in other words, would not have escaped conflict and change even if there had been no Second Vatican Coun-cil. Inner-city parishes would have felt the consequences of suburban growth and white flight. The religious patterns of immigrant sub-cultures would have been frayed by the educational and economic successes of the postwar generations. Catholic marriages, sexual mores, and attitudes about male and female roles would have been shaken by the pill, the sexual revolution, and the women's move-ment. But the Council magnified the theological repercussions of these developments. It emboldened critics within the church and le-

gitimated new thinking that ultimately touched even the most intimate recesses of spiritual life.

Americans, regardless of their religious loyalties, were fascinated
by the Second Vatican Council and by Pope John XXIII, the pontiff
who called it against the advice of his Roman bureaucracy. The
country had changed since anti-Catholicism contributed to the defeat of Al Smith's 1928 presidential campaign. Non-Catholics had
come to appreciate, although still with a trace of envy and forebod-
ing, the size of the church and its place in their communities. At the
same time, Catholicism retained for many people an aura of mystery,
of the exotic, even of the forbidden or sinister. And for Catholic and
non-Catholic alike, the church had come to symbolize unyielding
permanence, whether interpreted as an anachronistic obstacle to
modern progress or as a solid rock in a convulsive landscape. The
Council suddenly revealed the church less as the unmovable rock of
Peter than as the barque of Peter, a ship being trimmed and re-
trimmed to catch breezes and ride out tempests, stanching leaks and
undertaking repairs even as it navigated treacherous currents.

What happened in Rome when the world's Catholic bishops gathered in four separate sessions of roughly two months each from 1962
to 1965 summoned up deep feelings about permanence and change,
steadfastness and adaptation. Americans also realized that the Council and its aftermath had very practical consequences for their own
society. Almost immediately it eased long-standing tensions between
Catholics and Protestants and between Catholics and Jews. It promised to alter the tonality of the nation's morals, to create new al-
liances in civic life, to bring new energies to neighborhoods.

Yet enthusiasm about ecumenism and "aggiornamento" (John
XXIII's Italian for "updating") rather quickly turned to talk of "a
church in crisis." In the name of the Council, priests and lay leaders
were demanding changes that startled bishops and alarmed Rome.
Catholic scholars set about digesting two centuries of theological
thought and biblical exegesis that church authorities had managed
to keep at bay. A drawn-out debate about the church's condemnation

of contraception led a papal commission to urge a change in the teaching; and when, after several years of suspense, Pope Paul VI rejected the commission's conclusions, his 1968 encyclical, *Humanae Vitae*, only spurred questioning by the clergy as well as by the laity of the church's moral competence in matters of sexuality. Theologians publicly dissented from official teaching; priests quietly or not so quietly resigned from the priesthood to marry; nuns shed not only their peculiar head-to-foot garb but, in many cases, their traditional roles as schoolteachers and nurses, and not a few left their strife-ridden religious orders altogether.

All these developments were accompanied by volleys of accusations and counteraccusations along with dire predictions from all directions about the church's future. Church authorities had assiduously cultivated the image of a church united in its beliefs; now that image appeared shattered by poll data revealing wide differences between the faithful and official teachings. As the sixties passed into the seventies, moreover, the fact that the church became a leading actor in the bitter national dispute over legalized abortion meant that any evidence that the hierarchy was losing its hold on the flock would inevitably be underlined.

No wonder the word "crisis" was so widely heard. Catholicism in the United States, perhaps as much as anywhere in the world, was being swept by conflicting visions of everything from prayer and morality to the nature of the church, even to the nature of God. The church was prodded and buffeted not only by social movements and political moods but, since 1978, by a papacy that is at once dynamic in its leadership and conservative in its policies.

EVERY VISIT OF Pope John Paul II to these shores, in 1979, 1987, 1993, and 1995, has been the occasion for taking the church's pulse, blood pressure, and temperature—and for issuing ominous diagnoses. Yet each time, the crowds and the fervor marking the visits, combined with the documented reservations of many Catholics

about the pope's teachings, indicated how difficult it was to pronounce any simple verdict on the current strength and future
prospects of American Catholicism.

Quite apart from Catholicism's endurance through two millennia
of ups and downs, Catholics were continuing to grow in numbers in
the United States. By the end of the century, there were at least 12
million more American Catholics than in the years after the Second
Vatican Council. As a percentage of the national population, Catholics had fallen back in some years, rebounded in others, but overall
held their own. The record of recent years might be compared
unfavorably to Catholic growth rates at earlier points in the century,
but it could hardly be viewed as an augur of a diminishing population. The number of students in Catholic schools, having dropped
precipitously from the mid-sixties to the 1980s, leveled off and even
increased; new schools were started even though the system's underlying finances remained tenuous. And ironically, even as Catholic
schools, once the special object of non-Catholic suspicions, struggled
for survival, they were increasingly viewed as models of educational
effectiveness, particularly for disadvantaged children, and as anchors
of inner-city neighborhoods. Likewise, although the gap between
the hierarchy's official positions and the views of many Catholics on
topics like contraception, divorce, and the restriction of the priesthood to celibate males has continued to widen, the bishops issued
pastoral letters in the 1980s that became centerpieces for national
debates about the nation's defense policies and the workings of its
economy.

The instruments for carrying out these periodic checkups on the
health of Catholicism in the United States have been extremely limited. Opinion polls have concentrated on the news media's narrow
range of favorite topics—Catholic views on contraception, abortion,
the ordination of women, and a handful of other popular issues.
Lurking behind these measuring sticks has usually been the assumption that the church must modernize, become up-to-date, adjust to
America—or fall by the wayside.

I do not accept that assumption, at least not in the form it usually takes. While it would be silly to deny that to be meaningful a faith must have at least some plausible fit with its cultural surroundings, much talk of getting in step with the times cloaks unstated or unexamined beliefs about just what the times require, usually along the lines of accommodation to secular worldviews. That being said, I also do not accept what has increasingly become the opposing assumption: that only religious groups that define themselves sharply and stubbornly in opposition to the prevailing culture are destined to flourish and grow. Both assumptions, although rooted in important truths, are oversimplified and misleading. So are evaluations of American Catholicism based on nostalgia for a Catholic "golden age" of the 1950s.

THE STARTING POINTS for this analysis are somewhat different. First, any honest examination of what might be called "leading Catholic indicators"—church attendance rates, ratios of priests to people, knowledge of the faith, financial contributions—reveals a church at risk. On closer examination, some of these trends prove to be more ambiguous and susceptible to varying interpretations than may at first seem the case. Nonetheless, American Catholicism, to put it bluntly, is in trouble. Absent an energetic response by Catholic leadership, a soft slide into a kind of nominal Catholicism is quite foreseeable. Not that Catholics will suddenly flee from the church, repudiate its creed, or spurn the solace to be found when needed in its familiar ministrations. But they will participate in its communal worship and service more and more irregularly and occasionally. Their faith will become an increasingly marginal or superficial part of their identity, bearing less and less on the important choices of their lives—about work and career and sacrifice on behalf of others, about sex and marriage and how they raise children or forgive their parents for the way they were raised. At the outside, there is even the possibility of a sudden collapse, in a single generation or two—such as has been seen in Ireland and, earlier, in French Canada—of what appeared to be a virtually impregnable Catholicism.

Second, although the issues highlighted by the media as crucial to the future of American Catholicism are not unimportant, especially when they are recognized as symptoms of deeper questions, they give a very partial sense of the challenges the church faces. The standard topics—sex, gender, priest shortage, papal authority—must be supplemented, even framed, by other concerns, especially questions of worship and spiritual life, of religious education and formation, and above all, of leadership.

Third, just as the assumptions and topics featured in media coverage of American Catholicism have grown frozen over the years, so have the analyses favored by leading figures within the church itself. Liberals and conservatives raise the same fears, make the same complaints, offer the same arguments as they did twenty years ago. Has the world stood still, one wonders, since the Second Vatican Council? Can nothing be concluded from more than three decades of postconciliar experience? Wouldn't it be a remarkable coincidence if liberals were proven right about absolutely everything and conservatives wrong— or vice versa? The time has come for analyses and recommendations that freely cross liberal-conservative party lines—and that also seek insight in the experiences of other religious groups.

Fourth, and most important, while the future of the Catholic Church in the United States is by no means sealed, American Catholicism must be seen as entering a crucial window of opportunity—a decade or so during which this thirty years' war between competing visions is likely to be resolved, fixed in one direction or another or in some sort of compromise for at least a good part of the twenty-first century.

Change, of course, will continue; it always does. But at some moments in history the options narrow; the range of possibilities jells; and barring the jolt of an extraordinary event like the Second Vatican Council, any further breaks in the pattern or changes in direction become painfully difficult and excruciatingly gradual. The Catholic conviction that the church will persevere, in one form or another, until the end of time—"The gates of hell shall not prevail against it" (Matthew 16:18)—is compatible with both vigorous health and sorry decline. It is compatible with any number of alternative futures, just as it has been compatible with any number of contrasting pasts, eras of disarray and decay no less than eras of growth and influence.

WHY DO THE NEXT ten to twenty years constitute one of those moments when the mold is being set? The answer is that the church is currently and simultaneously negotiating two key transitions.

The first transition is a passage in generations. Already a leadership formed in the dense subculture that characterized American Catholicism before the Second Vatican Council (1962–65) is being replaced by a leadership formed entirely after the Council, indeed largely in the most tumultuous period immediately following that landmark event. This succeeding leadership generation arrives with new questions but increasingly without old knowledge. And the Catholic generations that follow, the twenty-somethings and thirty-somethings now inching their way toward leadership in Catholic thought and institutions, remain a religious blank. They await a definitive religious imprint, whether from the New Age or MTV culture, the media, the Vatican, or rival forms of liberal and conservative Catholicism.

The second transition is the passage from clergy to laity. At every level of Catholic life, from parishes to hospitals and universities, from administering dioceses to providing spiritual counsel, leadership has traditionally been in the hands of priests and nuns—that is, of people who underwent an intense, shared religious formation and who, because of celibacy, lived almost entirely within the framework of Catholic institutions. The ranks of those people are shrinking. Leadership is steadily passing into the hands of laypeople, and certainly at many levels of church life this change will be permanent.

The spiritual, intellectual, and psychological formation of these new lay leaders will be highly diverse; their loyalties (and economic ties) will be to families, communities, professional groups, and so on, in a completely different fashion than was the case with priests and nuns. As the papacy asserts the claims of central authority and uniform norms at the top, the conditions that traditionally allowed that authority to be exerted effectively are disappearing at the bottom. Will these contrary pulls balance one another—or prove mutually destructive?

The combined effect of these two intersecting transitions will be enormous, but the exact outcome is not predetermined. The transitions will generate a whole series of choices for American Catholics, leaders and faithful, but the future depends on what choices are made, or left to default, as this double passage is negotiated.

So far I have referred to the Catholic Church in the United States or American Catholicism, with only glancing mention of the pope and the Vatican. Obviously, it would be fanciful to suggest that the future of the church here might be determined without regard to the directions and decisions of the church's supreme pontiff. Those decisions will be major determinants of the eventual outcome. And yet to consider the church here (or in other parts of the world) as a passive recipient of papal policy is to misapprehend Catholicism, both theologically and sociologically. American Catholic leaders have repeatedly shaped both the way that papal policy is formulated and the way it is implemented. While this book will recognize the importance of papal initiatives and constraints, the emphasis will be on how the American church responds to them.

THIS BOOK, it should be made clear, does not aim at plumbing spiritual depths or proposing a new theological vision. If the news media tend to probe Catholicism by means of opinion surveys, there are a plethora of books, usually written by and for Catholic insiders, that diagnose the church's problem and prescribe solutions strictly in terms of spirituality or theology, with scarcely any attention to the nuts and bolts of Catholic life. Whether the perspective is conservative or liberal, the problem is bad spirituality or theology and the answer is good spirituality or theology (the author's). The emphasis here, by contrast, is frankly on the institutional rather than the profoundly spiritual or theological. There is a familiar gibe that Jesus came preaching the gospel and ended up with the church. The gibe expresses an important truth. Love of God and love of neighbor, discipleship, self-emptying service, forgiveness, life led in unending praise and gratitude, life modeled on Jesus' union with the Father, on his call to conversion, on his invitation to a new kingdom, on his teaching, healing, death, and rising—the church exists not for its own sake but to be the witness, the instrument, the locus of this Spirit-filled sharing in divine glory. In that perspective it is possible to dismiss everything in this book as superficial.

But there is another truth. Even Jesus relied on institutions to announce his message and propel it into the world. He was a Jew, thinking, speaking, and acting within the story of Israel. He spoke the language of that story, and with his followers he took for granted its patriarchs, prophets, practices, and Law. Whether in affirmation or innovation, he observed his covenanted people's holy days, read their scriptures, utilized their sacred spaces, employed their roles and titles. For the institutions of Judaism, it was a time of great flux. But institutions there were, nonetheless, and when Judaism and Christianity went divergent ways in the half century after Jesus' life, it was necessary for the fledgling Jesus movement to evolve its own institutions, often modifications or extensions of the old.

Despite the tendency of people to speak, usually dismissively, of the "institutional church," there is simply no church that is not an *institutional* church. What other kind could there be? The idea of a noninstitutional church is thought-provoking but also oxymoronic, like a non-food meal or a non-water rainstorm. The Second Vatican Council's description of the Catholic Church as "people of God" may have been attractive precisely because it seemed to minimize the formal structures that had come to burden Catholicism. But it certainly did not abolish them. A people is not a population. A people is not an undifferentiated mass but a group with a sense of itself, a collective memory, a solidarity, an anticipated destiny—all of which must be preserved in formulas, rituals, written or recited epics, lines of authority, prescribed and proscribed behaviors.

This book focuses on that institutional, practical dimension of Catholicism's life. It does not deny that an institution's vitality may begin in hidden wellsprings of prayer, insight, and mysticism, and that Catholicism's vitality must issue into lives of love, sacrifice, and worship. But every great church renewal has had an institutional expression and every great church failure has institutional sources. Mystical, intellectual, and charitable energies operate within institutional frameworks, indeed sometimes spring from the frustrations of institutional shortcomings. The Catholic Church can succeed as an institution while failing as a church. But it cannot succeed as a church while failing as an institution. That, at least, is the working premise of this book.

Part One

———————+———————

Chapter One

The Battle for Common Ground

N OT everything surrounding Cardinal Bernardin's funeral in November 1996 testified to the vitality of American Catholicism. The cardinal himself had become convinced that the future of Catholicism in the United States was seriously threatened by acrimony, polarization, and a paralysis of leadership. He had given much of his dying energy to addressing that threat. Yet his efforts had given rise to more discord. At one dramatic moment during his funeral, those divisions suddenly erupted into view.

Three months earlier, on August 12, 1996, with the backing of twenty-five prominent Catholics, including seven bishops, the cardinal had announced an initiative to restore constructive discussion between conservative and liberal factions in the Catholic Church in the United States. A little over two weeks later, he learned that the pancreatic cancer had returned and spread to his liver. Knowing he possibly had only a few months to a year to live, he remained determined, he told close associates, to make this project, known as the Catholic Common Ground Initiative, a final priority and part of his legacy. It was, in fact, the subject of his last major public address, on October 24, some three weeks before he died.

By that time, the Catholic Common Ground Initiative had generated wide attention in both the Catholic and secular press and stirred both enthusiasm and opposition. In announcing the effort, Cardinal Bernardin had released a three-thousand-word statement, "Called to Be Catholic: Church in a Time of Peril." The statement was the product of three years of discussions among a group of laypeople and clergy. Bernardin offered it as an accurate description of the church's situation and a guide to the Common Ground effort.

"Will the Catholic Church in the United States enter the new millennium as a church of promise, augmented by the faith of rising generations and able to be a leavening force in our culture?" the statement had asked. "Or will it become a church on the defensive, torn by dissension and weakened in its core structures?"

The outcome, the statement went on to say, depends on whether the church can reverse the polarization and overcome the ideological litmus tests that were inhibiting candid discussion. What kinds of problems were going unaddressed? The statement listed more than a dozen, without claiming to be exhaustive:

- the changing roles of women
- the organization and effectiveness of religious education
- the Eucharistic liturgy as most Catholics experience it
- the meaning of human sexuality, and the gap between church teachings and the convictions of many faithful in this and several other areas of morality
- the image and morale of priests, and the declining ratios of priests and vowed religious to people in the pews
- the succession of laypeople to positions of leadership formerly held by priests and sisters, and the provision of an adequate formation for ministers, both ordained and lay
- the ways in which the church is present in political life, its responsibility to the poor and defenseless, and its support for laypeople in their family life and daily callings

- the capacity of the church to embrace African-American, Latino, and Asian populations, their cultural heritages, and their social concerns

- the survival of Catholic school systems, colleges and universities, health care facilities and social services, and the articulation of a distinct and appropriate religious identity and mission for these institutions

- the dwindling financial support from parishioners

- the manner of decision making and consultation in church governance

- the responsibility of theology to authoritative church teachings

- the place of collegiality and subsidiarity in the relations between Rome and the American episcopacy

The list is interesting. It includes items typically of concern to liberals in the church (women's roles, sensitivity to minority groups, consultation and relations between Rome and the American church), along with items typically of concern to conservatives (religious education, the survival of Catholic schools with a distinct religious identity, theological accountability to authoritative teachings). The list includes problems that both conservatives and liberals equally recognize—the declining number of priests, for example—although they might diagnose the causes quite differently and offer dramatically different solutions. Areas of controversy like the quality of liturgies or the church's political role are indicated without suggesting a particularly liberal or conservative remedy. The statement points to the gap between church teachings and the convictions of many Catholics on human sexuality without taking sides on how it should be closed.

ONE DOESN'T HAVE to search far to find support for the statement's claim that the Catholic Church in the United States is polarized and beset by acrimony and suspicion. It is not at all unusual for leading conservative figures to suggest that liberals are preaching heresy and promoting moral corruption, and for liberals to charge that conservatives are betraying the gospel and rebuffing the Holy Spirit.

Driving this polarization of American Catholicism is a dynamic born of Vatican II and its aftermath. The drama of the Council itself sensitized Catholics, as never before, to behind-the-scenes maneuvering and to subtle shifts in church policy. Since those who had opposed the conciliar decrees remained entrenched in the Vatican, they were suspected of stubbornly sabotaging, or at least contesting, each effort to implement the Council. And rather than clearly seize the lead of the postconciliar momentum, Pope Paul VI preferred to take two steps forward, one backward, always trying to moderate the pace of change and maintain unity by placating contending factions. It was not an unreasonable strategy. But the fear that the Council's work was being undermined and might ultimately be reversed was never dissipated. Mounting distrust fed harsher, more radical criticism, and more radical criticism fed greater resistance. Stir in the highly political, questioning, confrontational mood of the 1960s and early 1970s. Soon every Vatican pronouncement, every new theological proposal or pastoral innovation, every critical observation from left or right was scrutinized through the lens of suspicion, interpreted as a shift toward one or another extreme.

Earlier in the year in which the Common Ground Initiative was announced and Cardinal Bernardin died, two popular novels exemplified the polarization tearing at American Catholicism. *White Smoke* was written by the Reverend Andrew M. Greeley, a distinguished sociologist of religion and prolific author of popular fiction and wide-ranging commentary. *Windswept House* was written by Malachi Martin, an Irish-born former Jesuit and Vatican official. Although he had left the priesthood in 1965, Martin's novels and nonfiction dealing with religious and geopolitical conspiracies made him a darling of some conservative Catholics (he served for a while as religion editor of the conservative biweekly *National Review*).

Both books could best be called papal potboilers. Greeley's conjured up the conclave called to elect a successor to Pope John Paul II. Martin's conjured up a plot in the Vatican to force John Paul to resign.

Appearing at virtually the same time, the two books were mirror images. The liberal heroes of *White Smoke* are advocates of pluralism in the church who want to decentralize papal power. The villains are members of a sinister "Corpus Christi Institute." (No informed reader could fail to think of Opus Dei, the controversial Catholic movement that flourished in Franco Spain and has formed an international elite of conservative Catholic leaders with the blessing of John Paul II.) Rich, secretive, and ultrareactionary, in league with thugs and criminal bankers, the institute has infiltrated the Vatican. In *Windswept House*, it is the liberal enemies of papal authority who have infiltrated the Vatican and are conniving with mysterious forces of global finance. The ultraconservative heroes are but a faithful handful, sustained by a wealthy family and forced to operate clandestinely.

What is arresting, however, is not just the symmetry but the starkness of the depictions. There is not a saving grace, for instance, among Greeley's conservatives. When they are not patent liars and vicious criminals, they are oafs or toadies. They are complicit with a kidnapping, attempted murder, and near gang rape. A woman-hating, psychotic antiabortion militant who tries to assassinate the new pope (for being insufficiently pro-life) is thrown in for good measure.

That turns out to be mild compared to Martin's villains. The leadership of the Catholic Church in *Windswept House* is riddled with rings of homosexual pedophiles and, yes, satanic covens. The novel begins with a blasphemous ritual in which high papal officials enthrone Satan within the very precincts of the Vatican. This brood of vipers is sapping the Catholic faith of millions and systematically replacing it with a humanistic enthusiasm for a new world order run by secret Masonic lodges and other shadowy string pullers. If Greeley's Corpus Christi Institute was intended to call to mind a real organization, some of Martin's satanic characters were thinly disguised renditions of real church leaders.

To be sure, this is the stuff of thrillers, and no one expects thrillers, even Vatican thrillers—maybe especially Vatican thrillers—to be realistic. But both these authors were also writing with didactic purposes. They were playing with characters and plots, but they were quite serious about the underlying conflict. Did they believe the bad guys were really that bad? I asked them separately, and each said yes. Historians have often viewed popular literature as a window on what is churning, often irrationally, below the surface of a society or institution. Greeley and Martin provided a glimpse into the fierce emotions—the overheated id, if you will—of American Catholicism.

THE COMMON GROUND INITIATIVE was premised on a conviction that not only was this polarization destructive, it was also deceptive. Feeding on itself, it suppressed a silent middle, made up of moderate conservatives and moderate liberals. Despite intuitive reservations, they were regularly appealed to and spoken for by more militant voices in their own camps, roped into the dynamic of mutual distrust and worst-case interpretations. The dynamic was powerful because the silent middle was by no means of one mind; yet even though the moderates who constituted it had serious disagreements among themselves, they chafed at the polarization. The initiative was meant to articulate their reservations and give them a platform on which to engage their differences while resisting the pressure to extremes.

Cardinal Bernardin was widely perceived as a leader of the liberal wing of the Catholic hierarchy as well as a skillful mediator between entrenched blocs. Both traits explained why he had gone out of his way to ensure that conservatives were visibly represented along with liberals on the committee overseeing the initiative.

Its charter members included Mary Ann Glendon, the Harvard Law School professor who had been tapped by the pope to head the Vatican's delegation to the 1995 World Conference on Women held in Beijing. The committee also included Sister Elizabeth A. Johnson, an award-winning feminist theologian. Archbishop Rembert Weakland of Milwaukee, who had overseen the drafting of the bishops' controversial 1986 pastoral letter on the American economy, was on the committee, along with Bernardin himself, who had done the same for the 1983 bishops' letter on nuclear arms. But so was Michael Novak, author and theological defender of American capitalism, who had spearheaded the opposition of politically conservative laypeople to both those documents.

The other cardinal on the committee, Roger Mahony of Los Angeles, and several of the other bishops on it were viewed as distinctly more conservative in church matters than either Bernardin or Weakland. And still other committee members had national reputations as opponents of abortion: former Pennsylvania governor Robert P. Casey had been shut out of the 1992 Democratic convention for his antiabortion views; the legal scholar and historian John T. Noonan Jr. had written critiques of legalized abortion that explained, at least in part, why President Reagan named him to the Ninth Circuit Court of Appeals. The committee had its businessman, Barry Sullivan, a Chicago banker and later public official and utilities executive in New York, and its labor leader, John Sweeney, president of the AFL-CIO. Some of its clergy members were best known for scholarship and spirituality, others for social activism.

What was missing from this committee was certainly the firebrands, but also just the regular standard-bearers of both left and right. This was a committee of moderate liberals and conservatives, men and women with strong disagreements who could be counted on to discuss rather than denounce. And with two cardinals, two archbishops, and three bishops on the committee, along with papal favorites like Glendon and Novak and certified right-to-lifers like Casey and Noonan, it was hardly a group to start endorsing heresy.

That is what made the immediate response from other high-ranking church leaders so startling. If there was any doubt that the American church was riddled by the kind of suspicion and conflict that the Common Ground Initiative set itself the task of healing, the reception given the initiative ironically provided more than ample proof. Although Cardinal Bernardin had included other bishops and another cardinal in the Common Ground Initiative, he had not wanted it to become an official episcopal project. The initiative was going to provide a forum for contending views, and to invest that with the episcopacy's collective authority would either put the bishops in an untenable position or remove all flexibility from the initiative's proceedings. Still, Bernardin, always the consummate diplomat, carefully informed Rome of his intentions, specifically the Vatican's secretary of state, Cardinal Angelo Sodano, and the head of the Congregation for the Doctrine of the Faith, Cardinal Joseph Ratzinger. Bernardin also gave Bishop Anthony Pilla of Cleveland, then the president of the National Conference of Catholic Bishops, and all the other active American cardinals advance notice of his plans, sending them copies of the "Called to Be Catholic" document and the names of those enlisted in the effort. Bernardin knew well two standard operating rules among the Catholic hierarchy: (1) Don't take your fellow bishops by surprise. (2) Settle differences privately rather than mount public disagreement.

WITHIN HOURS OF Bernardin's announcement of the Common Ground Initiative, Cardinal Bernard Law of Boston publicly criticized it, denouncing in particular the "Called to Be Catholic" statement, which he termed "unfortunate" and showing "an ideological bias which it elsewhere decries in others."

"The fundamental flaw in this document," Cardinal Law stated, "is its appeal for 'dialogue' as a path to 'common ground.'" Yet that "flaw" could hardly be tactfully limited to the document. It was central to Cardinal Bernardin's entire initiative.

"The church already has 'common ground,'" Cardinal Law continued. "It is found in sacred Scripture and tradition, and it is mediated to us through the authoritative and binding teaching" of the church. "Dissent from revealed truth or authoritative teaching of the church," the cardinal said, "cannot be 'dialogued' away. Truth and dissent from truth are not equal partners. . . . Dialogue as a way to mediate between the truth and dissent is mutual deception."

By the usual standards of episcopal protocol, Law's response was more than blunt; it was brutal. His rejoinder was designed to strike and strike hard. The next day Cardinal James Hickey of Washington, D.C., issued a statement repeating Cardinal Law's charges even more emphatically: "True 'common ground' is found in Scripture and tradition as handed on through the teaching office of the Holy Father and the bishops." Talk of dialogue only obscures these realities, he warned. "We cannot achieve church unity by accommodating those who dissent from church teaching."

Like Cardinal Law, Hickey read into the Common Ground statement the danger of determining church teaching by opinion poll. His closing salvo targeted "compromise" of the gospel and "the church's undiluted teaching," a remarkable rebuke to the integrity of a fellow cardinal. On August 22, Cardinal Anthony Bevilacqua of Philadelphia weighed in with a similar statement, and on August 23 so did Cardinal Adam Maida of Detroit. Both statements appeared on the front pages of their archdiocesan newspapers.

Cardinal Bernardin felt compelled to reply. On August 29, he released a statement composed in question-and-answer form. He provided more detail about the genesis of the "Called to Be Catholic" statement in conversations held under the auspices of the National Pastoral Life Center. Founded and directed by a New York priest, Monsignor Philip J. Murnion, the center was devoted to the improvement of parish life through consultations, publications, and research. The cardinal noted the many favorable responses his initiative had received, including ones from Bishop Pilla and other bishops. He then candidly addressed the criticism that had issued from his fellow cardinals and defended dialogue against the charge that it was a way to erode or elude church teaching.

"The primacy of Scripture and tradition is fully recognized" in the Common Ground statement, he said, and quoted its rejection of any approach ignoring the authoritative teaching office "exercised by the bishops and the chair of Peter." Cardinal Law had wound up his critique by complaining that the centrality of Jesus, the necessary beginning of any authentic church renewal, was not introduced into "Called to Be Catholic" until the eighteenth paragraph out of twenty-seven. Without naming Law or wondering how his Boston colleague could miss something in the first, not eighteenth, paragraph, Cardinal Bernardin noted that "the statement begins by asserting that the very first condition for addressing our differences constructively must be 'a common ground centered on faith in Jesus.'" This question-and-answer statement was released, as it turned out, on the day after Bernardin had learned that his cancer had returned. He was already working on the announcement he would make to the press the next day: he was dying.

ONE WOULD HAVE to go back to the nineteenth century to find such a public challenge of a high-ranking American Catholic official by equally high-ranking colleagues. Naturally people began to doubt that this campaign was entirely spontaneous. If it had been orchestrated, by whom? And why?

Rome was one answer, and Pope John Paul II's consistent worry about departures from unpopular church teachings. But Rome did not typically react so swiftly or with such imprecise scrutiny of a suspect document. Nor did Rome ordinarily countenance, let alone encourage, public disputes between cardinals. Sometime later, moreover, Cardinal Ratzinger was reported to have expressed puzzlement at the brouhaha to an American bishop, and the pope himself encouraged Cardinal Roger Mahony to participate in the project.

A simpler, if not mutually exclusive, explanation led not to Rome but to Cape Cod. Evidently, as Cardinal Bernardin sent out advance word of his initiative, three other cardinals—Hickey, Bevilacqua, and William Baum, Hickey's predecessor in Washington, who had gone to work in the Vatican—were on the Cape vacationing with

Cardinal Law. It seems likely that they had discussed the Common Ground proposal there and determined to oppose it.

That likelihood leaves unanswered the "Why?" of these cardinals' rebuke, and particularly the "Why so public?" Was it sheer power politics—Cardinal Law wishing to assert his emerging preeminence among the American cardinals over against Cardinals Bernardin and Mahony? Was it offended amour propre—Cardinal Bernardin, following other precedents, had given them notice of his plans but without asking for their approval? Was it the tug-of-war that had gone on for years between Bernardin and Law over whether policies for the American church should be established through the deliberations of the entire bishops' conference and its elected officers, as Bernardin firmly believed, or within the smaller circle of cardinals, named by the pope, as Law preferred?

Or was it, as several conservative Catholic publications suggested, something still more serious—the specter of a concerted liberal offensive, a drive to entrench views otherwise on the wane, possibly even to provoke an American schism? The year 1996 had seen a not very successful petition drive for a vague list of church reforms by Call to Action, a protean Catholic Church reform group that rather indiscriminately embraces thoroughly radical critics of the church alongside moderate Catholic liberals and even a few bishops, and by Catholics for a Free Choice, an abortion-rights lobby that consistently attacks the hierarchy. The same year, Archbishop John Quinn, the retired archbishop of San Francisco and a former president of the National Conference of Catholic Bishops, gave a lecture at Oxford diplomatically but unmistakably criticizing the centralization of power in the Vatican during John Paul II's papacy.

Only fanciful suspicions of court intrigue could link the petition drive, Archbishop Quinn's lecture, and the Common Ground Initiative. But suspicion had become the order of the day in many Catholic circles. The anti–Common Ground cardinals, though they probably did not sniff the sulfuric odor of schism, may have envisioned some snowballing of initiatives that, in one way or another, imperiled the existing lines of authority and all the doctrines that authority upheld. Hence their alarm. It is the same alarm that seven years later made conservative bishops in the United States and Rome immediately denounce the Boston-based lay group Voice of the Faithful that arose in the wake of the sex scandal.

Whatever the exact explanation, the episode confirmed the Common Ground Initiative's diagnosis of a church in which, at the leadership level if not in the pews, everyone was operating on hair trigger, mental muscles tensed to think the worst, ready to perceive a doctrinally cautious appeal for dialogue as a subversive act.

The reaction of his fellow cardinals deeply wounded Cardinal Bernardin and added another burden to his last months. His close associates were well aware of this, and a much larger group of Chicagoans and Bernardin sympathizers nationally felt the sting of the assault on "their" cardinal. Those were the feelings that momentarily but unforgettably erupted at the cardinal's funeral.

Monsignor Kenneth Velo was halfway through his homily. He had recalled many of Cardinal Bernardin's traits and deeds. He had just mentioned the cardinal's readiness to take "hard stands"—on nuclear disarmament, health care for the poor, racial injustice—even in his dying weeks protesting partial-birth abortions on the Capitol steps and writing to the Supreme Court in opposition to the legalization of assisted suicide. Both inside and outside the church, the cardinal "took initiatives," the homilist continued. That word signaled what was coming. "He had a hard time with people who directed lives by using rearview mirrors," Velo said. "He wanted people to come around the table to see not what divides us but what brings us together," he went on. *"He wanted to make common ground holy ground."*

The words "common ground" later appeared without capitalization in Velo's text. But the instant they were uttered, the cathedral shuddered with a flash of affirmation. Few people had any doubt about the reference. The congregation rose, applauding, hundreds of robed priests, choir members, and dignitaries. Facing them about

150 bishops sat in ranks behind the altar, prominent among them the very cardinals who had criticized Bernardin's Common Ground Initiative. Some bishops quickly—but many hesitantly, uncertainly—got to their feet; and then they too were all standing, even if a bit sheepishly. There was no escaping the crossfire of feelings in the American Catholic Church.

NOT EVEN A massive display of affection and grief for perhaps the most influential Catholic churchman in the United States since the Second Vatican Council could mask the deep divisions in the church. Ultimately, those divisions rest on divergent readings of what has been happening in Catholicism generally and the American church in particular. And what has been happening? The full answer, as Cardinal Bernardin's funeral demonstrates, involves psychological and spiritual realities that are very real although they elude easy measurement. Yet one simple starting point might be some leading Catholic indicators.

- In 1965, there were 46.6 million Catholics in the United States. In 2002, there were 65.3 million. In 1965, they constituted 24 percent of the population. In 2002, they constituted 23 percent.
- In 1965, approximately 65 percent of Catholics attended Mass every Sunday. In 2002, the rate was approximately 34 percent. In 1965, probably half or fewer of those attending Mass received Communion. In 2002, probably 90 percent received Communion.
- In 1965, there were 58,132 priests. In 2002, there were 45,713. In 1965, there were 994 ordinations. In 2002, there were 479 ordinations.
- In 1965, there was one priest for approximately every 800 Catholics. In 2002, there was one priest for approximately every 1,400 Catholics. Because priests are aging, there is one nonretired priest for approximately 1,900 Catholics.

- In 1965, the average age of diocesan priests in active ministry was 46. In 2002, it was almost 60. In 1965, almost half of all diocesan priests were under 45. In 2002, less than 20 percent were under 45.

- In 1965, there were 179,954 sisters in religious orders. In 2002, there were 75,000. In 1965, there were 12,271 brothers in religious orders. In 2002, there were 5,690.

- In 1965, there were no married or single men ordained to be permanent deacons and almost no laypeople employed full-time in pastoral work by the church. In 2002, there were 13,764 permanent deacons and another 14,000 full-time lay "ecclesial ministers" working alongside sisters in pastoral posts.

- In 1965, there were 17,637 parishes. In 2002, there were 19,496. In 1965, there were 15,00 Catholic parish elementary schools, with 4.5 million students, who constituted almost 50 percent of the Catholic school-age population. In 2002, there were 7,000 schools, with 2 million students, constituting less than 25 percent of the school-age population.

- In 1965, there were 304 Catholic colleges and universities, with 385,000 students. In 2002, there were 238 Catholic colleges and universities, with 724,000 students.

- In 1965, there were 952 hospitals and health facilities, treating 17 million individuals annually. In 2002, there were 1,000 hospitals and health facilities plus 1,500 special-care homes, treating almost 90 million individuals annually.

- In 1965, one person converted to Catholicism for every 362 Catholics. In 2002, one person converted for every 405 Catholics.

- In 1965, Catholics gave an estimated 2.2 percent of their income to the church. In 2002, they most likely gave less than half of that.

To ignore these indicators would be folly. To pretend that they are self-interpreting would be delusory. In some cases, the trends are confusing. In other cases, they have leveled off or possibly reversed themselves. In almost all cases, their meaning cannot be discerned apart from the factors that are proposed to have caused them. Should Catholics take comfort in the overall increase in their numbers? But if that increase is due largely to immigration from Catholic countries, what does it say about the health of the church here? What does it say about Catholic participation in the church's liturgical life of prayer if Mass attendance has significantly decreased but the proportion of worshipers receiving Communion has shot up? Can we interpret figures about Mass attendance without some theory about why it has declined—or why it was once so much higher? Can we interpret figures about increased reception of Communion without plumbing the meaning this has in the spiritual lives of the partakers? Does the change in the ratio of yearly conversions to the size of the Catholic population reflect a decline in evangelizing fervor—or an ecumenical spirit that has reduced the pressure on spouses in "mixed marriages" to convert? Given that ecumenism, isn't the number of converts impressively high?

A great many of these leading Catholic indicators appear to trace a pattern of decline and to signal the onset of crisis. When conservative Catholics have made these figures—for example, the decline in Mass attendance or the closing of Catholic schools—part of their criticism of recent changes in the church, liberal Catholics have often preferred to ignore the data or find silver linings in the clouds. When liberal Catholics have cited these figures—for example, the shrinking numbers of vocations to the priesthood—as grounds for further changes, conservatives have challenged the accuracy of the data or minimized their import. Those strained reactions strike me as whistling past the graveyard.

————

AT THE SAME TIME it must be admitted that the different interpretations of these leading Catholic indicators flow from something deeper and larger—from how they are fit into different narratives, different explanatory accounts, of what has happened in Catholicism over the last half century. The pivotal event in those accounts is always, and quite rightly, the Second Vatican Council.

One narrative line—it could be labeled ultraconservative—is entertained by a hard core of influential Vatican officials and ultraconservative American laity like those agitating for the restoration of the Latin Mass. For them, the Council was an unfortunate mistake, rooted in mischievous theological enthusiasms and perpetrated by naïve bishops. Events have amply demonstrated that the "prophets of doom" who warned Pope John XXIII of the Council's dangers were right. With perseverance, however, the Council's innovations can be restricted, then reversed, even if it requires the paring away of millions of nominal Catholics who are "American" rather than loyally " Roman." John Paul II's papacy has provided an opportunity for some of this restoration, but the pope, unfortunately in this view, has never endorsed the effort.

Far more widely held—in fact, possessing almost official status—is another, moderately conservative, story line: the Council was indeed the work of the Holy Spirit, a landmark event, but one badly misrepresented by politicized media, liberal theologians, and restless clergy.

On the one hand, the Council introduced badly needed reforms, gave the church a jolt of energy, and expedited Catholicism's transformation from a European-based to a genuinely global faith. On the other hand, in the name of a vague "spirit of the Council" rather than its actual documents, all sorts of established teachings and practices were opened to challenge. Hierarchy was to give way to democracy, traditional morality to current opinion, established doctrines to the latest consensus of theologians and biblical scholars. In the United States, conciliar changes accelerated the Catholic population's cultural assimilation and the erosion of a distinctly Catholic subculture and its supportive institutions.

This narrative takes a turn in 1978 with the election of Karol Wojtyla to the papacy. Pope John Paul II embarked on a firm course of consolidation. In tireless journeying and dramatic, media-friendly events, he reached over the heads of questioning clergy or independent-minded hierarchies to touch Catholic populations directly. He fired warning shots across the bows of those groups in the church that challenged Vatican leadership. Religious orders were put on notice when, in 1981, he suspended the Jesuits' internal procedures to put his own man temporarily at their head. Theologians were warned with official disavowals of a few leading dissenters. National conferences of bishops were reined in. Some, like the Dutch and Brazilians, were summoned to Rome for papal review; all were subject to firm instructions during papal visits and gradually reshaped by the pope's power to appoint men to his liking as bishops retired or died. A steady stream of encyclicals from the pope and doctrinal injunctions from the Congregation for the Doctrine of the Faith gave official cues to interpreting the work of Vatican II. A revised Code of Canon Law (1983) and a comprehensive Catechism of the Catholic Church (1992) codified the Council's actions, integrated them into past teachings, and signaled that the period of their open-ended interpretation was being brought to a close.

Consolidation, in this view, is by no means a return to the status quo ante. The church's advocacy of religious freedom and human rights, it is said, is a permanent conciliar gain. So is a new and fearless evangelization. If John Paul sometimes had a more confrontational edge than the Council fathers, that was only a necessary corrective, born of his Polish experience and the lessons of postconciliar disarray. In contrast to liberal accommodation, he exemplified a kind of heroic Catholicism likely to stir the hearts of young people. It will take time, of course. The resistance to his vision is deeply entrenched. The fruits of his papacy have barely begun to emerge, let alone ripen.

———

AT LEAST TWO opposing stories of the Council and its aftermath come from the other side of the Catholic spectrum. The first, the liberal narrative, is probably the most widely recounted. The Council was a singular inspiration, the Holy Spirit working through the "good" Pope John XXIII. The Council concluded a real armistice in the war that the church, for at least two centuries, had been waging against modernity. It tore down the ramparts that Catholicism had been erecting since the Reformation and the Scientific Revolution and within which it had felt almost claustrophobically besieged since the Enlightenment and the French Revolution. The Council had reversed the tendency to structure the church, whether in governance or at prayer, in ever more hierarchical, centralized, and juridical terms rather than communal, local, and mystical ones. The Council had affirmed freedom of conscience and religion, sought common ground with Protestant and Orthodox Christians, reached out to other faiths and especially to the Jewish people, and declared solidarity with the present age.

True, the Council fathers had reaffirmed past teachings. That was to be expected. What was stunningly new was something else. Arriving in Rome in October 1962, the bishops had been handed a conventional set of warmed-over condemnations and a tightly plotted procedure for approving them, all the work of those "prophets of doom." And the bishops overwhelmingly rejected it. They took charge of the agenda, they chose their own leaders, and they discarded the predigested texts in order to develop fresh ones. Again and again, in the course of the Council's work, the Vatican conservatives raised objections, forced delays, created obstacles—and were repeatedly outflanked and outvoted. The ambiguities and compromises in the Council's documents do not disguise the fact that the outcome represented a dramatic new thrust in the church's life and an unmistakable departure from the defensive past. The church had acknowledged its historicity. Change, not immutability, was recognized as the law of life. Dialogue, not condemnation, governed the church's relationship to the contemporary world. There was, indeed, an underlying "spirit of Vatican II" that quite legitimately provided an interpretative key to resolving the ambiguities in its documents and a framework for approaching other issues that the Council had not engaged.

Entrenched in their Vatican posts, however, the curial conservatives maintained their dogged opposition, bottling up legitimate change and provoking overreactions. It was this begrudging obstructionism, not a runaway zeal for adaptation to the zeitgeist, that was the context for the frustrations, excesses, and drift; for the loss of priests, nuns, and brothers; for the breakdown of institutions. Indecisive and fearful of breaking with the conservatives, Pope Paul VI had been bullied into paralysis or worse. And while John Paul II was an attractive figure of global stature who had shaken the foundations of the Soviet empire and challenged the complacency of the rich West, his internal leadership of the church had given new life to the old conservatism and only put off the day of reckoning with necessary changes that the Council had prefigured. Meanwhile, the essential struggle—between the party of the Council and the party against the Council—continues.

For the final, radical narrative of this history, the Council was certainly a break with the past but a halfhearted one, carried out in a naïve mood about the ease and extent of authentic reform and what it truly required. Since virtually the entire history of Catholicism has been shaped by Roman imperialism, Western racism and colonialism, modern capitalism, and the vast sweep of patriarchy, all of the church's scriptures, doctrines, and practices must be reexamined with a "hermeneutic of suspicion." The Council could be only the opening round in a series of ecclesiastical and theological revolutions. The postconciliar turmoil and setbacks were not really due to the Vatican's failure to be true to the Council, however exacerbating that might be, but to the inherent instability of the conciliar settlement itself. No one should pretend that the Council fathers would have approved of homosexual relationships, authorized the ordination of women, or identified the church with a revolutionary vanguard, let alone deconstruct the whole idea of hierarchical authority, a priesthood ordained and set apart for life, and most of traditional sacramental theology. Yet these are the kinds of far-reaching changes latent in the Council's actions, despite its failure to recognize them. The Council fathers unwittingly set the church on a revolutionary course, and conflict and dissatisfaction have been inevitable as long as the trajectory remains incomplete.

THOSE STORIES, of course, represent but four points on a spectrum. My own account would come closest to the third, with an admixture of the second, a touch of the fourth, and a whiff of the first. Yet all of these narratives strike me as much too preoccupied with defending the battle lines that have existed in the church since the 1960s or before. The plots of these stories are frozen in those early years and largely untouched by any sense of the ironic or unexpected that might spring from more recent events.

The Council, in my view, did signal a definite break with the immediate past but one that strongly affirmed a *ressourcement,* a reappropriation of earlier expressions of the faith that had been neglected in the polemics fed by the Reformation and the Enlightenment. There is, then, a legitimate "spirit of the Council" that provides an interpretive key to its documents and their application to unforeseen issues. The Council's affirmation of the active role of the laity as baptized believers, for example, has important consequences for the church's thinking about sexuality. A traditionally highly deductive reasoning about sexual morality and contraception must be tested against the lived experience of married Catholics. The dialogue with modernity that the Council proposed in place of repeated condemnations suggests that movements for political justice or women's equality, even when springing from secular ideologies, must be engaged without prejudice.

At the same time, part of that "spirit of the Council" is an appreciation and receptivity toward tradition at least equal to any hermeneutic of suspicion. Vatican II cannot be invoked to justify sweeping dismissals of whole periods and major themes in the church's history or all the Council fathers' caveats and compromises.

As for the postconciliar period, the resistance of curial leaders and the failure of Pope Paul VI to grasp the reins of reform and direct change rather than continually appear to be resisting it did create the conditions for a breakdown of authority and a promiscuous embrace of novelties. In particular, the encyclical *Humanae Vitae,* reasserting the church's official condemnation of contraception despite a papal commission's endorsement of change, precipitated a crisis of authority that sent tremors through the ranks of priests and bishops as much as of the laity. But the problems faced by Paul VI and his bureaucracy were not all imagined. Catholicism had indeed barricaded itself into so intricately constructed an edifice that one could not remove a stone here or an arch there without imperiling the whole structure. And once Catholicism admitted that its claim to be ahistorical and immutable was unfounded, or once it acknowledged that yesteryear's heretics were in fact today's "separated brethren," could historical consciousness and ecumenism stop short of total relativism?

What is more, the postconciliar years presented the church with questions that the Council fathers had really not foreseen or addressed. Chief among them were questions arising from what was only then being recognized as a world-historical change in the status of women and, related to that, in our understanding of human sexuality. The Council offers cues about approaching these topics in its deliberations, but clear answers cannot be derived from either the Council's documents or its spirit. It is much better to admit that in certain matters, Catholicism is entering uncharted waters.

The existing narratives stress developments internal to the church and tend to underestimate the independent impact of outside events. It was the Council's fate to have ended just as the most radical part of the 1960s was beginning. The Council's decisions had been made in one context—a European and American world enjoying unprecedented political freedom, social stability, and economic prosperity.

The Council's implementation took place in another context: established authorities of all sorts—moral, cultural, political, economic—were being challenged. In the United States, the civil rights and antiwar battles injected an almost unprecedented confrontational tone, and sometimes confrontational techniques, into internal church disputes. The youthful counterculture added utopia and libido to social critique. Not a few Catholic priests, nuns, and lay leaders, elated that the Council had liberated them from uncritically held dogmas, seemed to fill the void by seizing secular dogmas no less uncritically. Among the more venturesome, there was revolutionary theory for the body politic and psychobabble for the body physical. Down-to-earth types concentrated on obvious problems where the ideals of church and society seemed to converge: fighting racial injustice, mending marriages, countering adolescent alienation. At the average parish level, priests and parishioners often exhibited a good-willed if somewhat baffled acceptance that the rules had been changed—one had to be ready for whatever came along next.

Beyond noting the differences between Paul VI's and John Paul II's papacies, the prevailing stories of the Council and its aftermath unfortunately differentiate very little between distinct stages. In the United States, the period of greatest turmoil was ending by the late 1970s. The American hierarchy had been given a new coloration by the appointment of the so-called Jadot bishops, more locally rooted and pastorally oriented shepherds promoted by Archbishop Jean Jadot, a Vatican diplomat from Belgium then serving as Rome's representative in the United States. The National Conference of Catholic Bishops was getting its sea legs as an organization, and increasingly the bishops, rather than colorful inner-city or antiwar priests, appeared to be at the helm of American Catholicism. They were in the forefront of opposition to abortion. They conducted hearings on the state of the nation all around the country for the bicentennial, in 1976. They stirred national debates with pastoral letters on nuclear weapons (1983) and economic justice (1986). Decline in at least some of the leading Catholic indicators was leveling off.

Consolidation in the United States, in other words, was already under way when John Paul II's own agenda for consolidation began to kick in. In some ways, the two efforts coincided, especially in the pope's advocacy of both traditional morality and contemporary human rights and in his simple vigor, physical and intellectual. Yet in still more ways the papal campaign eventually worked at cross-purposes from the bishops'. It reignited disputes that had died down; it hardened divisions that were being negotiated; it dampened the initiatives of the bishops' conference; and it signaled that the days of the Jadot bishops were numbered. In my narrative of the postconciliar years, Rome and the United States are out of sync.

My narrative also differentiates between sectors of church life. Despite their otherwise contrasting accounts, conservatives and liberals alike see themselves as beset victims carrying on a brave resistance against entrenched establishments. But at least in the United States, in sectors like academic theology, religious education, liturgical theory, peace and justice centers, and many religious orders of men and women, liberal thinkers and activists are overwhelmingly the establishment. On the other hand, conservatives of one sort or another hold sway in sectors like seminary education, Catholic philanthropies, Catholic media, right-to-life networks, a few religious orders, and above all in the hierarchy itself—especially the cardinals and archbishops. Conservatives and liberals, in other words, are both "establishments" and "outsiders," depending on what part of American Catholicism you are examining. All the parties that emerged from the Council have their mixed records of successes and failures, their vested interests, and their turf to defend.

Perhaps no single point in this book is more important than this: the narratives that have framed the contending diagnoses of Catholicism's health are outdated and inadequate. It is time to cease forcing the data into simplified, partisan accounts, time to relax and expand the framing narratives to accommodate almost four decades of further experience.

Chapter Two

The Scandal

IN January 2002 the *Boston Globe* began an exposé of Boston Catholic priests who had sexually preyed on minors and a local hierarchy that, by ignoring warnings, rebuffing complaints, and reassigning priests, had allowed this abuse to continue. Over the next months, the public was bombarded with reports of molesting priests and inattentive, negligent, or accommodating bishops in dioceses throughout the country. During the hundred days between its initial story and the point in April when the pope summoned America's cardinals to Rome, the *Globe* alone carried more than 250 stories, many on page one. By the time the bishops met in Dallas in June to confront the scandal, more than twelve thousand sex-abuse-by-priests stories had been carried by the major TV networks, cable outlets, wire services, and newsmagazines and the nation's fifty top newspapers. What the papers spelled out day after day, newsmagazines packaged into cover stories, radio and television news distilled into a few brutal phrases, cable shows transmuted into shouting matches between talking heads, and hour-long TV specials dramatized with ugly details of predatory sex recounted against footage of stained-glass windows and priests raising the host in their consecrated hands.

Catholics were stunned, then outraged. Polls registered dramatic losses by Catholics of confidence in their leaders. Interviews surfaced raw anger. Catholics reported friends and family members who had started attending other churches. To be sure, most parishioners expressed shock and sorrow while declaring their faith unshaken. But that rock-bottom confidence did not reflect the continuing tensions between faith and doubt that are now the daily reality for millions of religiously thoughtful Catholics. Not even the most steadfast could escape the impulse to take some distance from a soiled church; indeed, it was often the *most* steadfast who were *most* shocked and aggrieved.

By year's end, a Gallup poll showed that Catholic church attendance had slid 7 percentage points since the previous March and the percentage of Catholics saying that their faith is "very important" to them had dropped from 61 to 49 percent over the course of 2002. (The comparable figure for Protestants was 70 percent.) Another poll, while confirming that most Catholics insisted that their faith had not been affected, reported that slightly over 20 percent had asked themselves whether they should leave the church because of the scandal.

It has been said that those first one hundred days of 2002 changed the history of the Catholic Church in the United States. That is not quite right. There is scarcely a known or likely result of the scandal that was not somehow already under way, from the drop in Mass attendance to the questioning of leadership, the reduced numbers seeking the priesthood, and the disaffiliation of young adults from church life. It would be more accurate to say that the scandal, although unprecedented for American Catholicism, did not so much change the course of that history as immensely accelerate it. It gave a new urgency to questions going well beyond the scandal. It revealed the distrust already simmering just beneath the surface of American Catholic life, ready to boil over into anger. Although it temporarily united left and right, liberals and conservatives, in criticism of the bishops, ultimately it supplied the polarized camps in the church with new reserves of outrage to fuel their conflicting outlooks.

THE AMERICAN CATHOLIC church's sex scandal of 2002 occurred
because terrible things had been done to thousands of children and
young people. It occurred because many church officials—different
ones at different times—failed to prevent those crimes and do everything in their power to repair the harm, whether acting out of ignorance, naïve piety, misplaced trust, indifference to children, clerical
clubbiness, fear of scandal, subservience to lawyers, concern for
church assets, diocesan prerogatives, sheer administrative incapacity,
or downright complicity.

Those things must be set on the record from the start, and Bishop
Wilton Gregory, president of the United States Conference of
Catholic Bishops, said as much in his address opening the bishops'
meeting at Dallas in June 2002. There is of course a great deal more
that must be said about the scandal, including ways in which it has
been misperceived and misunderstood. But there is no disputing the
appalling behavior of priest-perpetrators, the toll of pain wrought
on victims and their families, and the enormous gravity of the scandal. Nor should there be any question of reluctance to hold church
authorities responsible for their decisions.

There are, however, questions about which church authorities
should be held responsible for what decisions at what times, and such
questions are of paramount importance to any analysis of how the
scandal fits into the larger pattern of crisis in American Catholicism.
Ordinarily, that would go without saying. In the current circumstances, it has become difficult to say.

People react to few crimes more viscerally than sexual molestation of children. Parents, in particular, feel what one psychologist
who has dealt with abusing priests called "a kind of healthy
'parental rage' when their children are threatened or harmed"—or,
one might add, at the very thought of it. And though the extent of
such abuse in the United States (and probably elsewhere, too) is
mind-boggling, in 2002 the public, especially the Catholic public,

was confronted as seldom before with the loathsome details of abuse and its lasting effects, heightened by a grotesque association of child exploitation and religious authority.

The anger that resulted was understandable; nothing less would have been human. Yet this anger left little room for nuance or distinctions, although polls found the same pattern that often shows up in opinion about schools, representatives in congress, or physicians. The bishops as a group were censured, often in the most sweeping terms, though not in many cases one's own bishop, certainly not one's own parish priest. A letter to the editor of the *National Catholic Reporter* is not at all untypical. The bishops' way of responding to accusations of sexual abuse, the writer declares, "was to commit heinous crimes, with total disregard for the mental suffering of the victims, and to attempt to cover up the situation with money and coercion."

To introduce into this black-and-white landscape any shades of gray, any question of degrees of knowledge or responsibility, any recognition of forces beyond the villainy of bishops, any differentiation among bishops or between decades, any distinctions between naïveté, negligence, arrogance, and complicity, any uncertainty about human motives, any hint of legal complexities, any questions about media accuracy—is that anything less than making excuses, shifting the blame, even "revictimizing" the victims?

I can, as I said, understand this reaction. More than once, in reading accounts of predatory priests and their unavailing superiors, I felt it myself. But I remain convinced that this form of free-floating rage is a faulty foundation on which to construct either an understanding of the sex abuse story or an adequate remedy for what it revealed.

To begin with, the church's sex scandal cannot be understood without some sense of the distinct time frames in which it took place. Nor can the scandal be assessed as though all the essential facts are clearly known. Even after more than a year's worth of constant reports, a great deal remained unknown, thanks primarily to the church's closed-door procedures and the hierarchy's resistance, at least until recently, to full disclosure. If people have sometimes filled in the blanks with their worst suspicions, taken the most egregious failures of church leadership as representative, or been unwilling to credit any real changes in church policy, the bishops have, above all, themselves to blame.

"FOR THE ROMAN CATHOLIC CHURCH in the United States, reports of sexual abuse by priests of children and teen-agers have taken on the dimensions of a biblical plague," began a story in the *New York Times*. "Last week, for the first time, Pope John Paul II spoke out publicly on the problem. In a letter to American bishops, the Pope expressed sorrow for the harm inflicted on victims and for the shock and demoralization suffered by the whole church. The Pope's message confirmed what the bishops had implicitly acknowledged a few days earlier. . . . The crisis of confidence in church leadership was such that action could no longer be left for the local level."

I wrote that *Times* story, not in 2002 but in June 1993, almost a decade earlier. At that time, the church had been engulfed in stories about sexually predatory priests for almost five years. There was the Reverend Bruce Ritter, founder-hero of Covenant House, New York's refuge for runaway youth, and James Porter, a laicized priest from Fall River, Massachusetts, whose serial molesting was on a scale equal to the worst depravity revealed in 2002. There were scores of others. The scandals of those years, although never receiving the intense level of media coverage that occurred in 2002, also produced cover stories in the newsweeklies, bone-chilling exposés on prime time TV, public apologies from bishops, and impassioned exchanges among Catholics about celibacy, patriarchy, authoritarianism, and sexual repression.

Having covered that earlier episode, I found the avalanche of revelations in 2002 startling in a way different than most Catholics. To begin with, I was not seeing a new wave of post-1993 sexual abusers. I was seeing the same wave—risen, as it were, from the grave. The Father Geoghans and other priests whose names now became notorious were frequently not successors to the Father Porters, Father Gauthés, and other earlier predators; they were their peers, and their crimes against young people had often taken place at the same time.

Although the horror of molestations by priests was now driven home by a degree of explicitness unknown in the pre-Lewinski news media, there was nothing about the horror and extent of the abuse revealed in 2002 that had not been widely publicized and heatedly discussed before. In the story just quoted, for example, published on page one of the *New York Times*'s Sunday Week in Review section, I reported contrasting estimates that two Catholic priest-sociologists had extrapolated from data released by the Chicago archdiocese. The Reverend Andrew M. Greeley estimated that 2,500 priests in the U.S. had abused 100,000 minors over the previous 25 years. Monsignor Philip Murnion presented an alternative estimate of about 15,000 victims over 40 years. By comparison, on January 12, 2003, the *New York Times* published what it called "the most complete compilation of data on the problem available," counting 1,205 priests who had been publicly charged with abuse by 4,268 people—over the last 60 years. The *Times*'s figures, limited to documented or publicly reported cases, were surely a conservative minimum. They were not meant, and cannot be taken, to minimize the problem. The point is only that a full decade earlier, far larger estimates, from respected Catholic sources, were already appearing in the paper's columns.

This raises a lot of questions on top of those—about celibacy, secrecy, seminary training, the priest shortage, and the sexual maturity of candidates for ordination, for example—already being asked a decade ago. In 1993, experts had warned the bishops of "a sustained crisis in the church" if church authorities were perceived as unable or unwilling to deal decisively with sexual misconduct. Why did church officials, even those who seemed to hear and respond to that warning, nonetheless fail to forestall that crisis? Why had the crisis not erupted until a decade later? Why, when it did erupt, was it so much more severe than earlier, even though, as I would argue the evidence indicates, priestly crimes and episcopal failure, while by no means ceasing, had actually decreased in the ensuing decade?

THE PERIOD BEFORE 1985 could justifiably be termed the dark ages of sexual abuse. While bishops recognized the gravely sinful character of any sexual abuse of minors, especially by priests, they typically displayed a pious faith in repentance, forgiveness, and willpower. They remained ignorant, sometimes willfully ignorant, of the compulsive nature of this conduct and its shattering impact on victims. Priests' denials were routinely accepted and accusations dismissed without investigation. When faced with an admission of guilt or undeniable evidence of abuse, church officials responded by warning the priestly molester sternly, dispatching him to a retreat house for prayer and recollection, or ordering him into a brief medical treatment—and then reassigning him to another parish. Bishops and their subordinates took for granted the necessity of preventing scandal, relying on the widespread deference to religious authority to quiet parents and gain the complicity of civil authorities, which in fact was usually forthcoming. Pastoral concern for victims was subordinated to legal advice from insurers.

In this environment, serial molesters could find new assignments and new victims for years. Because of the shame and silence surrounding sexual abuse, this was true not only of Catholic clergy but of teachers, coaches, Boy Scout leaders, and others. But three factors made serial abuse by priests less likely to come to light. First, priest abusers and their superiors operated within an enclosed, self-protective clerical culture bonded by years of seminary formation and reinforced by celibacy. Second, priests moved from assignment to assignment without the open process of inquiry, interview, and evaluation that was characteristic of many other religious groups as well as professional appointments. Third, a powerful aura of being consecrated surrounded the Catholic priesthood, making these crimes all the more unthinkable to most people—and all the more devastating to the victims.

From the mid-1970s, the problem of child sexual abuse, whether in families or in institutions, began to generate public concern. Government hearings and studies, new psychological research, and in some states mandatory reporting laws reflected a new awareness that abuse was far more widespread than previously believed, that its effects could be extensive and lasting, and that perpetrators were not necessarily dirty old men skulking around school yards or snatching children into alleys. Perpetrators could be respectable citizens, family friends, educators—even clergymen. Catholic officials, tragically, were laggards and not leaders in this changing awareness. Between 1985 and 1993, they were dragged kicking and screaming into dealing with the issue. These were the years of transition.

The case of the Reverend Gilbert Gauthé in Louisana, reported in both the secular and the Catholic press in 1985, sounded the alarm bell. That year saw at least three initiatives to address the problem, including a closed-door discussion at the June 1985 meeting of the bishops' conference; but none caught fire. It took the drumbeat of widely publicized cases, the threat of huge financial losses, the doggedness and growing effectiveness of victims' groups, and the biting criticism of individuals like Andrew Greeley or publications like the *National Catholic Reporter* to overcome the inertia. Step by step, workshop by workshop, meeting by meeting, the bishops' conference nationally and many bishops locally did take action. They engaged experts, studied the medical realities, met with victims, revised local diocesan policies, and scrutinized the quality of treatment centers. The bishops began to emphasize pastoral care for victims and screening of seminarians; they struggled with the risks involved in reassigning offending priests after apparently successful treatment; they prodded Rome to ease church law so that recalcitrant priests could be more readily dismissed.

The watershed years were almost certainly 1992–93.

In late 1991, Cardinal Bernardin was appalled to discover his error in reassigning an accused, superficially treated priest who was accused of further offenses and was eventually indicted. Bernardin

apologized directly to the parishes involved and then assembled a
blue-ribbon committee that not only culled forty years of diocesan
records to identify potential abusers and remove those still active, but
in 1992 recommended a new model for handling accusations: a lay-
dominated committee (including a victim or a victim's relative), a
nonclerical gatekeeper, and a publicized hot line. The Chicago model
was imitated or at least adapted elsewhere.

The arrest in 1992, and trial and sentencing in 1993, of James
Porter, with victims and courtroom scenes dramatically portrayed on
television, galvanized many bishops to comb their files for possible
lurking Porters and to get them into treatment or out of the active
priesthood. In Boston, one such case was John Geoghan. Another was
the Reverend Paul Shanley, already on extended sick leave in California but serving part-time in a parish. It is no coincidence that the
more recent revelations of priests who abused minors in the 1970s
and 1980s, or even before, show many such individuals leaving
parishes or the priesthood altogether in 1993 or 1994.

In June 1992 the bishops' conference approved a set of "Five Principles" to guide dioceses: (1) Respond to allegations promptly. (2)
Immediately suspend anyone reasonably suspected, while proceed-
ing with an investigation and making use of "appropriate medical
evaluation and intervention." (3) Comply with civil law and cooperate with criminal investigations. (4) Reach out to victims. (5) Deal
with the issue "as openly as possible."

A year later, after sponsoring further exchanges with victims and
experts, the conference formed a special Ad Hoc Committee on Sexual Abuse to address the issue and fill out the Five Principles.

What did all this accomplish? In the years that followed, virtually
every one of the nation's Catholic dioceses overhauled its procedures
for investigating allegations of sexual abuse by priests and for dealing with victims. A majority of dioceses, according to a March 2002
survey by the *St. Louis Post-Dispatch,* began relying "on lay committees, not the church hierarchy alone, to assess allegations of sex
abuse." Many dioceses established hot lines, publicized their anti-

abuse policies, or undertook educational efforts in parishes. It is almost certain that bishops, having undergone the equivalent of crash courses in sexual dynamics, grasped the tragic inadequacy of previous "Go and sin no more" attitudes and ceased to shuttle known clergy offenders from parish to parish. Seminaries began seriously screening candidates and sought a middle ground between the older harsh suspicion of sexuality and the flouting of celibacy that marked some institutions in the postconciliar reaction.

At the beginning of July 1993, for example, the New York archdiocese made page one of the *Times* with its announcement of a new policy for investigating allegations, removing priests, and advising accusers to bring their complaints to law-enforcement officials. The policy left the investigation and preliminary decisions in the hands of a trained priest, who was to rely on a lay-dominated panel responsible for general oversight, special expertise, and "judgment calls" in hard cases. In that regard, the policy fell somewhat short of the Chicago model. But like the policies in Chicago and elsewhere, it followed what was the nearly unanimous therapeutic consensus of that time—that is, returning a priest guilty of sex abuse to a parish ministry was almost always out of the question, but a priest successfully undergoing extended treatment might serve in other ministries "under supervision and subject to certain limitations."

The *Times* editorial page quickly welcomed the New York policy, along with the actions by the bishops' conference, "as good news, not just for Catholics, but for Americans of all faiths." The church, the editorial continued, "is a bulwark of stability, especially in broken communities where its parishes and schools are often the only functioning institutions. The actions of the Cardinal and the bishops won't make the problem of sexual abuse disappear, but they are surely a comforting first step."

What June 1993 signaled, I believe, was a period of real but uneven and incomplete progress, despite the fact that there were undoubtedly dioceses that did little or nothing, or others where new policies on paper were never translated into different practices on the ground. This is one of many areas where the bishops' failure to gather data has unfortunately made it difficult to speak confidently.

A first step, the *Times* had written. What were the second and third? The church's real but uneven and incomplete progress turned out to be calamitously uneven and disastrously incomplete. The years of transition, it might be said, were followed by the years of unfinished business.

APPROVING THE FIVE GUIDELINES and establishing an Ad Hoc Committee on Sexual Abuse had been relatively bold steps for the bishops' conference. Those actions were in effect an admission that the crisis could no longer be left for the local level. That, however, implied some modification of established church law, which made each diocese independent in administrative matters, including disciplining priests. Bishops were in fact reluctant to tread on one another's turf, to institute policies that might infringe on their own prerogatives, or to do anything that could be used against them in lawsuits. Guidelines were useful, but the bishops stopped short of attempting what was finally done at their Dallas meeting in June 2002: drawing up a full-fledged policy that (with Rome's endorsement) would become mandatory throughout the nation. Cardinal Law was reportedly a leader in resisting anything of that nature.

Nor was it an auspicious sign that the new Ad Hoc Committee would be spearheaded not by a cardinal or archbishop but by a bishop from Bismarck, North Dakota. Bishop John F. Kinney was a respected prelate taking on a difficult task, but he hardly wielded the influence in the hierarchy that a leading prelate from a major archdiocese might have. He and his committee labored intensively for several years. They heard the testimony of victims of abuse. (More than once Bishop Kinney would return to his room after a meeting and weep.) They produced three volumes of valuable studies and some major recommendations—but never the thoroughgoing changes that might have prevented the 2002 shock wave.

The committee's recommendations for diocesan policies, for example, never made it to the floor of the bishops' conference for debate and a vote. Although far less stringent than what was voted at Dallas, the recommendations put some real meat on the bare bones of the Five Principles. The committee also proposed that accurate data be collected from dioceses about the extent of the problem, the numbers of perpetrators and victims, the disposition of their cases, the amount of money expended—data, in other words, that would have prevented much speculation and guesswork in the media. The committee proposed healing sessions along the lines of the collective encounter with victims that the bishops finally experienced at Dallas in June of 2002. These ideas were discussed in the Administrative Committee, the body of over fifty bishops that serves, among other things, as a kind of steering committee for the whole conference. But beyond that, Bishop Kinney said, the committee's proposals "never saw the light of day."

"It was clear that getting votes would be tough, so it was decided not to try." There was even a lot of "hesitation as to why this committee was needed," he said. Some bishops were uncomfortable with any committee named "on Sexual Abuse." Many bishops had suspicions about the conference infringing on the authority of each bishop to handle the affairs of his own diocese. Overall, there was "a lack of understanding of the gravity of the issue."

IF PRACTICES REGARDING reassigning priests, investigating complaints, aiding victims, and screening seminarians appear to have changed substantially in the 1990s, the unfinished business, besides the establishment of a clear-cut national standard, included many other questions—about reviewing old records and reevaluating allegations from previous decades; about reassigning priests who had undergone treatment even to limited ministries; about dealing with the criminal justice system; about sealing settlements with victims; and about ensuring that Catholics were thoroughly informed of what had transpired in the past and what church officials were now doing, including how many church dollars were being spent on suits, settlements, and treatment.

The point about informing Catholics proved crucial. Neither on the diocesan nor on the national level did church officials initiate credible investigations and issue full reports on the pre-1993 scandal. Where new sex abuse policies were put into place, they usually lacked mechanisms for public oversight that could assure Catholics that the procedures and safeguards were actually being followed. The absence of this kind of self-examination has meant that a great deal about the church's actions since 1993 remains unknown or, even where appearances suggest either genuine progress or extraordinary dereliction, unverified.

By the end of 2002, of course, it seemed counterintuitive to think that there were important things still not known about the scandal. If anything, many people felt they knew far more than they wanted. Especially during the first six months, revelations, accusations, admissions, and denials had rolled down day after day like an avalanche of mud.

For Catholics with a serious stake in their faith, it is hard to describe the nearly overpowering effect of confronting these stories, many of them featuring graphic descriptions of sexual acts and their psychological impact as recalled by victims. Every day new names with new offenses from new places. It took extraordinary concentration to focus on important details like the dates of the abuse or of reassignments, and by which bishop, living or dead, and whether to parishes or to restricted ministries, and whether treatment had been required or not, of what sort and with what kind of further supervision if any, and whether victims were spurned or given help. Extracting overall patterns from this churning flow of stories was virtually impossible. Many were complicated accounts of charges, denials, countercharges, and legal maneuvers. But some were bombshells, like the allegations leading to the resignations of two bishops, or the news that the Reverend Paul Shanley of Boston had publicly defended sex with minors and, while on a leave in California, operated a motel for a gay clientele. Not only did the bombshells convince one to believe the worst about the stories that were hard to understand, but most people, even journalists, appear to have made sense of this torrent of reports by taking one or two outstanding examples of predator priests or uncomprehending, even complicit bishops—a Geoghan, a Birmingham, a Law—as the paradigms for all.

No one needed details about exact dates or treatment, no one needed to extract overall patterns to be appalled at the crimes of individual priests. But such matters were at the very heart of determining the nature, degree, and extent of episcopal responsibility and institutional failure.

Given the rapid cascade of shocking revelations, blurring the time frames in which church actions might be accurately judged was almost unavoidable. Headline writers and broadcasters typically drop verbs or change tenses to convey a staccato sense of immediacy: "Pedophile priests—sex abuse rocking the Catholic Church." Even when the news media were quite precise in giving the dates of particular events ("The three brothers said the abuse had occurred from 1969 to 1974"), the connective tissue linking this story to all the rest often suggested a pattern of events continuing more or less unabated to the present ("The allegations added to the revelations of sexual abuse currently engulfing the Catholic Church"). The engulfing revelations may equally be of deeds done one, two, or more decades ago, but that is hard to keep in mind when such phrases occur in the context of "news"—that is, of events mainly happening yesterday or last week or at most last year.

A national survey of Catholics released in November 2002 asked whether the scandal was "about acts which occurred a long time ago, or are these acts still occurring today?" Over two-thirds answered "still occurring today" and only one out of five answered "a long time ago." The choice, as so often with polls, was not entirely happy. Sexual crimes by priests, or any other group, are unlikely to be totally eliminated at any time, so technically one could assume that these crimes still occur. But the evidence overwhelmingly showed that what the scandal was about was acts from long ago rather than today.

Acts from the past should not be ignored or minimized. Belated reports of atrocities committed by American troops in Vietnam justifiably make headlines, as do unethical instances of medical experimentation or fraudulent drug testing, even when they occurred years ago. We not only hold individuals responsible for such past acts; by bringing them to light, we learn important lessons about our institutions, ideologies, politics, and economics, and sometimes about human nature itself.

At the same time, legitimate distinctions between past and present cannot be brushed aside. However seriously the public might take fresh charges about a war crime allegedly committed three decades ago in Vietnam, a different reaction would be called for if the charges concerned current deeds in Afghanistan. Responsible reports on unethical medical experiments or fraudulent drug testing always emphasize whether the experiments are still continuing or the questionable drugs are still in use. So while molesting priests and negligent church authorities should be held accountable for actions done even long ago, it was unfortunate that the blurring of events occurring over several decades obscured changes that had occurred in the nineties. It disserved concerned parents, innocent priests, dismayed Catholics, and anyone trying to fathom the meaning of the scandal and propose reforms.

BLURRING THE RELEVANT time frames meant blurring the distinctions between priests who had been credibly accused of sexual abuse and reassigned without serious treatment, priests who had been sent into treatment and reassigned to restricted or supervised ministries, and priests accused of past abuse only in the course of the current scandal.

A strong theological case can be made, especially in hindsight, that any priest guilty of molesting a minor, no matter the nature or frequency of the deed, is unworthy to serve as a public minister of Christ and the church, regardless of whether he has repented and successfully reformed as an individual. That is more or less the position that the bishops eventually took at their June and November 2002 meetings.

But a different case was made in the mid-1980s and afterward, and it too was convincing. Many priests, it was claimed, could be successfully treated, and keeping them under supervision in ministry was in fact more responsible than just expelling them from the priesthood into the community. Much has been made of the paper circulated among bishops in 1985 in which the Reverend Thomas Doyle, a canon lawyer, the Reverend Michael Peterson, a psychiatrist, and F. Ray Mouton, a lawyer, warned the hierarchy of the potential scope of the scandal. Usually overlooked is that this paper, too, assumed that many abusers who were not true pedophiles—that is, attracted to prepubescent children—could be returned to some form of ministry; in fact, that was a major point of a paper by Peterson, given to all the bishops, to which the Doyle-Peterson-Mouton paper was an addition. In the early 1990s, I interviewed both Catholic and non-Catholic psychologists and psychiatrists treating and studying molesting priests and visited one of the treatment centers. Now and then I wondered whether these therapists were not, like many people of goodwill, overestimating their own professional powers and underestimating their own therapeutic bias; but overall I found their arguments and work impressive. It seems fundamentally inaccurate to lump decisions by church officials following those therapists' recommendations with decisions made, for example, out of blind loyalty to fellow priests, willful indifference to victims, or the reliance on totally amateur medical opinions typical of an earlier period. What happened in the 1990s has been muddled by routine phrases equating all such decisions—regardless of the time frame or treatment—as "relocating," "reassigning," "shuffling from parish to parish," "allowing accused priests to keep on working," or "protecting priests accused of sexual abuse."

But impressions of the 1990s have also been muddled by known instances of church officials who clearly ignored the recommendations of treatment centers or who grew inattentive to the restrictions and supervision the centers had prescribed. Was such negligence common, or exceptional? In the current atmosphere and without convincing information to the contrary from the church itself, even a few such examples were enough to cast doubt on the appearance of post-1993 change. Such doubts were intensified by cases where offending priests, although removed from ministry, seemed to be otherwise handled with kid gloves, fobbed off on other dioceses, or in the case of some in Boston, bid farewell with inexplicably lavish and pious praise from the cardinal.

AFTER 1993, even the most conscientious bishops had left two kinds of problems insufficiently examined and resolved. One involved the criminal justice system. The other involved settlements and secrecy. They were major items in the unfinished business that ultimately overshadowed the real achievements of this period.

"Comply with obligations of civil law as regards reporting of the incident and cooperating with the investigation": that was one of the Five Principles endorsed in 1992. Faced with evidence of current criminal acts, church officials no longer were willing to connive with civil authorities to block prosecution, as had frequently been the case decades earlier, or to pressure victims not to bring charges. But what should church officials do with allegations freshly made or belatedly unearthed of acts committed years before, never reported, and probably beyond criminal prosecution? When laws requiring mandatory reporting of sexual offenses against minors did not apply to clergy, as was the case in most states, should church officials report allegations anyway? Should that be done regardless of victims' wishes? Should that be done regardless of the allegations' credibility?

The New York archdiocesan policy welcomed by the *Times* in 1993, for example, mandated advising accusers that they could report the matter to legal authorities and underlined that priests and other church personnel in categories legally required to report allegations—like school principals or therapists—should fulfill their obligation; but it did not provide that all church authorities, including parish priests, automatically report accusations. "There are instances in which the family says we don't want this to go any further," an archdiocesan official said.

Anyone assuming that the answers to all such questions are obvious is innocent of the difficulties of balancing privacy, civil liberties, and the protection of children and minors. When a bill widening the obligations to report sexual crimes against minors was introduced into New York's state legislature in 2002 in the wake of the Catholic scandal, Planned Parenthood lobbyists objected that the law would make teenagers whose sexual partners or abusers were over eighteen less willing to seek medical help or abortion counseling. Many courts and states are currently tangled in debates about the civil rights not merely of suspected or accused abusers but of *convicted* sex offenders who have served their sentences, versus the rights of communities to publicly identify these individuals as a means of protecting children.

The bishops might have been excused for failing to hit upon simple and satisfying answers. Unfortunately, they never seem to have grappled seriously with the problems. Neither nationally nor locally did the bishops justify their policies on reporting with a well-developed public rationale that, even if debatable, could be seen as resting on factors other than institutional self-interest.

Far more damaging, however, was their failure to confront the problems of secrecy, openness, and publicity, first of all in regard to civil settlements. Here too the right course of action is not obvious. The revelations of 2002 may at least partly fall into the category of "No good deed goes unpunished." During the 1990s many bishops chose to reach settlements with accusers that a decade earlier would have been resisted, and probably successfully: many victims had led troubled lives and would not have made the best witnesses. There were many plausible reasons for reaching secret or sealed settlements. Secrecy undoubtedly facilitated payments in borderline cases instead of the prolonged, costly, and painful litigation that might have ensued when priests' or victims' reputations were at stake. The church could also provide assistance in cases where officials felt the victim's claims of diocesan responsibility, as opposed to the molester's responsibility, were questionable. Secrecy was frequently requested by victims themselves, who did not want to display their traumatic experiences to neighbors, employers, or children and other family members. While one legal expert who worked on church matters for decades told me, "Eighty percent of the time it was victims who asked for confidentiality," I am not at all ready to accept that number. Until someone manages to study a random sample or sufficient number of these settlements, no one will know for sure. Yet, even if the percentage is much smaller, the point is a fair one. My guess is that the secrecy emerged from a complicated mix of motives: standard legal practice advising against setting precedents for future lawsuits, and the common interest of defendants and plaintiffs, insurers and church lawyers in avoiding prolonged and risky litigation and ugly publicity.

There were church lawyers who advised against making secrecy a condition of settlements. There were victims' lawyers who refused to seek or agree to it. On both sides, they were in the minority. The problem was that sealed settlements may have allowed some predatory priests to molest again, although that appears rare. More likely, identifying abusers would have encouraged other victims to come forward for help, healing, or simply vindication in knowing they were not alone. Again, the trade-offs are not simple. In September 2002 a group of federal judges in South Carolina, spurred by the Catholic sex scandal as well as cases involving business corruption, liability for dangerous products, and medical malpractice, proposed barring secret settlements as a way of protecting the public. The proposal set off a fierce debate among lawyers, and by year's end the idea had dropped from sight. But again there is no indication that the bishops, in their reform efforts of the early 1990s, ever seriously examined the potential dangers of secrecy.

Even if the question of sealed settlements was complicated, the bishops shied away from other opportunities for disclosure. With few exceptions, they did not report publicly how many priests had been accused, pressured out of the active priesthood, sent into treatment, or returned to supervised assignments if the treatment centers so advised. Bishops did not, in fact, explain clearly and publicly what state-of-the-art therapy was then telling them about treatment and recidivism, and what treatment and reassignment policies they were following. Nor did they reveal the number of settlements, quite apart from any further details, or how much money had gone into them and into treatment. In far too many cases, bishops did not reveal to pastors or other supervisors the history of priests being reassigned after treatment. Undoubtedly this reticence was sometimes motivated by considerations of confidentiality or by the naïve assumption that every Catholic had paid close attention to the extensive news coverage that had made the bishops wince. But sharing information of this sort did not come naturally to bishops. Most of this failure to disclose—indeed aggressively to inform and educate Catholics about—the sex abuse scandals revealed after 1985 almost certainly sprang from deeply ingrained habits of holding information within a very narrow circle of advisers and decision makers. In 2002, the church would pay dearly for this failure.

THE YEARS OF unfinished business ended on January 6, 2002, when a team of investigative reporters at the *Boston Globe* opened its series of stories on the case of John Geoghan. "Church Allowed Abuse by Priest for Years," ran the headline. The year of the scandal had begun.

The church's leadership was completely unprepared.

"I believe that if you were to have conducted a poll on January 5, 2002, of communications directors, priest personnel directors, or even bishops on how their diocese had handled or were handling cases of abusive priests, they would have honestly told you that they believed that things were fine in their diocese," Joseph Zwilling, communications director for the archdiocese of New York, wrote a year later.

> Indeed, in the last decade, much progress had been made in how dioceses had responded to accusations of abuse. As a member of the Archdiocese of New York's priest personnel advisory board from the early 1990s until last year, I can tell you firsthand that we had made great strides in our understanding of the nature of sexual abuse, and in knowing how to respond whenever we received an accusation of abuse against a priest. Our policy, which had been developed and publicly released in 1993, had enabled us to deal with allegations of abuse in a careful and consistent manner. I know that the Archdiocese of New York was not alone in this, and that our experience was shared by virtually every diocese in the country. And so we believed, naively perhaps, that we were "doing well."

One of the things contributing to that sense of doing well, despite the major failures noted above and obvious enough in hindsight, was the aftermath of the false accusations launched against Cardinal Bernardin in November 1993 and recanted 108 days later. It was hard to ignore the possibility that the timing of the accusations and the filing of a lawsuit against the cardinal had been orchestrated by the accuser's lawyer and CNN to get massive publicity both for the charges and for a CNN sex abuse special. Although the lawyer and CNN denied any such manipulation, the fiasco undoubtedly embarrassed and sobered the media. It injured the credibility of those leaders of victims' groups who had been among the bishops' chief critics but had now precipitously hailed the accusations against Bernardin. The story of predatory priests was soon demoted from nightly news to occasional revivals during a sweeps week or following extraordinarily large settlements. In the nearly eight years between the recantation of Bernardin's accuser, in February 1994, and January 2002, the *New York Times* published about three dozen articles on priests and sex abuse in the United States, compared to almost twice as many in the four years before. With the pressure off, church officials focused on handling current cases and preventing future ones by screening and educational initiatives for seminarians. There was much less thought about the problems posed by the backlog of cases from earlier decades. In 2002 it was largely on those cases that the bishops would be judged.

Not only were the bishops unprepared, they were taken by surprise and overwhelmed. The *Globe*'s exposé, when it came, came like a flash flood. The pace of the story, and the void it created in Catholic leadership, was the second major factor of the scandal in 2002. If there is one thing that the Catholic hierarchy is not built for, it is speed. Decisions about even noncontroversial matters creep through multiple stages of deliberation. It is the exceptional prelate, like New York's late Cardinal O'Connor, who is given to spontaneous sound bites. Staffs for public affairs, communications, or press relations are small and vary greatly in their professionalism. And the unfolding of the scandal in Boston posed a particular problem for the structure of a church that is viewed as highly unified and centralized, which it is doctrinally and liturgically, and yet is remarkably decentralized administratively. As bishops learned to their dismay, headlines about "the church" had an impact in the Midwest or Northwest, even when they referred to events in New England. Yet the national bishops' conference, let alone other bishops of national stature, had no mandate or effective mechanism for injecting their responses into a local matter in Boston. The Boston archdiocese itself, already in an adversarial relationship with the *Globe,* simply battened down the hatches. Cardinal Law's initial efforts at response proved inept or inaccurate. As reporters all over the country followed the *Globe*'s lead, looked into local records, and were alerted by accusers' lawyers, the story quickly became national. But the blitz of stories had already thrown church officials so much on the defensive that almost anything they said beyond apologies had the ring of self-serving rationalizations. Many took to cover. Some, I was told, welcomed even unfair attacks as a kind of expiation for what they knew were past failures, an attitude that might have satisfied a personal craving for martyrdom but did little to inform Catholics and the public. In sum, for the first three months of the year, Catholic officialdom was mainly paralyzed. Not until April did the leadership of the national conference begin to make itself visible on the more civilized television shows. Catholics, in the meantime, were deprived of any assurance that the church's leadership nationally had registered the seriousness of the scandal and were preparing any kind of response.

ONCE DOUBT WAS CAST on almost all church leaders' trustworthiness, of course, it is unclear what they might have said that would get a hearing. Could they have said anything to clarify the different stages of episcopal awareness and indicate that policies about allegations, treatment, and reassignments had really evolved? Could they have suggested that sealing settlements or turning over information to legal authorities raised issues that might be more complex than they first appeared? The one kind of official response that could have received a hearing was hard data: How many dioceses had established lay-run review boards? Screening in their seminaries? Counseling programs for victims? Exactly how many instances of predatory priests had come to light, over what period of time, and how had they been resolved? Tragically, this was precisely the kind of information the national bishops' conference had never been mandated to collect.

If the bishops were unable to give the public hard answers to these questions, they might have at least promised to get them. Early in 2002 they could have established a blue-ribbon commission to examine the problem, from its pre-1985 through its post-1993 stages. Leading bishops, chosen by the conference, might have served on such a panel, providing it with inside knowledge and hierarchical authority; but the commission would have had to be dominated by public figures, lay Catholics and possibly non-Catholics, respected for their judgment, independence, experience, and integrity. By not taking such a step or something similarly dramatic and decisive, the bishops condemned American Catholicism to be battered by almost six months of increasingly global, all-encompassing, and unanswered accusations.

The void in leadership extended to Rome. Loyal defenders of this papacy admitted that the Vatican had scarcely a clue about the gravity and import of the scandal. The pope's ill-considered summoning of the American cardinals to Rome raised enormous expectations—based on the popular misconceptions about the centralized nature of Catholicism—that he would somehow resolve matters with a solemn utterance or a stroke of the pen, when in fact it was not the cardinals but the bishops' conference, not scheduled to meet until June, that had to take action. The Rome meeting closed with a disastrous press conference and two statements that Vatican officials insisted on larding with technical language from church law that was predictably misunderstood and set off more furors.

TO WHAT EXTENT was the scandal shaped by the media? That is a legitimate question and deserves a dispassionate study. For most people, after all, the sex scandal was the scandal *as they knew it through the media*. Obviously such a study would have to distinguish serious investigative reporting in major newspapers from tabloid sensationalism, and thoughtful panel discussions on the Public Broadcasting System's nightly news from shouting heads on shock TV and cliché-ridden television specials. Preposterous claims by prominent Vatican officials that the scandal was manufactured by an anti-Catholic media only discourage any such examination. Likewise the comparison by a Honduran cardinal, considered a possible papal successor, between the American media's reporting of the scandal and persecution of the church by Hitler and Stalin. Bishops and other church leaders in the United States almost unanimously reject such fantasies, although there is a widespread conviction that the coverage distorted the record. There is also widespread recognition that without the press, going back to the *National Catholic Reporter*'s pioneering articles and editorials in 1985, much of the abuse and the failure to prevent it would never have come to light. Indeed, the church would have escaped its present mortification and many victims spared their suffering if there had been more pursuit of this story rather than less.

However, the news media did contribute to the blurring of time frames, the equation of all reassignments of priests, and the lumping together of all sealed agreements, refusals to turn over internal records, and long-standing, though debatable, closed-door procedures under prosecutorial terms like "cover-up," "payoff," and "hush money." Ultimately, the better news outlets did take up some of the important distinctions and nuances involved in the scandal. Nonetheless, the basic frame of the scandal story was established in the first three months of 2002, and it was a frame or story line that journalists found hard to escape.

Whatever shortcomings the news media suffered, they were vastly magnified by the final two factors that helped shape the 2002 scandal, which speak loudly to the overall situation of Catholicism in the United States.

One was the near unanimity—and in many instances vehemence—of the commentary appearing in editorials and columns or heard on the air. Not that one expected editorial writers, commentators, or columnists to defend sex abuse! Yet one might have expected a few voices moderating the sweeping denunciations of bishops, pointing out some of the actions they had taken as well as some of the dilemmas they faced.* Instead, columnists and commentators

---

*The importance of the commentary in influencing how the scandal story was framed is illustrated by an exception that proves the rule. Rather late in 2002, conservative Catholics finally focused attention on the apparent fact that most victims of molester priests were not prepubescent or female but adolescent boys—evidence, it was claimed, that the real problem was homosexuality. With homosexuals rather than bishops in the line of fire, a num-

settled numerous scores with the Catholic Church, from the way they were treated in parochial school to the church's opposition to abortion and refusal to ordain women to its lobbying for poverty programs and against armaments. If there were pundits inclined to sympathy with the church—and I believe that there were—they kept their heads down, perhaps wondering, in view of Catholic officialdom's congenital secrecy, whether anything they wrote might be blown out of the water by the next day's revelations. The one-sidedness of the commentary indicated, on the one hand, just how antagonistic to Catholicism the media culture has become and, on the other hand, just how nervous Catholicism's remaining friends in that culture are about going out on a limb for the church's leaders.

EVEN MORE TELLING than the almost uniformly critical and frequently vehement views of media commentators in general were the no less critical and vehement views of Catholics themselves. Liberal and conservative Catholics vied in attacking the bishops. Each found the sex abuse scandal proof of their preexisting diagnoses of what ails the church. For the liberals, that meant celibacy, a flawed attitude toward sexuality, the refusal to ordain women, and the lack of a real voice for laypeople in church governance. For the conservatives, that meant theological dissent, a breakdown in clerical obedience and sexual discipline, and the toleration of homosexuals in the ranks of the clergy, if not even among the hierarchy. The polarization of leading Catholics was blatant.

The vehemence of these polarized Catholic activists and intellectuals resonated in the less polarized ranks of ordinary Catholics. Something more diffuse was at work, it seemed, than rival agendas.

---

ber of commentators immediately warned, quite rightly in my view, of scapegoating gay priests or gay people generally. The result was not that the conservative diagnosis went away but that it was handled with a tentativeness and nuance not characteristic of how the story was otherwise framed.

Throughout the year, bishops lamented that the sex abuse scandal had undermined Catholics' trust in church leadership. But the truth was almost certainly the opposite. A preexisting erosion of trust had shaped the way Catholics perceived—and in some respects misperceived—the scandal.

Conservatives and liberals might have different lists of complaints. What they had in common was a festering sense that church leaders too often said one thing in public, believed another in private, and acted in ways not necessarily consistent with either. Distrust is built on this kind of fissure between appearance and reality. The point was brought home to me in a conversation with a man representing a Catholic publisher at a convention. In his home parish, it turned out, not one but two priests had been removed for suspicions of sexual misconduct. Yet within a few minutes he slid easily from those rather striking events to the marriage annulment obtained by the spouse of a close relative. It was all of a piece: the suspicion that the church was not on the up-and-up in handling failed marriages, and the suspicion that it was not on the up-and-up in handling wayward priests.

Catholics' distrust, anger, and alienation were also the product of years of irritations with what looked like the indifference, incompetence, or arrogance of church leaders. Embarrassing statements from on high, inept, ill stated, or ill explained; embarrassed acquiescence at lower levels. The center of gravity of the American Catholic populace is middle class and moderately liberal, which means they believe that tolerance, pluralism, open discussion and inquiry, the equality of men and women, the ideal of intimacy in marriage, and many other typically modern values are authentic ways of living one's Christianity. For years these Catholics have felt that many high church leaders, some in Rome, some in the United States, entertain an incomprehension for this outlook bordering on contempt. Other leaders, these Catholics sense, comprehend but comply, publicly endorsing positions that are privately questioned.

If the sex abuse scandal had never occurred, the Catholic Church in the United States would still face a crisis. The problems illumined by the scandal were present in other forms and in other parts of American Catholic life. The clergy's fading authority, the disappearance of the ethnically reinforced Catholic subculture, the impact of the Council (both disruptive and renewing), the divisions about sexual teachings, the priesthood, and above all the bishops' leadership—these would have remained areas of contestation and pressing decisions even if no priest had ever molested a young person. The sex abuse scandal revealed some egregious examples of negligent, incompetent, duplicitous, and even corrupt Catholic leaders. But the underlying problem was not bad leaders. It was a vacuum of leadership, and it would manifest itself in area after area, from the church's public role to its internal reform.

———+———————+———

Chapter Three

The Church and Society

T HROUGHOUT American history, the role of the Catholic
Church in politics has been the source of endless fascina-
tion and fear. Although overshadowed in recent years by attention given the Christian right, political actions taken under the
banner of Catholicism, whether by bishops or prominent laypeople,
are almost certain to be noted—and to stir controversy. In election
years, pollsters track the "Catholic vote." The Republican Party pur-
sues a "Catholic strategy." On issues ranging from immigration to
war, from abortion to school vouchers, from biomedical research to
welfare reform, from the death penalty to debt relief for poor nations, the views of the church are thought to matter.

Yet the Catholic Church and Catholic voters occupy a strange position in American political life. Just as Catholic voters are increasingly
"swing voters," the Catholic church is a "swing advocate." Its positions, as articulated by the hierarchy and leaders on the diocesan and
parish levels, defy many of the standard assumptions about liberals
and conservatives. Catholic leadership and organized activists have
deep differences with both major parties. They find themselves being abandoned by some of the church's traditional allies and courted
by some of its traditional critics. They also find themselves whip-
sawed by different currents in the church itself, often along genera-

tional and gender lines, and more recently by victims and their advocates in the sexual abuse scandal. The scandal threatens to impede the influence in public policy debates of both the bishops and social justice activists, although the staying power of the church in these matters should not be underestimated: in late 2002, support for going to war in Iraq dropped by almost 10 percentage points among Catholics after pollsters mentioned the bishops' questioning of an American intervention.

ACTUALLY, THE ENCOUNTER between the United States and the Catholic Church is seldom recognized for what it is, one of the most remarkable episodes of modern history. During the stormiest period of that encounter, when Catholic immigrants and American nativists were regularly facing off in riots and armed battles, both the new nation, whose time was yet to come, and the old church, whose time was thought to have gone, were perched on the margins of history. Then, by the second half of the twentieth century, when the new nation and the old church had emerged as almost uncontested superpowers, the one political and the other religious, the alignment between them seemed so extensive and so natural that the earlier discord was virtually forgotten.

The waves of nativism, No Popery, and Know-Nothingism that excited the country between 1830 and 1860 and provoked anti-Catholic pogroms in any number of cities cannot be explained as simply the fearful aversion of ignorant Americans to an influx of foreigners. Enlisting, alongside many cheap demagogues, some of the country's leading citizens, these movements were energized not only by sheer prejudice but by impulses common to some of the country's leading reform movements. The anti-Catholic impulse often overlapped with the antislavery one; abolitionists regularly equated popery with slavery, which did nothing to attract Catholics to their cause. But the real point is that a growing Catholic presence in the middle decades of the nineteenth century threatened America's idea of itself in a profound way. Catholicism was not just different; in the popular mind, it was what this country had defined itself *against*.

On the other hand, Catholicism, ever since the Reformation, had also defined itself *against*—against Protestantism, Enlightenment rationalism and optimism, constitutional liberalism, egalitarianism, individualism, and democracy, all the components, in sum, at the heart of this new American experiment. Catholics had come to the United States nonetheless, desperately and for the most part gratefully. The United States provided a refuge from oppression or starvation or both. But it was a troubling refuge, not just because of the hostility but because the very advantages the new nation offered, its freedoms foremost, constituted a challenge to many of the church's teachings and a temptation to abandon them. Catholics could not help but be of several minds about their new home.

The end result for American Catholicism was summed up nicely by Charles Morris, in his lively history *American Catholic,* with the phrase "prickly apartness." Beginning in the middle of the nineteenth century, the controlling faction within the American Catholic hierarchy effectively created a society within a society and a culture within a culture. The church became an all-enveloping cocoon of institutions, beliefs, and practices that, to quote Morris, was "*in* America, usually enthusiastically *for* America, but never quite *of* America."

This prickly apartness notwithstanding, in a little more than a century Catholicism was transmuted from alien danger to typical emblem of Americanism. Morris uses two visible symbols to frame the remarkable passage.

The first is the Washington Monument and the fact that one-fourth of the way up its height, the stone changes color. The change can be indirectly attributed to Pope Pius IX. As a gift to America, he had donated a stone from the Temple of Concord in Rome to be used in the monument. "Nativists were horrified, and rumors quickly spread that the completion of the monument would be the signal for a papal coup d'état." Early on March 6, 1854, the stone was stolen; and the next day a Know-Nothing faction took over the private society building the monument. Congress in turn backed away from an appropriation, and so for twenty-eight years, until construction began anew—this time with stone of a different tint—the 153-foot stump stood as a monument not to Washington but to paranoid fear of popery.

The second symbol was no less visual: the slew of movies with Catholic themes and heroes that were nominated in 1943, 1944, and 1945 for thirty-four Academy Awards and won twelve. Catholic priests, it seemed, had metamorphosed from sinister figures seducing young women in the confessional to cinematic models of American manhood. From Spencer Tracy's Father Flanagan in *Boys' Town* to Bing Crosby's crooning ex–baseball player Father Chuck O'Malley in *Going My Way* and *The Bells of St. Mary's*, Karl Malden's labor priest in *On the Waterfront*, and assorted roles by Pat O'Brien, there emerged a superpadre, virile, wise, good-humored, compassionate, and in emergencies possessed of a remarkable knockout punch. The superpadre was part of a larger change in image. In the 1940s and 1950s, the Catholic Church was to morality and uplift what General Motors was to industry and the Yankees were to baseball. On television, from 1952 to 1957, Bishop Fulton J. Sheen, with a peak audience of 30 million, became the most popular inspirational speaker, as he would now be labeled, in the nation's history.

How had this unforeseen convergence between Catholicism and the American image come about? Sheer numbers of Catholics, urbanization, a loss of Protestant authority and confidence, the Cold War—all played a part. But paradoxically that very prickly apartness which had once made the church so suspect now enabled it to step forward as a repository of the old-fashioned, tried-and-true American values that had lost some of their grip on the rest of the culture.

The acceptance of Catholicism as genuinely American should not be exaggerated. In the years between Catholicism's Hollywood triumphs and Bishop Sheen's TV successes, Paul Blanshard published, first, a series of articles in the *Nation* and then two books, *American Freedom and Catholic Power* (1949) and *Communism, Democracy, and Catholic Power* (1951). Blanshard's overall thesis was simple: the Catholic church posed a threat to American democracy parallel to that of Stalin's Communism. Seen from a distance, that seems as implausible as ravings about the Antichrist and the Whore of Babylon. But Blanshard was no unlettered backwoods preacher. He was a skilled polemicist whose intelligence and liberal credentials won accolades from eminent intellectuals such as John Dewey, Albert Einstein, Bertrand Russell, McGeorge Bundy, and Horace Kallen, and gave him an influence among Supreme Court justices. He could exploit not only the church's undeniable opposition to liberal and democratic liberties in the past but also its continuing inconsistencies about church-state relations in the present, its clinging to privileged positions in states like Spain, Italy, and Ireland, and to official teachings that contradicted the practice of most Western Christians.

Blanshard's was only the latest version of the argument that Catholicism was incompatible with American democratic freedoms. The argument rested on three legs: that Catholics owed ultimate political loyalty to a foreign ruler (and despot), the pope; that the Catholic Church rejected freedom of religion, merely tolerating the separation of church and state as long as Catholics were in the minority but intending to become the established church should the faithful ever constitute a majority; that a hierarchical church claiming to teach doctrines as absolutely true and demanding obedience and assent from its faithful destroyed the independence of mind and conscience necessary in democratic citizens. Around these charges, opponents of the church wove an abundant folklore of Catholic hypocrisy and depravity, which, as with other suspect groups like blacks, Jews, and Mormons, commonly focused on sex and the violation of women—in the Catholic case, on the celibacy of priests and nuns, an "unnatural" sham that rendered convents "priests' harems" and "Roman brothels."

In fact, Catholicism did differ from Protestant America in its understanding of how conscience should be formed and exercised. For Catholics, determining the truth could not be separated from determining what community of faith was the bearer of truth. Non-Catholics complained that the church did not want the believer to think for herself; Catholics responded that, yes, the believer should think for herself—but not *by* herself. The church honored autonomy but neither in the way nor to the extent that Protestant America did. Autonomy had a different weight and place in the Catholic constellation of virtues than in the Protestant one. But was autonomy the only virtue pertinent to citizenship? Did the Catholic constellation make for poorer citizens? Or possibly, as Catholics thought, for better citizens?

SUDDENLY, BETWEEN 1960 AND 1965, all the residual stress points between Catholicism and America's public ethos seemed to collapse. The campaign of John F. Kennedy for president had first revealed how much of the old suspicions remained alive. But Kennedy's victory rendered all that anachronistic. The liberating effect on American Catholicism was enormous. It was gospel truth among Catholics that Al Smith had been defeated in 1928 because of his religion, and the memory weighed heavily. For a Catholic boy like myself, the classic daydream was not to become president but to become the first *Catholic* president.

Catholicism had more than arrived, it seemed. The year of Kennedy's election saw the American Jesuit theologian John Courtney Murray on the cover of *Time* magazine. Murray's collection of essays *We Hold These Truths* went beyond denying incompatibility between Catholicism and the nation's constitutional framework. Catholicism, Murray argued, would rescue the founders' vision from the secularism, materialism, and relativism that was undermining it. Again, it was a case of that prickly apartness: the church had preserved belief in an objective order of truth, a natural law discoverable by human reason and dialogue, and a transcendent basis for human dignity; now it offered these principles as the basis for a public consensus that would put American freedom on a firm footing in an age of pluralism.

Kennedy's victory and even his elevation to the pantheon of assassinated martyrs were soon overshadowed by the Second Vatican Council. The Declaration on Religious Liberty explicitly affirmed what American Catholics had long held: there should be no coercion of conscience in matters of religious belief; the state need not profess or privilege the one true church; all faiths, rather, could enjoy civil tolerance. The declaration not only reflected the American experience of church-state separation; it was framed to a significant degree by Father Murray, and it rescued American Catholics from the equivocal position in which they had always been placed, at least on paper, by older church teachings.

Beyond the Declaration on Religious Liberty, the Council did three other things with major implications for the role of the church and of Catholic citizens in civic life. First, it shifted the understanding of the church's mission from one almost exclusively focused on preparing individuals to attain eternal life to one that emphasized witnessing to God's love and compassion by striving to bring justice and healing to the world right here. Second, the Council changed the church's stance toward modernity, from one of almost blanket suspicion and antagonism to one of critical sympathy and engagement. The church shared the joys and hopes, grief and anguish of the age rather than tsk-tsking them from afar—a shift in attitude of obvious relevance to a culture as self-consciously modern as America's. Third, the Council announced a new, positive attitude toward the other branches of Christianity. Conciliar documents acknowledged the need for church reform, emphasized the place of scripture in the church's life and liturgy, stressed the calling of the laity and the need for collegial structures in church governance—all implicit bows to features of Protestant Christianity. Relations with Protestant America were placed on a dramatically new footing. Certainly these last two shifts sounded a death knell for prickly apartness.

Catholicism's political face changed dramatically during the decade of the Council. The country was caught up, first, in the civil rights movement and then the anti–Vietnam War campaign. Nuns in habits marched on picket lines. Priests joined black-led demonstrations in the South and then returned home to mount inner-city protests in the North and engage in civil disobedience. The Reverends Daniel and Philip Berrigan and Sister Elizabeth McAlister put a distinctly Catholic stamp on the seizure and burning of draft records and other dramatic nonviolent protests that religious activists carried out in several cities. This more radical current of Catholic political engagement was not without precedents—primarily in the pacifist, anarchist Catholic Worker movement, led since the early Depression years by Dorothy Day. Its "houses of hospitality" not only provided food and shelter for down-and-outers in numerous cities but became nurseries for radical theological and political thinking.

Radical sixties Catholicism left a permanent mark on the church's presence in the public square. It melded the imperatives of the Council with the civil rights movement's techniques of civil disobedience and nonviolent direct action and with the antiwar movement's nearly apocalyptic mood of urgency. Added was the influence of Latin American liberation theology. Where Catholic social and political thought had typically stressed cooperation and rejected conflict, Latin American liberationists, borrowing from Marxism and from the reality of their social situation, insisted that conflict was unavoidable and the church's traditional posture of impartiality sided in reality with the status quo. Theology had to be political, had to be done from the perspective of victims, from shantytowns instead of university classrooms; and the church had to exercise a "preferential option for the poor." Given the turmoil and confrontations of the sixties, this was explosive stuff, sometimes embraced uncritically by priests and nuns who, having just freed themselves from doctrinaire piety, now substituted a no less doctrinaire ideology. Almost inevitably the momentum of radical Catholicism was lost as the fevers of the time were lowered, conservative and neoconservative counter-movements arose in response, and Catholic belief confronted a new challenge, the Supreme Court's 1973 ruling on abortion, *Roe* v. *Wade*. The politics of Catholicism would take on a new complexity.

THE NEW COMPLEXITY, too, had its precedents. As a church of immigrants, Catholicism had always leaned both left and right. It supported forces that promised to relieve Catholics' material hardships; it opposed forces that promised to undermine fundamental moral teachings embedded in the traditional outlooks of immigrant communities. The problem, of course, was that often enough these forces could not be neatly sorted out.

In 1884, Cardinal James Gibbons of Baltimore staved off a Vatican condemnation of the rapidly growing Knights of Labor, a group that he considered an understandable response to the grievances of workingmen. His action is often credited with positioning the church as a friend of labor; consequently, in the United States, unlike in much of Europe, the church retained the loyalties of its working class. Catholics did play an enormous role, as leaders and as rank-and-file members, in the labor movement. The church produced outstanding "labor priests" who rallied behind hard-pressed union organizers and frequently served as mediators in industrial conflicts. Religious orders operated "labor schools" offering introductions to Catholic social teaching as well as practical training in organizing and parliamentary procedure. Yet all this activity was hedged around with cautions, concern about social disorder, defense of traditional male and female roles, and the desire to fend off more radical alternatives. The American church was following the lead of the papal encyclicals that endorsed unions and condemned rapacious capitalism but also defended private property and condemned class conflict and socialism.

The Bishops' Program for Social Reconstruction, promulgated in February 1919, foreshadowed the New Deal in urging government provision for public housing; minimum wages; unemployment, disability, and old-age insurance; health and safety regulation; child labor restrictions; fair labor laws overseeing unionization and bargaining; high taxation and other measures to limit or regulate monopoly. When Monsignor John A. Ryan drafted this list of reforms, which two decades later he vigorously supported from his position as a prolific writer and as director of the bishops' Social Action Department in Washington, he managed to align Catholic natural law principles with Progressive Era politics. The alignment broke down, however, when Ryan took up topics like birth control and marriage—or eugenics, a pet Progressive cause. And even Ryan, in campaigning for laws restricting child labor, found himself struggling against powerful Catholic leaders like Cardinal William O'Connell of Boston, who feared that "this soviet legislation" would interfere with the rights of parents.

There were plenty of political crosscurrents churning the Catholic world long before *Roe* v. *Wade*. Catholic voters were a loyal component of Franklin Delano Roosevelt's New Deal coalition, but they were suspicious of New Deal "brain-trusters" given to "social engineering." Catholics were strongly anti-Communist, and from the 1920s through the 1950s, almost everything, from the persecution of the church in Mexico and in Civil War–torn Spain to the expansion of Communist power in Eastern Europe, China, and Vietnam—or even in American labor unions—fed into a vision of global struggle between Communism and Catholicism. One segment of Catholic citizens was susceptible to the Depression-era anti-Semitic blandishments of the popular radio priest, Charles Coughlin. In the 1950s, a much larger segment rallied to the demagoguery of Wisconsin's Senator Joseph McCarthy. Race, too, roiled Catholic politics. From a distance, Rome had always pressed Catholics to reject American racism. A few pioneering Catholic clergy and activists, black and white, had done the same, their numbers swelling in the 1960s. The hierarchy vacillated, caught between their principles and the fears and prejudices of many parishioners, particularly in ethnically defined neighborhoods. Some bishops led; others lagged.

At the voting booths, Catholics liked Ike, but not quite as much as most other voters. Catholics rallied behind JFK, then followed national trends in the elections of Johnson, Nixon, Carter, Reagan, and so on. Democrats, winners or losers, almost always did better among Catholics than they did altogether—and this has remained even truer at the congressional and local level—but the margin has steadily diminished. In 2000, exit polls showed Catholics voting 50 percent for Gore, 46 percent for Bush, 2 percent for Nader, and 1 percent for Buchanan. Non-Hispanic weekly Mass goers favored Bush; less regular Mass goers as well as Hispanic Catholics favored Gore.

A postelection study of the religious vote showed that non-Hispanic Catholics who attended Mass once a week or more (33 percent of the Catholic voters) voted 57 percent for Bush and 43 percent for Gore. With the somewhat larger group (42 percent of Catholic voters) who attended Mass less frequently, the reverse was true: 43 percent voted for Bush, 57 percent for Gore. Hispanic Catholics voted an overwhelming 76 percent for Gore and only 24 percent for Bush, while nominal Catholics followed a similar pattern, voting 65 percent for Gore, 35 percent for Bush. Leaving aside the Nader or Buchanan voters, for the Catholic community the overall split between the two leading candidates was 49 percent for Bush, 51 percent for Gore. This pattern reflected the higher turnout of weekly Mass attenders and the lower turnout of others, especially Hispanic and nominal Catholic voters. Republican analysts stress the weekly Mass-attending segment of this vote, which nonetheless shows a continuing Democratic edge.

EARLIER IN 2000, a study of American Catholics in the Public Square tried to determine not just which way Catholics were voting but whether their political views were shaped by their religion. Representative samples of Catholics were polled in January and February and then again in September. Meanwhile, Catholics were asked to talk about politics and religion in eighteen focus groups formed in fifteen cities, comprising different socioeconomic and ethnic groups of the faithful. (The mid-September poll showed Catholics leaning to Gore more than they actually did in the polling booths, although an exceptionally large percentage was still undecided and the poll accurately predicted an extraordinarily close presidential contest.)

Although these studies confirmed that Catholics were "less reliably Democratic" than in the past, realignment with the Republican Party was also far from a fact. In fact, the two polls showed Catholics still more likely to consider themselves Democrats than Republicans (35 percent to 26 percent), with over 30 percent calling themselves independents or other. When independents and others were pressed on whether they felt closer to the Democratic or Republican Party, the "leaners" followed more or less the same proportion of Democrats to Republicans, with roughly a third continuing not to choose. (Not surprisingly, this percentage of "stubborn" independents decreased, from 17 to 10 percent, between the poll taken in the beginning of the year and the one taken in the middle of the campaign season.) When the Democrats and Republicans were asked whether they were "strong" or "weak" members of their parties, almost as many said "weak" as said "strong." Altogether, then, one gets the picture of continuing Democratic loyalty, but with large percentages of Catholics on both sides of the political divide falling into the categories of "weak" party members or " independent leaners." Although 52 percent considered themselves Democrats or (in the case of independents) closer to the Democrats, only 19 percent considered themselves "strong" Democrats. While 38 percent called themselves Republicans or closer to Republicans, only 15 percent called themselves "strong" Republicans. This is indeed the profile of a swing vote.

Ideologically, Catholic voters appeared equally poised between camps, in keeping with the church's hybrid mix of both upholding traditional morality and endorsing governmental activism to repair inequities. Catholics proved similar to other Americans in preferring the label "conservative" to that of "liberal," and 42 percent of them called themselves conservative rather than liberal or moderate on "moral issues like abortion." But only 29 percent described themselves as conservative regarding "social welfare programs that help the poor and needy." Asked which was more important, "improving government services such as education and health care, even if it means higher spending" or "cutting taxes and reducing government spending," 62 percent chose improving government services and 38 percent cutting taxes. Asked which statement came closest to their own views—"The responsibility for getting out of poverty rests primarily with the poor themselves" or "Society has a responsibility for helping poor people get out of poverty"—63 percent emphasized society's responsibility rather than that of poor people themselves. The typically liberal positions on government services and social responsibility for combating poverty had considerable resonance among Republican Catholics and, of course, even more among the Democrats.

It is one thing to identify distinctive patterns in Catholics' political attitudes. It is yet another thing to connect those specifically to their faith, rather than, say, to factors that might set Catholics apart but not be strictly religious, like their particular socioeconomic status, ethnic histories, regional and urban concentration, and so on. In the poll taken early in 2000, about a quarter of a representative sample of self-identified Catholics replied "very much" when asked how much they drew on their faith in making political choices. Another 38 percent replied "somewhat"; 14 percent said "not much"; and 21 percent said "not at all." How much, in the opinion of these Catholics, did various elements in their church life—Catholic education, their parish, homilies and prayers at Mass, and statements by church leaders like bishops and the pope—influence the way they connected their faith and politics? Catholic education was far and away the most influential, with 44 percent saying it was very influential and a total of 77 percent saying it had influenced them politically "very much" or "somewhat." (About half the sample had attended Catholic schools at some time.) Homilies and prayers at Mass ranked an interesting second, with parish and leaders like the pope and bishops not far behind. Catholics were more or less evenly divided as to whether they wanted priests to bring up political issues in the pulpit, recommend contacting elected officials, or even urge support for specific laws—but they drew a sharp line against endorsing or opposing a candidate or a political party.

The picture that emerges from Catholics' testimonies about the influence of their faith on their political choices is obviously ambiguous. The portion saying they were influenced "very much" was equaled by the portion saying "not at all." The largest group was the one saying "somewhat." If graded on success in shaping Catholics' political views, the church's report card might record anything from a C plus to a B plus. When asked to choose which of several "Catholic teachings" they found most important for political decisions, many more picked "the need for moral values in society"—a rather anodyne, catchall phrase—than "the sacredness of human life" or "the need to care for the poor and needy" or "the importance of personal responsibility," all phrases associated with particular political stances, whether right-to-life or antiwar activism, liberal support of antipoverty efforts at home and abroad, or even a kind of tough-love commitment to rewarding individual and social discipline. On issues like vouchers allowing parents to choose their children's schools, the use of U.S. troops for peacekeeping missions even when national security is not at issue, legalizing physician-assisted suicide, forgiving the debts of third world nations, and ending capital punishment, Catholics overwhelmingly aligned themselves with church statements only on the first. When it came to using U.S. troops in peacekeeping missions, opposing the death penalty and physician-assisted suicide, and forgiving third world debts, the most that could be said was that Catholics were probably less at odds with the positions endorsed by Catholic leaders than were most other Americans. One interesting finding was that while the percentage of Catholics recalling that they had actually heard about statements by church leaders on assisted suicide, the death penalty, or debt forgiveness for poor nations varied greatly from issue to issue, in every case most

Catholics accurately identified the church's official position—even though they didn't agree with it. So much for the consoling thought of some Catholic leaders that such divergence stems only from ignorance of the church's stance rather than conscious disagreement.

The 2000 polls also explored the ambiguities and complexities of Catholic voters' attitudes about abortion. For it was the Supreme Court's 1973 decision overturning whatever laws limited access to abortion in all fifty states that created the present perplexity. The Catholic Church, its teachings, and many of its most active members have become pieces that simply don't fit into the puzzle of American politics.

THE MAIN REASON why the abortion issue has so deeply affected the church's political stance is that it is about life and death. True, the context is sex, and attitudes toward sex and women have undoubtedly colored Christian moral teaching on abortion over the centuries. But the moral principles governing abortion are first and foremost the principles governing killing. If, as the church maintains, what is being killed is a human life, that brings the issue to a whole new level of gravity. Abortion involves a woman's body and a woman's life; but in this view it also involves another body and another life—or, currently in the United States, over a million such lives a year. These are matters that even many Catholics in disagreement with church teachings on sex or with church practices toward women cannot take lightly.

That is not to imply that Catholics are of one mind on abortion and its legality. Everyone knows otherwise. *Roe* v. *Wade* actually came at a particularly difficult moment for American Catholicism, less than five years after the prolonged reexamination of the church's rejection of contraception had ended in confusion and bitterness. The credibility of the church's teaching on sexual matters took a blow from which it has yet to recover.

In those circumstances, even the nation's Catholic bishops, although swift to declare opposition to *Roe* v. *Wade* and call for a constitutional amendment to protect unborn life, were slow to organize, and appear to have been prodded into a full-scale organized campaign by grassroots antiabortion activists. When the bishops did undertake their 1975 "Pastoral Plan for Pro-life Activities," which included education among Catholics and provisions for aiding women with problem pregnancies, along with a much more visible campaign to shape public policy, the public-policy plank met a cool reception among more liberal Catholics still smarting from *Humanae Vitae*, still disappointed with the hierarchy's ragged efforts to implement the reforms of Vatican II, and still rankled by memories of past crusades, whether against dirty movies or godless Communism, that seemed to identify the church with right-wing rhetoric. Liberal Catholics had also reconciled the church's insistence on universal moral principles with a pluralist America by cultivating those strands of Catholic tradition, highlighted by John Courtney Murray, that distinguished between law and morality, neither divorcing the one from the other nor equating them either. This was the basis of the case New York governor Mario Cuomo made, in a September 1984 speech at the University of Notre Dame, for acting in accord with *Roe* v. *Wade*'s legalization of abortion despite his personal conviction that abortion was immoral. Among many Catholics, these attitudes—skepticism about church teaching related in any way to sex, distaste for whatever seems to put the church in bed with conservative militants, and awareness of the distinction between what might be immoral and what should be illegal—still suffice to keep the church's antiabortion exhortations from full acceptance. In addition, despite church teaching, Catholics share a widespread intuition that unborn life is more deserving of protection as it is more fully developed. Catholic women, in particular, aware that burdens from problem pregnancies are often left on the mother's shoulders, have frequently voiced support for legal access to abortion while simultaneously deploring abortion as immoral—an escape hatch or life preserver, hopefully never to be used, but there just in case. Then there are many Catholics who, being human, have simply accustomed themselves to accept what is now part of the culture.

For many other Catholics, especially those knowledgeable, reflective, and conscientious about their religious beliefs, the abortion issue has drastically altered the political landscape and vastly complicated the way they relate their faith to their politics. For one thing, the church's antiabortion campaign did *not* initiate a massive conservative shift. The bishops took more highly visible liberal positions in the decade and a half after *Roe* v. *Wade* than perhaps at any other time in history. They were regular critics of the Reagan administration's military involvement in Central America. "The Challenge of Peace," a 1983 pastoral letter on the morality of war in a nuclear age, was debated in prime time and on front pages as it passed through several drafts. Its immediate effect was to question the administration's arms buildup and associated talk of nuclear "war-fighting" strategies. Its long-range effect was to bring traditional categories of just and unjust warfare to bear on modern issues of nuclear weaponry and deterrence so persuasively that this discourse has been taken seriously by the armed forces and become an inescapable element in foreign policy debate. A year later, in the wake of Ronald Reagan's sweep of forty-eight states in the presidential race, the bishops released the first draft of what, two years later, became their pastoral letter on the U.S. economy, "Economic Justice for All." For a while the bishops' avowal of government responsibility for economic equity appeared to be the only alternative to market-dominated Reaganomics still standing.

These two major letters were not followed by others, mainly because their very public character made Rome nervous. The Vatican began choosing a new kind of bishop, oriented more toward assuring internal church order than embarking on controversial political initiatives. Nonetheless, the bishops did not swerve from less visible advocacy of what would generally be seen as liberal programs to aid the working poor, immigrants, welfare recipients, the homeless, the medically indigent, and crime victims as well as imprisoned criminals. In recent years, the bishops, nationally and locally, have become outspoken in opposition to the death penalty. In international affairs, they have pursued a cautious, moderately liberal course, struggling in particular with the ethics of "humanitarian interventions" and playing important roles in the successful movements for banning land mines and for debt relief. Repeatedly the bishops' conference has elected to its major offices prelates associated with this political, economic, and international agenda.

NONE OF THIS is totally surprising. The hierarchy's course is in line with a legacy of church teaching on social and economic matters. It reflects the church's direct contact with the poor in inner-city parishes and among new migrant communities—and globally with populations tottering on the edge of survival. And of course, it echoes positions taken again and again by Pope John Paul II.

Beginning in December 1983, seven months after ushering to passage the bishops' pastoral on war and peace and one month after being elected to head the bishops' committee dealing with abortion, Cardinal Joseph Bernardin tried to articulate the coherence of what others might see as a schizoid civic posture. A whole range of "questions along the spectrum of life from womb to tomb," he said in a public lecture at Fordham University, now "creates the need for a consistent ethic of life. For the spectrum of life cuts across the issues of genetics, abortion, capital punishment, modern warfare, and the care of the terminally ill." He went on: "Our moral, political, and economic responsibilities do not stop at the moment of birth. Those who defend the right to life of the weakest among us must be equally visible in support for the quality of life of the powerless among us: the old and the young, the hungry and the homeless, the undocumented immigrant and the unemployed worker. . . . Consistency means we cannot have it both ways." That notion of consistency also lay behind the bishops' unhappiness with the government's reliance on military force and downplaying of human rights in its Central American policy.

The consistent ethic certainly did not end arguments about how the church or Catholic voters should rank issues. Many right-to-lifers, who had frequently been more militant than the bishops, considered it a dodge and a way for liberals in the church, including in its agencies, to continue supporting liberal politicians who were pro-choice. Certainly, the consistent ethic threw up a firewall between the church and single-issue politics, which was exactly what angered those Catholics who believed that opposing abortion ought to be the single decisive issue. Others, like Bernardin himself, insisted that, rather than dilute the stand against abortion, "the credibility of our advocacy of every unborn child's right to life will be enhanced by a consistent concern for the plight of the homeless, the hungry, and the helpless in our nation, as well as the poor of the world."

The consistent ethic of life was an idea that Bernardin continued to develop in major addresses to the very end of his life, and it became the watchword, although not without controversy, of the American church's public posture.

BERNARDIN ALSO TOOK UP another issue perturbing Catholic politics—the relationship between politicians' religious convictions and their public responsibilities. Hadn't John F. Kennedy laid this matter to rest in his 1960 presidential campaign talk to the Houston Ministerial Association? As president he would be accountable to the Constitution he had sworn to defend, not to his religious faith; he foresaw no conflict between his faith and his constitutional oath, but if one arose, his only option would be to resign rather than break his oath. Oddly enough, after the emergence of the religious right, Catholic politicians sometimes did face conservative Protestant leaders, no longer complaining that the politicians conformed docilely to church doctrine but that they didn't. Primarily, however, the critics of Catholic politicians were not distrustful Protestant ministers but their own Catholic bishops. "I do not see how a Catholic in good conscience can vote for an individual expressing himself or herself as favoring abortion," the newly appointed Archishop John O'Connor of New York said during a televised press conference in June 1984. The context for the questions tossed at O'Connor was the fact that New York's Governor Mario Cuomo, a Catholic, had signed rather than vetoed legislation providing state funding of abortions. The garrulous O'Connor, who would be made a cardinal the following year, made matters more complicated when a journalist from a right-wing Catholic paper asked whether the archbishop would excommunicate the governor. O'Connor replied that he would have to think about it.

This remark set off one of the biggest, most public, and most prolonged brawls between a Catholic politician and a leading Catholic prelate in memory. Cuomo happened to be at home watching the press conference with his wife and thirteen-year-old son. "I thought the question was offensive, and I expected him to brush it off," Cuomo later told Charles Morris. "But he *didn't*. He actually *considered* it!"

"Dad, is that true? Could you be *excommunicated?*" Cuomo recalled his son asking. The governor was aghast; he was not going to let the matter rest.

In retrospect, the battle of headlines that indeed did begin between the governor and the archbishop might be seen as a key moment in the altered relationship between post–Vatican Council laity and the hierarchy. Catholic public figures had often diverged from their church leaders' wishes in political affairs, a step rendered easier by the fact that those leaders were rarely unanimous themselves. But apart from a few intellectuals, these Catholics had not challenged high-ranking bishops publicly on the principle of the thing—what could be considered theological turf. Cuomo, though a politician first, was a man of considerable learning and intellectual acumen. Some people also thought it significant that he was Italian and O'Connor Irish.

Cuomo put weeks of feverish labor and consultation into preparing his formal reply. The talk, delivered at the University of Notre Dame, sounded well-developed liberal Catholic themes about the complex relationship between morality and law appropriate to a pluralist society. "There is no church teaching that mandates the best political course for making our belief everyone's rule," Cuomo insisted. Translating moral conviction into effective public policy is something that demands prudential judgments. Is the effort likely to succeed? Will the resulting law be effective and enforceable if it does not spring from a wide moral consensus? Are there other, more attainable goods that should not be foregone in a quixotic effort to institute a controversial public policy? Cuomo believed that legally banning abortion was "not a plausible possibility and even if it could be obtained, it wouldn't work. Given present attitudes, it would be Prohibition revisited, legislating what couldn't be enforced and in the process creating a disrespect for law in general." He offered similar arguments against lesser antiabortion proposals that he had been attacked for not supporting.

Cuomo's argument could be twisted into the crude formula "I am personally opposed to abortion but I don't want to impose my view on others"—and that is exactly what less subtle politicians said. Here and there Cuomo's language lent itself to that interpretation. He did tend to personalize the source of his opposition to abortion, either as strictly "private" Catholic teaching or some quirk of his (and his wife's) conscience only modestly explained beyond their being Catholic. While he avoided the dubious language of "imposing" (as though virtually every democratically voted law didn't impose something unwanted—whether higher taxes or lower speed laws or fewer meat inspectors—on someone), he did stress opposition to abortion as a specifically Catholic cause with little note of the considerable numbers of Protestants, Orthodox Jews, and other Americans similarly concerned. Still, Cuomo's case finally rested not on some absolute wall of separation between personal faith-based morality and public policy making but rather on his insistence that the two could be joined only by way of mediating prudential judgments. Bishops like O'Connor could not slide from morality to law without acknowledging, as they regularly did in areas other than abortion, those prudential judgments, judgments on which the churchmen were no more expert than politicians and had no business treating as absolutes.

CUOMO'S NOTRE DAME SPEECH occurred in a presidential election year. In 1984, the religious right was riding high. More important for Catholics was the Democratic Party's nomination of Geraldine Ferraro, a Catholic, for vice president. Ferraro shared Cuomo's abortion politics but not his theological or polemical acumen. Moreover, she had signed an invitation two years earlier to a breakfast briefing sponsored by Catholics for a Free Choice, an aggressive pro-choice lobby that was deeply entangled, and now entangled Ferraro, in challenging not just church opposition to the legalization of abortion but Catholic teaching about its morality. When this letter surfaced, O'Connor added criticism of her to his criticism of Cuomo, with perhaps more justification had it not been in the midst of an election campaign. He was joined by other bishops—to the point that the elected president of the bishops' conference, Bishop James Malone of Youngstown, Ohio, had to reemphasize publicly the hierarchy's neutrality in presidential races.

Under these circumstances, Catholics with liberal or Democratic loyalties were primed to welcome Cuomo's argument, which in fact set off a spate of editorials and other public declarations: Malone's statement; a counterlecture at Notre Dame by Catholic congressman Henry Hyde, the Republican right-to-life standard-bearer from Illinois; a talk by O'Connor at Fordham; and about six weeks after Cuomo's speech, another major lecture by Bernardin, given at Georgetown. Without mentioning the New York governor, Bernardin granted much of Cuomo's argument, which was after all quite traditional. Separation of church and state did not mean separation of religion and politics, the Chicago cardinal said. Both the church itself and individual citizens had the right to bring their moral visions into the public debate. In this sense, he defended not only the Catholic hierarchy's engagement with questions like nuclear war and abortion but also what was then the religious right's relatively new and fiercely criticized presence in politics. But Bernardin distanced the Catholic Church's approach from the religious right's.

The church, he said, recognized both the complexity of public questions and the need to translate religiously rooted positions into language and arguments suitable for the public discourse of a religiously pluralistic society. He seconded an observation of Bishop Malone, which was also one of Governor Cuomo's, that there is a distinction between a moral principle and the best political or legal strategy for realizing it in public life. The bishops had advocated both moral principles and specific solutions in their letter on nuclear arms, but they had acknowledged the great room for debate about the latter. The church needed a similarly open discussion about specific legal responses to abortion. The deepest moral convictions of individual political leaders should infuse their policy choices, but exactly how remained complex. Bernardin limited himself to saying that politicians declaring themselves personally opposed to widespread abortion were minimally obliged to declare themselves for some change in public policy.

Six years later, in another Georgetown lecture, Bernardin spelled out the point in negative terms. He rejected "the position of a public figure who is personally opposed to abortion, but not publicly opposed in terms of *any* specific choices. . . . I do not pretend to know in every circumstance which tactics such a figure should use, but moral consistency requires that personal conviction be translated into *some* public actions to validate the personal view" (my emphases). By this time, however, the Catholic political dilemma had grown acute.

———

THE REASON LAY with the bishops, but even more with the politicians. When it came to abortion, church leaders never made themselves perfectly clear on the room between moral principle and specific strategies in politics or policy. Did they fear that clarity would cancel their leverage, or did they fear incensing loyal right-to-lifers? Whatever the reason, politicians with moral objections to abortion but also doubts that most antiabortion measures were viable had little reason to see gains in anything they did or said short of those measures.

In reality, politicians of that sort were already becoming scarce. Fewer and fewer Catholic politicians with pro-choice positions made any effort like Cuomo's to reconcile their political choices with church teaching on abortion or with the consistent ethic of life. Mostly Democrats, they were simply wholeheartedly pro-choice. Between 1984 and 1990, for example, it became obvious that Cuomo himself was not going to spend any political capital whatsoever on the abortion issue. Having argued that he was constrained by lack of a public consensus opposing abortion, he backed away from even the mildest proposals that might have shaped such a consensus. His stance was in stark contrast to the one he took on capital punishment, where he was outspoken in trying to cement a consensus against it and adamant in vetoing the legislation that reflected the consensus for it. Catholics who had taken his Notre Dame speech as heartfelt were hard pressed to find either similar courage or consistency in his abortion policy.

Meanwhile, the Democratic Party, which had supported *Roe* v. *Wade* in its platforms since 1976, added a call for government funding of abortions in 1984. In 1988, the platform dropped an earlier concession that Democrats "fully recognize the religious and ethical concerns which many Americans have about abortion." In 1992, at the Democratic National Convention, Governor Robert P. Casey of Pennsylvania asked to present a minority report challenging the party platform's endorsement of legal abortion as a "fundamental right" deserving government funding. Casey was not allowed to address the delegates. At the party's national level, opposition to abortion was becoming literally unspeakable. Democrats with national ambitions like Al Gore, Jesse Jackson, and Richard Gephardt had all jettisoned previous reservations about abortion.

If Cuomo's refusal to defer to O'Connor was emblematic in one sense, the Casey silencing was emblematic in another. For Catholics who had already cast their fortunes with the Republican Party, the Democrats' sidelining of Casey meant little more than another opportunity to say, "We told you so." But for those who found Republican policies, especially since Ronald Reagan's terms in office, an ill fit with Bernardin's consistent ethic of life, the silencing contained a harsh lesson. In Pennsylvania Casey had battled for universal health insurance and, failing that, gained coverage for poor children whose families became ineligible for Medicaid. He backed labor rights and tax breaks for the poor, improved the workers' compensation system, boosted funding for public schools, mandated trash recycling, and upgraded local sewer and water facilities. He even pushed through a controversial tax increase, keeping Pennsylvania fiscally strong during a stretch of recession and eventually passing on a financial surplus to his successor. He looked like the consistent ethic of life personified—and to boot he won reelection in 1990 by the largest margin in Pennsylvania history. If Casey's credentials as a liberal, and a politically successful liberal, couldn't earn him a hearing for an antiabortion case, what could?

THE ABORTION DEBATE created even wider problems for Catholic presence in political life. As Yale constitutional scholar Stephen L. Carter put it, *"Roe* changed the rules."

"The public rhetoric of religion," he writes, "which from the time of the abolitionist movement through the era of the 'social gospel' and well into the 1960s and early 1970s had largely been the property of liberalism, was all at once—and quite thunderously, too—the special province of people fighting for a cause that the left considered an affront. Since the 1970s, liberals have been shedding religious rhetoric like a useless second skin, while conservatives have been turning it to one issue after another." An influential school of liberal thought now demands that in political affairs only strictly secular arguments be considered legitimate. To join the political debate, citizens who are religious must either bracket their beliefs or repackage them in sufficiently secular terms.

This is a long and complicated subject, and Catholics have been caught in the middle. As Bernardin suggested, the church has recognized the difference between the shared religious language appropriate within the community of believers and the language appropriate for civic discussion in a pluralist setting. The church's own moral tradition, moreover, rested as much on philosophical as on theological premises. The abortion debate, for example, turned in large measure on exactly how to perceive and evaluate the life terminated in the abortion procedure. For the church, the principles pertaining to the nature and rights of that life are not derived from the Bible or church pronouncements in ways that those with a different view of the Bible or who are outside the church can rightly ignore. Those principles arise from the intrinsic nature of human life and community and can be known by human reflection, however much aided by religious texts or doctrines. Working within this framework, Catholics thinkers might even disagree about aspects of the abortion question, especially about the moral status of the very earliest stages of a developing life. The point is that Catholic moral reasoning about abortion is no different, no more or less religious, no more or less secular, than Catholic reasoning about racial discrimination, the justice of warfare, capital punishment, or obligations to the poor. To exclude this form of reasoning in the one case is to exclude it in the others.

When critics, because they saw this reasoning as backed by church authority, dismissed it as religious, they were not only dismissing the Catholic position on abortion but challenging a specifically Catholic public presence much more broadly. At the same time, Catholic leaders like Bernardin wanted to preserve the difference between the church's approach and that of some antiabortion evangelical allies, who relied on biblical injunctions and, in fact, used the Bible in ways quite foreign to Catholicism (and mainline Protestantism), let alone to non-Christian Americans. When media attention made militant groups like Operation Rescue at least temporarily the public face of the antiabortion movement, the difference tended to be obscured—and pro-choice adversaries lumped both approaches together as indistinguishable and equally illegitimate.

Conservatives and Republican Party strategists also lumped together the two approaches—while welcoming rather than disparaging them. That was one of the reasons that, at least until the George W. Bush presidential campaign, the faith-friendly face of the Republican Party and American conservatism did not offer an alternative to which church leaders and Catholics who were both theologically and politically reflective could respond wholeheartedly. Of course, inherited Democratic loyalties, often rooted in ethnic experience, were a factor. But the Bible-citing, born-again style was not Catholicism's. In Jimmy Carter's case this style was tempered by a kind of political humility and a caution that Carter owed to the theologian Reinhold Niebuhr's strictures about national self-righteousness. But in Ronald Reagan and his successors the born-again style more frequently manifested itself in an ebullient certainty, and this religiously infused politics seemed to short-circuit those prudential judgments and consequent compromises that Catholicism respected. Style might have been overlooked, were there not those differences in substance. One can tick off specific issues on which church representatives have regularly butted heads with conservatives lodged predominantly in the Republican Party—the death penalty, arms trade, gun control, immigrant and refugee benefits, minimum wage and maternal leave, poverty programs, health care, housing, environmental protection, and so on. Behind the specifics stand larger themes: Catholicism's positive attitude toward active government and parallel suspicion of profit-driven market competition collide with Republican denigration of government and celebration of free markets. Catholicism's refusal to distinguish sharply among the needy collides with Republican stress on character as a criterion for assistance. Catholicism's internationalism collides with Republican Americanism. Catholicism's stress on community and social obligations collides as much with the economic individualism of the American right as with the lifestyle individualism of the American left. Every four years the Catholic bishops' conference distributes a "statement on political responsibility" to stimulate reflection by Catholics during presidential election years. "Faithful Citizenship: Civic Responsibility for a New Millennium," the year 2000 edition, highlights dozens of concerns, some normally associated with conservatism and others with liberalism. Nowhere, however, does that brochure-length document mention what, far more than abortion, has become the signature issue of the Republican Party—cutting taxes.

IS IT IMPLAUSIBLE that the political landscape for American Catholicism could be so drastically altered by one issue like abortion? Isn't it true, to begin with, that Catholics are divided among themselves, much like other Americans, about abortion? Aren't a majority of Catholics at odds with church officials' pronouncements? Opinion about abortion is notoriously difficult to estimate. As in other cases, small differences in the wording of questions can have large consequences for the interpretation of results; but more than in other cases, wording about abortion frequently seems to reflect the prior understanding of the pollsters or their sponsors about what is the primary issue at stake—human life, women's rights, respect for the Supreme Court and the Constitution, legality, or morality.

Early in the September 2000 poll for the American Catholics in the Public Square study, the Catholic respondents were asked, "If you had to choose, would you describe yourself as more pro-life or more pro-choice?" They were almost evenly divided, with 46 percent opting for pro-life, 49 percent opting for pro-choice, and 5 percent unable or unwilling to respond. Asked whether they "personally approve" of abortion under a variety of circumstances, high percentages of Catholics approved when a woman's life or physical health was endangered or when she had been raped, about half approved in the case of a serious birth defect, and large proportions disapproved in cases of late abortions or abortion for sex selection. Sizable majorities disapproved "personally" in what research shows are the circumstances accounting for most abortions—emotional or financial distress or simply not wanting the child. At the same time, when asked, "Regardless of your own views on abortion, do you think abortion should be legal?" two-thirds of the Catholics said yes.

Other polls, other details—but one conclusion is firm. Like many other Americans, especially evangelical Protestants, Catholics are far from morally comfortable with a great number of the abortions that do occur; but unlike evangelical Protestants, a majority of Catholics have withstood their leaders' identification with the pro-life movement and its goal of restoring legal bars to abortion.

Quite apart from this division in Catholic ranks over abortion, aren't political veterans correct in claiming that most voters vote their pocketbooks, their fear of crime or war or cultural disarray, their ethnic identity, or their impressions of candidates' character, with abortion scarcely on this list of dominant concerns? Pro-life organizations—and sometimes pro-choice ones, too—produce polls in which sizable numbers of voters declare that candidates' positions on abortion would be of critical importance. But election exit polls seldom confirm that abortion made that kind of difference in the voting booth.

Taken together, the degree of support among Catholics for legal access to abortion and the low priority that the abortion issue seems finally to have for most voters on election day might cast doubt on the importance of this question for the church's future presence in American political life. Won't this internal division and this external indifference make abortion gradually drop away as a hot-wire issue for Catholics? Won't the church adjust to those realities and concentrate its efforts on matters where it enjoys greater consensus within its fold and greater interest within the society?

That conclusion overlooks two things already mentioned: the life-and-death gravity of the abortion issue and the kinship between the moral reasoning on abortion and that on other matters, especially the broad "life" agenda sketched by Cardinal Bernardin. Divisions in the church on abortion are sometimes compared to the laity's widespread rejection of the official condemnation of contraception, but the comparison is misleading. Not only is contraception not a life issue in the sense that abortion is, but a solid majority of Catholic moral theologians appear to find the official teaching on contraception as thoroughly unpersuasive as do most Catholic couples. Even a papally appointed commission voted overwhelmingly for change. In the case of abortion, disagreement with the official teaching, though not unknown, is much more limited—largely to questions about the protection owed the very earliest stages of embryonic life and, as seen in the Cuomo-O'Connor-Bernardin debate, about the obligation to bring the civil law into closer alignment with this moral understanding of the value of unborn life. The gap between even liberal church thinkers and the principles and practice governing abortion in the United States since 1973 remains enormous. However pastorally the church responds to women who have felt compelled to seek abortions, there is little ground for thinking that its teaching itself will be significantly modified or downplayed, let alone abandoned. A considerable number of Catholics may choose to reject or ignore that teaching, but they will not be able easily to compartmentalize that rejection from an adherence to church positions on public issues in other areas.

As for the possibility that other priorities will keep abortion on the margins of electoral battles, that view scants primary contests, where pro-choice and antiabortion stances can matter mightily because activists who mobilize and donate funds exercise disproportionate influence. That view also underestimates the way in which attitudes toward abortion can make voters feel at home or not in a political party, even though, asked to pinpoint their major concerns, they might name something else. Finally, that view also underestimates the importance of activists and networkers whose enthusiasms or antagonisms are conveyed, deliberately or not, to wider circles. Some years ago, immediately following a major election, I covered a meeting attended by Catholic bishops and many of their diocesan staff workers, the kind of people who oversee social service agencies or lobby state legislatures on behalf of migrants or poor people or assist parish committees who recruit volunteers for soup kitchens. One evening, I went to dinner with about ten of these people. Almost all were registered Democrats, and yet almost all either had not voted or had written in symbolic names ("Joe Bernardin"), both in the presidential contest and in state or local liberal-conservative face-offs that had received national coverage—so alienated were they by the pro-choice identification of their party's candidates. Several had been particularly antagonized by Democratic primaries in which candidates vied to be more pro-choice than thou, that being the test, evidently, of who was the truest Democrat. One can hear or view political ads with that message only so often before concluding that, hey, this party doesn't want me. It is one thing to be a minority; it is another to be a pariah.

NOT ONLY HAS abortion become a litmus test for the permissibility of a Catholic style of moral reasoning in politics, it has become the forerunner of other issues regarding control over human life: euthanasia, physician-assisted suicide, stem cell research, cloning, genetic interventions. On many of these issues, Democrats are increasingly committed to an individualism in choices about lifestyle, and Republicans, although divided between social conservatives and libertarians, end up committed to the individualism of market forces. Both Democrats and Republicans generally share the nation's traditional enthusiasm for science and technology and the disinclination to let philosophical worries, no matter how serious, dim the promise, no matter how uncertain, of tangible benefits to specific individuals: your elderly parent, my friend's child, some admired celebrity. Is this an environment where church leaders and Catholics who take their tradition seriously are doomed to political homelessness and irrelevance?

Homeless, but not irrelevant: that would be the analysis of political commentator E. J. Dionne. Dionne believes that Catholics reflecting the church's defiance of the standard American alignments can constitute a corrective presence, a "ginger group, a kind of leaven," in each of the major parties. "Catholics can talk of the limits of free markets among Republicans and the need to temper lifestyle individualism among Democrats."

Homeless, but not for long: that would be the analysis of a number of the architects of a Republican "Catholic strategy." In this view, regular churchgoing Catholics will find a natural home in a Republican campaign for "moral restoration" in the United States—if only the party learns to speak Catholic. By articulating its vision in the language of the church's social teaching as well as in the language of evangelical Protestants and Main Street businessmen, and by damping down anti-immigration, anti-Hispanic, and starkly laissez-faire Republican sentiment, the party can encourage Catholic ties to conservatism while neutralizing the Catholic voices that would retain Catholic ties to liberalism. Liberalism itself, with its pro-choice and secularizing tendencies, can be counted on to do the rest—driving religious Catholics into Republican arms.

Homeless, and steadily disintegrating: that would be the analysis of David Leege, a political scientist for many years at the University of Notre Dame. Leege is skeptical about how much religion itself, as distinguished from ethnicity and other factors affecting American Catholics, ever shaped their political outlook. Leege is also doubtful about the Republicans' Catholic strategy, not because he denies the appeal of moral restoration to Catholic weekly churchgoers but because weekly churchgoers are a declining part of the Catholic population. Can an effective political strategy ignore the large—and increasing—numbers who identify themselves as Catholic, hold to most major Catholic doctrines, and do attend Mass at least once a month although not weekly? More suggestive for the future, in any case, is the emphasis Leege puts on gender and generational change. Young Catholic men and women in their twenties and thirties appear to be traveling in different directions politically. The men, attracted by appeals to entrepreneurialism and no-nonsense market discipline, are being drawn to Republican ranks. The women, attracted by appeals to social welfare, to abortion rights, and to tolerance in sexual and lifestyle matters, are leaning toward the Democrats. What is interesting is that young Catholic adults put concern for the poor and needy very high in their understanding of what Catholicism requires, yet in the aggregate neither men nor women appear to translate that concern into political attitudes in the ways their parents and grandparents have.

OBVIOUSLY THE CHURCH'S PLACE in the nation's public life is being reconfigured by a change in generations and the passing of a largely clerical leadership. The role of priests, nuns, and bishops in creating Catholicism's political face actually grew to an unprecedented degree from the 1960s through the mid-1980s, and has declined sharply since. Not that some bishops and priests weren't highly political earlier, but before the Second Vatican Council, Catholics tended to differentiate the political sphere from the religious one. Political morality was a question of getting one's fair share, and it was best left to lay political leaders. Religious morality was a question of personal virtue and sacramental practice, and that was the domain of the clergy. Of course, the two spheres overlapped—for example, in matters of sex, censorship, and public decency. Of course, individual clergy, like the left-wing Father Edward McGlynn in the nineteenth century or the right-wing Father Charles Coughlin, could be politically influential, though more by dint of their eloquence (or populist or patriotic demagogy) than their clerical collars. When pastors opinionated politically in their pulpits, parishioners either nodded or nodded off, depending on their preexisting prejudices. Heaven and hell were not at stake.

That changed when the Council insisted that this world was a place of God's presence and not only a place of preparation for the next. The Council brought politics closer to the core of religious concerns that had always been the clergy's business—but the Council also emphasized the responsibility and the autonomy of laypeople in carrying their faith into public affairs. It was the former change that had an immediate impact. Activist priests could trade on their "sacred" status to get leading visible roles in the civil rights and antiwar movements. Nuns walking picket lines were a novelty in 1963. By comparison, the bishops gave much more thought to the proper limits of their authority in political matters (abortion excepted) and consulted extensively with lay Catholics. Nonetheless, the bishops could still combine their long-standing theological authority with their expanding sense of political responsibility when they took on complicated topics like nuclear warfare and the working of the economy in the 1980s. Antidotes were already at work. As noted, Cuomo's Notre Dame speech on opposing abortion was a challenge because it set out a theological argument as well as political conclusions. At about the same time, conservative and neoconservative laity mobilized by Michael Novak, himself a theologian, issued "lay letters" countering the bishops' pastoral letters on nuclear defense and on the economy. Cuomo and Novak could find ample justification for their initiatives in Vatican II. By the late 1980s, under pressure as well from a papacy that preferred reserving political initiatives to itself, the day of highly visible episcopal and priestly leadership in political matters had faded.

The generational change has been slightly more complicated. If the generation of Catholics formed in the preconciliar Catholic culture was predisposed to take bishops and priests seriously, the generation formed in the postconciliar period, which coincided with the politically tumultuous late sixties and 1970s, was predisposed to take political morality seriously. In this way, there may be more continuity in linking faith and politics between the older generation now retiring from leading places in American Catholicism and the generation succeeding them than in other areas. Catholics in their sixties and seventies and Catholics in their forties and fifties often have similar social justice concerns, and often feel the same need to integrate their convictions about abortion and about war or poverty. The discontinuity emerges with the post–baby boomers, the so-called Gen X and Gen Y Catholics for whom Ronald Reagan was their childhood president, the 1960s are ancient history, and the whole sense of the relationship between Catholicism and political responsibilities appears much more nebulous.

Catholicism's future role in American public life turns on three things: how it negotiates the present impasse with liberalism and the Democratic Party over abortion and related issues; whether it can incorporate laypeople, broad consultation, and open debate into the process of articulating Catholic positions on public issues; whether it can find fresh voices and fresh formulas to do for the next decade what Cardinal Bernardin and his consistent ethic of life did for the 1980s and 1990s.

Chapter Four

Catholic Institutions and Catholic Identity

Today we call them megachurches—huge institutional complexes capable of sponsoring groups and activities that embrace virtually all aspects of their congregants' lives. American Catholics had already invented megachurches a century ago and created thousands more in the decades that followed—imposing parishes, often ethnically based, sometimes occupying several city blocks with their elementary and secondary schools, gymnasiums and community centers, convents and rectories, some with a fully equipped parish theater or a roller-skating rink, some with an affiliated orphanage or even hospital. One such parish, Our Lady of Victory in Lackawanna, New York, near Buffalo, was the industrial town's second largest employer, surpassed only by Bethlehem Steel. Like today's megachurches, these parishes offered a panoply of clubs and activities for every category of parishioner and stage of life: youth groups, men's groups, women's groups, sports teams, choirs, devotional and burial societies, book clubs, charitable organizations. Parish processions defined the neighborhood as sacred turf. Parish carnivals were quasi-civic events.

These urban parishes were only one expression of American

Catholics' instinct for institution building, which extended to schools, hospitals, charities, publications, and dozens of other enterprises. Feeling excluded and threatened by a Protestant-dominated public school system, Catholics established their own. Responding to the needs of struggling immigrant communities, bishops, pastors, and religious orders of priests and nuns founded an extraordinary array of hospitals, orphanages, and social services. Catholic fraternal societies provided insurance while preserving ethnic cultures. Catholic reading circles and Catholic summer school programs of lectures, concerts, and dramas mirrored the nineteenth-century Chautauqua Movement for cultural improvement. Catholic newspapers by the hundreds were printed in a babel of languages, often for small ethnic readerships but sometimes with national impact. Catholic publishers sprung up to serve a growing market for Bibles, prayer books, catechisms, religious novels, and pious nonfiction.

From the nineteenth to the twenty-first century, that network of institutions has evolved and metamorphosed, expanding here, shrinking there; but its sheer extent is still astonishing.

Consider health care. Along with hundreds of nursing homes and other Catholic health care facilities, for example, six hundred Catholic hospitals—the nation's largest group of not-for-profit hospitals—care for 90 million inpatients and outpatients annually. In the radical reconfiguration of health care that has occurred in recent years, Catholic institutions have tried to keep pace: of the ten largest health care systems produced by mergers and purchases, four are Catholic.

Consider social services. There are some fourteen hundred local Catholic Charities organizations, which every year assist 9.5 million people with emergency aid, food, clothing, child care, family counseling, drug rehabilitation, summer camps, job training, pregnancy and maternal care, adoptions, and refugee and immigrant settlement.

Or consider schooling. Seven thousand Catholic parochial and private schools, plus Catholic secondary and higher education, constitute the nation's largest private educational system.

MOST AMERICANS ARE FAMILIAR with parts of this network. They see parishes, schools, and hospitals. They read about the local Catholic bishop or the United States Conference of Catholic Bishops. They know of religious orders like the Jesuits or the Sisters of Charity. Of course, they are aware of the pope and of the Vatican, the enclave that is his command center in Rome. But they are far less certain about how all these pieces, usually described in news stories as "the church," actually fit together.

It is easiest first to conceive of the Catholic Church's structure geographically and then to overlay some elements that are not geographical. The entire United States is divided into 177 dioceses and archdioceses of the Latin Rite, the major, Western form of Catholicism that once celebrated its rituals in Latin and looks to the pope for ultimate leadership. Each of these dioceses is headed by a bishop. The bishops are named by the pope, after a consultative process usually influenced by other church leaders. Bishops, however, are not simply agents or deputies of the pope: according to Catholic theology, they are successors to Jesus' twelve apostles, loyal to the leadership of "Peter" while exercising their own independent mandate for leadership, especially within their own dioceses. Thirty-one of these American dioceses, because of size or historical importance, are designated as archdioceses and their bishops known as archbishops. From among these archbishops, usually, a handful are named cardinals, or special advisers to the pope and electors of a future pope.

Each of the dioceses is divided geographically into parishes, and most parishes are headed by diocesan priests, ordained by a bishop, pledged to celibacy and obedience to their local bishops. In densely populated and highly Catholic cities, a parish may consist of a dozen or two dozen square city blocks; in sparsely populated areas, where the Catholic population is thin, a single parish may consist of hundreds of square miles. One way or another virtually every square inch of inhabited American territory falls within the boundaries of a Catholic parish. When the number of parishes changes over time, it is because a growing number of Catholics within a given area has led a parish to be divided, and a new one established, or on the other hand, because the Catholic population has shrunk and one parish may be merged with another. Parish closings of this kind are traumatic and get more attention than the establishment of new ones, even though the latter occurs more frequently, since the Catholic population continues to grow.

This geographical dimension is important. With some exceptions, Catholics are to belong to the parish within whose boundaries they live. Although an increasing number of Catholics skirt this norm to seek a parish more congenial to their own taste or outlook, this geographical dimension still gives Catholic parish life a special character. Protestant or Jewish congregations are defined by their members, not by a stretch of turf. They can up and relocate the congregation in suburbia if that is where the congregants have moved. Catholic parishes stay, whether or not the parishioners do, and that gives parishes and sometimes the parishioners a substantially different relationship to their neighborhoods. Major developments in urban history have hinged on this fact.

But the overlay to Catholicism's geographical structure is equally important. There is a Latin Rite military archdiocese, for example, responsible for military chaplains and serving Catholics in the armed forces anywhere in the United States or overseas. There are also fifteen eparchies, or dioceses that oversee Catholics who belong to rites stemming from Eastern Europe or the Middle East and retaining different forms of ritual and organization than those developed in the Latin West. The eparchies, some regional, some covering the entire country, are the equivalent of dioceses for Ukrainian, Ruthenian, Romanian, Syrian, Melkite, Chaldean, Maronite, and Armenian Catholic parishes wherever these are located.

The United States Conference of Catholic Bishops is the collective instrument of all the nation's bishops. The entire hierarchy meets for several days twice a year to discuss internal church business and moral issues facing society. The bishops elect their officers from among their ranks. They serve on committees dealing with everything from doctrinal questions to public policy. They hire permanent staff. They represent official church positions before the public, in forms ranging from congressional testimony to major pastoral letters that are painstakingly drafted, debated, revised, and ultimately approved, or less authoritative statements issued by top officers or standing committees. The national conference conducts studies, sponsors programs, and publishes material that can be used by dioceses or parishes. But the powers of the conference are strictly limited. No bishop has to use conference materials. Any bishop is free to disagree publicly with conference statements. If such conflicts happen rarely, it is because the conference normally proceeds on the basis of overwhelming consensus and bishops normally prove to be team players. Only in regard to liturgical practices, like choosing the scripture translations used at Mass or establishing uniform rituals for the sacraments, is the conference empowered, as a matter of course, to set policy binding on individual bishops, although it can also act with authority in some special cases, like the policy on priests who sexually molest minors. Conference decisions in these cases as well as liturgical matters must be ratified by the Vatican.

Among the church structures that cross diocesan and parish lines, by far the most familiar and most important for the overwhelming majority of Catholics (who, after all, belong to the Latin Rite and are not in the armed forces) have been religious orders. Benedictines, Carmelites, Trappists, Franciscans, Dominicans, Jesuits, Christian Brothers, Sisters of Charity, Sisters of Mercy, Little Sisters of the Poor—these names and many more come quickly even to the minds of people who have only a vague sense of what defines such religious communities, how one differs from another, and how they are linked to bishops or parishes.

The history of celibate men and women who join together in communities, live in accordance with a common rule, and devote themselves to particular forms of prayer or good works dates back to the church's earliest centuries. Different orders, founded at different times, have focused on different activities: liturgical prayer, silent contemplation, penitential sacrifices, manual labor, missionary work, or the search for knowledge, both of God and of God's creation. Inspired by charismatic founders or responding to the needs of their place and time, some religious orders have specialized in preaching, others in educating the poor or nursing the sick and dying, still others in theological learning and advanced scholarship. Some men's orders consist entirely of priests; others of brothers, who take vows but are not ordained; some men's orders include both brothers and priests. Orders of women, for whom ordination has never been possible, have varied more in the extent to which they remained largely within their convents or conducted more public lives in nursing and teaching. Although public vows of poverty, chastity, and obedience are common to religious orders, each order's own rule dictates precisely how the group will be governed and how its members will live. Once these rules have been approved by Rome, orders have considerable autonomy and independence from local bishops in managing their internal affairs or deciding whether or not to undertake some task within a diocese. Tensions between religious orders and local bishops are one of the long-running dramas of Catholic history.

In the United States, the men and women of religious orders played a central role in creating the vast network of Catholic institutions. In some ways, while bishops and diocesan priests kept the existing parishes going, the priests and sisters in religious orders were the entrepreneurs, the adventurers, the experimenters, who broke new ground, founding hospitals and colleges, staffing primary schools, launching missionary efforts, starting publications, and guiding new organizations for laypeople.

The Official Catholic Directory devotes a half dozen pages to na-

tional organizations that have some relationship to the bishops' conference. These include associations of theologians, canon lawyers, religious educators, campus ministers, pastoral musicians, Scout leaders,
cemetery administrators, church fund-raisers, and heads of religious
orders, as well as ethnic, occupational, and devotional groups. It includes Catholic Relief Services, the church's arm for international development and overseas aid, and Catholic Charities USA, the umbrella
group for local Catholic social services. And then there are national associations of local institutions, like the Catholic Health Association and
the Association of Catholic Colleges and Universities.

That official list turns out to be only the tip of an iceberg. Missing,
for example, are the Knights of Columbus, a giant fraternal society
that provides insurance and sponsors charitable activities across the
continent. The Knights' absence is a reminder of hundreds—more
probably thousands—of Catholic organizations, less visible to be
sure and less affluent as well, that operate across the boundaries of
parishes and dioceses: missionary societies, movements for social
change or for renewal within the church, professional groups, devo-
tees of particular saints or spiritual practices, Catholic philanthropies, publishers, magazines, and on and on. They may have the
formal approval and institutional backing (money!) of a local bishop
or a religious order. Others may be independent, or simply not disapproved. National media, such as *Commonweal*, the *National Catholic
Reporter*, and the Eternal Word Television Network (EWTN), offer a
diversity of views on Catholic matters. The more conservative Lega-
tus vies with the more liberal Call to Action in shaping an agenda for
church reform.

CATHOLICS ONCE TOOK PRIDE, perhaps excessive pride, in this network of institutions, especially when manifested in the solid, brick-
and-mortar structures that filled so many town and city blocks.
Outsiders, on the other hand, oscillated between envy and nervousness.
Since the Second Vatican Council, Catholics have viewed their institu-

tions more matter-of-factly, alert to the danger that heavy institutional responsibilities can dull the vigor of the faith, just as the letter killeth the spirit. But there is only dawning awareness that the future of this network is uncertain. Its economic base, to begin with, is precarious. In the case of the parochial school system, of course, the financial strain has become a matter of widespread discussion and even political controversy as Catholics and sympathetic school reformers have argued that these schools should be eligible for government support in the form of vouchers or tax credits. Health care and social services confront different but equally daunting problems. Precarious finances are an old story for many of these Catholic institutions.

The new story is the crisis in Catholic identity.

To put the matter bluntly: What is Catholic about Catholic health care? Is it different in its healing methods? What is Catholic about Catholic higher education? Is it different from the courses and programs offered by the state university down the road, which now probably has a religious studies department and a Catholic student center? What is Catholic about Catholic social services? When a local Catholic Charities finds emergency housing for the victims of a fire, advises immigrants on their legal status, or offers safe refuge to abused women, is this help significantly different from services offered by other agencies? Questions like these go to the very raison d'être of this vast network of Catholic institutions.

Questions like these are not questions for Catholics alone. Other Americans have a stake in the extensive network of Catholic institutions and their policies. In addition, many Americans are asking similar questions about their own institutions and whether they can maintain religious, ethnic, or other cultural distinctiveness without cutting themselves off from the American mainstream. In other words, these are questions, at some level, about the nature and future of American pluralism.

For a long time, Catholics did not have to ask such fundamental questions. Most of these Catholic institutions were primarily serving Catholics and were directly controlled and managed by bishops, clergy, or men's and women's religious orders. Besides, Catholics entertained a confident (and often defensive) sense that whatever was Catholic was clearly different from whatever was not, and was probably better.

Today, however, Catholic hospitals and Catholic social services serve constituencies and catchment areas that are as likely to be non-Catholic as Catholic. Although at many Catholic colleges and universities Catholic students are in the vast majority, at other schools Catholics are a distinct minority. Inner-city parochial schools often have student bodies predominantly from other faiths, Baptists in many African-American neighborhoods, Buddhists in New York's Chinatown. Equally important, the staffing of such institutions, even at the highest levels—hospital administrators as well as physicians and nurses; social agency directors as well as case workers; deans and principals as well as professors and classroom teachers—has been rapidly shifting from the priests and nuns of yore to lay professionals, many of them hired strictly on the basis of skills and with little or no regard to their religious commitment. Priests and nuns themselves, let alone the lay professionals that are taking their place, no longer view their institutions as spiritual rivals to benighted non-Catholic counterparts.

What is the church accomplishing with its considerable investment of resources in these institutions? Are they continuing to be fed spiritually, intellectually, and financially by the American Catholic community—and to feed it in turn? Or are they spinning off into a kind of separate planetary system, where they will support themselves on the basis of government funding, medical insurance payments, tuition, and fees for services, where they will continue to do good work, but where their relationship to the religious life of the nation's largest church would be minimal and peripheral?

Questions of this sort are increasingly pressing. And the answers are not simple. Does it matter whether there is no such thing as a Catholic X ray, appendectomy, or hip replacement? Does it matter that there is no specifically Catholic way of teaching reading or doing advanced algebra? Perhaps it is enough, in circumstances where other institutions, usually public ones, are somehow absent or wanting, that Catholic hospitals provide good surgery or that Catholic schools effectively teach reading and the multiplication tables, regardless of whether the operating room procedures or the third-grade pedagogy differ one whit from what others might provide, if others were able or available to do the job. Perhaps it is important for Catholic institutions simply to carry out what the church calls the corporal and spiritual works of mercy—healing the sick, sheltering the homeless, instructing the ignorant—and thereby give a corporate witness to the church's valuing of health, learning, and science. Perhaps Catholic hospitals, schools, and social agencies can draw on religious motivation in staff and volunteers to carry out with greater dedication and effort the same tasks that their secular counterparts perform.

On the other hand, it could be argued that while a Catholic hospital might not differ from a non-Catholic one in the way a hip replacement is performed, it might possibly differ in the way the patient is treated before and after. An X ray is an X ray, but maternal care, treatment for AIDS, and care of the dying could be significantly affected by religious commitments and convictions. Likewise for family counseling, helping slow readers, or teaching literature to adolescents. If Catholic institutions are to be alternatives to public or nondenominational ones, rather than their mirror images, what will make them real alternatives? Isn't it some specifically religious dimension that might create a different manner in which health care or social services are provided, a different discipline and atmosphere in inner-city schools, a different emphasis or ethos in higher education? It doesn't seem satisfactory to reduce that dimension to a few codified essentials—that Catholic hospitals abstain from performing abortions, for example, or that Catholic colleges require a semester or two of theology. Nor does it seem satisfactory to recast that dimension in elevated but cloudy terms—respect, personal attention, ethical standards—so religiously neutral that they might as easily apply to the Red Cross blood bank as to Holy Cross Health Clinic.

The problem of defining and maintaining Catholic identity is complicated not only by the new clientele of these varied institutions and the changed character of their professional leadership, but also by their funding, which now frequently mixes public moneys with fees from those directly served, both Catholic and non-Catholic, and with private philanthropy, also both Catholic and non-Catholic. To make the identity issue still more complicated, the hard questions and difficult choices shift somewhat as one moves from sector to sector, from Catholic social services, for example, to health care or to higher education.

Each sector has its own character arising from different histories, "products," and forms of organization. Catholic hospitals and health care facilities were usually founded by religious orders of women, sometimes with the sponsorship of bishops. Under the supervision of sisters, most of these institutions long operated independently. A Catholic hospital run by one order on the west side of town might have nothing to do with the hospital run by another order on the east side. Today the number of sisters has declined dramatically, and with almost no new recruits to the convent, many of these religious orders are destined to disappear. Meanwhile, health care is undergoing radical changes in organization, marked by multiple mergers and the emergence of profit-making hospital chains and corporations.

Although women's religious orders also founded many small colleges, major Catholic universities were largely the creation of men's orders, especially the Jesuits. Compared to health care institutions, Catholic colleges and universities have been fewer in number and never as fragmented. Like orders of sisters, religious orders of priests, monks, and brothers have been shrinking in size, but they were fewer, and thus often larger, to begin with. If numbers were all that mattered, men's orders would have a somewhat better chance of maintaining some kind of presence in their schools than women's orders do in either their schools or their hospitals, but the advantage is only relative.

Catholic social services, by contrast, are not generally in the hands of religious orders, although many sisters played important roles in their development and still can be found on their staffs. Having often evolved locally from initiatives on the parish and diocesan level, most Catholic social services have been brought together in diocesan Catholic Charities offices under the authority of the bishop.

So the effective decisions about Catholic identity rest in somewhat different hands from sector to sector. Likewise, questions of Catholic identity will take different forms depending on whether the product is scholarship, medical care, or refugee resettlement—as a swift overview of the issues in Catholic health care and social services and a more detailed examination of those Catholic higher education will make clear.

What remains constant across the board is a sense of what would constitute failure: not that some of these institutions might cease to exist or even consciously and deliberately cease to be Catholic—for institutions, too, there is a time to live and a time to die—but that they would mindlessly drift into essentially secular simulacra of their religious selves, still bearing the insignia but no longer sharing the allegiance, their Catholic identity hollowed out and their links to the worshiping millions in parish pews reduced to historical memory and maybe the word "Saint" or "Catholic" at the portals.

ORGANIZED CATHOLIC HEALTH CARE began in catastrophe—a response to the plagues that swept over medieval Europe and especially to the Black Death that reduced the continent's population by perhaps one-third during the fourteenth century. Heroic groups of religious men and women risked their lives to provide the victims with some modicum of care and, in the usual course of things, with last rites and burial. Vowed to voluntary poverty and a common life, some of these groups became a regular part of the urban landscape in the late Middle Ages and early modern era. Not only did they minister to the sick and bury the dead when plague swept their communities; they also founded hospitals, not for curing the ill, of course, which was still largely beyond anyone's powers, but as refuges for society's outcasts—the indigent, abandoned, helpless, deranged, and dying. For women's orders like the Daughters of Charity and the Sisters of Mercy, this required a break from a spiritual life nurtured strictly behind convent walls. It was from Irish Sisters of Mercy, for example, that Florence Nightingale, despite her suspicions of their Catholic loyalties, learned important lessons about nursing during the mid-nineteenth-century Crimean War.

The early history of Catholic health care in the United States is mostly the story of selfless women who nursed victims of cholera and yellow fever, cared for soldiers during the Civil War, and brought medical care to the frontier. Whether cleaning maggots from wounds or assisting at amputations under battlefield conditions, running small hospitals in mining-town cabins or creating almshouses, orphanages, and asylums for the mentally ill, the common task was tending without stint to the bodily needs and the psychological states of those without family or resources until either change in circumstances, natural recuperative powers, or death itself relieved the situation. The sisters often maintained small pharmacies, but their paramount skills were not scientific. Rather they brought to their patients devotion, discipline, order and cleanliness, calm, and companionship in the face of pain and death.

Naturally a considerable amount of these sisters' efforts were directed toward the Catholic community. Catholic immigrants were disproportionately among those without funds and family, who depended therefore on the sisters' help. In addition Catholic doctors and, even more often, Catholic priests found themselves barred from Protestant-dominated institutions. So Catholics created their own. Despite this concentration on fellow religionists, it is surprising how extensively the nursing orders staffed or even ran institutions serving the whole public. When physicians at the University of Maryland opened the Baltimore Infirmary, a fifty-bed institution, in 1823, they invited the Sisters of Charity, founded by Elizabeth Seton fourteen years earlier, to manage and staff it. A decade later, the same group was caring for the sick and dying at the Maryland Hospital, a municipal almshouse. Throughout the nineteenth century and across the country, sisters became the medical caregivers at many a public hospital, almshouse, prison, and orphanage. Sometimes they bumped against anti-Catholic prejudices, but these could be eclipsed quickly by the exigencies of an outbreak of typhoid or smallpox. The sisters were fervent, certainly, but there is ample documentation of their sensitivity to the religious convictions of non-Catholics, particularly those rendered vulnerable by illness and dependency. Pluralism was respected at bedsides long before it was explicated in seminary theology manuals or dreamed of in Rome.

The links between bodily care and spiritual comfort were obviously tight so long as health care was mostly prescientific and pretechnological. In most circumstances, sisters trying to offer hope and solace could take for granted a common Christian culture, even if it was tinged with anti-Catholicism. Among Catholics, sisters could draw on an extensive and intricate set of shared beliefs, images, and rituals, from the popular religious art and symbols that might adorn hospital walls to the saints and blessings that were associated with recovery from various illnesses, and of course, the sacraments of Eucharist and anointing. Nonetheless, this pervasive religious atmosphere always had its fault lines, conflicts between expectations of reserve and modesty on the sisters' part and the indecorous realities of care for frequently indecorous, especially male, patients. Tensions regularly emerged between the sisters' restricted patterns of life and their increasingly professional calling to health care. In the early twentieth century, there was even a major debate over whether sisters in hospitals could substitute more washable white habits for their traditional forms of garb. The most important question, however, was whether Catholic health care could reconcile its spiritual emphasis and distinctive religious identity with the new, science-based standards for medical education and hospital practice demanded by professional accrediting agencies in the wake of Abraham Flexner's landmark 1910 report on reforming medicine. The unqualified answer, given by the Catholic Hospital Association, newly formed in 1915, was yes. As medicine moved into one new era after another, Catholic health care would move with it, and so would the challenges for religious identity.

Some of these challenges confronted all health care but had special significance for care offered in a religious context. Incidents from a Catholic hospital illustrate one of the major changes of the last half century: Two men had heart attacks, one in 1954, the other in 1974. Both were taken to Mercy Hospital in South Buffalo. In 1954, the patient was placed under observation in a medical ward; thirty-nine days later he was released, with a weakened heart that would burden his existence for years. In 1974, with emergency resuscitation equipment ready at hand, the patient was immediately placed on an EKG monitor and taken to intensive care; after fifteen days, he was released with an excellent prognosis. The first patient declared that a "whole atmosphere of caring permeated the institution." The second patient reported that the care was impersonal and left him feeling lonely and isolated.

Those two experiences illustrate gains and losses as the American hospital metamorphosed from a place of care to a place of cure. But they also illustrate the impact of high-tech medicine on a specifically Catholic institution, one founded by the Sisters of Mercy in 1904. Fifty years after that founding, it was still extensively staffed by sisters and filled with patients drawing on a shared religious, ethnic, and neighborhood culture. Twenty years later, in 1974, that ethos had dissipated significantly. No one was willing to reject the real gains in medical outcome, but no one could deny that something had been relinquished as well.

The quarter century since then has witnessed even more striking changes as the number of Mercy nuns declined, treatment grew more dependent on medical technology, and market forces reshaped hospital practice. Mercy Hospital is now joined with two other hospitals as part of Mercy Health System in western New York and, in turn, is affiliated with a still larger Catholic Health System embracing twelve hundred physicians, eight thousand employees, and almost fifty different hospitals, clinics, and centers for primary, diagnostic, surgical, or long-term care.

Catholic Health System, moreover, has a joint operating agreement making it part of Catholic Health East, one of the largest systems in the nation. Founded at the beginning of 1998 by a dozen groups of women religious, soon joined by a thirteenth group, Catholic Health East acts as a vehicle to serve and maintain their health care ministries in a network that stretches from Maine to Florida. The system has also created an entity under church law to which existing institutions or programs could be transferred by religious orders that were simply going out of existence or, for some other reason, chose to leave health care altogether.

IN FEBRUARY 2002, a group of Catholic leaders and scholars met at a Franciscan mountaintop retreat center in Malibu, California, the remnant of a family estate that once covered much of the surrounding valleys and mountainsides. Organized by the Commonweal Foundation, the lay Catholic publishers of *Commonweal* magazine, the meeting was part of American Catholics in the Public Square, a project examining different aspects of Catholicism's presence in American public life. A major topic for this weekend was Catholic health care. With bright sunlight flooding the grounds and with views that stretched from the ocean to the rooftops of lavish homes owned by Hollywood stars, it was hard to be gloomy. But Clarke Cochran, a political scientist at Texas Tech University in Lubbock, Texas, opened the session with a rather bleak assessment. Having studied Catholic health care's public role and identity for years, Professor Cochran found the Catholic identity of institutions like Buffalo's Mercy Hospital seriously challenged by "market forces and medical technology."

"Internally," he stated, "the business practices of Catholic institutions look very much like the business practices of for-profit institutions." The CEO "is most likely to be a non-Catholic layman with an MBA from a state university, instead of a Catholic nun with an MDiv from Fordham." The realities of the bottom line left little room for the attention to the poor, the immigrants, and the outcasts that had been a central concern of Catholic institutions. At the same time, modern medicine has stressed acute care, heroic efforts to defeat illness and extend life, and reliance on machines and pharmaceuticals rather than touch and voice. Largely eclipsed was "healing modeled on Jesus," which Professor Cochran described as "personal and incarnational," valuing "care more than cure, regarding death as an enemy but by no means the most dangerous enemy."

"What would be the consequences of taking quite seriously the claim that sacramentality is central to Catholic identity?" he asked. By this, he meant the capacity to convey through the visible and tangible a message about the presence and action of the invisible and mysterious. "If health care is to be *Catholic* it needs to look, feel, smell, and taste Catholic. This demand is difficult to measure. How many crucifixes and statues does it take (per bed? per floor?) to make a hospital Catholic? Does sacramentality reside in the visible primarily, or in the tangible, the touch that passes between healer and patient? Or is it in the voice, compassion embodied in words and tones?"

However questions like those might be pursued, another participant at the meeting, Sister Patricia Vandenberg, feared that there were simply not people able to pursue them. Sister Vandenberg, who now teaches hospital administration at Baldwin-Wallace College in Berea, Ohio, is an experienced health care administrator. As a member of the Congregation of the Holy Cross, she has had to oversee mergers and closings of some of her order's hospitals. In the 1970s, when women's religious orders realized their ranks were thinning, they began promoting or recruiting Catholic laypeople to fill executive positions. But in time, this "gave way to the notion that a qualified, committed Christian," she said, "would be an appropriate candidate, and eventually that gave way to anyone who was committed to the mission and had the skills." No one planned such a shift in leadership: "A decision is made on the East Coast; a decision is made in the Midwest; a decision is made in good faith on the West Coast, and at the end of the day, you have your scorecard, and you say, 'Whoa, look at this!'"

"I am not taking exception to this evolution to lay leadership," Sister Vandenberg was quick to note, "and I'm really not taking exception to the inclusion of non-Catholics." But "if you expect someone to bear the heritage in the present moment, have it in their gut . . . and transmit it to the next generation, you cannot realistically look to somebody who has not grown up in the heritage and is not . . . sacramentally connected to the life of the church."

A similar worry has been expressed by Dr. Ann Neale in *Health Progress,* a publication of the Catholic Health Association (CHA). She urged "continuous grappling with the meaning of our Catholicity and its import for the health ministry today. Such an undertaking," she wrote, "cannot be the project of a few individuals or occasional seminars."

"For some in Catholic healthcare," she warned, "Catholic identity is something of an embarrassment. . . . These individuals' goal is to be part of the mainstream, and they believe that pursuing the meaning of Catholic identity will undermine that objective. . . . Expert as they are in business and finance, [some executives] may be uncomfortable with a mode of discourse that ponders religious convictions and values, reflects on personal experience and current reality, and attempts to discern practical mission implications for what they have always considered purely business matters."

Informal conversations at the Malibu meeting underlined the problem of who could carry on this heritage. No one has really gathered figures on the religious affiliations of the leaders of Catholic health care institutions, a significant lacuna in itself. But one conference participant, well placed to know, estimated that, of the ten largest Catholic health systems, half had non-Catholic CEOs. Of sixty-plus systems that then constituted well over 90 percent of Catholic health care, at least one-third had non-Catholic CEOs. At the local hospital level, where the turnover in CEOs is extraordinarily high, new ones, it was estimated, were increasingly non-Catholic.

Not that the distinction between Catholic and non-Catholic is necessarily critical. Catholic CEOs, as Dr. Neale's article suggests, are often as reluctant or ill equipped to address questions about Catholic identity in health care as non-Catholic ones. Both Catholics and non-Catholics may privately hold deep religious or at least humanitarian convictions, and they are typically goodwilled toward their enterprises' historic mission, however vaguely they comprehend it. But what priority do they give it, especially when it creates complications for other tasks? To whom do they delegate responsibility for Catholic identity and mission, and how much real authority do those figures have? Are there knowledgeable and dedicated people throughout these large, complex organizations on whom they can rely?

SOME PEOPLE HAVE argued that the time has come for the church and religious orders to withdraw entirely from running their own health care institutions. This is an argument that did not appeal to another participant at the Malibu meeting, the Reverend Michael D. Place. As president of the CHA, Father Place heads what is, in effect, Catholic health care's national trade association. The association represents over fifteen hundred hospitals, long-term care facilities, home health agencies, hospice groups, adult day care and assisted living programs, HMOs, physicians' groups, outpatient clinics, and foundations, sponsored by 260 groups of sisters, brothers, dioceses, and other sponsors. With others, Father Place believes that health care is an obvious area for the church to give an institutional witness. Market pressures and technological imperatives that make the task more difficult also make it all the more necessary. As both providers and political advocates, Catholic health care has a particular responsibility to those shunted into second-rate care or without care. As bearer of a sophisticated tradition of reflections on ethical issues in medicine, Catholic health care has an important contribution to make to some of the twenty-first century's most daunting problems. The church cannot address questions of medical access and bioethics effectively from the sidelines. It needs the hands-on involvement of Catholic health care both to deepen its own understanding of these questions and to speak credibly in society.

In 2000, the Catholic Health Association mustered its member organizations into composing a simple statement of identity. The statement is two paragraphs long and fits on one side of a three-by-five-inch card. The other side has a handsome illustration, reminiscent of a medieval manuscript illumination. It shows Jesus healing the paralyzed man who had to be lowered through the roof of a house because entry was blocked by a crowd. The statement itself speaks of "continuing Jesus' mission of love and healing"; of "bringing together people of diverse faiths and backgrounds"; of giving life to "the Gospel vision of justice and peace"; of attending to "the whole person"; of acting "in communion with the Church"; and of treating all people with compassion, "with special attention to our neighbors who are poor, underserved, and most vulnerable." This statement is the centerpiece of an array of booklets, videos, posters, and discussion guides distributed by the CHA.

All this could be read as praiseworthy but also rather obvious and lacking in specificity. That is not the case (as will be seen in Catholic higher education). Jesus, scripture, prayer, and other suggested rituals are prominent in all these materials. Nor is the diversity of those working in Catholic health care and those being served as patients ignored. A rabbi's testimony to his place in one hospital's ministry (and to his wife's treatment) is featured in the discussion booklet accompanying the CHA's brief statement of identity. That identity, according to the statement, goes beyond normal medical services and church ties: Catholic health care must serve the poor medically and as a public advocate. The accompanying materials signal a special Catholic interest not only in abortion and sexual issues but in genetics, euthanasia, physician-assisted suicide, pain control and care of the dying, access to health care for all, protection of conscience, and the maintenance of a pluralism of health care systems respecting the particular traditions of different groups of Americans.

Besides promoting an array of orientation sessions, workshops, discussion groups, and retreats for exploring Catholic identity, the CHA initiated a "benchmarking" project aimed at translating the ideals of Catholic identity into measurable practices or outcomes, surveying Catholic institutions to gauge the extent to which these outcomes are being achieved, identifying "best practices," and building a database to use in measuring future performance.

How reliable is the information volunteered by CHA member facilities under this program? How strong will be the temptation to put the best spin on the findings rather than ring alarm bells? The association's reports on the first round of findings, from acute care facilities and long-term nursing residences, are glowing. Whatever the final outcome, which no one can predict, this is unquestionably a serious move from the inspirational rhetoric that often obscures a sapping of Catholic identity to concrete measures.

If Catholic health care has recently felt its religious identity eroded from within, that identity is now also being threatened from without. The reason is abortion. Pro-choice networks, funded by Ford and other major foundations, are seeking to make the provision of abortions, sterilizations, and contraception a condition for participating in publicly funded health care programs like Medicare, Medicaid, or their equivalents at the state level. The immediate spur to these campaigns has been mergers between Catholic and secular hospitals (whether public or private) resulting in agreements not to provide abortions or tubal ligations (sterilizations).

It is doubtful that such mergers have significantly reduced access to abortion or other reproductive procedures barred by Catholic teaching. Most abortions do not take place in hospitals. Where hospitals are the only institution in their communities, fewer than 1 percent are Catholic, and even most of those turn out to be within twenty-five miles of a non-Catholic facility. In some mergers involving Catholic hospitals, moreover, the non-Catholic partner did not offer such services to begin with; in other cases, the merger is so limited in scope that the non-Catholic partner retains organizational independence and continues to offer the same services. But for pro-choice groups, a matter of principle is at stake: that abortions be accepted as normal medical care. In this view, not offering them disqualifies an institution as medically legitimate. A matter of politics is involved as well: to reduce the presence in health care of a church that keeps alive moral objections to abortion. For Catholic health care, what is at stake is similarly a matter of principle—that traditions with differing moral convictions not be excluded as health care providers, especially as medicine poses more and more fundamental questions about defining and exercising control over human life, beginning with abortion, perhaps, but encompassing euthanasia, cloning, sex selection, surrogate motherhood, and genetic therapies and enhancement. The CHA is determined to make the case for accommodating religiously and morally distinctive health care institutions on the basis of American traditions of pluralism and respect for conscience.

Making that case in response to pro-choice pressures has been complicated by simultaneous pressures from the Vatican and conservative Catholic forces. A number of Catholic health care providers had made their own accommodations to the variety of moral stances among their staffs and their patient populations, allowing procedures to be performed on their own or associated premises that the church continued to condemn. The issue was not abortion, a life-and-death matter about which willingness to contravene church moral teaching was virtually nil. The issue was sterilization, prohibited in official teaching by arguments that, like those against contraception, leave even some rather traditionalist moral theologians, let alone the average Catholic, unpersuaded. In a 1994 revision of the "Ethical and Religious Directives" governing Catholic health care, the American bishops attempted to create greater leeway for Catholic institutions to cooperate with non-Catholic partners having different policies on several controverted issues, especially sterilization. Rome began pressing the bishops to tighten the directives, and in 2001, after several years of jostling, they did. The theological arguments are subtle, the practical impact on access to sterilization hard to ascertain; some tubal ligations are performed in hospitals immediately following childbirth. The campaign to tighten the directives clearly gave ammunition to critics of Catholic health care, who were able to point to restrictions in Catholic hospitals on procedures far less controversial than abortion. To at least some of those already engaged in the uphill struggle to retain their institutions' Catholic identity, the Vatican demands added to the burden.

IN THE SUMMER OF 2002, the Catholic Health Association and Catholic Charities USA, two organizations that were almost a century old, held their first joint meeting. The convergence reflected a growing recognition that the two groups, along with Catholic Relief Services, the church's arm for overseas emergency aid and long-term development efforts, needed to cooperate on common concerns. Large among those concerns was Catholic identity.

Each organization had its specialized workshops, on topics like domestic violence and substance abuse (for the charities participants) or assisted living and measuring health outcomes (for the health care participants). They came together to worship in Eucharistic liturgies, and both separately and jointly they addressed issues of Catholic spirituality, religious belief, and public advocacy in a pluralist society.

Like the Catholic Health Association and its member institutions, Catholic Charities USA and the diocesan social services that belong to it have been giving new attention to their religious identity. A

Catholic Identity Project task force began meeting in the mid-1990s and by 1997 had produced a major manual, *Who Do You Say We Are? Perspectives on Catholic Identity in Catholic Charities.* The manual stated quite clearly the source of the present concern: the emphasis on professional skills and standards in staffing rather than on religious vows or devotion; the shift in clientele from a large Catholic one to a heterogeneous, indeed often largely non-Catholic one, and a concomitant shift to a diverse staff; the growing reliance on tax dollars, through fee-for-service payments or government contracts, and on general community philanthropy rather than on specifically Catholic funding; the consequent web of government requirements and regulations as well as social norms focused on protecting diversity and preventing discrimination; and finally the replacement of priests and sisters by laypeople at the very top of Catholic Charities agencies as well as in the staff ranks.

Along with historical, theological, and legal overviews of the relationship between charities work, the church, and faith, the manual includes the Catholic Charities USA Code of Ethics and study guides and model programs culled from different dioceses' efforts to engage their staff and their boards in discussion and prayer bearing on Catholic identity.

At a raucous dinner one evening during the convention and then at a more orderly breakfast in the coffee shop the next morning, I was able to gather diocesan Catholic Charities officials from around the country and quiz them about the problems of identity their agencies faced and the policies they had adopted. Between the two meals, some fifteen dioceses were represented: Milwaukee, Phoenix, Denver, Chicago, Raleigh, Trenton, Sante Fe, Galveston-Houston, Saint Paul–Minneapolis, Saint Cloud, Portland (Maine), Saint Petersburg, Yakima, Paterson, Joliet.

The stories they told paralleled those in health care but with some differences. Some of the crucial changes in Catholic social services dated back to the New Deal era. Already, Catholic agencies had become professionalized, had recognized responsibilities reaching beyond Catholics in need, and had welcomed collaboration with broadening government programs. But unlike health care, social services did not become high-tech. It was easier for large numbers of priests and nuns—even bishops—to pursue professional training in social work than to combine religious life and responsibilities with, for example, the study and practice of surgery or internal medicine. While certain problems were decades in the making—above all, the separation of professional social services from the personal contributions and face-to-face charitable activities of people in the parishes—as long as priests and nuns were plentiful, the decision makers remained a tightly integrated part of the hierarchical structure.

It was telling that almost all the diocesan officials joining me at the two meals were laypeople. At dinner, when several proposed that the bishops' heightened sensitivity about Catholic identity stemmed from the recent loss of clerical leadership, there was no dissent. "Are they really part of 'us'?" was how one charities director described the bishops' worry about lay leadership. Comments around the table revealed some anxiety about narrow or heavy-handed episcopal views of who or what was "Catholic."

Overall, however, these officials expressed a matter-of-fact, businesslike attitude. Assuring Catholic identity in their agencies was a necessity and a challenge; there were differences about the extent of the problem, but no one dismissed it as insignificant—and no one considered it intractable either. Government funding, it was generally agreed, was not the problem outsiders often imagined. Catholic agencies and government funders had a lot of experience working together and a good sense of what each could or could not do. Indeed, several officials reported more problems with private foundations than government. One recalled foundation offers to fund programs that were accompanied with, "Oh, you won't call this Catholic Charities, will you?" or, "You won't have any crosses visible, will you?" Faced with such assumptions, he said, "We walked away from $25 million."

More than in Catholic health care or higher education, where the role of religious orders created some distance between institutions and the hierarchy, Catholic social services are largely answerable to the local bishop. And much more than in health care and higher education, fields where certain organizational models dominate, the organizational charts of social services appear to vary greatly from diocese to diocese. Here a single Catholic Charities corporation with its own board and director reporting to the bishop embraces a nicely symmetrical set of agencies, each specializing in a distinct area of service. Elsewhere a jumble of agencies, projects, and institutions— some with independent histories as orphanages, say, or settlement houses but now absorbed into the diocesan structure—requires a director (and ultimately the bishop) to oversee multiple corporations, boards, and overlapping ministries.

These local variations will affect questions like whether board members should be Catholics or, if not, should meet some other criteria to ensure Catholic identity. It is generally understood that the top level of Catholic social services leadership should be Catholic— although some advocates of strict church-state separation reject that as illegitimate for an organization receiving government funds— and equally understood that hiring at other levels should proceed without regard to religion, as long as staff members are willing to abide by the Catholic agencies' mission and ethical code.

At our two meetings, the directors' assessments of their staffs' acceptance of Catholic standards and identity followed a certain pattern. Two or three of them would point out that non-Catholic staff members were often highly appreciative of the charities' religious and ethical commitments. It was not uncommon, for example, for African-American workers from an evangelical background to be much more comfortable than Catholics themselves with public expressions of religious sentiments or opportunities on the job for prayer and reflection. After several observations along these lines, another director would break in with a warning against being Pollyannaish—and an anecdote about staff members chafing at indications of Catholic identity. Not surprisingly, flash points were agency bans on advocating contraception and abortion, especially in teenage pregnancy counseling—and in some cases policies against serving on boards with representatives of Planned Parenthood or otherwise collaborating with it. A kind of professional social service ideology of religious neutrality and nondiscrimination sometimes proved problematic: one director mentioned a non-Catholic staff member who complained, with intimations of a lawsuit, that articles with a religious element in her agency's newsletter were creating a "hostile work environment."

Joseph F. Duffy, executive director of Catholic Charities for the diocese of Paterson, New Jersey, later sent along materials from the employee handbook his agency used in orienting new employees, volunteers, and board members. It emphasized Catholic identity right from the start. While it was true that the agency might be described in secular terms—drug treatment programs, day care centers, food banks, or a network of social service providers, especially with its religiously and culturally diverse workforce and population being served—"that is not all that we are." What "we are" is stated forthrightly and theologically: "a faith-based organization" that exists "to give witness to the Gospel message of Jesus Christ. That message calls us to recognize Jesus is in every man, woman, and child on this earth and . . . to serve Him through our brothers and sisters and to exercise a preferential option for the poor," guided by scripture, Christian tradition, and Catholic social teachings. The statement is similarly forthright about Catholic Charities' accountability to the bishop of Paterson and to Catholic beliefs, practices, and canon law.

The handbook is similarly forthright about its intention to welcome and respect people of other traditions and beliefs: "Our posture is clear. The Catholic Charities Agencies of the Diocese of Paterson are unashamedly Catholic organizations that welcome people and organizations of all faiths, and no faith, to share in our mission. . . . Explicit in our invitation . . . is the understanding that we do not intend to evangelize. We do not require conversion for them to become involved in our ministry. . . . Also explicit is the fact that we will not deny our faith in order to recruit volunteers or accept support." In fact, the handbook goes on to warn against the temptation to blur or veil the organization's Catholic character in order to attract funds or recruit skilled workers. "Honesty . . . requires more than silence: it requires clarity and candor about who we are." The mission, values, and identity of Paterson's Catholic Charities "should be discussed with each new employee, volunteer, and board member, and time should be regularly set aside during board meetings, annual retreats, or planning sessions to review these matters."

"Something else that I forgot to mention at dinner has to do with some practices that you find here," Mr. Duffy also noted later. "Specifically we pray before meetings. Most often it is Catholic and/ or Christian orientated but we have also used Muslim prayers and Jewish prayers. . . . For years we had an annual employee retreat/re- flection day, which fell into disuse until last year. In September and October of the year 2001 we reintroduced it as an annual event. . . . During the year we occasionally have prayer/worship services which sometimes include prayer and reflection, Mass, reading materials, etc."

Paterson may not be representative, and undoubtedly its orienta- tion of staff and board members does not always work in practice as well as it appears on paper. My impression was that other directors, although they might tailor that approach to their own circumstances or make a pragmatic case for alternative means to the same end, would not object to the Paterson policy in principle.

Indeed, their worries seemed to focus less on any growing gap be- tween their professional and volunteer staff, whether Catholic or not, and Catholic faith than on the older problem of the gap between their agencies' operations and the Catholic community—that is, the parish congregations. Directors spoke of various initiatives and staff assignments all aimed at reknitting Catholic Charities' ties with parishes, many of which are now geographically, economically, and psychologically distant from those most desperate for social support.

It is a task, furthermore, that can no longer rely on networks of fellow priests but requires lay Charities leaders to mobilize older pastors, younger and often more conservative priests, and parish lay leadership.

Those around the tables seemed mostly to be in their middle forties and fifties, not at all on the verge of retirement. But they voiced worries about their successors. Diocesan directors, it was felt, are coming to their posts with less seasoning in Catholic Charities work. It was the same question I heard sounded in Catholic health care and higher education: Who would be the next generation of leaders? Who would pass on the ethos and the identity?

SHORTLY BEFORE THE DINNER HOUR on November 16, 1999, I stood and watched the nation's Catholic bishops swarm out of a ballroom at the Capitol Hill Hyatt Regency Hotel in Washington, D.C. A mass of black suits breaking into clumps, smiling, chatting, heading for elevators, or leaving the lobby for restaurants, they had emerged from an executive session at their annual Washington meeting. Although a pro forma debate and public vote wouldn't come until the following day, the bishops had just agreed, behind closed doors, to make a 180-degree turn in their policy toward Catholic higher education.

In principle, the bishops had resolved a decade of debate over how to apply to the United States *Ex Corde Ecclesiae* ("From the Heart of the Church"), the Apostolic Constitution on Catholic Universities issued by Pope John Paul II in 1990. Only three years earlier, the bishops had approved, by a lopsided vote of 224 to 6, a process of applying the general principles set out in *Ex Corde Ecclesiae* largely through consultation and dialogue with Catholic educators rather than through strict requirements and formal lines of authority. The Vatican had sent back the American bishops' scheme, insisting on a controversial requirement in church law that Catholics teaching theology receive "mandates" from their local bishops, and insisting, as well, that Catholic colleges and universities develop clear-cut ties with the hierarchy and that other measures—like numerical quotas for Catholics on faculties and boards of trustees, and oaths of doctrinal fidelity for presidents—be put into place to assure the institutions' Catholic identity. Now in 1999, conditioned to be good soldiers, the bishops were dutifully carrying out the Vatican's wishes, reversing their own earlier position by an equally lopsided 223 to 31.

The bishops'—and the Vatican's—concerns about the Catholic identity of Catholic higher education were important and real, but their complete reversal was self-defeating, as likely to undermine Catholic identity as to strengthen it. The bishops, it seemed to me, were playing fast and loose with a network of Catholic colleges and universities unique in the world. In most nations, one could count the number of Catholic colleges and universities on the fingers of one or two hands. In the United States, there are 238 of them. A handful are research universities or liberal arts colleges of national stature. Georgetown, founded in 1789, and Notre Dame, founded in 1842, typically battle for ranking in the top twenty-five by *U.S. News & World Report*. Boston College rivals them academically as well as athletically. Holy Cross is one of the nation's finest liberal arts colleges. Other Catholic institutions are outstanding regional schools that have kept the liberal arts tradition alive or urban universities with professional schools that prepare many of their cities' lawyers, teachers, civil servants, and business leaders. Some departments and professional schools within all these institutions rank even higher among their peers. Among the women's colleges, or former women's colleges, many have shifted from a largely traditional-age student body to midlife or returning students.

The 725,000 students at these schools constitute about 5 percent of the nation's college and university enrollment. It could be argued from those numbers that Catholic higher education is not as important a piece of the nation's infrastructure as Catholic health care or social services. But those schools are probably an even more important part of the *church's* infrastructure—and hence of those other institutional networks as well. For one reason, more than Catholic health care or social services, Catholic higher education still serves Catholics—and often those Catholics likely to be among the most active church members. For another reason, a church that insists on central doctrines and bears a long tradition of highly sophisticated theological and philosophical thought is going to put a lot of store in higher education. Obviously, that concern with doctrine and an enormous intellectual inheritance is going to complicate questions of Catholic identity in ways not present in health care and social services. Hardly had medieval Catholicism given birth to what became the modern university when squabbling broke out between this unruly child and church authorities.

Another complication arises from the jumble of functions that higher education performs in the United States. It is not only a laboratory where the learned and their apprentices pursue new ideas and test old ones; it is also a character-forming (or -deforming) arena for late adolescents and young adults, offering them a kind of rite de passage through which to separate themselves from parental homes and encounter new values and ways of living; it is an important locale for ventures in friendship, courtship, and mating; it is a source of the credentials, skills, and contacts that sort people out occupationally and economically; and it is a symbol of the modern liberty of thought that had often been pitted against Catholic authorities. Finally, as the bishops' on-again, off-again votes suggest, the effort to maintain a network of distinctively Catholic institutions of higher education, more than the parallel efforts in health care and social services, revealed the cross-purposes of Vatican and American leadership.

ON MAY 1, 1991, the front page of the *New York Times* carried an article with my byline describing the difficulties faced by Catholic colleges and universities in maintaining any distinctive Catholic identity. I had worked on the story for many months, interviewing dozens of educators, revising my drafts, repeatedly setting the project aside for more pressing assignments. By the end of the decade, scores of other papers and magazines were following this issue with the intensity of sports coverage. In 1999, controversy about Catholic higher education and its religious ties often made page-one headlines in major newspapers in Boston, Washington, New York, and Chicago, as well as in *USA Today,* the *New Republic,* and the *Chronicle of Higher Education.*

In 1991, I felt no danger of being scooped. The lack of urgency did not keep me from becoming, in the years that followed, as absorbed by this issue as any bishop. When visiting Catholic campuses, I grilled as many professors, deans, provosts, or presidents as I could reach—and of course students, too—about the subject. I passed from being a reporter to being an advocate, and duly recused myself from writing any news stories on the topic.

Actually, the roots of my interest went back further. As the student editor of a Catholic university newspaper in the early 1960s, I had naturally been ready with ideas about how to run a better school. At the paper itself we had to evade a system of censorship that fit right into the absurdities of Eastern European Communist regimes described by Milan Kundera and Vaclav Havel: a ban, for example, not only on reporting the findings of Gordon Zahn, a distinguished Catholic sociologist, about the German Catholic hierarchy's accommodation to Hitler's foreign policy, but on acknowledging in print the very existence of Professor Zahn in any activity whatsoever. Since we never had occasion to run a group photo in which he appeared, I don't know whether we would have been expected to airbrush him out. Similarly we had to plow our way through official objections to publish a critical survey of religious attitudes and theology courses at the university.

What is striking in retrospect, however, is that none of our youthful rebellion was aimed at diminishing the Catholic character of our university. Quite the contrary. We wanted to report on Zahn's *German Catholics and Hitler's Wars* because we hoped that fellow students might become more thoughtful and morally vigilant

Catholics, not doubting or cynical ones. We wanted to report on dissatisfaction with the numerous required theology courses not to abolish the requirement but to improve the courses.

Catholic colleges and universities had been founded to preserve the faith and to help the newly arrived get ahead in a supportive atmosphere. At a time when secondary school academies, seminaries, and colleges often overlapped in facilities and purposes, Catholic schools opened and closed, some founded directly by bishops but most under the quasi-independent sponsorship of religious orders of priests, brothers, and sisters. Well into the second third of the twentieth century, undergraduate Catholic education at these schools featured heavy doses of theology and philosophy, usually reflecting a supposed "neoscholastic synthesis" based on the medieval writings of Thomas Aquinas. As a 1959–63 undergraduate at Loyola University in Chicago I was required to take one theology and one philosophy course each semester. The working supposition seemed to be that any priest still breathing could teach theology. Many philosophy courses, by contrast, were superb, reflecting a phase when traditional Thomism was cross-fertilizing with existentialism and phenomenology. In either case, the sheer load of such courses sent an unmistakable message that theological and philosophical reflections counted for how one lived.

Catholicism did not stop with those courses. It cropped up in history and literature, in sociology, and sometimes in science. At times its appearance was apologetic, protective of the church, its beliefs, and its actions. Just as often, the approach was demanding, questioning, self-critical. In many cases, what was involved was a different choice of topics or emphases than one might encounter in other colleges. Medieval thought, Latin America, the Reformation, laments over the antagonism between religion and science, discussions of the morality of warfare and of the Christian roots of anti-Semitism undoubtedly had a greater prominence in my college courses than if I had gone to the University of Chicago or the University of Illinois. So did certain French, British, or American Catholic writers, like

Paul Claudel, Georges Bernanos, Evelyn Waugh, Graham Greene, Thomas Merton, and Flannery O'Connor.

Beyond the course work, all Catholic schools maintained their own version of in loco parentis. Unisex dormitories or even coed visiting hours were unthinkable. A yearly retreat and a few other religious exercises were obligatory for Catholics. Although many courses were even then taught by lay faculty members—the majority, in my case—the goodly numbers of priests and sisters from the sponsoring religious orders were visible reminders of Catholic schools' special character.

None of this assured piety or intellectual conformity. Whether students were personally devout or skeptical, morally rebellious or even cynical, depended largely on the convictions and attitudes they brought with them from their homes and parishes. Vocal scoffers were rare although not unknown; quiet questioners were numerous. For the most part students concentrated on getting their degrees and hiking themselves up one more rung on the economic ladder. In the major urban universities, the majority of students were commuters, which set limits on the school's oversight of their conduct.

Although Catholic academia harbored outstanding scholars in those years, many of its leaders felt that it suffered from a sheltered or isolated existence. Well before the Second Vatican Council opened in 1962, American Catholicism experienced a wave of intellectual self-criticism that crested and crashed into churning breakers with the turmoil of the sixties. Core curriculums stressing theology and philosophy gave way to student choice. The buyers' market in faculty, which allowed Catholic schools in the hinterlands to hire young scholars with Ivy League degrees and Ivy League ambitions, coincided with American Catholicism's new demand for academic excellence and inclusion in the intellectual mainstream. Many schools transferred governing authority from the religious orders to boards controlled by lay majorities. The church was recognizing new roles for its laity, and school officials realized that loosening the mechanisms of church control might appeal to new sources of funds, both private and state. Schools similarly pledged themselves to the same norms of academic freedom that prevailed in secular higher education.

All these developments provoked worries and complaints, but often the criticism was undercut by what seemed like a nostalgia for a supposed golden age that to many Catholic educators meant, in fact, a defensive, isolated, ghetto Catholicism. What might be the long-run consequences if most of the bright young scholars flooding the best Catholic campuses weren't Catholic themselves or, Catholic or not, shared the strictly secular scholarly interests dominating their chosen disciplines rather than anything particularly bearing on Catholicism or even religion in general? Merely to raise such a question sounded suspiciously like a retreat from academic rigor and openness into a rejected parochialism.

MY DOZENS OF INTERVIEWS with Catholic educators at the beginning of the 1990s consistently revealed two states of mind: denial and fear.

An official at one university sent me a national study he had made of the Catholic character of Catholic colleges and universities. A priest and member of the religious order that had founded the university, he had defined Catholic identity in terms of a concern for individual students' whole well-being and not only their intellectual achievement, the promotion of service to the local community, and so on. By this definition, the results showed that the religious identity of Catholic campuses was in fine shape. When I pointed out that almost all humanistically inclined, liberal arts schools would affirm the concerns he had defined as distinctively Catholic, he seemed oblivious to the implicit question behind my observation—and nonplussed when I spelled it out. In the same interview, he proudly volunteered that the university had just hired a dean of students without any consideration of her religious background.

The more common note, however, was not denial but fear, fear that putting a premium on anything distinctively Catholic, or even generally religious, in recruiting a faculty, designing a curriculum, or regulating student life would risk one's standing in the academic community.

When I asked the head of a biology department at a Catholic school whether an otherwise well-qualified candidate for a post would profit from also having a scholarly interest in the long-standing discussions of the relationship between science and religious faith, the reply was that the candidate ought to keep such an interest under wraps. Otherwise, it was explained to me, the candidate might seem to be trading on something besides the biology discipline's strict definition of professional qualifications in genetics, cell biology, or whatever was the candidate's chosen specialty.

Philosophy departments, I discovered, were particularly nervous. Precisely because of the rich heritage of Catholic philosophy and its close ties with Catholic theology, philosophy departments at many Catholic schools felt pressed to distance themselves from any religious coloration that might threaten their academic respectability— some of them to the point, I was told, that anyone with a background in Catholic philosophy was at a positive disadvantage in seeking a position.

At many schools, one tactic for relieving these anxieties was simply to relegate the institution's Catholicity to extracurricular student organizations, liturgies, retreats, and other activities organized by campus ministry offices, or to the counseling provided in residence halls or psychological services.

I also began noticing how many Catholic institutions downplayed their Catholic connection in student recruiting ads and brochures, fund-raising appeals, and job announcements. What was stressed was their city, region, history, or founding religious orders. Jesuit schools evoked their order's historical association with Renaissance humanism and rigorous learning. Franciscan and Vincentian schools recalled the images of all-embracing charitable service associated with Saint Francis of Assisi and Saint Vincent de Paul. In a culture warm to vague spirituality but suspicious of institutional religion, it was evidently considered the better part of marketing to go lightly on the links of these religious orders and schools to a *church*—especially one that was demanding and controversial. Catholic institutions not only wanted to escape their own narrow and sometimes authoritarian pasts; they felt burdened by the often exaggerated stereotypes of these traits that existed in their publics.

BETWEEN 1994 AND 2001, I spent five years teaching at two of the nation's premier Catholic universities, Notre Dame and Georgetown. My interest in how religious identity could be retained and expressed at schools like those, aspiring to the first rank of American research universities, was generally welcomed. When I visited Notre Dame in 1994 to discuss an invitation to spend a year as a visiting professor of American studies, I had the sensation of faculty members lurking in doorways ready to pluck at my sleeves and enlist me in this or that faction of campus debate about Catholic identity. At Georgetown, where I was a visiting professor of history, the general campus mood was indifferent to the topic; nonetheless faculty and administration leaders had set in motion two important studies of it, and I served on a task force commissioned to propose practical steps for strengthening the university's Jesuit and Catholic character.

The campus cultures at the two institutions diverged considerably, primarily as a result of their location, Georgetown in the nation's capital, Notre Dame in South Bend, Indiana. Georgetown is deeply shaped by Washington's local industry, government. Notre Dame, on the other hand, *is* the local industry in South Bend. Both faculty and students have been drawn to Georgetown because of the school's proximity to the nation's political life. Religion, beginning with the university's name, is less a factor in the school's public profile. It was not remarkable that the graduate who became president of the United States, Bill Clinton, was a Southern Baptist. Furthermore, thanks to Georgetown's School of Foreign Service and other programs that have been natural allies to it, like linguistics and international business, there is a strong presence of international students and international politics. The school's important Center for Muslim-Christian Understanding, for instance, is overwhelmingly in the public eye for its work on Islam, especially in relation to political issues, and very little for matters having to do with Christianity or Catholicism specifically. There is a large theology department but no graduate program in theology.

Partly because of its role as a symbol of striving American Catholicism, partly to compensate for its out-of-the-way location in the Midwest, and partly because Midwest Catholicism itself was always much more open than the East Coast variety, Notre Dame has long been a host to some of the church's most important spiritual and social movements. In recent decades, it has become a kind of crossroads for global Catholicism. Where Georgetown bustles with speakers, scholars, and conferences pertaining to the world's political superpower, Notre Dame bustles with speakers, scholars, and conferences pertaining to the world's religious superpower.

Students at both schools are excellent. The undergraduate body at Georgetown is now less than 55 percent Catholic, and it is certainly more cosmopolitan than the overwhelmingly Catholic undergraduates at Notre Dame. The Notre Dame faculty is 55 percent Catholic. Georgetown does not keep such a figure. I often met faculty members at Georgetown who told me that they had come to the university with little awareness that it was Catholic or Jesuit. That would be a very rare case at Notre Dame. That other members of the Georgetown task force on which I served would stereotype Notre Dame as a provincial, dogmatic place revealed more about the self-image of Georgetown than about Notre Dame.

Despite these differences, my impression was that the problem of Catholic identity on both campuses was strikingly similar. On both campuses I encountered scholars who never read a news report of a Vatican statement without seeing the shadow of the Inquisition fall on their office door. Many faculty members at both schools considered Catholic identity the responsibility of the theology department, campus ministry, or the founding religious order, and a good number ascribed to the religious order a degree of mysterious power that seemed highly exaggerated. On both campuses I encountered many excellent students who said they felt deeply Catholic but were not very sure what that meant or entailed intellectually. Both schools offered an impressive array of theology courses, required two semesters of theology, and produced not only a significant number of theology majors but a very great number of students majoring in other subjects but minoring in theology. Yet even the latter group, although enthusiastic about their Notre Dame or Georgetown education in general, not infrequently declared themselves intellectually undernourished in terms of their faith.

At bottom, the resistance to meaningful affirmation of Catholic identity had similar sources at both universities, as it has in many other schools with serious scholarly aspirations. That resistance arises from the assumption that there is really only one model for academic excellence and authentic inquiry, which is represented by the benchmark secular universities and liberal arts colleges. The measures of excellence within these leading institutions are, in turn, largely set by the separate academic disciplines. Though the overall atmosphere claims to be one of untrammeled discussion and investigation, in practice it is strongly biased toward a conventional political liberalism (with barely a sprinkling of radicalism) and a reflexive suspicion of traditionalism in belief and moral conduct.

At Catholic institutions, only a small minority hold this view as a well-articulated conviction, with the correlate that any extensive attention to religion in the school's life is baggage threatening to impede the institution's excellence. For many more, this view is a kind of intuition that operates negatively. For them, Catholic identity is perfectly fine, even praiseworthy, until that point in a particular decision—choosing a provost, designing a core curriculum, recruiting students or new faculty, budgeting for special scholarly programs or research, mounting a major fund-raising campaign, advertising the school, governing student behavior—where it could make the institution's profile clearly distinct from the benchmark schools. At that point, the fears kick in. The fears are many—of losing academic reputation, of blighting one's marketability, but most of all of simply slipping back toward the two other familiar models of religiously affiliated higher education: either the preconciliar Catholic model, subject to serious church supervision through sponsoring religious orders, or the strictly confessional colleges of evangelical Protestant persuasion.

BY THE TIME the bishops cast their 1999 vote on *Ex Corde Ecclesiae,* the topic of Catholic identity was no longer being dodged. Instead, it sometimes seemed as though the chief feature of Catholic identity was to be endlessly brooding over Catholic identity.

On campus after campus, the question of Catholic identity has been taken up by official committees or ad hoc groups. Boston College, the University of Dayton, and other schools have established faculty institutes, seminars, and summer workshops that explore the relations between faith and scholarship and encourage faculty in a variety of disciplines to develop courses or pursue research of likely relevance to the Catholic tradition. Campuses are sprouting new initiatives in "Catholic studies." They include full-fledged departments, endowed chairs, or interdisciplinary programs offering undergraduate majors or minors or graduate certificates. To differing degrees, they attempt to communicate and advance scholarship about Catholicism that extends beyond theology, ethics, and philosophy to embrace literature, history, art, the social sciences, and even the natural sciences.

One major forum for discussing the identity and mission of Catholic schools has been the Association of Catholic Colleges and Universities, an organization enrolling all but about two dozen of those institutions in the country. In August 1995, for example, it brought together four hundred presidents, deans, and other officials to review findings from studies examining everything from curriculum to student life policies and counseling practices. In the six months directly preceding the bishops' vote in 1999, hundreds of educators from Jesuit campuses across the country came to Saint Joseph's University in Philadelphia for "Jesuit Education 21: Conference on the Future of Jesuit Higher Education"; over a hundred Catholic intellectuals gathered at Holy Cross College in Worcester, Massachusetts, for "A Conversation About the Future of American Catholic Intellectual Life"; and the Erasmus Institute at Notre Dame drew academic stars from Great Britain and the Ivy League to perform at a conference on "Higher Learning and Catholic Traditions." The Erasmus Institute is itself an example of the new movement: it supports scholarship bringing Catholic traditions to bear on contemporary issues in the humanities, social sciences, arts, and professional fields like law. The hope is to bridge the gap between secular learning and the church that has grown up in recent centuries, to the detriment, the institute believes, of both.

One obvious explanation for all this activity is *Ex Corde Ecclesiae*. Unquestionably the prospect of such a document, long in the making, and its final arrival in 1990 concentrated the minds of not a few Catholic educators who might otherwise have preferred to avoid an uncomfortable topic. At the same time, the document—or the fears associated, not entirely without reason, with virtually any Vatican document—was often an albatross around the neck of campus advocates of reasserting Catholic identity. Like the majority of papal documents, *Ex Corde Ecclesiae* is the work of many hands and far from seamless. It reflects compromises between competing interests and priorities; it retains ambiguities, inconsistencies, lacunae, and loopholes. Yet the bulk of the text itself, addressing the nature and mission of Catholic higher education, also reflects the experience of a pope who had been a university chaplain and professor. It is a rich source of ideas about university life and its intersection with Christian faith. At least, to those who actually read it.

Unfortunately, that part of the text, with both its strengths and weaknesses, has been almost entirely eclipsed by the set of "General Norms" that follow it. For two decades, Vatican officials had sought to compensate for the diminishing presence and authority of religious orders on Catholic campuses by introducing provisions governing higher education into the 1983 revised Code of Canon Law and by devising rules (norms) that would bring colleges and universities under the authority of local bishops and ultimately of the Vatican, much as was the case with seminaries. After interminable jousting with Rome over academic autonomy and freedom, and differences from nation to nation in legal systems and government funding, Catholic educators breathed a sigh of relief. The number of norms appearing in the final document was reduced by at least half from earlier drafts. Moreover, it was left to national conferences of bishops to draw up specific plans, taking local circumstances into account, for implementing these norms—subject, of course, to Vatican approval.

The relief was premature. Rome was determined to make an example of American Catholic higher education—and would accept nothing short of the juridical application of the norms set out in the papal document, while the bishops' conferences of other nations were given a pass. The controversies that resulted—especially those around the question of whether Catholic theologians at Catholic schools would have to obtain some kind of certification, or *mandatum*, from their local bishops—pushed the issue of Catholic identity into the headlines: "Catholic Colleges See Peril in Vatican Push for Control" (*Boston Globe*); "Catholic Church, Universities in Power Struggle" (*USA Today*); "Catholic Campuses Face a Showdown on Ties to Church" (*New York Times*). *Ex Corde Ecclesiae* guaranteed that questions about Catholic identity did not sink from sight, although it is doubtful that the cause was helped by Vatican intransigence.

BUT THE PAPAL DOCUMENT was far from the only factor at work. During the same years that it stirred debate on Catholic campuses, other religiously affiliated colleges and universities had been caught up in a similar self-examination of their religious heritage and what it means for their religious future.

My original *Times* assignment had not been limited to Catholic schools. I also talked to administrators and faculty members at institutions sponsored by Methodists, Baptists, Mormons, Presbyterians, Lutherans, Church of Christ, Disciples, Christian Reformed, Mennonites, Quakers, and Jews. Emory, Baylor, Brigham Young, Pepperdine, Valparaiso, Earlham, Calvin, Yeshiva, and Brandeis were some of the better known targets of my obsessive questioning. Through all these discussions and many others, I learned about schools whose religious ties were purely honorific, schools where they were alive and well, schools where they were struggling for renewed life. At many of these campuses, the challenge of maintaining a distinctive religious identity dwarfs the questions haunting Catholic campuses. Nonetheless, the effort was being made—and it was not limited to Christian traditions. New chairs and programs in Jewish studies have been established on many campuses. New Buddhist and Muslim institutions of higher learning have been founded.

Obviously, these are not responses to the pope.

There is, in fact, a larger ferment active in American culture. It involves a simultaneous desire for inclusion and for particularity. It has been seen in the civil rights struggle, with its opposition to restrictions but also its emphasis on retaining racial and ethnic heritages. It has been seen in the women's movement, with its opposition to gender-based barriers but also its demand that women's experience must now be taken seriously in shaping social norms. Struggles over sexual orientation and even those over physical disabilities have combined demands to be treated just like everyone else with reassertions of the right not to be just like everyone else. All these groups are saying, We want entry and equal respect, but we do not agree that the price must be the extinguishing of all distinct identity. On the one hand, these movements fear discrimination as one form of exclusion. On the other hand, they also fear homogenization as another, more subtle form of exclusion. The result has been a new understanding of the relationship between faith-related institutions of higher learning, pluralism, and multiculturalism.

One can see the beginning of that new understanding in the demise of the image of the melting pot. Concern for a multicultural pluralism has produced new popular images: a mosaic, a great quilt, even a flavorful stew. The idea is the same: different components or ingredients retain their special colors, patterns, or flavors while contributing to the beauty or taste of the whole.

But human beings are not solid, unchanging, or passive, like pieces of mosaic, patches of cloth, or chunks of food. People are alive and they are social. A pluralism of people requires not just diversity, but diversity of a special sort, a diversity of communities, of living traditions, bound together by their own memories, convictions, and ways of life—but also renewing those memories, convictions, and ways of life under the challenges of changing circumstances. (A zoo is diversity. A forest, an ecology of living species, is pluralism and multiculturalism.) But for these communities of memory, conviction, and ways of life to renew and reproduce themselves as living species, not captured or stuffed specimens, they need to bring together a certain minimum population. They need institutions of learning, transmission, research, inquiry, criticism, and discussion. One fundamental institution of that sort in our age is the university.

Universities themselves, of course, assume a certain internal diversity and pluralism. But if a university is unable to maintain a distinctive profile and identify for itself—if every university feels compelled to re-create within itself an identical pattern of diversity and pluralism—that will be destructive of the larger pluralistic and multicultural project. It will strip communities and living traditions of a powerful resource. It will raise the prospect that the demand for diversity and pluralism may paradoxically issue in a bland conformity or at most a melee of superficial and ornamental differences churned up by the manufacturers of cultural novelty.

So an authentically multicultural pluralism, the argument goes, demands the survival of diverse and distinctive forms of faith-based higher education.

This position has been strengthened by the growing recognition that there is no search for truth standing totally outside all presuppositions and all communities of searchers. Nor is there any such thing as *the* university, in the sense of a pure Platonic model existing outside a historical and cultural context. All thinking, the philosopher Alasdair MacIntyre has argued, is tradition-based and all inquiry is tradition-directed, an obvious point once one recognizes that modernity, too, represents a tradition. Building on MacIntyre's point, David B. Burrell at Notre Dame notes that "there are different kinds of universities, beholden to diverse educational traditions." The kinds of research universities dominant in the United States since the early twentieth century take their presuppositions about truth and the purpose and nature of inquiry and education largely from the traditions of natural science and the Enlightenment, sifted through pragmatic and populist aspects of American culture. There is no reason why other models, although they might necessarily share a great deal with those traditions, would not enrich higher education.

Of course, this broad argument for pluralism in higher education and for the value, in general, of maintaining distinctive institutions reflecting different communities of memory, conviction, and ways of life applies to every major faith tradition. It would be true of Baptist identity, Methodist identity, Orthodox Jewish identity, Buddhist identity, and so on. It does not speak to the question of what specifically *Catholic* identity would mean or what it could contribute to higher education, let alone how it could be realistically fostered or maintained.

PERHAPS IT WOULD HELP to stop thinking about Catholic identity as though this were something univocal across the enormous variety of Catholic colleges and universities. There may be some overarching principles like those in *Ex Corde Ecclesiae*, but there is no single way of embodying them, and it might be wiser to speak of Catholic identities in the plural. Nationally ranked research universities like Boston College or Georgetown or Notre Dame have the potential to be a Catholic presence in the university world—and might therefore conceive of their mission and shape their identity—in a different way than, say, regionally important universities like Seattle or my alma mater, Loyola of Chicago, and certainly differently than, say, the former women's liberal arts colleges that currently serve nontraditional-age students, sometimes in urban settings with a preponderance of minority and non-Catholic students. A Saint John's University in Collegeville, with its Benedictine monastic matrix and regional roots, might well conceive of its mission differently than the Vincentian Saint John's University in Jamaica, New York, an important starter school for many students who are the first generation to attend college from immigrant families. Traits and objectives will emerge in schools depending on their own histories, their constituencies, their founding inspiration, their locales in city or country, this region or that.

This reverses the way Catholic identity is often approached. Is it wise to discuss it as a big template against which individual institutions measure themselves, rather than begin with the individual institutions and a process in which they ask themselves: "At this individual institution, with its own history, location, socioeconomic niche, and everything else, what do we mean by our distinctive Catholic identity and mission? What goals and standards are we willing to articulate, concretely and specifically enough so that we would be able actually to know whether we had failed to meet them?"

In a few cases, those questions might still center around the students being served. Undoubtedly the student body was once a key, if not *the* key, to the identity and mission of Catholic colleges and institutions. There are cases where the student population remains distinctive today, where Catholic schools can justly claim a distinctive mission in reaching students likely to be excluded or marginalized by non-Catholic colleges and universities. On the other hand, if the Catholic mission is defined in terms simply of reaching Catholics, the church's attention, energies, and resources ought to be radically reallocated to the Catholic campus ministry centers of our state and community campuses, where the vast majority of Catholic college and university students, at least 80 percent, are to be found. If, on yet another hand (the third, I confess), the mission is seen in terms of preparing a core elite, whether as undergraduates or professional students, for responsible roles in the Catholic community and American culture, that too seems like a justifiable basis for identity and mission. But then, one must add that that concern should be given a candid place, alongside SAT or GRE scores and strictly academic recommendations, in admissions policies. And that concern would have a major bearing on the curriculum.

Which raises the second and probably the most obvious of the questions that any Catholic college or university might ask itself in the process of concretely examining identity and mission: what is being taught? Are the catalogue of courses; the core curriculum; the research interests that faculty share with both undergraduates and graduates, with their peers and the public; the programs of professional education in law, education, business, medicine—are any of these in any significant way distinct, distinct in any significant *Catholic* way, from what might be offered in a corresponding state or secular institution?

Andrew Greeley has argued that both at the research level and in undergraduate courses there should be an emphasis, though not an exclusive emphasis, on Catholic aspects, themes, and topics—in history, social theory, literature, art, spirituality, ethnic studies, political science, and philosophy—and areas of interest not likely to be available elsewhere and by no means limited to the discipline of theology. "Build the program and they will come," he wrote in an issue of *Commonweal* magazine. Of course, being no stranger to academic politics, he almost certainly knows it may be a bit more complicated.

If the answer to "What is being taught?" turns out to be "Nothing significantly different than in corresponding secular schools," there is clearly a problem of Catholic identity. Catholic identity must be centered in the Catholic university's intellectual life, and not assigned exclusively to campus ministry, the dean of students, and counseling services as a tempting way to dodge problems of academic freedom and faculty responsibility; nor can it be assigned exclusively to the theology and philosophy departments. The standard one or two introductory courses in theology or philosophy are not a sufficient answer. Catholic identity should somehow, even if indirectly, pervade the curriculum of the university as a whole.

What is being taught cannot be neatly separated from how it is taught. This *how* suggests approaches not so distinct from those at other good schools but nonetheless faithful to Catholic tradition: personal attention to the whole student, concern for the social consequences and ethical dimensions of what is being studied, learning through community service, and opportunities for the disadvantaged. A philosopher and former president of Bucknell and the University of Rochester, Dennis O'Brien, among others, has argued something more far-reaching: that religious truth (or as he puts it, "iconic truth") has its own logic and demands its own method, distinctive from those appropriate to scientific truth—which generally sets the norms for modern secular higher education—and from those appropriate to artistic truth, which squeezes with some difficulty into that model. The *how* of the teaching in O'Brien's Catholic college or university, at least in some of its curriculum and associated activities, would directly address questions of love, commitment, and decision making in ways significantly different from the standard model. In this sense, Catholic colleges and universities would be a "contrarian" alternative to secular ones. They would offer a different understanding of "the real," how one knows it, and what that knowledge means for one's life. Some teachers at Catholic institutions probably once intuited in practice much of what O'Brien justifies in theory, but may have moved away from this more personal, participatory *how* and toward the appraisive, neutral *how* of other institutions.

Finally, *how* the teaching occurs bears on the quality of the scholarly community and the character of campus culture. More lasting learning may arise from those sources than from classroom assignments. What is distinctive here about expectations in relations between the sexes? About compassion for the isolated or alienated? About creating an environment that treats moments of prayer and reflection—before eating in the dining halls, for example—as natural rather than eccentric, or that integrates the liturgical rhythms of the week and the seasons into campus life? Again, these are questions that should be answered in the ecology of specific schools, their traditions, settings, student bodies, and so on.

Questions about the character of the campus community and culture cannot be narrowed to university positions on controversial speakers or student groups. Should honorary degrees or other awards be bestowed on pro-choice or pro-capital-punishment politicians? Should groups advocating access to abortion or calling for an end to marriage laws distinguishing between heterosexual and homosexual couples receive student-government funding? Such positions involve judgment calls: the case of Andrew Sullivan being invited, as a self-identified gay intellectual, to speak at Notre Dame on Catholic teaching and homosexuality may be different from Larry Flynt, publisher of *Hustler,* being given a platform by the Georgetown student Lecture Fund to rant about the Catholic Church and sex. What counts is the spirit and public rationale behind school policies and their application. What counts even more is the *overall pattern of vibrant engagement* with Catholic concerns and traditions in the intellectual and communal life of the institution.

However one tries to think through Catholic identity in concrete terms of particular schools, their curriculums, and the tenor of that academic community, one cannot escape the question of personnel. As in Catholic health care and Catholic social services, *who is going to do it?* Catholic identity cannot be imposed from the top down, let alone by authorities like the bishops, outside the scholarly community. Some religious orders, no longer possessing the numbers to constitute a significant presence in the faculty, are quietly rewriting the bylaws of the schools they founded or devising complicated patterns of boards and inner boards in hopes of maintaining a kind of absentee landlordism. These efforts are doomed. Ultimately, as a number of veteran educators and scholars of higher education have observed, the religious character of colleges and universities will be determined by the faculty. Faculty members stay longer than students or administrators. They do the teaching and research. The grandest schemes for curriculum and course content have to pass through their passive-aggressive hands. Perhaps the president, the dean, or the department chair could order that religion be seriously attended to, say, in Western-civilization core courses, but there is no way around the readiness and capacity of the individual professor really to do that.

The future of Catholic identity in higher education is inescapably linked to hiring practices. Some years ago, George Marsden, the leading historian of the secularization of American higher education, distilled this issue to its essence, at least for major religiously affiliated universities. Once such an institution, he wrote, adopts the policy that it will just hire "the best qualified candidates" without any regard to religion, "It is simply a matter of time until its faculty will have an ideological profile essentially like that of the faculty at every other mainstream university. The first loyalties of faculty members will be to the national cultures of their professions rather than to any local or ecclesiastical traditions. Faculty members become essentially interchangeable parts in a standardized national system."

The fact that a few schools have dared to broach the delicate but crucial question of "hiring for mission" or "mission-centered hiring" is another dramatic change from the early nineties. Are there ways to factor faith-related priorities in research and teaching into the recruitment of faculty without erecting doctrinal litmus tests, surveillance of private conduct, or limits on open inquiry? No other issue is as explosive—but also as central to Catholic identity—on many Catholic campuses.

In the most basic sense, of course, colleges and universities always hire for mission. What else would a rational organization hire people for than their capacity to carry out the organization's mission? To be sure, sometimes hiring faculty is very complex. Administrators work out package deals involving a position in the chemistry department for the spouse of a prestigious star scholar that the sociology department is determined to land. But the package is contrived—whether wisely or not, whether to the benefit of the chemistry department, whether in undue thrall to considerations of prestige—ultimately because it is believed that, overall, the package will contribute to the mission of the university.

Ordinarily, then, it would be anything except hiring for mission that would demand an explanation and justification. It is the *religious* dimension of hiring for mission in religiously affiliated colleges and universities that provokes objections.

The objections to hiring for mission—or more accurately, to incorporating religious factors in the process of hiring for mission—are at first glance formidable:

"It imposes orthodoxy."

"It requires monitoring private conduct."

"Religious faith is a matter of inviolable conscience."

"True religious commitment is unfathomable."

"Bringing religious faith into hiring invites hypocrisy."

"Religious commitments change over time."

"Hiring for mission at Catholic schools would mean discriminating against non-Catholics."

"It would render currently employed non-Catholics second-class
   faculty members."

"Is there such a thing as Catholic mathematics, cell biology, or
   physics anyway?"

Some colleges, of course, *want* to impose orthodoxy; they believe
that monitoring private conduct is the responsible thing to do. They
may recognize the rights of conscience, but think that those whose
consciences change over time or are different to begin with should
simply seek employment elsewhere. Those schools can simply brush
these objections away. Very few Catholic institutions of higher education fall into that category. Nonetheless, they must acknowledge
the concerns behind those objections even as they answer them, as I
believe they can. Their answer would encompass at least four components: achieving clarity about mission, distinguishing between hiring for Catholic identity and hiring Catholics, embedding concerns
about the religious dimension of mission into the entire hiring
process and beyond it, and eschewing mechanical or inflexible rules.

If Catholic colleges and universities are going to take religious
factors into account in hiring for mission, they are going to have to be
clear about what that mission is—and perhaps even clearer about
what it is not. The brief exercises known as mission statements, often
largely rhetorical or written with an eye toward marketing, will not
do. The even briefer phrases—"Savonarola University is a Jesuit (or
Christian Brothers, etc.) school in the Catholic tradition"—are
equally unhelpful.

Imagine that all applicants for a faculty opening received, with
the acknowledgment of their applications, a succinct, attractive,
carefully written brochure explaining in some detail what significance for teaching and research at Stylites University or Holy
Penance College derived from its institutional commitment to viewing reality in terms of creation, incarnation, and redemption in Jesus; what responsibilities this entailed to the Catholic community;
how this shaped the curriculum; and how this influenced the campus

ethos. The brochure could explain why this commitment demanded rigorous scholarship; why this commitment did not restrict academic freedom or inquiry, although it might encourage certain lines of research; why this commitment in fact welcomed diversity and especially diverse religious perspectives prepared to engage in conversation and dialogue. The brochure could direct the curious or the nervous to further, more developed articles or books on Catholic identity. From the start, such a brochure could open a conversation about Catholic identity that might run through the entire search and hiring process, alongside, to be sure, all the usual explorations of a candidate's work in demography or Ottoman history or neuropsychology or Renaissance Italian literature, with its dossiers of scholarly publications, interviews, guest lectures, and so on.

In that whole process, beginning with the brochure, it would be important to emphasize that the school's Catholic identity may be linked to hiring *but not necessarily to hiring Catholics.* The primary issue would be public scholarship, not personal creed, the workings of one's mind and not the state of one's soul, even if at some subtle point the two may not be separable. Candidates' scholarly research and teaching agenda should be the threshold critical issue, not baptismal certificates or Mass attendance. Besides being a first-rate cell biologist and teacher of cell biology, does the candidate have scholarly interests in the ethics of her field, for example, or in how it intersects with theological or philosophical questions, or does she have a teaching style that has regard for the humanity of her students or their potential for service—qualities obviously related to the institution's mission as a Catholic university? Having to choose among competing specialists in modern French politics, or in international relations theory, or in the sociology of popular American culture, the relevant search committees may weigh the fact (along, of course, with much else) that one candidate has cultivated an interest in the church and the Vichy regime, another has spent time working on the ethics of warfare or the intersection of religion and nationalism, another has written on religious themes in films. There should be no passing over an outstanding French historian who has broken new ground in the economic aspects of colonization for a mediocre candidate who has written on the church and Vichy. But applied deftly over time, such considerations would result in a faculty that in no way slighted excellence in essential areas and yet, without establishing any doctrinal criteria, would construct a distinctive profile of scholarly interests reflecting the institution's Catholic identity.

The truth is that non-Catholics often exhibit such mission-related priorities in their scholarly interests and teaching style to a greater degree than do Catholics. Paul Ramsey, a Methodist ethicist at Princeton, did much to revive interest in Catholic just-war theory. Scholars of many religious backgrounds and of none have employed, refined, and criticized Catholic concepts in medical ethics. Light has been shed on important figures in Catholic thought or movements in Catholic history by scholars of diverse religious views. That fact, as well as the arrival of a new era of dialogue between world religions, means that Catholic identity must embrace scholars of other faiths and of no faith not simply as admissible presences in Catholic higher education but as essential to its purposes. Protestant, Eastern Orthodox, Jewish, Muslim, and other religious and nonreligious perspectives are intrinsic to a Catholic university, not something external against which Catholic identity is balanced.

Is such an approach likely to produce a faculty with more than the 25 percent of Catholics, both nominal and active, that could be predicted on the basis of American demographics? Probably. Maybe 40 percent, maybe 50 percent, maybe more or less. Who knows? Is that a problem? I don't think so. Jews are disproportionately represented in many elite faculties, and only anti-Semites are troubled. We should be beyond the point, furthermore, when it is assumed that Catholics think alike, even on religious issues. The bottom line is this: although each faculty member's personal stake in the Catholic dimension of the school's mission might change over time or vary with his or her discipline, the great mass of the faculty, Catholic or not, would have been hired with some reference to that dimension and would be regularly engaged in the process of hiring others with reference to that dimension.

This note of an ongoing process embedded in the faculty and its deliberations is essential. When I first began to inquire about the religious mission of faith-linked schools, I encountered more than one provost, academic dean, or president who assured me that the institution's Catholic mission played a critical role in hiring. How did that actually take place? I would ask. "Oh, I interview every candidate for a position," the reply would come. "I have them read the mission statement, and I ask them if they are comfortable with that."

Now, why did I suspect it would take a pretty dull and well-fed job candidate not to find an acceptable way of answering that question? Or that it would take a pretty awful answer to make an academic vice president tell the psychology department to start their ten-month grind of recruitment, reviewing dossiers, conducting interviews, and reaching a consensus all over again? If questions about a new faculty member's fit with a school's religious identity were to be part of that process, they could not be left to a last-minute conversation; they would have to play a role from the initial point when a job opening was defined, and then exert some steady influence throughout the entire process of recruiting and reviewing and interviewing. Obviously, this would require some general faculty consensus, even some well-honed skills building on the ones that academics learn by apprenticeship and their own experiences in hiring and being hired.

Just as this process cannot be condensed into a single interview, it should not conclude with a letter of appointment. Currently, schools vary greatly in offering (and sometimes requiring) orientation sessions, videos, workshops, or off-campus retreats for new faculty members. Most religious orders are willing to welcome faculty, whether Catholic or not, into some sharing of their spiritual practices and traditions. On Jesuit campuses I have met many non-Catholic faculty and staff deeply affected by their exposure to the Spiritual Exercises of Saint Ignatius Loyola through short or extended retreats. But continuing education in Catholic identity must be intellectual as well as spiritual, with lectures, film series, panel discussions, seminars. People hired with minimal potential to contribute to the religious dimensions of the university's mission may turn out to be major contributors if their knowledge is deepened, their intellect and curiosity piqued, and maybe their spiritual needs addressed. People hired with interests clearly supportive of Catholic identity may let them languish if there is no continuing stimulation and encouragement.

Weighing potential contributions to Catholic identity in the hiring process does not imply any mechanical principles or procedures that apply without nuance or deviation to all appointments, fields, and disciplines, as though issues of special interest to Catholicism were relevant to chemistry and accounting to the same degree and in the same way as to political theory, literature, and history. Nonetheless, even chemistry and mathematics, let alone business administration, might be hospitable to certain philosophical, ethical, or cross-disciplinary reflections and conversations in a Catholic university that are far less likely to occur elsewhere.

Assembling the best possible faculty is an art form, not a science. Hard-and-fast rules will never do. A department rich with sterling classroom teachers can afford to hire an individual renowned for her research but only a passable teacher. Likewise, a department well supplied with faculty members whose research has some bearing on questions related to Catholicism, ethics, social justice, world religions, and so forth, and whose teaching style reflects the characteristics singled out by the university's religious identity, need not give much thought to such matters in its latest job search. A department lacking such faculty members should be required to give these research and teaching emphases a high priority in its next search. If a department or professional school had an opportunity to land a star with little or nothing to offer in terms of the university's religious identity, there would be no reason not to do so. The gap could be compensated for later. Obviously, such flexibility implies that someone is tracking and steering the whole pattern—departmental chairs and deans, with perhaps some faculty committees in between.

I am convinced that with these four steps, hiring for mission—or once again, more accurately, hiring for the religious dimension of mission—is both practical and compatible with academic freedom and diversity:

- being clear that the religious dimension of the institution's mission does not imply proselytism and an enforced orthodoxy
- emphasizing that what is primarily to be weighed in regard to that dimension is the contribution of scholars' research and teaching agendas rather than personal faith or practice
- integrating these considerations into the whole process of job definition, recruitment, interviews, hiring, and continuing campus life
- eschewing mechanical rules or quotas for flexibility

Will that overcome the hostility entrenched in many disciplines, and in the academic environment generally, to any consideration whatsoever of religious factors in hiring? Probably not. That hostility is both a legacy of justified suspicion and a product of unjustified prejudice. It will be hard for individual Catholic colleges and universities, which are competing for faculty and standing in that larger environment, to counter these objections as separate institutions. They need to undertake collective initiatives, perhaps alongside representatives of other faith-related schools. The Association of Catholic Colleges and Universities, a major foundation, or some other prominent body should sponsor a blue-ribbon committee of eminent scholars with impeccable credentials, from both faith-affiliated and secular institutions, to draw up guidelines regarding the appropriate and inappropriate weighing of religious factors, whether personal commitments or scholarly interests, in hiring and promoting faculty. Such a report, which could make all the necessary distinctions between different kinds of schools, would be an invaluable guide and reference point for hiring and for future discussion.

Although faculty hiring for mission is essential, it is not sufficient. Ultimately, there is in fact no panacea, no silver bullet, no once-and-for-all solution to ensure the Catholic identity of Catholic higher education. Episcopally credentialed theologians, new institutes, programs in Catholic studies, inner-city service projects, peace and justice programs, faculty retreats, faculty seminars, student retreats, ethics across the curriculum, special chairs, prestigious lecture series—no one thing will do it, but rather a constant alertness to opportunities, initiatives on many fronts, with some successes, some failures, no quitting.

NONE OF THIS can be accomplished without leadership. That means presidents of Catholic colleges and universities who don't make Catholic identity an afterthought but rank it with the top concerns (primarily financial) that daily occupy their attention. That also means second-tier and middle-level staff in administrations and faculties who do not view fostering their school's Catholic identity as a burden—or as someone else's task—but as a challenge to be creative and reflective.

In March of 2002 I spoke at the Seminar on the Mission and Character of Boston College, a remarkable series of meetings at which the vice presidents and deans of that Jesuit university, along with its president, the Reverend William Leahy, were pursuing the topic of Catholic identity. After the lively session, Father Leahy chatted with me and the Reverend J. A. Appleyard, Boston College's vice president for university mission and ministry (the title itself is indicative of a heightened concern). The two priests ticked off a long list of top posts that were opening or soon to be opening at other Jesuit universities—presidents, academic vice presidents, provosts, deans of graduate programs. Where would suitable candidates with a concern for Catholic identity and the sensitivities and skills to foster it be found? The Jesuits' own numbers were shrinking, especially of those with sufficient academic qualifications and experience. The year before, after a prolonged search, Georgetown had surprised many people by choosing a layman for its president for the first time in its over-two-hundred-year history. The choice made sense: John J. DeGioia, a Georgetown alumnus and a philosopher, had served in the administration as a dean and vice president for many years. He was immersed not only in the university's culture but in Jesuit spirituality. Unfortunately, men and women like DeGioia may be as few on the ground as qualified Jesuits or other members of religious orders, unless, that is, Catholic higher education and the church generally make a determined effort to identify and nurture such people in their careers and in their religious interests and commitments.

Sister Patricia Vandenberg said the same thing in her reflections on the Catholic presence in health care: "Do we have the people who are capable of doing this?" she asked. "Who are they, where are they, and how are we making sure that we are tending to that stream, the human resource capacity?" The same questions are being asked in offices of Catholic Charities. The same questions are being asked—not philosophically but often in the very practical context of seeking, hiring, and promoting technically skilled staff and executives—by Catholic magazines, Catholic publishers, Catholic foundations, community groups, local and regional as well as national associations, all the small and large institutions in the imposing network that it has been the genius of American Catholicism to create.

Nor can this leadership succeed without a vision of Catholic identity that is neither a vestige of preconciliar circumstances and theology nor a vague affirmation of good intentions from which anything distinctively Catholic has been drained. What the theologian Monika K. Hellwig has said regarding Catholic higher education applies equally to the other institutions in that network: Discerning a Catholic identity appropriate today "is not a matter of something we have lost and must retrieve. It is a matter of discovering how to do something we have never done before."

Part Two

Chapter Five

———————|————————————|———

Around the Altar

O<small>N</small> an average Sunday, approximately 20 million Catholics go to Mass. It is here at the liturgy, not in the bedroom, that the future of Catholicism in the United States will be determined.

Lex orandi lex credendi, declares an ancient Christian maxim: the law of prayer is the law of belief. Worship precedes theology. Or better, the two realities are intimately and inextricably entwined. Many of the most powerful and moving declarations about God and Jesus in the earliest New Testament texts are in fact hymns and acclamations, professions of faith, and other sacramental formulas that Paul of Tarsus incorporated into the letters that became Christianity's foundational theology. "Liturgy is the self-expression of the church. When we gather for worship, we give the simplest, most immediate, most condensed statement of our beliefs," explains Sister Kathleen Hughes, one of the country's leading liturgical scholars.

This is particularly true for Catholics. For Catholicism, more than for many other forms of Western Christianity, religious life is sacramental, organized around ritual moments, from baptism to marriage, that visibly mark an inner transformation. Chief among these sacraments is the Eucharist, when the church gathers to receive Christ present in the word of scripture and in the sacramentally changed bread and wine. And though the Eucharist, or Mass, is celebrated daily in most Catholic parishes, preeminent among Eucharists is the one celebrated on Sunday, the day of the Lord's resurrection. This Sunday Eucharist is not a means for improving the rest of life, a time-out when individuals seek inspiration or moral instruction. That may occur, of course. But the Eucharist is, first of all, an end in itself—core, continuation, and culmination of daily existence, "source and summit of the Christian life," according to the Second Vatican Council. It is a memorial of Christ's Last Supper, of his life, sacrificial death, and resurrection. It brings together the faithful around the altar with all their labors, sufferings, and joys, and in praise and thanksgiving unites them and their efforts to the redemptive acts of God in Jesus.

Although exalted, that language really does capture what many devout Catholics, despite distractions and dissatisfactions, not only believe in principle but experience subjectively at Mass. The centrality of Sunday worship has obvious consequences for the church as an institution: at no other time are so many Catholics in such contact with one another and with church leaders. This is the prime moment for Catholics to reaffirm their faith and deepen their knowledge and understanding of it. This is the time when Catholics become most aware of their corporate existence, when they welcome new members, pray for the ill and deceased, and mobilize themselves for activities on behalf of those in need. With its cycles of readings and liturgical colors and seasonal prayers, Sunday worship provides a living calendar that gives Catholic life a rhythm of preparation and celebration: Advent, Christmas, Lent, the solemn paschal liturgies of Holy Week and Easter, Pentecost, and other major feasts. To pass from the sublime to the utterly mundane, the Sunday gathering is also the major occasion when Catholics offer their resources for the church's financial support, partly because the weekly donation, rather than quarterly or yearly contributions, has been customary and partly because it appropriately accompanies the offering of bread and wine as symbolic of the faithful's labors and life's necessities.

Study after study shows that Catholics who attend church weekly or almost weekly are distinctly more knowledgeable about their faith and committed to the church. And the children of Catholics who attend Mass regularly are far more apt to practice their faith than children of infrequent attenders. Indeed, Catholics who report attending Mass, receiving Communion, and praying frequently as children are at least eight times more likely to report such frequent practice as adults. In thoroughly Catholic cultures, where images and monuments of faith are part of the landscape, where religious beliefs are deeply woven into family and folk practices, Catholicism has persisted despite occasional or even infrequent attendance at Mass. The idea that this can occur in a pluralistic society like the United States, replete with competing worldviews and allegiances, is highly unrealistic. Any probing of the church's future vitality must begin with this truth, and hence with Sunday worship.

SINCE 1965, the Roman Catholic liturgy has been radically reshaped. Over that same period, Catholic Sunday Mass attendance has declined by at least a third and perhaps closer to a half, depending on which figures one trusts. Strangely enough, these two developments are not directly related. Virtually all the evidence indicates that the reshaping did not cause the decline. Whether the decline can be halted and reversed, however, depends very much on what the church does with the reshaping.

Of all the changes in the church's life stemming from the Second Vatican Council, nothing else touched ordinary Catholics so immediately and tangibly as the changes in the liturgy. In the popular mind, these changes are often equated with the replacement of Latin by local languages—and the squabbles over the accuracy and eloquence of the newly authorized translations. Certainly, to many Catholics, the disruption of familiar words and gestures could not help but be wrenching. But in fact the changes went far beyond that. They constituted a kind of Copernican revolution in Catholic worship. The

basic truths—the sun, stars, Earth, and other planets of the faith—
were still there, but they were strikingly reconfigured. The break
with the past was by no means total. Indeed, the changes were made
not in the spirit of designing something new but of returning to an
essence that the world's bishops at the Council feared had become
obscured by centuries of accretions. After the Council, Catholics
could still justly repeat traditional definitions of the Mass and other
sacraments. Nonetheless, the new rites incorporated an altered understanding of God, church, priesthood, and salvation. *Lex orandi
lex credendi*.

The reconfiguration was, to begin with, physical. Consider most
Catholic churches in the United States before the Council. The area
that Catholics termed the sanctuary was clearly separated from the
congregation's pews by a step or two and by the waist-high Communion rail, where the faithful knelt in a row and received the small
wafer, or host, on their tongues. At the back of the sanctuary, on a
platform at least several steps higher, stood the altar, not a table as
much as a massive counter projecting from a whole wall of ascending
ledges and niches for matching sets of candles and carved figures of
angels and saints. Surmounting the altar, beneath a crucifix and centered amid the candles and carvings, was the richly decorated and
veiled tabernacle, where the Blessed Sacrament was kept. During
much of the Mass, the priest faced this counter-altar and the tabernacle, his back to the people. Occasionally he turned to offer a symbolic (because in Latin) greeting, to which the altar boys returned an
equally symbolic Latin response.

Most churches also contained side altars, modest or elaborate, in
front of a statue or mural of Our Lady on one side of the church, of
Saint Joseph on the other. Stained-glass windows tended to be purely
decorative or instructive, with scenes from the life of Christ or the
saints; but statues and other images throughout the church served as
focal points for special devotions and supplications. Around the walls,
fourteen Stations of the Cross portrayed a sequence of moments in
Jesus' final sufferings, from judgment by Pontius Pilate to burial.

Metal stands of vigil lights, ranks of candles burnt as a sign of personal petition or thanksgiving, occupied prominent places.

The whole church was clearly *sacred space*, marked off from the ordinary world by its subdued light, the array of images, the flickering candles, and the red altar lamp indicating Christ's presence in the tabernacle. The sanctuary, the domain of priest and altar boys surrounding the altar, was even-more-sacred space. The altar constituted a kind of throne for the enshrined Blessed Sacrament, and the whole church a throne room. Acts of reverence like genuflecting and making private visits to the Blessed Sacrament for silent prayer fit naturally into the atmosphere of a court audience. Sunday worship, no less than personal prayer, was at its core internal and silent, and though it would be mistaken automatically to equate those characteristics with passivity, it was easy enough to become a passive audience to the priest's action. The spirituality fostered was strongly individualistic—God and I locked in gaze or interior conversation.

All this was radically altered after the Council. The Council fathers' objective was at least twofold: to restore the sense of the Eucharist as communal and to invite the active participation of the whole congregation. The priest now led the prayers in a language understood by all. He celebrated Mass facing the other worshipers across a free-standing altar, with the pews grouped, where possible, in something like a semicircle. Where the Communion rail was removed, the division into priestly and congregational areas disappeared. The tabernacle was frequently relocated on a side altar; even when left in place, it was now literally upstaged by the free-standing altar, so that the entire church no longer felt like a divine abode. The altar furniture, from candlesticks to pulpit, was simplified, and in new churches, so were the Stations of the Cross. Sometimes vigil lights and statuary disappeared entirely. More often they were reduced in prominence, keeping with the idea that the Mass and sacraments and not a host of private devotions should be the focus of the church's prayer.

Much more could be said about this remodeling of Catholic churches, which like so much else in American Catholicism has become the subject of fierce controversy. The significant point here is that modified churches manifested physically and spatially a reconsidered faith. With the position of the priest reversed and the people gathered around the altar, God was now experienced in the midst of the assembly, not someplace above or beyond it, or residing in the tabernacle in front of it. The church at worship was now experienced more as an egalitarian assembly sharing a common baptism and engaged in a common public prayer. God's presence was felt as much temporally as spatially within the church building and the tabernacle. To the extent that the physical arrangements stressed the communal and reduced sharp distinctions between the sacred and the profane, salvation was apt to be understood more in terms of service in everyday life—the worshipers actively and publicly giving witness to God's reign—and less as the individual soul's escape from a sinful world.

Of course, these shifts in understanding were not conveyed by the physical changes alone. The switch from Latin into vernacular languages—English, Spanish, and so on—was more than a practical switch from what few understood into what most understood. It was a symbolic move from a special, sacred, Sunday language to ordinary weekday tongues. The change was accentuated by the first translations into English, which strove for the familiarity of ordinary speech and avoided the kind of archaic or solemn language that typically lives on in ritual when it has expired everywhere else.

The reformed liturgy provided new roles for laypeople, women and men alike, as readers of scripture, leaders of song, distributors of Communion. Women proclaimed readings from the pulpit and offered the chalice to communicants. This, too, reduced the priest's monopoly on sacred actions and shortened the distance in status between ordained and the baptized. So did the practice of receiving Communion in the hand and taking the chalice oneself. Rather than kneeling, eyes closed and tongue outstretched like a baby bird being fed, the communicant stood eye-to-eye with the priest or Eucharistic minister, touching objects previously handled by the priest alone.

What the Council had called "the aim to be considered before all else" in reforming the liturgy was "full, conscious, and active participation in liturgical celebrations" by all the faithful. Not just the altar boys but all the worshipers together were to respond to the priest's greetings and invocations, affirm prayers made by him in their name with a collective "Amen," exchange the sign of peace—a handshake or embrace—throughout the church, and raise their voices in song.

There were other important changes. The old Mass had been defined as offertory, consecration, and Communion—all focused on the elements of bread and wine and their presentation, transformation, and reception. One could arrive late, after the gospel was read, for example, or after the sermon was preached, but before the offertory. Although such tardiness was frowned upon, the latecomer was not considered to have actually "missed Mass." By contrast, now the scripture readings and a homily were held to be integral parts of the liturgy. This "liturgy of the Word" preceded and paralleled the "liturgy of the table," the latter, in effect, the liturgy of the Word made flesh. The liturgy of the Word included readings from the Old and New Testaments—a much greater variety of scriptural passages than before—followed by a homily, by prayers for peace, justice, and the needs of members of the congregation, and by the creed. The liturgy of the table included the offering of bread and wine, the Eucharistic prayer invoking the Spirit and Jesus' words at the Last Supper, and Communion. This new balance placed the otherwise isolated "miracle" of the Eucharist in the broad context of God's dealings with Israel, the message of Jesus, and the witness of the early church. And the proclaimed and preached scripture, along with the congregational praying and singing, was part of another shift in the liturgy, from a chiefly visual rite, with inaudible prayers but dramatic gestures, to one both voiced and heard. In both ways, the liturgy ceased to be private, passive, otherworldly, ahistorical; the readings, homily, and prayers reminded the worshipers that they were part of a people chosen to be disciples, light and salt for the world.

OR SO IT WAS in theory. What was the impact of these radical changes in practice? The answer is immensely complicated and, in some respects, still unknown. It is known that, despite some initial cries of outrage and a great deal more of bafflement and loss, the new, reformed liturgy has been widely accepted.

What, then, explains the decline in Sunday Mass attendance? One thing above all, but it had little to do with alterations in the liturgy: Catholics stopped thinking of the Eucharist as their Sunday obligation, something done under pain of committing a mortal sin and at the risk of eternal damnation. As Bishop Kenneth Untener of Saginaw, Michigan, put it, "When I grew up you had two choices: go to Mass . . . or go to hell. Most of us chose Mass." On the books, at least, that is still the case. The official Catechism of the Catholic Church states that missing Mass on Sunday without a serious reason is a grave sin; and grave sin, the catechism indicates elsewhere, makes one liable to "eternal punishment." But somewhere along the line church leaders stopped preaching this, and church members stopped believing it. In 1998, Pope John Paul issued *Dies Domini,* a lengthy and eloquent letter on the Lord's Day. Of its eighty-seven numbered sections, only one focuses on the history of church law regarding Catholics' Sunday obligation, and only one sentence declares, somewhat obliquely, "This legislation has normally been understood as entailing a grave obligation." The pope is evidently no more willing than the neighborhood pastor to get people to church out of fear of damnation rather than love of the Eucharist.*

If the force of the Sunday obligation has faded, that only sets a higher standard for a ritual that must now draw people because they

---

*Exactly why and how this momentous shift occurred is not clearly established; indeed, the whole subject of belief in hell and damnation, especially among Catholics, is badly understudied. Suffice it to say that at some point enough Catholics found this belief a greater obstacle than incentive to faith. After that, discretion appeared the better part of fervor.

Other reasons have been advanced to explain the drop in Mass attendance. Andrew Greeley, for example, has claimed that much of it was a onetime dip caused by negative reaction to the 1968 papal reassertion of the condemnation of contraception. It seems highly likely that these two phenomena, teaching about damnation and rejection of the teaching that contraception sent one to hell, are connected.

really want to be there. And if requiring people to worship under threat of eternal punishment now strikes many Catholics as reflecting badly on the God who would enforce such a threat, at least the requirement sent a message about the importance of Sunday worship—a message that must now be signaled by the liturgy itself.

Attendance, however, is not the chief topic of the passionate debates that the new liturgy and its impact continue to stir among important segments of Catholic leadership. Even the remaining, highly vocal critics of the liturgical reform seldom deny its popularity. To them, that means about as much as the popularity of Oprah Winfrey or *Monday Night Football* or fast food. If anything, such popularity is just another symptom of the church's decline, of a general dulling of Catholic belief and sensibility, a collapse into banality characteristic of the culture at large that the new liturgy has abetted rather than resisted.

At the extreme, this critical minority believes that the new Mass falls just short of not being a Mass at all. They do not fully agree with the excommunicated followers of the late French archbishop Marcel Lefebvre that the so-called Tridentine Mass, authorized in 1570 by Pope Pius V in the wake of the Protestant Reformation and the Catholic Council of Trent, was established for all time and that any departure from it, like the new liturgy, is invalid. But these critics share the Lefebvrites' attachment to the Latin Tridentine rite, which they consider the fullest if not the only expression of Catholic faith. They campaign for its reinstatement; they flock to it wherever it is allowed to be celebrated as an option; they look with suspicion on the whole reforming effort of Vatican II and even more on the actual rites that were authorized in its name. These they hold to be, if not actually heretical, then leaning dangerously in that direction.

How many American Catholics share these views? One scholar estimated there were over 375 centers celebrating Tridentine Masses in the United States as of 1995, accommodating no more than twenty-thousand Catholics. That is a much smaller number than the publicity given to advocacy of the Latin Mass might suggest, although the advocates insist that many more would attend if more such Masses were readily available. At the other end of the theological spectrum, a similarly small but similarly vocal movement of militant feminists wants nothing to do with any liturgy over which only male priests can preside. Some Catholic feminists reject altogether the idea of a distinct priesthood as incompatible with feminist egalitarianism. They have begun to celebrate their own liturgies, which sometimes owe as much to New Age syncretism as Christianity. A much milder degree of egalitarian and feminist sentiment expresses itself in demands for more inclusive language in the prayers and scripture translations or for minimizing the distinctions between priestly and congregational roles that still hold in preaching and the liturgy of the table.

But dissatisfaction is not limited to the extremes. A broad swath of centrist to conservative commentators, many of them sympathetic to the basic thrust of the Council's reforms, have also been dismayed by how those reforms were put into practice. They object to a dumbing down of the rites. In striving for intelligibility and familiarity, they complain, the translations from Latin into English achieved only banality. In the name of congregational participation, the church's treasury of chant and polyphony was traded in for guitar-accompanied pseudofolk and soft-rock hymns. Solemnity and silence gave way to a frantic set of calisthenics: stand up, sit down, sing along, shake hands. Liberated from Latin and the old rubrics, priests started acting like emcees, and music leaders like martinets.

There is no doubt that the earlier years of the reformed liturgy were marked by incomprehension in most ordinary parishes and giddiness among many church activists. Having been taught the supposed universality and immutability of the Latin Mass, most priests were ill prepared to turn around and explain the new liturgy in terms other than "the Council says." Activists, on the other hand, often overwhelmed the cadre of veteran, scholarly liturgical reformers with enthusiasm, frequently taking the changes as carte blanche for wild ventures in making worship "relevant" with heavy doses of

1960s politics or countercultural expressivism. "Hootenanny Masses" with guitar music were a widespread, moderate innovation. Here and there children's Masses began to feature clowns. Catholics engaged in radical civil rights or antiwar activities or simply frustrated by the minimal impact of the Council on their parishes began to style themselves an "underground church" and to hold Masses in their homes, where sympathetic priests set aside vestments and official rites for informality and spontaneity. Horror stories from those days about Eucharists using beer and pretzels (or Coke and potato chips) soon attained the status of urban myths.

By no means was all the experimentation irreverent or pointless, but much was ill conceived and ultimately tiresome. Adding to the confusion, these efforts shared certain weaknesses with the ordinary parish. In 1990, Thomas Day, a liturgical musician and head of the music department at Salve Regina College in Newport, Rhode Island, published a small polemic, *Why Catholics Can't Sing*. Interestingly, liberal Catholic publications like *America* and *Commonweal* that had long supported liturgical changes had already published articles by Day, and liberal Catholic thinkers blurbed his book. Day skewered the sentimental Irish-American musical heritage that he argued had actually found new life in what passed for contemporary church music. He analyzed self-congratulatory lyrics and crooning song leaders who blasted aside congregations with their overamplified microphones. Day named names and took serial numbers. He listed many of the most popular new hymns and hymnals and cut into them with detailed criticism.

But Day did not stop with music. His most important criticism was aimed at the connected phenomena of "de-ritualization" and "display of personality." Deritualization purposely broke the sense of actions that were out of the ordinary. Day gave the example of the solemn entrance procession with resounding organ, followed by a moment of silence while the priest adjusts the microphone. And then: "Good morning, everybody."

"THUD! You can almost hear something collapsing," Day writes.

"Later on, just for symmetry, the celebrant will conclude the liturgy with a cheerful 'Havernice day.'"

Ritual traditionally and literally cloaked the Catholic celebrant in a special garb, but beyond that it cloaked him with a set of words and actions belonging to the whole community regardless of the individual at the altar. Deritualization, in Day's view, opens the door to a display of personality. Charm, folksiness, dramatics—in one form or another the personality of the priest becomes the center of attention. Whether in the person of chatty Father Hank or emoting Father Histrionic or Mr. Caruso, the parish song leader, "Ego Renewal, this tendency to put 'me' in the center of the liturgical landscape, is the single most influential thing to happen in the way Catholics have worshiped since the Second Vatican Council."

Why Catholics Can't Sing outraged liturgical specialists, as the author almost certainly hoped it would. In fact, having advocated reform in the teeth of entrenched habit and misunderstanding, liturgical experts had become highly defensive about what had been achieved and often seemed to close ranks against almost any serious criticism. And in fairness, some criticism, though not Day's, has suffered from a continuing confusion about the very nature of the liturgy, still conceived, at least for the laity, as essentially a time of private prayer, with which the new rites interfered, rather than a communal act of the whole congregation.

Even more of the criticism, though again Day should be excepted, suffered from a distorting nostalgia, reflected in talk about a lost sense of mystery, solemnity, and beauty. Yet there was very little that was solemn or mysterious, serene or aesthetically elevating, about the Tridentine Mass as it was actually celebrated by the average priest in the average parish. Quite the contrary. It was frequently hurried, graceless, with slurred prayers and jerky gestures. Priests were known for twenty-minute specials. There was no music, or perhaps a struggling organist who sang one or two sentimental hymns in a struggling voice. (High Masses, Day recalls, were subject to "yodeling sadists up in the choir loft.") Most weekday Masses were the unchanging Mass for the Dead in the unchanging black vestments rather than the Mass of the day's saint or of the liturgical season. Sunday Masses, except at the bigger urban parishes with trained choirs, were only a little better.

Wistful laments for the reverence and beauty of the preconciliar Mass rest on myth or highly selective memory. There were such Masses, of course. But the solemn high pontifical Masses at Chicago's cathedral that I attended a handful of times as a boy were the exception, aesthetically worlds apart from the thousand parish Masses I served as an altar boy. Deritualization, as Day notes, did not begin with Vatican II. If some priests diligently observed all the rubrics and exhibited a heartfelt fervor as they whispered the words of consecration over the bread and wine, they otherwise lumbered through the Mass mechanically, bowing and turning and kissing the altar and stabbing the air in signs of the cross and intoning the Latin as though these gestures and sounds had no other meaning than obligatory steps for validly completing the rite. And those were the better celebrants. Other priests quickly communicated to the altar boys a smug familiarity with all things sacred, a kind of authorized irreverence in which we were privileged to share. Yet even as a rather jaded seventh-grader, I remember being startled by one pastor's habit of reducing whole portions of the prayers to a brief hum or grunt. While other priests were saying Mass, the same pastor would stroll into the sanctuary with a screwdriver and putty knife to scrape the melted wax out of the bottoms of the glass cups for vigil lights. Only God can judge that pastor's interior attitude (and long since has), but his behavior, exuding an arrogant proprietorship of the liturgy, was as superficially blasphemous as that of any self-appointed postconciliar experimenter.

Horror stories, in sum, are not new. What is new are higher standards—standards imposed by the reforms themselves, by the Council's decree that the rites should be marked by "noble simplicity" and manifest their meaning with a minimum of explanation, by the impossibility of disguising a slipshod, expressionless, or eccentric manner of celebrating Mass now that the gestures are visible and the language understandable. The preconciliar liturgy had its power. It deserves to be understood rather than dismissed. But holding it up as an ideal seriously discredits criticism of current practice.

STRIPPED OF THIS NOSTALGIA, an unusual amount of criticism is now being voiced by thoughtful liturgists who have been at the very heart of the liturgical reform. Retired archbishop Rembert G. Weakland of Milwaukee once served as abbot general of the Benedictines, the order of monks that pioneered much of the liturgical revival in Europe and the United States. He is a trained musician and an expert in liturgical chant. And he was one of the 140 official consultors appointed to recommend specific changes in Catholic rites to implement the Council's general instructions. In an analysis prepared for a 1999 meeting of the Common Ground Initiative, Archbishop Weakland worried that "something that should be a point of unity in the church, the Eucharist, has now become the most conspicuous point of disagreements and tension." Not surprisingly, he criticized some conservative critics for still treating the Mass as private prayer or an occasion for aesthetic exaltation. More unexpected, perhaps, was his interrogation of the liturgical reformers: Have the reforms, and all the efforts to be "creative" in worship, he asked, obscured the sense that God rather than the community is the primary actor in the Mass? Have they diminished "respect for and belief in the real presence in the Eucharist?" Ultimately, "have we reduced the sense of the transcendent and an appreciation for God's presence and role in the liturgy?"

Sister Kathleen Hughes, no less than Archbishop Weakland, is identified with the cause of the reformed liturgy. As professor of word and worship at Catholic Theological Union in Chicago; biographer of the Reverend Godfrey Diekmann, O.S.B., one of the great Benedictine pioneers of the liturgical reform in the United States; and longtime adviser to the International Commission on English in the Liturgy (ICEL), as well as to the American bishops' Committee on the Liturgy, she was a leading member of the liturgical establishment, a fact that often exposed her to the attacks of conservatives. It was particularly significant, then, when she began a book, published in 1999 to deepen Catholics' understanding of the new liturgical forms, with a frank confession: "Especially for those who have invested their time and talent in one or other aspect of the reform—bishops and worship office personnel, pastors and administrators, musicians and artists, writers and teachers—there is a deeply disheartening suspicion that something is very wrong."

"In the process of the reform have we lost touch with the heart of the liturgy?" she asked. "Has the reform lost its soul?"

"So much ferment," she noted. "So much upheaval." But what had been the results? "Has the transformation of our liturgy transformed us?" Has it "helped us to pray more deeply?" she wondered. "Are we more just? More loving?" She recognizes "places where the renewal of worship has achieved wonderful results, where reverent and hospitable worship attracts hundreds, where the environment and the music, the proclamation and preaching are all executed with great care, where the presider and all the ministers are prepared and prayerful as they invite a community to grow in God's grace week after week."

But then there are also the parishes where "Sunday after Sunday, dwindling numbers gather for lifeless, dispirited worship."

Finally, there are the vast majority of parishes, neither outstanding nor lifeless. They have appointed the laity to liturgical roles, established liturgy planning committees, sent parishioners to innumerable workshops, remodeled the worship space, bought new vestments and hymnals, found a new music director, incorporated into the liturgy the languages or special traditions of different ethnic groups within the parish, fostered the communal dimension of the sacraments of baptism and reconciliation. Yet the demands outstrip the energy. "Pastors, particularly, are feeling the pressure of a far more demanding, better educated, and mobile flock, while their duties are multiplying and their own numbers are diminishing and aging." And the outcome so often seems to be rancor, over what to sing, when to stand or kneel, whether to avoid addressing God as "he," how to honor the Blessed Sacrament—a whole "minefield of competing and conflicting theologies, pastoral strategies, and sometimes simply aesthetic sensibilities."

Obviously it is difficult to generalize about nineteen thousand parishes, large and small, urban, suburban, and rural, serving congregations differing widely in class and cultural heritage. Almost every diocese will have one or two or perhaps a half dozen parishes outstanding for their worship. Saint Monica's in affluent Santa Monica, California, has become known for a music-driven evening Mass drawing young adults from all over the city, while other Masses in the same parish were traditional in the best sense; indeed, some parishioners gathered on weekday mornings to chant the morning prayers inherited from monastic life. At the other end of the socioeconomic spectrum, the Mexican Indian parishioners at Saint Thomas the Apostle church in Los Angeles's Koreatown neighborhood used to spill out onto the sidewalk for the Mass with mariachi music; when a disgruntled homeless man torched the church, the new building had to be enlarged. At Holy Cross Catholic Church, a Jesuit-run, largely African-American parish in Durham, North Carolina, where I found myself one Sunday, the liturgical fervor was palpable, but so was the careful preparation and the reflective, literary quality of that day's preaching. I have been caught up by the colorful "smells-and-bells" high liturgies in the Basilica of the Sacred Heart on the campus of the University of Notre Dame, but also by the quiet early morning Masses celebrated in the basilica's crypt.

Then there are the truly awful liturgies. At an upstate New York parish, a visiting priest, an older man who had probably put his persona of Father Good Guy to some good purposes as a boys' high school teacher, actually broke off the prayers from time to time to tell jokes, in one case an anti-Semitic joke. This had nothing to do with the hypertrendiness that those still disconsolate with Vatican II blame for every liturgical failure. But I have seen plenty of that, too: congregations of graying survivors of the sixties that seem mainly to be celebrating themselves and their superiority to morally benighted church authorities. The watchword is "inclusivity"—and yet the strictest left-wing unanimity is presumed in prayers and homilies.

Such sorry cases are now the exceptions. What is so crucial to the future of American Catholicism, however, is the great in-between, parishes becalmed in mediocrity or parishes mixing thoughtful and effective liturgical efforts with elements that grate like fingernails on a blackboard.

Here is Saint Suburbia's in the Midwest. A few years ago it undertook a $3 million renovation of the church, aimed at creating a church in the round. The renovation pitted volunteers and professional staff claiming liturgical expertise—and a pastor impressed by the design of a local megachurch—against parishioners who were either more religiously traditional or simply budget conscious. Meant to heighten congregational participation and a sense of community, the renovation probably had the opposite effect, at least in the short run. Architecturally, the compromise that emerged from years of squabbles and consulting placed the altar, pulpit, and chairs for the presider and servers on a raised island in the middle of what was once the nave. Hovering over them is a futuristic canopy (technically known as a baldachino) containing lights and a sound system and held in place by a spiderweb of cables. The effect is closer to a starship command center than to a communal table. The pews—reduced in number and with ample space between them because of the declining church attendance—are grouped around this altar, but its height and complexity separate people from the presider and readers almost as completely as the traditional Communion rail.

The actual liturgies at Saint Suburbia are distinguished mainly by a lack of distinction. A neighborly informality prevails. A few years ago, the pastor at that time would stroll through the church before Mass in his black clerical shirt and carrying over his arm the white vestment he would later don. He greeted parishioners. He recruited an altar server from the congregation. The parishioners spread themselves loosely throughout the pews, each family group keeping a proper distance from other groups. A pew was seldom filled, although at Christmas and Easter, I am told, the reduced amount of seating suddenly becomes insufficient.

At Saint Suburbia, the rubrics are observed—nothing experimental. The music is, well, nice—planned and performed by devoted musicians with good voices but eliciting little response from the congregation. A very generous estimate would be that half the congregants join in, and weakly at that. The preaching, too, is nice. No hellfire and no heavy theology, simply friendly messages about loving one another linked loosely to the scripture readings and brightened with the homilist's anecdotes. There are intimations of the church's concerns with peace, economic justice, racial inclusiveness, but nothing so specific as to be distressing or controversial. It is hard to imagine well-educated, professional suburbanites being either repelled or attracted by this preaching, or remembering it the next day.

This is mediocrity. But how bad is mediocrity, or even how mediocre is mediocrity?

In 1997, *Commonweal* magazine asked fourteen of its writers to report on one of the liturgies celebrated at a nearby church on Sunday, October 19. For the most part, the writers sensed a deep spiritual longing in their fellow worshipers and a sincere striving among the celebrants. Although noting a good amount of ragged music and disappointing preaching, the writers seemed wary of their own potential for spiritual snobbery and determined not to distance themselves from these all-too-human congregations. Good try, and God have mercy on us all, was the general reaction.

Those reports contrast with a cri de coeur from the writer Paul Wilkes, who visited parishes across the nation as part of a study. "In Boise, Idaho, and suburban Chicago, and hard by the Massachusetts Pike in Newton," he wrote, "I have worshipped with people who couldn't wait to get to church on Sunday, who willingly tithed, who even enjoyed meetings." But these are the tantalizing exceptions, he suggests, "to the staid mediocrity that too often passes for parish life." American Catholics, Wilkes says, have "come to accept lifeless liturgies" and "clueless, noteless sermons that appear to be warmed-over term paper memories from a poorly taught New Testament 101 class."

ARE WILKES'S IMPRESSIONS accurate? Are Sister Hughes's? Are *Commonweal*'s? Are mine? One of the startling things is how little effort is being made to find out. Experts in Catholic worship regularly fill scholarly journals with articles on liturgical history and theory, but there appears to be an almost complete lack of empirical study of what actually is happening in parishes.

In 1988 the Reverend Lawrence J. Madden, S. J., had overseen a study of fifteen English-speaking parishes by a number of liturgical experts. The study found that twenty-five years after the Council the surveyed parishes could be said to have made "a splendid beginning" but that there was also a striking degree of dissatisfaction with how the liturgies were actually being done. The longtime director of the Center for Liturgy, Spirituality, and the Arts at Georgetown University, in the year 2000 he was finishing a term as pastor of Holy Trinity Parish near the university. A dozen years after the study, what were his overall impressions of the grassroots reality in the nation's nineteen thousand parishes? "Optimists say there are two thousand good parishes," he replied. "Pessimists say two hundred!" A range, in other words, between one out of ten and one out of a hundred.

Stranger even than the lack of large-scale empirical studies is the apparent lack of parish self-examination. How many pastors ever experience Mass as a member of the congregation does? How many parish worship committees systematically observe their own services? How many, that is, actually register what proportion of the congregants are singing, and which hymns? Or when people do or do not join in the prayers? Or even whether the sound system works? For years I have been asking widely traveled priests and church officials how many parishes build such simple reporting—leaving aside more sophisticated inquiries into the effectiveness of homilies or ritual actions—into their staff responsibilities and regular meetings. The consensus is "almost none."

The contrast between the standards for worship and the standards that Catholics expect to be met in the rest of their lives is dramatic. Once a priest is ordained, he evidently has a license for forty years of liturgical malpractice—or superb liturgical leadership. One way or the other, he is accountable to no one, at least this side of egregious violations of the rites; and no one is charged with checking on him or his parish. Paul Wilkes reminds us of the professional competence that we demand from surgeons or cobblers or journalists. Leaving a Mass where many things have been done right but one or two elements have seriously marred the possibility of worship—execrable music, perhaps, or an ill-prepared, poorly reasoned homily—I often compare it to my experience as a magazine editor and newspaper reporter. It is as though one page out of thirty-two were to come out upside down or with smudged ink, making it unreadable—I think to myself—and we would simply congratulate ourselves that at least the other thirty-one were all right. Every day's issue of the *New York Times* is subject to a postmortem critique, and the editors circulate memos flagging shortcomings and pointing up successes. Why doesn't parish worship rate as much?

THE QUALITY OF A parish's worship can be usefully examined under four headings: presiding, preaching, participation, and music.

In the years immediately after Vatican II, presiding (the grace, appropriateness, and effectiveness of the priest and other worship leaders in their physical gestures and speech) was a disaster zone. Few priests possessed a ritual sense; few had ever infused the physical gestures of the Mass with meaning. Nor did the worshipers expect to find anything but the vaguest meaning in those actions, any more than in the Latin phrases. But when the liturgical reforms turned the presider around to face the congregation during Mass, those gestures were brought into full view, just as the prayers were brought into understandable English; and both demanded a way of moving and speaking, a posture and a presence, a choice of vocal and facial expressiveness that were suited to the action. Unprepared for this challenge, some priests celebrated Mass in flat tones and with jerky, mechanical movements. Others, as Thomas Day complained, became emcees or flamboyantly made themselves, not the ritual, the center of attention.

It is my strong impression that presiding at worship is much improved. The idiosyncrasies and excesses are much diminished, although that very fact may make those remaining stand out as inexcusable. There continues to be an unresolved tension in presiding between projecting an inviting warmth and fostering a sober solemnity, but there is also a large, reasonable middle ground in which more and more priests can be found.

Preaching, too, has improved. How could it not? There was nowhere to go but up. Catholicism, in this country as elsewhere, always boasted its great preachers. Yet traditionally, in the preaching league Catholic clergy occupied last place. Before the Council the sermon was considered a more or less optional part of the Mass—it would have been in Latin, after all, if it were really important—and Catholics in the pews almost certainly treated it that way. Restoring emphasis on the Word in worship, the Council insisted on the essential role of the homily expounding on the readings from scripture. Again, Catholic priests, trained far more in dogmatic and moral theology than in scripture, were caught unprepared. The improvement since then has been marked, thanks in good measure to a myriad of workshops, publications, and just plain embarrassment. Unfortunately, with a Catholic population better and better educated, the bar may be going up faster than preaching can improve. Catholics clearly expect more from their homilists than they are getting. Worse, an aging, overworked clergy can improve only so much.

Active participation in Eucharistic worship was at the center of the liturgical renewal, and here the change has been undeniable. The part that should be played by the entire worshiping assembly has been structured right into ritual: congregational responses, collectively recited prayers, the petitions of the people, presentation of the offerings of bread and wine, greetings of peace. Active participation, as conservatives have pointed out, is more than outward activity. On that level alone, however, a glance around most Catholic congregations leaves a very mixed impression. If the Lord's Prayer is recited rather than sung, worshipers typically join in heartily, just as most share the greeting of peace heartily. Beyond that, I find the response in most congregations highly uneven. A distinct minority appears in genuine interaction with the celebrant, while a sizable number of worshipers, often a majority, are silent or barely moving their lips. The effect is hardly inspiriting. More important, it raises questions about the deeper meaning of active participation: Do Catholics worship with the conviction that they are themselves, together, offering this great thanksgiving? Or, their occasional assigned words and motions notwithstanding, are they essentially watching and hearing someone else do it for them? Both theologically and experientially, there is a gulf between those attitudes.

Music is a special form of participation. Whatever boasts the church could make of great preachers, it could make far more of its musical heritage. Yet like preaching, music was long considered something optional in parishes, an adornment to worship, not the thing itself. Some immigrant groups brought strong traditions of congregational hymn singing from their homelands. Those traditions did not implant themselves well outside ethnic neighborhoods, and there they were more apt to enliven devotional services than Sunday Masses. The Council's call for congregational singing as part of the liturgy posed a serious challenge to American parishes.

And still does. Every time a Protestant denomination tries to revise its hymnal, there is thunder in the pews. It would be easier, one suspects, to revise the creed. And maybe for good reason. The hymns worshipers sing probably give form to their faith as much as the clauses of the creed. At least, that may be true for Protestants. One hopes it isn't true for Catholics, whose resistance to full-throated song, again with the honorable exceptions of a few ethnic communities, is legendary. Thomas Day stirred a hornet's nest of critics with the provocative arguments of *Why Catholics Can't Sing,* but almost none of his critics challenged the title itself. Although Archbishop Weakland criticized Day's book in 1991, he later complained: "Most of the new music created for the liturgy has been and continues to be trite in both musical form and text. . . . New music of limited value and with no one in charge of 'quality control' keeps being introduced, so that there is little stability. . . . Children learn no consistent repertoire of liturgical music that belongs to the Catholic tradition and that will serve them for their whole lives."

Much of the new music falls into two categories. One is what Day called the "sweet song," singsong tunes that, beneath a veneer of scriptural phrases or 1960s sentiments, are reincarnations of the gushy hymns of preconciliar days, which were in turn religious versions of the sentimental dance-hall ballads of Victorian America. They give song leaders ample opportunity for notes held longer than the average, untrained congregation is capable of. They also communicate a mild, comforting, carefully inclusive spirituality that stays away from strong theology or strong emotion.

The other category of new music is a kind of driving, rhythmically tricky hymn irresistible to young musicians like the ones at a Sunday evening Mass I sometimes attend. They are talented, they are dedicated, they are loud, and they are spirited. They have their own distinctive sound, and they have cut a tape or two. The congregation, which is heavy on the young adults for whom this late Mass is designed (although the church is still far from filled), inevitably applauds them at the end of the Mass. The applause is the giveaway. This is a performance, and the audience appreciates it. During the liturgy, however, very few people are actually singing, nor could they. The worshipers are obviously grateful for the effort made on their behalf, and the pastor, an extremely intelligent and overburdened man approaching retirement, is not going to disrupt something that appears to be working and welcomed. He cannot get too exacting over whether there is really much of a communal experience, a church truly worshiping together. If the church is half empty, well, at least it is half full.

Music is perhaps the weakest link in Catholic worship today. The problem is not that some, maybe much, of the music is an affront to good taste, although that is true. The problem is that the worshipers don't sing, and when they don't sing, the result is worse than if they had never been expected to. Imagine a birthday celebration where two or three out of ten family members actually sang "Happy Birthday" and the rest stood silent or barely moving their lips. What would be the message?

The ragged, halfhearted, dutiful singing that marks so many Catholic Masses is more than a lost opportunity; it is a distinctly dispiriting experience, a positive obstacle to worship. Those few with strong voices don't know whether to stand out as quasi soloists. Those with uncertain voices hesitate in the absence of a collective sound into which they can blend.

Catholics are not unaware of the widespread failure of their sung worship—but by and large it is treated as peripheral: it would be nice, of course, to have better singing, just as it would be nice if the church had a new paint job, but it is hardly essential. So while there are fierce debates about music, they are debates, by and large, about the aesthetic quality of the music and the theology of the lyrics—debates that could as well take place on the basis of comparing hymnals alone and quite apart from experience of worshipping congregations.

THE OTHER CHIEF TOPICS recently provoking heated debate and sharp divisions about Catholic worship are translations of the liturgical prayers and Eucharistic adoration outside of Mass.

Following the Council, all the sacramental rites were swiftly translated from Latin into local languages. Translation is an enormously complicated undertaking and one inevitably giving rise to disputes. But a consensus soon formed that these first translations, certainly the English ones, had been rushed and executed without sufficient appreciation of the requirements of ritual and the validity of a heightened language for sacred matters. So when the International Commission on English in the Liturgy undertook a new round of translations in the 1990s, the thrust of their work took, in many ways, a traditional direction. It might well have been welcomed by conservatives, except for two factors.

One was the question of gender-neutral, or inclusive, language that had arisen since the original translations. Should the translations abide by the growing sense that "man" and "he" were no longer acceptable English usage for all people, male and female included? Should the translations take sides in the theological wars set off by feminist criticism of masculine images for the Godhead? The new translations generally followed the prescription of the bishops of the United States and several other countries to minimize masculine pronouns when language referred to people, while retaining the masculine imagery of God the Father and God the Son. Occasionally the proposed translations seemed to push beyond this by substituting repeated references to "God" for male pronouns for the deity. With conservative theologians and their Vatican supporters convinced that even this concession to current usage is a needless and dangerous surrender to a feminism and a culture fundamentally hostile to Christianity and its Trinitarian formulas, the proposed translations were put under minute scrutiny for all kinds of doctrinal deviations.

The other factor was precisely the growth of this organized conservatism during the papacy of John Paul II. This conservatism looked on the guild of liturgical specialists as a hotbed of questionable theology, and included among its adherents many wed to the preconciliar Roman rite. They felt on a roll, so that even though the new round of translations responded to many conservative insights about language, why not hold out for more, for something still closer to the older, Latin forms?

The American bishops were not willing to accept this kind of delay, which would have deprived a generation of badly needed revised translations. Year after year they approved additional segments of the new translations, covering not merely the unchanging prayers of the Mass and other sacramental rites but all the prayers specific to each Sunday, the holy days, and the feasts of different saints. The process was often not pretty. Conservatives insinuated that liberal liturgists were covertly importing heresy into the church's sacred rites. Liberals were sometimes disingenuous about their emphasis on inclusive language. Bishop Fabian Bruskewitz of Lincoln, Nebraska, speaking at a meeting of the bishops, once compared the new translations to Nazi-inspired revisions of the Bible under Hitler.

ICEL and the majority of American bishops appear to have won those battles but lost the war. In 1994, the Vatican began withdrawing approvals it had already given the American bishops' choice of biblical translations for use in the liturgy. Then, joining the relentless conservative attacks on ICEL's work, the Vatican targeted the commission with a barrage of criticism and demands for restructuring, effectively subjecting it—and the English-language bishops' conferences it served—to much tighter control. Finally, in May 2001, the Vatican office overseeing matters of liturgy and sacramental life, the Congregation for Divine Worship and the Discipline of the Sacraments, issued a lengthy set of guidelines for translating liturgical texts. Titled *Liturgiam Authenticam,* the document's norms for translations in accord with "authentic liturgy" challenged years of work by ICEL and the bishops' conferences. It called for translations from the Latin that were as literal as possible, echoing Latin syntax and style; using to the greatest extent possible the same vernacular word to translate a given Latin word, regardless of context; and not hesitating to retain expressions that were arcane or incomprehensible to contemporary ears, if the phrases were sufficiently literal, theologically precise, or time-honored. The Vatican instruction appeared to brake efforts to make liturgical language more inclusive, barring many of the translating strategies employed to minimize inherited and obtrusive masculine formulations. Rather than measuring the accuracy of scripture used in the liturgy against the best manuscript texts available in Hebrew, Greek, and Aramaic—the original biblical languages—the instruction insisted that the determinative standard should be the Neo-Vulgate, a recent, updated version of Saint Jerome's fourth-century Latin translation, which was given official status by the Council of Trent in the wake of the Reformation. To many biblical scholars, this proposal bordered on the bizarre. (Not even the Pontifical Biblical Commission had been consulted.) Finally, the instruction asserted much greater Vatican control over the entire process of translating liturgical texts, reserving not only the right of final approval but also the congregation's right to intervene at many points along the way, approving (or blackballing) consultants and translators, for example, or even producing its own translations without involving the bishops.

Liturgiam Authenticam made many valid points about the special character of liturgical language, the value of uniform familiar texts for purposes of memorization and private prayer, and even the way in which odd terms or unfamiliar phrases in worship can "provoke inquisitiveness in the hearer" and spur religious education. The parts of the instruction clearly dealing with the problems of nations splintered by many languages and dialects were a healthy reminder of the Vatican's global responsibilities. But there was no question that, symbolically, *Liturgiam Authenticam* was a slap in the face to liberal liturgists, a preemptive strike against feminism, and a vote of no confidence in the English-speaking bishops. In its own way, the instruction was a kind of coup, composed and issued not only without consulting the world's conferences of bishops but without even canvassing all the individual bishops and cardinals who were members of the Congregation for Divine Worship and the Discipline of the Sacraments.

Most important, *Liturgiam Authenticam* cast into limbo more than a decade's effort to create a more solemn (but also gender-neutral) language of worship. Perhaps the Vatican guidelines will prove to have a bark worse than their bite, and this work will go forward without major revisions or delays. For the time being, it is unclear exactly how *Liturgiam Authenticam* will affect the prayers Catholics will be saying at Mass twenty years from now—affect, that is, not only the wording of those prayers but how many Catholics are praying them and whether they are praying them actively or dutifully, fervently or without spirit.

THE SECOND TOPIC PARTICULARLY roiling Catholics concerned about worship has to do with Catholic understanding of Christ's presence in the bread and wine sacramentally transformed at Mass. Over the centuries, where Mass was celebrated in Latin, its structure as a communal meal was obscure to laypeople, who rarely received Communion in any case. Attention naturally focused on the miracle of the changed bread and wine and the worship of Christ present in the Blessed Sacrament, quite apart from the other actions of the Mass itself. The more that medieval or Reformation-era controversies swirled around whether or how the bread and wine were actually changed, the more the church focused piety on the round consecrated host, which more than the consecrated wine could be easily seen and preserved. Immediately after the moment in the Mass when the priest repeated Jesus' words at the Last Supper, the host was solemnly elevated so that worshipers could gaze on it. The consecrated host was also displayed at the center of the golden rays of the magnificent vessels known as monstrances, carried in processions, or was locked behind the golden doors and richly decorated veils of the centrally placed tabernacles, before which a candle permanently flickered. Theologians could explain endlessly why the Mass represented a sacrifice or a meal, but what its structure really communicated was the hushed arrival of God, ruler and savior, and the obeisance of his devoted servants in a court setting, whether modest or majestic.

The Council's reforms were in no way aimed at diminishing Catholic belief in the transformation of the bread and wine and in Jesus' real presence in the Eucharist. They did aim at placing that presence squarely within the actions of the communal meal and the recollection of the Last Supper and Christ's paschal passage through death. The reforms aimed at linking Christ's real presence on the altar with Christ's presence in the biblical Word and Christ's presence around the altar, in the gathered people. At the same time, Catholic education and preaching ceased to stress the sharp differences over Eucharistic theology—transubstantiation versus memorial, for instance—that had thrown up polemical barriers between Catholics and Protestants. The feeling that distinctly churchy behavior rendered worship insincere and irrelevant encouraged an informality in dress and demeanor that hardly reinforced the belief that communicants were receiving divinity itself under the forms of bread and wine. The step-by-step abrogation of the old requirement that Catholics neither eat nor drink from midnight before receiving Communion also seemed to reduce the awesome nature of the sacrament.

By the late 1980s, therefore, first traditionalists and then a more diverse group of church leaders were pressing the question whether Catholic Eucharistic doctrine had not been seriously undermined. I myself contributed to this anxiety in April 1994 when the *New York Times* surveyed Catholics in connection with a series of articles on the church. Determined that the national poll would contain questions beyond what had become a rather routine repertoire of inquiries about birth control, abortion, homosexuality, married priests, ordination of women, and the like. I urged at least one question concerning worship. We settled on a question about Catholic views of the Eucharist, and the results were rather striking. Considerable thought went into the wording of the question. The goal was not to spell out exact theological understandings of the Mass but simply to identify the general direction of Catholics' beliefs by posing distinct alternatives that would be clear and brief over the telephone.

The actual question asked on the phone was, "Which of the following comes closest to what you believe takes place at Mass: (1) the bread and wine are changed into the body and blood of Christ, or (2) the bread and wind are symbolic reminders of Christ?"

The results took both Catholics and non-Catholics involved in overseeing the poll by surprise. For all those identifying themselves as Catholic on the poll, 34 percent said "changed into the body and blood" came closest to their belief, while 63 percent said "symbolic reminders." Among Catholics between eighteen and twenty-nine years of age, 29 percent said "body and blood"; 70 percent said "symbolic reminders." Among Catholics who reported attending Mass every week or almost every week, approximately half of those queried, 44 percent, said "body and blood"; 51 percent said "symbolic reminders." Only among Catholics aged sixty-five or older did the traditional belief gain a bare majority: 51 percent said "body and blood," with 45 percent saying "symbolic reminders."

Were we undervaluing the meaning Catholics read into the word "symbolic"? Would the results have been different, for example, if the first choice had included the phrase "under the appearances of bread and wine," echoing the formulation that older Catholics learned in their catechisms?

We also recognized that there is no empirical baseline—no similar survey from, say, 1930 or 1950—against which these results can be evaluated. Some Catholics in the past, even those leading pious lives of devotion to Jesus and the saints, may have been hazier about the Eucharist than is supposed. And finally it must be stated that at least one other national poll did *not* confirm the *Times*'s findings. Given a simple choice of agreeing or disagreeing with the statement "The bread and wine used at Mass are actually transformed into the body and blood of Christ," over 80 percent of the Catholics polled either strongly or mildly agreed.

Nonetheless, these well-publicized and widely (sometimes inaccu-

rately) repeated findings strengthened the impression of a significant falling off in traditional Catholic belief about the Eucharist.
Some conservative Catholics were already rallying around the celebration of solemn Benediction, a traditional devotion in which the
consecrated host is displayed and honored in a monstrance and then
used to bless the people. Likewise they promoted perpetual adoration, or round-the-clock silent prayer before the Blessed Sacrament.
In some ways this has been a grassroots movement, one of many
ways, from yoga to Marian pilgrimages, by which Catholics have
filled in a vacuum created when the Council's emphasis on a renewed liturgy seemed to downplay the many devotional practices
that gave an organized structure to personal prayer. But bishops, worried about eroding beliefs, also became increasingly ready to support
these Eucharistic practices and encourage others, like revived neighborhood processions on the feast of Corpus Christi (Body of Christ).
These practices, in turn, worried many Catholics who had worked
to institute the Council's liturgical reforms. Weren't they throwbacks
that threatened to shift spirituality away from the Mass and the community?

Architecture has become the latest battleground for the worries
about Eucharistic spirituality. The bishops have discussed new
guidelines that, in one way or another, try to guarantee the tabserna-
cle some of the physical centrality often lost when churches were remodeled or rearranged to allow for free-standing altars so that
priests could face the worshipers. This, too, has caused consternation
among liturgical specialists.

IT WOULD BE MISTAKEN to think that there is nothing at stake in
these battles over inclusive language and Eucharistic spirituality—
but there is less, I would argue, than many of those engaged in the
struggles imagine. The outstanding fact about today's worship wars
is that they are peripheral to the most pressing problems and a terrible displacement of energy.

The inclusive-language issue has unfortunately been rubbed raw by both proponents and opponents. A single reference to God as "he" can make many feminist Catholics angry, let alone generic references to the "men" for whom Christ died or the fool who says in "his" heart that there is no God (Psalm 14). Meanwhile the repetitions and circumlocutions aimed at circumventing masculine pronouns make traditionalists wince. At Mass, minor shouting matches sometimes break out in adjacent pews. When the priest prays that "our sacrifice may be acceptable to God," the congregation responds, "May the Lord accept the sacrifice at your hands for the praise and glory of his name, for our good, and the good of all his church"—except that some voices, male as well as female, emphatically say "for the praise and glory of *God's* name . . . and the good of all *God's* church." A minute later the competition is renewed. The priest declares, "Let us give thanks to the Lord our God," and the congregation divides between those content to respond, "It is right to give *him* thanks and praise," and those responding, "It is right to give *God* thanks and praise."

Common sense suggests that rigorously excluding feminine images of God and sticking to the supposedly generic use of masculine pronouns to cover both men and women diminishes women's sense of their own presence in scripture and worship. Refusing to retranslate the Nicene Creed recited at Mass so that the eternally begotten Son comes down from heaven "for us and for our salvation" rather than "for us *men* and for our salvation"—on the grounds that "men" still really means "men and women"—is simply to beg for noncompliance. On the other hand, when bedrock Christian formulas begin to be altered ("In the name of the Creator, Redeemer, and Sanctifier" instead of "Father, Son, and Holy Spirit"), resistance is appropriate. The burden of proof certainly rests with the innovators.*

The challenge of aligning Catholicism with the world-historical changes in women's roles can neither be won nor lost on the playing

*The issue of inclusive, or gender-neutral, language is explored further in Chapter Seven.

fields of liturgical language. Polls show that the vast majority of Catholic women, unlike those who have become hypersensitized to language questions, are not dismayed by traditional wordings. Nor is there any evidence that the American bishops' 1990 policy of encouraging gender-neutral language generally while retaining masculine references to the deity has created a slippery slope toward goddess worship rather than a barrier against it.

The same sort of false dichotomy has pumped energy into the conflict about Eucharistic presence and spirituality. At the outside, the return to solemn Benediction and perpetual adoration could again separate the Eucharist from the church's assembly. And yes, these devotions are sometimes promoted as an implicit, occasionally even explicit counter to a liturgical renewal thought to have downplayed aspects of Catholic belief about Christ's real presence that are at odds with contemporary doubts about the supernatural and to have crowded out, with communal participation, meditative, individual forms of worship.

These criticisms can be exaggerated, but they also contain truths, and liturgists would be wiser to pay attention than to denounce the messengers. What tension exists between these devotional practices and the renewed liturgy may also be clearer on paper than in practice. The piety engendered in Eucharist adoration outside of Mass might just support active participation at Mass. Human psychology is not as either/or as liturgical theories.

The energy invested in these most recent liturgical wars would be better devoted to more basic and less doctrinally divisive questions about Catholic worship. If Catholics are drawn to Mass less and less, or if they continue to go while the experience makes less and less impact, inclusive language and Eucharistic devotion will be moot issues. The real focus today ought to be on questions of practical competence, of implementation, and insofar as things of the spirit can be observed or measured, of empirical examination—in short, what in sports is called "execution."

If athletic terminology sounds inappropriate, another word could also serve: "craftsmanship." In 1995, Cardinal Godfried Danneels of Brussels told a conference at the University of Notre Dame, "In order to take one's place in the liturgical enterprise, one has to know one's craft." That meant a good helping of spirituality, insight, pastoral awareness, and instruction, he said, but the fact that "there is no lack of engagement or dedication or imagination" had not proved sufficient. "Perhaps the reason for the evident liturgical poverty in so many places throughout the world," the cardinal said, "is simply a lack of competence."

What, concretely, would emphasizing empirical observation and practical competence mean? One example comes from the diocese of Saginaw, Michigan, where Bishop Kenneth Untener began working with his priests and lay ministers first on preaching and then on the Sunday celebration generally. A short, trim man with fine features always on the verge of a mischievous grin, he is known for bringing up in print—or on the floor of the bishops' meetings—questions that most bishops prefer to avoid, like the laity's resounding rejection of official statements on contraception. He is also known for a unique lifestyle. At one point he began constantly traveling among his diocese's parishes, residing in each for a brief period and either commuting to his office and the cathedral or keeping in touch by phone.

All that makes Bishop Untener a liberal. Ask him to talk about social justice, however, and he doesn't talk long before bringing everything back to the Sunday Eucharist. "We get it correct on multiple choice that liturgy is the most important thing in a parish," he told me in April 2000, "but that's not where we invest our thought and energy."

In 1993, he decided to do something very practical about the quality of Catholic preaching. He first proposed the idea to his priests' council and obtained their unanimous endorsement. Then he began working his way alphabetically through the diocese's roster of priests, four at a time, plus a deacon or lay preacher. He asked them to tape a live sermon and send him the tape. He added a tape of a sermon of his own to theirs and sent out copies, along with transcripts, so that the whole group had heard one another's tapes, including the bishop's, before meeting for two hours to discuss them. The diocesan communications director, a trained journalist, joined the sessions. Having edited two of the transcripts the way a tough-minded editor would, she came with explanations of her changes. The first edited transcript to be examined was the bishop's, "And I tell her, 'Be ruthless,'" he said. A second professional woman present was a theologian and spiritual director. Six laypeople from a different diocese (and therefore unfamiliar with any of the preachers) constituted a final source of comment; each one listened to a tape and sent in written observations.

Bishop Untener described the sessions as doing "what golfers do after a match. We compliment, console, offer tips, and try to figure out how we can preach better." The key, of course, was honesty—and the fact that the bishop himself was as much on the line as others. "On the whole, honesty prevails and we have wonderful conversations, at times from the depths of our souls." Each person would leave with a blank tape, so that the whole process was run through three more times.

Bishop Untener had begun the preaching project "with trepidation"; it was, after all, "very sensitive." But the response was overwhelmingly positive: "Priests started asking, 'When's my turn?'"

Success regarding homilies encouraged him to look at the Mass. He began having priests videotape a whole liturgy, with the camera focusing on the priest but also looking around at the congregation. Again, he met with priests, in groups of four, after they all received copies of their videos and took notes. An expert in liturgical theology was there to help with the underlying theory. "The conversations can get very spiritual," Bishop Untener said; "for example, how hard it is to pray, really pray, in front of other people, not just *performing* prayer."

The early sessions convinced Bishop Untener that "the liturgy wasn't working, wasn't having the effects it's meant to have." So he had parishes do another video, this time focusing on the congregation from behind the altar. Using a stopwatch to measure exactly how much time the congregation spent in speaking or moving, he realized why the worshipers were inert. "The people hardly get to do or say anything. We think they're involved because more individuals are involved, as lectors reading scripture or as ministers helping to distribute Communion." But the worshipers in general have little more to do than in the preconciliar liturgy. "They're no longer even beating their breasts," he said.

He began some experiments—in three parishes, with the liturgy of the Word, and in another group, with the Eucharistic prayer. Some of the experiments were modest. Working with a scripture scholar and journalist, for instance, he wrote introductions setting the context for the first two biblical readings: "Six hundred years before Christ, the Israelites are in captivity." Or "Paul is answering questions he received in letters." Instead of passing collection baskets, the experimenting parishes involved the whole congregation in bringing forward their Sunday offerings. Other experiments went further. After the first two readings, congregants were invited to share their thoughts with the persons next to them. ("Now they listen to the readings differently.") During the Eucharistic prayer, they were invited to join in some of the priest's gestures, like holding out their hands and calling forth the Spirit.

These experiments were not about making worship "interesting" with novelties. "The last thing I want," Untener insisted, "is a gimmick for each week." The question was always, "What is it we're trying to do at this point in the Mass?" The aim was always to make that clear and tangible. Nor did the efforts neglect the very mundane aspects: for example, terrible sound systems, inability to catch the words of the responsorial psalm that the cantor sings between scripture readings, or the choice of music.

Departing from the assumption that the reformed patterns of worship would be self-explanatory, the bishop himself, a masterful, low-intensity teacher, began celebrating "teaching Masses" in parish after parish. That meant taking time at the beginning of each liturgy, and then interrupting its distinct parts if necessary, to explain the actions and symbolism. His view: "People are immensely thirsty for understanding."

SURELY, BISHOP UNTENER'S approach is only one of many possibilities. The important thing is that without neglecting theological understanding and official rubrics, it emphasizes the pastoral, the concrete, the practical. It remains grounded in the experience of the worshiping congregation and its leaders. It takes the reforms of Vatican II as its mandated framework, but it is not caught up in redebating the Council, criticizing or defending its implementation, accusing people of distorting or betraying its intentions, or using the liturgy to promote other causes. A pastoral, practical approach does not assume that having a liturgically correct position on Vatican II's reforms, whether of a more liberal or more conservative character, substitutes for truly effective, intellectually and emotionally transforming worship.

Such an approach, focused on presiding, preaching, and music, would also frankly ask whether the priority that parishes and dioceses claim to give worship is reflected in commitments of time and resources. How much of the budget is really devoted to liturgical matters? How much attention, energy, and staff do the pastor and staff direct to the quality of worship? One study of preaching found Catholic priests admitting that their sermons were a low priority. They reported spending an average of three hours in preparation, a figure that I suspect comes closer to their ideal than to their average, compared to the eleven hours spent by Protestant ministers. Congregants, on the other hand, both Catholic and Protestant, said the sermon was crucial. "I need more than a nice little talk that tells me how to be a good person," said one. "I can get that from Oprah." But despite this desire for good preaching, preachers had to operate in a vacuum. The vast majority of worshipers said that their comments to the preacher never went beyond "Nice sermon," while their real reaction was closer to "Ho-hum."

Another example of the need for parishes to consciously and deliberately plan arises in the case of those life-cycle events—marriages and funerals, above all—that foreseeably bring to the pews family members and friends who, for one reason or another, have drifted from the church. These are extraordinary opportunities for extending welcome, healing wounds, restoring ties—or for confirming alienation. A thoughtful, eloquent liturgy can revive the spark of faith; a sloppy, mechanical liturgy reminds people why they exited in the first place.

Lex orandi lex credendi. If the ancient maxim reminds us that in some sense worship is primary and that belief articulates it, it should also remind us that the relationship is reciprocal. The experience of worship is shaped by the belief one brings to it, as well as by the conduct of the service. The Mass is a different experience for the person who comes to it convinced that the gospel demands collective witness to the promised kingdom as well as individual piety. A routine or even slipshod Mass is a different experience for the worshipers who come convinced that, regardless of the liturgical competence of the priest or the enthusiasm of the congregation, the living Jesus Christ becomes immediately present to them in the consecrated bread and wine. Whether the Catholic Church successfully passes its faith to new generations will depend on their experience of the church's worship, but the very experience of worship also depends on what convictions new generations bring to it. Which raises the next question: how well is the church communicating and fostering those convictions?

Chapter Six

———————|———————————|———————

Passing on the Faith

E VERY generation of Catholic leaders—and probably of parents, too—worries that the next generation will "lose the faith." For Catholics, losing the faith once implied a crisis of belief or a conversion to some other, conflicting outlook. The process of losing the faith might be prolonged, but ultimately the point came when one rejected Catholic beliefs and practices and adhered to some alternative, whether religious or not. What worries Catholics today, however, is different: not that the faith will be consciously abandoned but that it will simply be lost in the more literal sense, the way one loses a piece of jewelry or an old memento—by casually setting it aside, mislaying it, leaving its absence long unnoticed, finally discovering that it is irrecoverable.

Religious education, like so much else in the Catholic Church, underwent dramatic changes in those first decades after the Second Vatican Council, changes involving a profound reexamination of the meaning of faith itself and the kind of education it implied. Not surprisingly, the first consequence of that reexamination was to disrupt an older system without substituting a new one. The search for an effective approach to passing on the faith has lurched forward, stalled, swerved this way and that ever since. The parochial school system, immigrant Catholicism's remarkable invention for inculcating the church's beliefs and practices into rising generations, passed through what can justly be called a near-death experience. Meanwhile, formal theological studies, always a wellspring for popular religious education, changed from a discipline pursued largely by priests teaching in seminaries to one pursued in equal measure by lay scholars, both men and women, based in colleges and universities, a transmutation with major implications for Catholicism's self-understanding in the future.

"I CONSIDER MYSELF A Catholic. I like being a Catholic. I'm proud to be a Catholic. But I don't really know what being a Catholic means." Any number of undergraduates at Notre Dame and Georgetown said that to me during the 1990s. Any number of teachers at other Catholic colleges and universities report that their students say more or less the same thing. Conversations with these teachers often become laments about "religious illiteracy," a phenomenon that came home to me some years ago when I asked a young relative (now in his thirties) something about the seven sacraments, a rather basic element in Catholic doctrine and practice. Embarrassment took over, and I changed the subject. Although he had attended Catholic schools for most of his elementary and secondary education, it was clear he had no idea of what, besides baptism and Eucharist, might be called sacraments in the Catholic tradition. It would be nice to think that he nonetheless possessed a spiritually profound understanding of sacrament even if he couldn't identify seven of them. After all, I could assure myself, it has been a mere eight centuries since Catholic theology settled on seven rituals in particular as sacraments! But there was no sign of that either. The same was true for young couples presenting themselves at a Manhattan parish to prepare for the *sacrament* of matrimony. First task, one of the priests told me, was to introduce them to the very idea of sacrament.

Similar laments are common about younger Catholics' knowledge of scripture; of doctrine about God, Trinity, or Jesus ("They barely know it exists," one college theology teacher said of his students); of saints, major events in church history, the structure of Catholic institutions and the operation of church authority, the significance of liturgical seasons; even of once familiar personal prayers. These laments need to be seasoned with skepticism, but they are more than the grouching of old folks. On the contrary, they are echoed by younger Catholics, often in scathing terms.

In the most extensive study to date of Catholics who were in their twenties and thirties in 1997, intensive interviews and focus groups produced almost universally negative judgments on the religious education experienced by these Catholics:

"Teachers aren't prepared."

"Nothing in depth, just Jesus is love."

"No content; touchy-feely."

"A baby-sitting session."

"Emphasis was on social issues."

From experiences like these—and they could be multiplied almost indefinitely—one might conclude flatly and without qualification that over the last several decades Catholic religious education has been a colossal failure. There is much to be said for that conclusion. It would set off sirens for bishops, pastors, parents, and religious educators. It would signal the need for a no-holds-barred assessment of the situation and a massive infusion of resources to remedy it.

Unfortunately, it might have destructive consequences as well. First, the degree of success or failure in passing a Catholic faith to new generations is not all that clear. Sociologists have claimed that when it comes to "core" Catholic teachings about God, Jesus, and the sacraments (unlike the controversial teachings about sexual morality, ordination of women, and so on, that polls often dwell on), younger Catholics no less than their parents appear quite orthodox. The same study of young Catholic adults that reported such biting views of religious education also found that over 90 percent of its sample affirmed the divinity of Jesus, at least 80 percent expressed belief in "a divine judgment after death," and about 90 percent either "strongly" or "moderately" agreed that "in Mass the bread and wine actually become the body and blood of Christ." These findings, too, require qualification, but that only underlines that little is clear when it comes to the state of beliefs.

For four hundred years, the basic tool of Catholic religious education in the West had been the catechism. Catholic bishops, meeting in Baltimore in 1884, authorized the writing of what became known as the Baltimore Catechism. From its succeeding editions, generations of American Catholics memorized crisp doctrinal formulations, numerous definitions, and daunting lists of sacraments, sins, virtues, graces, and commandments. There were few concessions to pedagogical technique. Much the same could be said of catechisms used in other nations.

By the 1930s in Europe and the 1950s in the United States, objections were increasingly raised to this treatment of faith largely as an intellectual assent to a set of theological propositions. Too many Catholics, it was complained, viewed God primarily as a rule maker and their own religious life as a matter of legalistically fulfilling precise obligations. Faith, it was countered, was a relationship of trust to a person, to God as revealed in Jesus Christ. Faith was the response to a call, as exemplified by Abraham, Moses, Peter and the other apostles, and finally Paul—all of whom accepted a call from God before they accepted any set of teachings. Faith involved a conversion, a reorientation of the whole person. Education in faith had to engage the affections as well as the intellect—here religious educators were influenced by developmental psychology and related theories about learning, growth, and character development.

In short, the Baltimore Catechism was dead before Vatican II. Indeed, the very language of religious education changed, familiar classroom terms supplanted by terminology drawn from the Greek of the New Testament. What was going on was no longer instruction but *catechesis*. Those doing it were no longer teachers but *catechists*. The whole field or discipline was no longer religious education but *catechetics*. Except for the related word "catechism," these were terms "unknown to most Catholics before 1960." The new language signaled the new approach, concerned not just with information but with "formation and transformation," to use a formula of one leading catechetical expert. Although the professionals who supervised catechetical programs in many parishes continue to be titled directors of religious education (DREs), the term "religious education," smacking of traditional classroom learning *about* religion, seemed to scarcely do justice to such a fundamental and total endeavor.

Though dead, the venerable Baltimore Catechism was not buried. It continued a shadow life, in two forms. For those who found the new catechetics wanting either pedagogically or theologically—who suspected, for example, that more depended on those memorized distinctions between actual and sanctifying grace or between perfect and imperfect contrition than these newfangled followers of John Dewey realized—the Baltimore Catechism was a kind of gold standard of solid religious education. For proponents of the new catechetics, it was just the opposite, a gold standard in reverse, a lead standard, maybe, that defined what catechetics was *not*.

Therein lay the problem. Postconciliar catechetics had a better idea of what it wanted to achieve than of how to achieve it. The *how to* was mainly how not to, and the *how not to* was all the things associated with the old catechism: memorization, repetition, abstract concepts, mysterious-sounding terms, precise definitions, doctrinal details and emphasis. Teachers and texts searched for child-friendly ways to introduce young Catholics to God, Jesus, scripture, sacraments, grace, sin, commandments—at the very time when long-standard theological ways of presenting each of these elements of Catholic faith were being debated and modified. Wave after wave of new theological ideas washed over the catechetical movement, which was primed to welcome them, sometimes uncritically. It was naturally receptive to critiques of dogmatic systems that seemed stifling to the new understanding of faith. It was poised to embrace alternatives that could connect with the familiar human experiences of students, sometimes at the cost of minimizing what did not fit easily into those cozy categories. At the same time, the whole culture was being swamped with wave after wave of movements for social, political, and psychological liberation. All this made its way, in highly diluted and sanitized form, into the vacuum created by the demise of the old catechism classes: activities, games, exercises, videos, storybooks, coloring books, usually simplified, psychologized, sentimentalized, and politically correct. Teachers were caught in the flux. Even if they did not latch on to some fad, they often lacked the confidence to insist on more than an acceptable common denominator.

WHICH BRING US BACK to the study mentioned above. Published in 2001 and based on research conducted in the late 1990s, *Young Adult Catholics* contains a number of surprises.

Even when these young adults were at odds with the church and disconnected from parish life, the high percentage "who called themselves Catholic surprised us," the authors write, "since research on American Protestants has depicted higher rates of switching and lower levels of denominational loyalty than we found here." Only 10 percent of Catholic adults under age forty have actually ceased to consider themselves Catholic, the authors found, and this was as true of Latinos as of non-Latinos. Furthermore, the fraction who consciously considered themselves no longer Catholics, whatever their ethnicity, were not falling prey to secularism. For the most part, they did not leave in rebellion against Catholicism but because of intermarriage or the positive attraction of another, often more conservative church.

Unfortunately, the findings of *Young Adult Catholics* are far from unambiguous. A random sample of over eight hundred young adults who had been confirmed in parishes years earlier were tracked down and interviewed by phone in either English or Spanish—and then the results checked against other national surveys of young adult Catholics, plus focus groups and in-depth interviews. A great deal of effort went into this design, especially to get a reliable sample of Latinos. Focusing on those who had been confirmed has the advantage of using a group that had a common starting point: some roughly similar degree of documented and more-than-nominal church involvement during adolescence. At the same time, because only about 60–70 percent of non-Latino youth and 30–40 percent of Latinos were confirmed during the 1980s and 1990s, the young adults of this study do not represent all current young adult Catholics. Both the non-Latino and Latino samples turn out to be somewhat more educated, more white collar, and more involved in church life than the average for Catholics aged twenty to thirty-nine.

It is safe to say, then, that the study's findings are slightly rosier than the reality. Not that they are overwhelmingly rosy to begin with. *Young Adult Catholics* is such a mix of good news and bad news, reassuring findings and alarming findings, that the authors themselves often seem hard pressed to reach a clear judgment.

Young Adult Catholics concludes on a sobering note. If these young adults, ten or fifteen years after their confirmation, are largely remaining Catholic, their Catholicism can look increasingly attenuated. That may not be true for the 10 percent whom the authors label "core Catholics." But much larger percentages are distanced from parish life and church institutions, have little sense of church authority, and are not sufficiently versed in the distinctive symbols, narratives, and vocabulary of Catholicism to articulate to themselves a coherent Catholic identity. Moreover, the fragmented Catholic identity they do possess appears to be less and less central in their lives. They are not, as the authors point out, "irreligious scoffers," but neither is there much evidence, for all the talk of being "spiritual," that they are serious seekers. Through no fault of their own, they breathe in a culture of religious individualism, while at the same time they are no longer tied to the Catholic community by their most important friendships or even their spouses. (Half of the married non-Latino Catholics under forty married non-Catholics.)

"The implications are portentous," the authors write. "If many young adults now believe that Catholicism is simply another denomination, that it 'doesn't really matter whether you're Catholic or not,' that there is nothing unique or distinctive about Catholicism, or that all that really counts is a generic Christian lifestyle, Catholicism's institutional vitality, public witness, and capacity to retain its young are in jeopardy."

The authors, it should be stressed, do not see their findings as an indictment of either the church or of young Catholics. They see many positive signs—and points of opportunity—in that tenacious, if not very coherent, self-identification as Catholic, in that residual sacramentalism, in the fact that even while these young adult Catholics berate their own religious education, they almost unanimously want their children to receive one. "A flashing yellow light" is the way one author described the study.

It would be foolish to blame this state of affairs on the shortcomings of postconciliar religious education. The age groups under examination, which will soon define American Catholicism, have been shaped by major shifts in the nation's culture as well as in the church—dramatic changes in family life, in the roles of women and in male-female relations, in attitudes toward government and confidence in other social authorities, in the lines drawn between private and public spheres, in the scope of pluralism and the understanding of tolerance, in the nature of information and entertainment. It did not take the new catechetics to sow ideas and reflexes problematic for the maintenance of Catholic identity. The most that could be said, in many cases, is that the new forms of religious education did not respond successfully—and it is improbable that the old forms would have done any better.

FROM THE MIDDLE OF the nineteenth century to the middle of the twentieth, Catholic leaders believed that the key to passing on the faith was a separate system of Catholic schools. Obligatory reading of the Protestant King James translation of the Bible and a residue of blatant anti-Catholicism in textbooks spurred this attitude, but the deeper concern was not Protestant proselytism in public schools as much as the avoidance of religion there altogether. "Listen not to those who would persuade you that religion can be separated from secular instruction," declared the bishops at their historic First Plenary Council of Baltimore in 1852. "Encourage the establishment and support of Catholic schools; make every sacrifice which may be necessary for this object." Prodded by uncompromising proponents of Catholic schools, in the 1870s the Vatican even came close to insisting that the bishops deny the sacraments to Catholic parents who sent their children to public schools, pressure that the bishops had the good sense to ignore as impractical and almost certainly counterproductive. But in 1884, at the Third Plenary Council of Baltimore, the same one that authorized the Baltimore Catechism, the hierarchy decreed that every parish had two years (!) in which to build a school, every pastor had to carry out that plan under pain of being removed, and every family was bound to send its children to Catholic schools under pain of sin.

Officially, Catholic education became the norm. Here, as in so many other areas of church life, "officially" was only half the story. Many parishes simply could not afford schools. Many pastors simply did not comply. Many parents found justifications for not observing the church law. In reality, the majority of school-age Catholics were almost always educated in public schools. Today that is true of 80 percent.

Nonetheless, the Catholic school system was a remarkable invention and a remarkable achievement. In the century following the Civil War, a largely immigrant, working-class church created a private, faith-based network of schools that, by the mid-1960s, educated more than one out of eight of the nation's schoolchildren, and in some major cities as much as 25 percent of the school-age population. Once frequently derided as a second-rate set of schools stubbornly supported by a pliant population that valued faith over intellect, parochial schools have been belatedly recognized as having successfully maintained the identity and morale of uprooted ethnic communities and instilled the discipline and skills needed for entry into the American mainstream.

Yet in some ways, the last several decades of this system are the most remarkable of all—demonstrating that these schools will surely have an important role in the religious formation of future Catholics, even if not the same role as in the past.

At the very height of their success, having more than kept up with the postwar movement of parishioners to the suburbs and finally enrolled slightly more than half the Catholic school-age population, Catholic schools entered a thirty-year stretch of unprecedented turmoil and dramatic change. Following the Council, they experienced a mass exodus of what, traditionally, constituted the mainstay of their teaching staff, the members of religious orders, especially of women's orders.* Between 1965 and 2002, the number of sisters, brothers, and priests teaching in these schools declined from 114,000 to 9,000. Today, almost 95 percent of the teaching staff are laypeople, Catholic and non-Catholic.

That was the first domino to fall. Combined with a growing cost of education generally, it greatly increased the cost of Catholic schooling. Parishes that had historically covered the bulk of school budgets could no longer do so. Tuition rose dramatically. So another domino fell: An enrollment in 1965 of approximately 5.6 million students at all levels had fallen by 38 percent within a decade, and by 1995 had dropped to 2.6 million students, where it has more or less remained. The number of schools declined from over 13,000 to a little over 8,000.

*For more discussion of the turmoil that shook women's religious orders after Vatican II, see Chapter Seven.

Population shifts and an altered sense of the church's mission drastically changed the profile of the student body. The number of African-American, Asian, and Hispanic students more than doubled, and by 2002 constituted over a quarter of the students. The number of students from non-Catholic families more than quadrupled, constituting over 13 percent of enrollment by 2002. Among the vast majority still identifying themselves as Catholic, religious practice was weakening.

In sum, Catholic elementary and secondary education lost its traditional teaching staff, had to shift the major burden of funding from parishes to parents, closed almost 40 percent of its schools, and suffered more than a 50 percent decline in enrollment. Yet, battered but transformed, it survived. It did so, in part, by taking on a new and challenging group of students. It did so despite changes that would have paralyzed or capsized many public bureaucracies or private industries. Indeed, it not only survived but achieved a prominent and positive place in the nation's educational consciousness. Long viewed as a suspect and alien presence in American life, at the very time when Catholic schools were passing through the strains of transformation, they suddenly received the respect they had never enjoyed.

Throughout the 1980s, prominent social scientists concluded that Catholic schools served urban minority students better than their public school counterparts. Against the timeworn complaint that Catholic schools were divisive, it was even suggested that in some respects Catholic schools fit the traditional "common school" model better than many public schools. These views were contested, to be sure. But Catholic schools were suddenly injected into debates about public education, about government versus market strategies, about racial progress and disparities. Catholic schools became a measuring stick for criticizing public education or the model for improving it. Catholic schools were offered as a potential tool for overhauling public education through competition for students and funds. Catholic schools were hailed as the hope for the black underclass. Catholic schools were upheld as a rebuke to teachers' unions. Catholic schools were a regular feature of political agendas and scholarly polemics. A long-standing debate about the legitimacy of vouchers or indirect support for religious education took on a new character. Previously centered on questions of church-state separation and religious freedom for groups desiring religious schooling, the debate now became a more mainstream one about reform of the nation's schooling.

Yet, whatever the important role Catholic schools can play to serve the educationally underserved or to repair failing school systems, they enroll only about 5 percent of American students. They need to be justified in their own terms and not just as adjuncts to the struggles about public education. Passing on the faith has not been their only function, but it is hard to imagine them apart from a central concern for religious formation.

Catholic schools provided much of what, in the view of contemporary catechetics, the catechism did not. In conjunction with the practices and celebrations of family and ethnic communities, schools rendered faith affective as well as intellectual, a matter of mentoring as well as memorization, of conduct as well as convictions. An entire environment preached to the students daily, from the crucifixes and religious art on the walls and the saints' days and liturgical seasons signaled on the bulletin boards to the prayers before class, the discipline in the corridors, the religious exercises before Christmas or during Lent, the preparation for First Communion and confirmation, the very strangeness of the nuns' garb as symbols of lives set apart for God.

Theologically and psychologically, a lot of this would now be found wanting. The understanding of God and the particular virtues that were once inculcated have been criticized, sometimes to the point of caricature and with little sense of their connection to the culture and needs of immigrant working-class populations. A generation or two of comics have squeezed laughs out of memories of how dragon-lady nuns nearly amputated the hands of miscreants with steel-edged rulers or, contrariwise, harbored hearts of gold beneath the Batman garb. Even the shopworn humor implicitly testifies that, pedagogically, this was a religious formation that qualified for the later catchword "holistic." And though Catholic schooling only briefly embraced as much as half the Catholic school-age population at one time, in reality it touched a far greater proportion, who perhaps spent some of the early grades in parochial schools before switching to public schools or switched from public schools to Catholic high schools. After all, the rare Catholic public school student who attends a parish catechetics program for an hour a week for ten years probably spends less time formally studying religion than he or she would in three years or so in a parochial school. When it comes to immersion in a Catholic learning environment, all ten years of one hour per week equal less than half a year of Catholic schooling.

Along with the total environment of a Catholic school, the texts, materials, and methods for teaching religion have improved immensely. Gone is not only the Baltimore Catechism. Gone are the content-light materials produced in the zeal of reaction. Textbook series differ in quality, and they will always be subject to new criticisms. But the ones I have seen systematically, solidly, and attractively introduce students to the full range of Catholic belief and practice at appropriate age levels, skimping on neither doctrine nor morals nor scripture nor prayers, sacraments, saints, holy days, and even popular though unofficial customs.

If religion texts were the measure, there would be little doubt that Catholic schools were well equipped to pass on the faith. But textbooks don't make a religion class, let alone a faith-forming environment. Not a few Catholics have wondered whether these schools can sustain their Catholic identity without the nuns who previously administered and staffed them and without the religious and often ethnic homogeneity of their student population.

So far, given the drastic changes of recent decades, the record is good. But the long-range outcome is by no means certain. If there is one thing, for example, that educators seem to be agreed upon, it is the crucial role of principals. Already, by the middle of the last decade, the majority of principals, both in grade schools and high schools, were laypeople. Both lay principals and those belonging to religious orders have been shown to have a strong sense of their capacity for spiritual leadership, find considerable satisfaction in that spiritual leadership, and are firmly committed to their schools' religious mission. However, by their own self-assessment, the principals most equipped to maintain the Catholic identity and mission of their schools were those with longer experience in Catholic schools and those belonging to religious orders. Principals belonging to religious orders and lay principals were similarly frequent worshipers, but lay principals were significantly less likely to declare that religion was extremely important in their lives or that a personal relationship with Christ was extremely important, two factors that appeared related to carrying out the religious mission of Catholic schools.

What about religion teachers in today's parochial classroom? In the mid-1990s, the typical Catholic-school teacher of religion was white, female, married, over thirty-four, and had taught religion for ten years or less in Catholic schools. Almost nine out of ten of these teachers were Catholics, eight of them from birth, and most had been exposed to years of religion classes in Catholic schools. Three out of four had some graduate study beyond their bachelor's degree, but only one out of four any graduate credits in theology. A little over half had received certification to teach religion, for the most part through courses offered by dioceses or other nonacademic programs.

The transition to lay leadership affecting every area of Catholic life constitutes "a cataclysmic shift," wrote the educator who studied these religion teachers. Through the 1960s, most teachers in Catholic schools "had lived within the culture of religious communities," he noted, while today most are "enveloped in the culture of the family. . . . The priorities and mundane obligation of these two groups are different, and . . . the wealth of experiences they bring to their classrooms are also varied. . . . The transmission of religious faith is in the hands of a new group of artisans, and this means that the future of religion and even theology itself will be reshaped because of this shift."

Overwhelmingly these lay teachers want to teach religion (over 80 percent would do it even if it were not part of their contracts) and they find doing so satisfying—but not as much as do the sisters still teaching in these schools. Lay teachers clearly bring a less intense life of prayer and of religious activities to their work than do the religious. Compared to the sisters, lay teachers are somewhat more concerned with affecting how their students behave (such as by helping others) than how their students feel (for example, their trust in God) or what they know (doctrines).

How good was these teachers' knowledge of church teachings? Did the teachers in fact agree with those teachings? Anyone worried about the teaching of religion might find it reassuring that 99.8 percent of these teachers know that the church teaches "God is a supreme, omnipotent Being," although a God who is "fallible and subject to change" was the personal belief of 1.8 percent. Views on the resurrection were slightly wobbly; although 95 percent understood "Jesus rose bodily from the dead" as church teaching, one out of ten chose "Jesus rose only in spirit from the dead" as her personal belief.

On the familiar gender- and sex-related issues—male-only ordination, remarriage, abortion, and of course, contraception—it is not surprising that many teachers identified the church's teaching accurately but disagreed with it. While 99 percent knew that the church teaches, "Premarital sex is always morally wrong," only 61.4 percent held that position themselves. Where significant percentages failed to identify the church's position correctly, the alternatives they chose were often ones that could be read as more stringent or conservative—for example, a more expanded view of papal infallibility than the church actually holds or a more restrictive view of the church's attitude toward people with a homosexual orientation. In many cases, the teachers' personal position, which they thought differed from the church's, was in fact the church's.

While some of these findings are reassuring and some worrisome, one should be cautious in drawing conclusions. The wording of the choices may have been confusing or obscure or even debatable in many cases. I suspect that quite a few of the sisters in the generation who taught me catechism would have done miserably on this questionnaire. The truth is that one can be a wonderful fifth-grade religion teacher or catechist without knowing exactly what the church teaches about providing nutrition to the dying patient or even whether the church prohibits abortion without exception or allows it to save a mother's life. Conversely, one could know all the right answers and be a disaster as a catechist.

More important for the future are the trends revealed here. First, the well-documented disagreement of Catholic laity with church positions on issues touching on gender and sexuality cannot be excluded from the Catholic classroom; the gap cannot help but introduce a note of reserve, uncertainty, dissimulation, or even hypocrisy into teaching. Good teachers have probably worked out ways of preserving the integrity of both the church's teaching and their own convictions—but can this be discussed in an open way that would help others?

Second, both accurate knowledge of church teachings and personal agreement with them were higher among the remaining members of religious orders than among lay teachers. Accurate knowledge and personal agreement were also higher among teachers who (a) were older, (b) had attended Catholic schools longer themselves, (c) had taught longer in Catholic schools, (d) had undergone more formal programs of certification, such as those requiring college theology credits, (e) taught upper grades, where they had to engage in more discussion about religious matters.

These findings point both to potential problems and potential solutions. Future teachers will almost entirely come from the laity and not religious orders. Younger lay teachers will be less apt to have attended Catholic schools or to have been exposed to a solid catechetical formation. Catholic schools must reinforce the factors working in the opposite direction: they must increase retention of principals and faculty, giving them more exposure to the Catholic environment;

provide opportunities for spiritual growth parallel to what once came as part of life in a religious order; and develop a serious certification process including college credit courses, and engage teachers in active discussion of their faith.

What a study like this does not directly measure is the capacity of lay teachers, as compared to their religious predecessors, to imbue the whole educational experience with a sense of sacramentality— God's presence in all things—or of gratitude, of celebration, of shared joys and burdens, of sensitivity to suffering and oppression, of concern for justice. Quite possibly, lay teachers could bring to this task insights and experiences not as available in religious life, but only, one suspects, with the encouragement and preparation essential to building confidence and skills.

IRONICALLY, WHILE EDUCATORS, parents, and politicians have been looking to Catholic schools for clues about improving public education, Catholics themselves have raised questions about the future of this historic enterprise. In 1964, during the Council's reassessment of so much in Catholic life, Mary Perkins Ryan published a book asking *Are Parochial Schools the Answer?* The author's conclusion was a firm *no.* The book sparked an often acrimonious debate. In retrospect this challenge seems inevitable. Fueled by a booming and increasingly prosperous Catholic population, in the two decades after World War II Catholic schools had grown at roughly twice the rate of public education—and still couldn't meet the demand. The strain was enormous. Classes were overcrowded, many with more than fifty students. Parents and educators were demanding more by way of quality. Hiring of lay teachers had begun, with all the associated costs, even before the decline in the numbers of teaching nuns.

Parochial schools, Ryan argued, reflected the "siege mentality" of a bygone day. They made the parish child-centered. They shortchanged students attending public schools. They absorbed energy, talent, and treasure that should be directed toward liturgy, social justice, and the education of older youth and adults, particularly parents who would make the home the locus of religious education. All told, parochial schools had come to impede rather than enable the church's witness to the world.

At about the same time as Mary Perkins Ryan was throwing her "stink bomb into the old schoolhouse," as one reviewer delicately put it, Andrew M. Greeley was publishing major studies indicating the effectiveness of Catholic education in transmitting the faith, although with some more-than-insignificant limitations. His findings were confirmed by more research in the early and late 1970s. The debate, however, was swiftly changing. No longer was it "Are parochial schools the answer?" but "Can Catholic schools survive?"—the title of a 1970 book by Greeley and William E. Brown.

The fundamental terms of the discussion have not much changed over the last twenty years. Catholic schools have indeed survived. The system steadied itself after nearly capsizing. But it remains financially precarious. Bishops and priests remain highly supportive of Catholic education—in principle. In practice, there are limits to what they can or will sacrifice to subsidize schools that cannot pay their own way. Parents are supportive, too, but also limited in the sacrifices they can make; and the explicitly religious reasons that parents once expressed for choosing Catholic schools may be giving ground to academic advantages over public schooling and a general concern for discipline and good values. There is a widespread sense that Catholic schools do effectively transmit the faith, although in fact the evidence is mixed. Father Greeley and others have marshaled impressive evidence in favor of effectiveness. Other studies, including *Young Adult Catholics*, have found only minor effects of Catholic schooling. Explaining the differences in these findings would probably require another major study in itself. Meantime, a rough consensus has probably solidified in favor of Catholic schools, if only because that seems dictated by common sense and by the impression that the alternative—the parish catechetics programs for public school students—has floundered. Finally, there is the recognition that this is not a zero-sum game: resources available for Catholic education would not necessarily be available for other endeavors, and Catholic schools may expand the resources available for other endeavors as well as compete for them. There could be a synergy rather than a trade-off between a vibrant parish school and an effective parish catechetical program.

After decades of shakeout in Catholic education, only one-third of the country's parishes maintain schools. On average, the school's budget now equals the parish's. Expenditures have been driven up not only by the end of the contributed services of sisters, brothers, and priests and the need to employ lay teachers. Class sizes have been reduced, and equipment improved; concerns about quality have evidently not been ignored in the struggle for survival. But it is no wonder that parishes have gone from subsidizing almost two-thirds of their schools' costs in the early 1960s to around a quarter three decades later.

Relying on parents to pick up the difference means pricing Catholic education out of the reach of many families, particularly low-income ones most in need of an alternative to failing public schools. Catholic officials have long argued, without success, that at least some government aid to all schools meeting educational standards is required by simple justice. Parents should be able to choose the environment in which by law their children spend a huge portion of their time and absorb many values. As things now stand, families availing themselves of Catholic schools provide a huge subsidy to public education. The case for aid to private schools has made headway but on different grounds. The Supreme Court in 2002 narrowly ruled that vouchers allowing low-income parents to choose other schools than their local public ones passed constitutional muster. For Catholic education the ruling was welcome but limited. Legally, voucher proposals still face provisions in many state constitutions barring state funds from going to religious schools; politically, vouchers face fierce opposition from public-school teachers' unions.

The question of government aid has put Catholic educators in a quandary. They do not want to be forced into an adversarial stance toward public education, where most Catholic young people are, after all, being schooled; and they are divided over what role the possibility of government funds should play in their efforts and planning. Some Catholic leaders advocate an aggressive campaign for such support as a key to the long-term survival of Catholic education. They believe that Catholic education should take advantage of a widespread sense that improving schooling cannot be accomplished without a major reconfiguring of educational funding and organization. Some of these leaders even propose refocusing the mission of Catholic schools primarily on providing students, regardless of their religious background, with a values-laden but not explicitly Catholic alternative that could complement and maybe influence public education. This, they argue, would be in line with the educational underpinning Catholic schools gave earlier immigrants but also in line with the new way that church institutions like health care and human services have come to understand their mission—not primarily as serving a still largely set-apart Catholic community but as the church's witness in serving the underserved regardless of faith. To still other Catholic educators, this sounds like a recipe for suicide. They don't question the merits of serving not only Catholics but also non-Catholics lacking access to good schools, or of accepting government aid if it comes without dangerous strings attached. They simply believe that detaching Catholic education from the self-interest Catholics have in their own children and in transmitting the faith will undermine support for the schools and sacrifice a valuable resource for the church. If reducing the Catholic identity of these schools and their rootedness in the Catholic population were the price of obtaining government aid, they argue, it wouldn't be worth it. In any case, such aid remains a highly iffy proposition. Catholic schools should not count on it or let the prospect distract them from developing an independent basis for financial survival. There are ways of combining these differing viewpoints, of course. Almost all

Catholic educators, for instance, are cultivating new sources of private support to supplement tuition and parish subsidies. Grade schools and high schools are doing what higher education has long done, turning to alumni, foundations, and business leaders for donations, and justifiably emphasizing different facets of their schools' missions—from maintaining the Catholic heritage to stimulating change in public schools or creating an educated work force—to different audiences.

The future of Catholic schools is sure to be complicated. They cannot be written off as a major source of Catholic vitality. They will remain an important component in any strategy to transmit a meaningful faith to twenty-first-century generations. But it seems unlikely that these schools can ever attain their previous centrality in carrying out this essential task. For the foreseeable future, eight of ten Catholic young people under eighteen will get their education in public schools. What about them?

OVER A FOUR-DAY STRETCH in mid-February 2002, over thirty-eight thousand people, including thirteen thousand high school students, flooded the Anaheim Convention Center across from Disneyland. With programs, notebooks, and bottles of water in hand, they trekked from meeting room to meeting room, choosing among over three hundred talks, workshops, concerts, Masses, and prayer services, some held in three nearby hotels as well as on three floors of the convention center.

This was the annual Los Angeles Religious Education Congress. If one were to judge by the energy, enthusiasm, teaching talent, organizational skills, sheer sprawl, and cultural diversity on display, then not only religious education, one might conclude, but American Catholicism itself must be in good shape.

On Sunday, February 17, thousands filled the center's arena for the afternoon closing liturgy, celebrated by Cardinal Roger Mahony of Los Angeles. Scripture was read in Vietnamese and Spanish as well

as English, and the cardinal began his homily by signing a welcome
for the hearing impaired. There were hymns with verses in Spanish,
English, Vietnamese, Tagalog, and Tongan—and the bread and wine
were brought to the altar while the choir sang in Latin a Palestrina
rendering of the Forty-second Psalm.

Most of the congress's hours, however, were filled with addresses
and workshops, over 275 of them, forty-four in Spanish and a handful in Vietnamese. They ran the gamut, from theologically straight-
forward analyses of scripture, sacraments, and contemporary social
and ethical issues to how-to-do-it ideas for classroom and counseling,
especially dealing with adolescents and family crises. Theologically,
the program represented the broad middle of American Catholicism, tilted somewhat to the left.

With a couple of dozen workshops going on simultaneously in
three shifts daily, preceded by major addresses in the morning, musical entertainment at lunchtime, concerts and social events in the
evening, it was no wonder that one speaker laughingly spoke of the
congress as a circus. A jamboree, said another. A zoo, said a third. A
Catholic Disneyland, said a fourth—he was referring specifically to
the huge exhibition hall where major publishers of serious theology
and religion textbooks were displaying their wares alongside booths
purveying religious key chains, holy cards with the appropriate saint
and prayer for each of life's trials, and other items of Catholic kitsch.

A Catholic Noah's ark might have been a better image, with every
species of American Catholic life rounded up and coexisting peace-
fully side by side. Whatever one might think of the complaint by a
Chicago priest, the Reverend Robert Barron, that postconciliar reforms had created a kind of "beige Catholicism" in the United
States, it was not supported by a stroll through the exhibition hall.
(One need hardly add that Father Barron, too, was a speaker at the
congress.) An outfit called Holy Rocks Inc. offered "rocks from the
Holy Land." There were icons for those drawn to Orthodox Christian
spirituality; the unrestrained crucifixes of Hispanic piety, with the
Savior's body scarred and bleeding; folk art from missionary-based

cooperatives in Latin America, Africa, Asia, and the Middle East. One booth featured something called Fun Nun—I decided not to ask. Then there were the less colorful, businesslike booths for theological training institutes, publishers of church music, and Catholic organizations providing social services to the poor, the sick and homebound, prisoners, young people, people with AIDS, and other groups in need. More than a half dozen booths offered computer systems, software, and online services for parishes—to keep track of their members, produce their bulletins, simplify their bookkeeping, improve their fund-raising, and maybe even write the homilies.

Events like the Los Angeles Congress are what makes thinking about American Catholicism so challenging: on the one hand, the commitment, seriousness, diversity, and vibrancy of these tens of thousands of participants, and the talent, dedication, imagination, and competence of its organizers and speakers; on the other hand, the many sorry reports about religious education and its apparently lackluster impact on younger Catholics. How can the two realities be fit together without denying one or the other?

THE LOS ANGELES Religious Education Congress makes it easy to forget that parish programs for the vast majority of young Catholics not attending Catholic schools have long been the stepchildren of Catholic religious education. CCD classes, they were once called and sometimes still are. The name stems from the Confraternity of Christian Doctrine, an organization founded in sixteenth-century Italy to carry out religious instruction. In 1905 it was revived by Pope Pius X—he called for a CCD program in every parish—and it was established as a national organization in the United States in 1935. The confraternity remains an office in the bishops' conference with important publishing rights; but it no longer provides the brand name for the very diverse forms of parish catechetical programs.

When directors of religion education meet at the Los Angeles Congress or the annual convention of the National Catholic Educational Association, they exchange sad stories about parents of parochial school pupils who don't want their children to make their First Communion along with the "CCD children" who attend public schools. The latter—and it seems their families, too—are something short of full-fledged members of the parish; or as one parent recalled the attitude in his neighborhood, "they weren't quite as Catholic."

Having invested so much, not only financially but psychologically, in parochial education, the church is only slowly coming to terms with the reality that Catholic schools, however valuable, can no longer be the norm. In 1950, less than 20 percent of all Catholic children of school age were in parish catechetics programs, compared to 33 percent in Catholic schools. In 1998, 52 percent were in parish catechetics programs, compared to only 16 percent in Catholic schools. Obviously, parish catechetical and religious education programs must now be given the kind of focused energy and mobilized resources that were once directed at parochial schools.

There are parishes where that has already occurred. In general it is clear that most programs are far less impressive. How far less? Unfortunately, not much is established beyond well-educated guesses. To be sure, there is not quite the dearth of empirical research that marks the study of liturgy. For over twenty-five years, the National Catholic Educational Association has been refining sophisticated tools so that both Catholic schools and parish catechetical programs can evaluate their success. These paper-and-pencil "assessment instruments" (the creators assiduously avoid calling them tests or examinations) have measured students' knowledge of church teachings about God, Jesus, worship, sacraments, scripture, and morality, and of religious terms. But in keeping with an understanding of catechetics going beyond simple knowledge about teachings, the assessment also queries students (anonymously) on what they actually believe and what their own attitudes and perceptions are in areas like relationship with Jesus, morality, Catholic identity, and relationships with others. Besides providing considerable feedback to programs using these assessments, the NCEA has accumulated data from hundreds of thousands of these assessments over a quarter century. The results showed that students were generally knowledgeable about God, Jesus, and sacraments, and personally affirm the basic gospel message of God's love for all people revealed in the saving life and death of a Jesus who is both divine and human and with whom they feel a personal relationship. What they knew and what they believed regarding scripture, morality, worship, Catholic identity, and traditional theological terms and categories were much more mixed. Students' rates of Mass attendance and agreement with church teaching on some moral issues had declined in the 1990s, as had their parents'. Not surprisingly, students spending more time learning about religion—that is, in Catholic schools—did better on the knowledge section than those in one-hour-a-week parish programs. Regular Mass attendance, a sense of being personally linked to Jesus, and a strong Catholic identity—measured by questions about the importance of being Catholic, the Eucharist, the desire to learn more about one's religion, among other topics—seemed crucial to high rates of both religious knowledge and religious practice. The students' general inability to identify key terms in Catholic theological vocabulary, from "paschal mystery" and "incarnation" to "grace" and "ecumenism," disturbed both proponents and critics of contemporary catechetics. Every field of thought has its carefully developed vocabulary, its code words, that facilitate serious discussion, wrote one leading religious educator surveying early results from these assessments in 1978. To minimize the value of this "institutional language," he complained, in the name of mystery and openness, is "nonsense and rubbish."

Despite these shortcomings, the report card on catechetical programs emerging from these assessments is not half bad. Maybe even B plus. Certainly better than the shrugs and sneers these programs have inspired in so many graduates as well as critics. Unfortunately, one can reasonably assume that the schools and parish programs seeking these self-evaluations (and paying for them) are among the better, more serious ones. Particularly in the upper grades and especially among high school students, many students drop out of parish programs, so that those remaining to fill out these evaluations are apt to be a select group in already select programs.

Perhaps the most important—and most distressing—data in this whole area are the numbers of children and young people who participate briefly, intermittently, or not at all. In any given year, the total percentage of young Catholics of elementary and secondary school ages who are enrolled in Catholic schools *and* in parish programs has grown over the decades, but not only has there been a shift in percentages from the more thoroughgoing religious environment of the Catholic school to the less intense involvement of the parish programs; about 40 percent of the Catholics in public schools still remain unenrolled.

So while the NCEA assessments are impressive diagnostic tools for the DREs and catechists in individual parishes, a true picture of the effectiveness of *all* catechetical programs nationwide, or even diocese-wide, remains uncharted. So do comparisons between different types of programs, those primarily employing traditional classroom styles of instruction, those engaging parents and focusing on catechesis in the home, those preferring retreats or summer sessions to weekly hour-long sessions, and so on.

One thing that the NCEA assessment instrument indubitably reveals has nothing to do with students but everything to do with the people who have constructed it. It shows what leaders of the catechetical establishment consider important to measure, and that turns out to be far from the caricature that some critics have presented.

Yes, there is a catechetical establishment, just as there is a liturgical establishment. There are leading graduate programs and institutes, senior scholars and popular gurus, respected credentials, professional organizations, newsletters, conferences, scholarly journals, how-to magazines, and so on. The catechetical establishment is liberal, loyal to a liberal view of Vatican II, and like the liturgists, has had to withstand a good many suspicions and denunciations. Over the years, critics have complained vociferously about textbooks, curriculums, and teaching materials. These are said to be watering down the faith or even propagating insidious heresies. The catechetical movement itself has been portrayed as a cabal skirting and subverting the authority of the bishops and the papacy, replacing true faith with politically liberal and radical secularism. Here and there, such hyperbolic criticism may have been justified—religious education could not have undergone such a major reorientation without throwing up some really bad ideas. Occasionally, the attacks have provoked useful rethinking, but just as often, I suspect, they have only reinforced defensiveness, overshadowed and discredited more nuanced criticism, and slowed rather than spurred the necessary correctives to postconciliar floundering.

Currently, such undiscriminating onslaughts seem particularly wrongheaded. Over the years, the textbook series and associated materials, either identical or similar to those used in Catholic schools, have been substantially revised and their content fortified. Half the dioceses spell out what books and materials can be used; even more give parish programs specific guidelines for their curriculum. The latest version of the NCEA assessments specifies over two hundred "fundamental terms in the Catholic vocabulary"—from "act of contrition," "Advent," and "annulment" to "Vatican II," "vocation," and "Yahweh"—that students should know as they progress from level to level. If children and young people absorbed and retained the key concepts, biblical themes, liturgical and sacramental symbols and actions, moral principles, major events and figures in church history, and personal spiritual practices outlined here, they would have as complete a grasp of their Catholic heritage as any generation has and certainly a better balanced one than the generations raised on the Baltimore Catechism. Catechetical directors and pastors rank their programs more effective in conveying knowledge of the Catholic faith and scripture than in fostering the spiritual and moral habits of the young or connecting them to the parish's worship and service or to the larger church.

THOMAS GROOME'S OFFICE is located on the second floor of a building near the Boston College campus. Once a house, it is now the
Institute of Religious Education and Pastoral Ministry. Groome, a
professor of theology and religious education at the university, is one
of the more influential figures in contemporary catechetics. He was
born in Ireland and raised on the Penny Catechism there, earned advance degrees at Fordham University, Teachers College, and Union
Theological Seminary in New York, and has developed a best-selling
series of catechetical textbooks as well as works in catechetical theory. Now, chatting in the summer of 2002, in the very epicenter of
the sex scandal, a relatively short distance from Cardinal Bernard
Law's residence and chancery office, Groome tries to put the postconciliar history of catechetics in some perspective. Between the late
1960s and the early to mid-1980s, "some people overreacted to the
arid, rote character of the catechism era," he allowed.

"Good things happened then, but religious literacy suffered
tremendously." By the mid-1980s, a new model emerged (he didn't
hesitate to cite his own textbook series) that tried to restore a balance
between the tradition's content and personal experience. "That paradigm has become fairly dominant," Groome said, but as to how effectively teachers use it, "we have miles to go."

The average level of religious literacy among sixth- and seventh-
graders, he believes, has become fairly good regardless of whether
they were in Catholic schools or parish programs. Of course, there
were great differences between parishes and between dioceses.
Groome estimated that 10 percent of the catechetics programs still
stuck by the highly cognitive approach of the catechism era and 10
percent stuck by the highly affective, experiential approach of the
early postconciliar years. The rest tried to relate knowledge and content to the life experiences of students.

Michael Corso, a younger colleague who has edited a book with
Groome, had somewhat different estimates. I spoke with him at a

coffee shop across from the Boston College campus. He doubted that even 5 percent of parishes had programs that were still fixed in what he termed the "happy face" phase of catechetics, unless they were totally devoid of resources and could only put together a minimal effort in lieu of doing nothing at all. More programs were taking a highly cognitive approach, not infrequently led by articulate younger catechists who tended to be more conservative, especially if they had received their training in a few highly conservative schools. The vast majority of programs were in the middle, using "very sophisticated" curricula, he said.

But that did not mean the programs, any of them, were successful. Corso described the frustration of catechists with a lack of parent involvement and even such a basic matter as nonattendance. "When skiing seasons begins," Corso said of his affluent parishioners, "attendance drops." In his experience, most parents of school-age children ended their religious education in the eighth grade, except for a minority who went to Catholic high schools. "They went on in the rest of life," he said, "starting to have adult questions and eighth-grade answers." They send their children dutifully now, maybe even desperately—hoping that their children will find something richer than they themselves received—but with no great confidence in the classroom experience. Young Catholic parents may express eagerness in polls about religious education for their children. But parents born after 1960 appear to be sending their own children to Catholic schools or parish programs at even lower rates than when they were young themselves.

A staple of catechetical programs is preparation for the sacraments, primarily for First Communion and reconciliation (confession) at around age seven and confirmation in the early teens; and curriculums are often designed with these events in mind. Again, getting parents genuinely involved in the preparation appears to be a challenge. In too many parishes, they all attend one pleasant but perfunctory group meeting, after which the catechist takes charge of faith matters and the family concentrates on buying the clothes and planning the party. The fact that Catholic parents feel that their children must receive these sacraments is something that catechists welcome and try to build on; but many a DRE, Corso told me, has discovered that for all too many youth in their early teens, confirmation is a kind of graduation: they stop coming to religious education events altogether.

Groome faults catechetics itself for this lack of parental involvement. The Baltimore Catechism at least gave parents something they knew, he said, something that allowed them to be engaged in their children's religious homework and track their children's progress. Now, Groome reports, parents throw up their hands and say, "I wouldn't know what to tell them anymore." When Groome included "family pages," sections requiring parental involvement, in the latest revision of his textbook series, the initial reaction was negative. Parents protested at being asked to participate. "This is why I send them to the parish CCD program or to Catholic school," they complained, although over time those sections came to be accepted.

"We need to give parents back the confidence and capacity to educate their children," he said.

THROUGH MOST OF CHRISTIAN history, faith was not transmitted to the ordinary person through schooling, which was reserved for a small elite. Only as schooling expanded in modern times has there been "a tendency to confuse what schooling can do with what can be achieved only through initiation." For Catholic educators that became particularly the case in the mid-twentieth century. According to Thomas P. Walters, a professor of theology and religious educator at Saint Meinrad's Seminary in Indiana, "An almost perfect match existed between what was said in a religion classroom and what Catholics practiced in the community," so it was natural to attribute to schooling what was in reality the initiation taking place in homes and parishes, which schooling only had to reinforce and render explicit.

Some religious educators, Walters believes, assume that "schooling can accomplish that which can only be achieved through initiation," while others assume that "focusing solely on the initiating community will solve any need for formal instruction." In this day and age, both approaches are needed to transmit a tradition or achieve a Catholic identity, he maintains, but schooling must articulate and develop what is ingrained by practice and by example, by witnessing and by participating—in sum, by "the company one keeps."

Whatever one's theory, the basic question is: can it be done within the existing structure of most parish programs? And the basic answer is no.

Here is the nub of the matter, so obscured by all the squabbles over the orthodoxy of textbooks, and obscured, too, by the good intentions of catechetical leaders who proclaim, in the most eloquent New Testament language, lofty goals of conversion or transformation that are, realistically speaking, quite frequently beyond the reach of their limited programs.

In Tom Walters's mind, 390 hours is a key figure. That is how many hours a student would spend in a parish religious education program if he or she came to a one-hour class for thirty weeks a year, every year from kindergarten to senior year in high school. He likes to compare that figure to the eleven thousand hours that, he says, students spend in their public schools over that period of time (or the fifteen thousand hours they reportedly spend watching television by age eighteen). Of course, the exact numbers are not as important as the relative orders of magnitude. And 390 hours is itself a hugely generous total: very few Catholic public school pupils actually participate in parish catechetical programs for all thirteen years.

Time is only part of the problem. The classroom model is another part. So is the fact that these programs depend almost entirely on volunteers.

No wonder that there is so much searching for alternatives to the K-to-12, classroom, 390 hours model. Family-centered programs are the most obvious. They aim at enabling parents to form their children's faith not by formal lessons but by the art and symbolism in the home; by children's books, bedtime prayers, and entertainment; by family rituals at mealtimes, on holy days, saints' days, or in the liturgical seasons of Advent and Lent; by service to others carried out together by parents and offspring; by family conversations about religious questions; by deliberate exposure to the motives and morals involved in adults' everyday working lives. This is not simply a matter of urging parents to do these things but of actually helping them, with ideas, materials, instructions, and opportunities to share their experiences and questions with other parents. Classroom- or textbook-based catechetics are not eliminated, especially as children grow older, but they are launched from the home, an extension of family faith life, rather than an exercise in religious expertise not possessed by parents.

Besides encouraging and assisting religious formation in the home, some parishes run intensive schools or camps for two weeks in the summer and, in place of weekly classes, involve families in monthly or seasonal liturgical, instructional, and service activities during the school year. Good catechetical programs make time for prayer and thoughtful worship and integrate children and young people into the liturgical events of the whole parish; good programs bring their youthful participants into service projects like soup kitchens and helping the homebound. It is noteworthy that retreats are one element of religious education programs to receive a positive grade from young adults—suggesting the value, as students head for adolescence, of more intense, out-of-the-ordinary experiences for adolescents as well as activities with a strong peer role.

This search for an alternative to the 390 classroom hours is sound, almost inevitable; yet a few caveats should be noted. Walters emphasizes the fact that Catholics are no longer united about beliefs and practices in the way that initiation by osmosis assumes. Those stressing family-centered catechetics should recall that among young Catholics, one of every two marriages is to a non-Catholic. That may not be an obstacle to religious education, certainly not among ecumenically minded couples from different branches of Christianity. Among couples sensing that religious differences may create marital tensions, however, family-centered or home-based catechetics is fraught with difficulty. Likewise with many unstable or broken families. So, too, the appeal for "total catechesis" that would make religious education a dimension of all parish activities, from liturgy to social justice campaigns, makes wonderful sense in principle. The danger in practice is that spreading responsibility so widely can make no one feel truly accountable: if the pastor is a poor preacher or the parish social justice committee is dormant, the DRE has a ready explanation for failure. Parochial schools, in their heyday, often enjoyed an independence that allowed strong principals to keep them operating at peak performance through the tenures of mediocre or abysmal pastors as well as good ones. Can catechetics programs get along without some of that stand-alone independence?

OBVIOUSLY THE SKILLS demanded of DREs and of catechists are enormous. Too often these have been reduced to enlisting a sufficient number of volunteer catechists, lining up the classrooms, and purchasing the essential texts and supplies. Those are indeed fundamental responsibilities; but DREs must also be able to judge which parishioners make good catechists and which do not, get them trained and forged into a team, supporting them personally and encouraging their religious growth. Both DREs and catechists need imagination and a capacity for hospitality and for dealing with parents as well as students. They need real religious knowledge and a personal spirituality that communicates itself to students. Since successful parish catechetics programs require much more integration into parish life, they demand extensive collaboration with pastors, which often must be skillfully elicited.

Who are these DREs and the army of mostly volunteer catechists that they supervise, over 350,000 of them by one count? They represent a leading example of the massive transition of leadership in postconciliar Catholicism from leadership by priests and sisters to leadership by laity in old and new positions of church ministry.

About two-thirds to three quarters of the nation's Catholic parishes have someone filling the responsibility of DRE—the uncertainty arises from differences in the way the job is defined or whether it is full-time, part-time, or merged with other positions. In approximately a third of those parishes, director of religious education is a full-time paid position (the average salary in 1999 was $28,000). In another third, it is paid but part-time (the salary is about $15,000). In the final third, it is voluntary. Full-time DREs are experienced: on average they have worked in catechetics for nineteen years. Over half of them have master's degrees. Part-time and volunteer DREs are only a few years behind in length of service, and only a third of them have master's degrees.

"Compensation lags behind DREs' educational level and expectations," Michael Corso said. "Individuals can put up with low income only so long, then they go elsewhere." With an average of eight years in their current positions, they appear fairly patient, however. The establishment of a new but increasingly standard parish position obviously raises questions not only of pay levels but also of credentials, career patterns, job security, relationships with pastors, and morale. One gets the impression that solutions are steadily, if sometimes painfully, emerging. One also gets the impression that the quality of volunteer catechists has been steadily improving, and turnover decreasing.

Yet as a professional field, catechetics remains insecure, full of dedication and bright ideas but nervous about its relations with increasingly conservative church authorities, and consequently defensive about its perennial critics. This is not an environment that encourages intellectual debate or rigorous assessment. At the parish level, DREs and catechists often have to live with the feeling that their programs exist on the margins of the parish's real concerns—not quite as important as the broken boiler, the leaky roof, the fights about music at Mass, the marrying and burying, certainly not as important as the parish school. Budgets confirm this. Despite the fact that tuition payments must now provide the bulk of parochial school budgets, in the mid-1990s parishes with schools still used about a quarter of the parish budget to subsidize them. At the same time, according to one survey of DREs, 83 percent of the catechetics programs received less than 20 percent of the parish budget, and over half received less than 10 percent.

WHETHER THE SEARCH for new catechetics models points to parents at home or to the whole parish, it is pointing toward adults. In November 1999, the American bishops approved a document, "Our Hearts Were Burning Within Us," declaring adult faith formation to be at the heart of the catechetical effort. The Vatican's *General Directory for Catechesis* had made the same point. Reaction among catechetical leaders was enthusiastic. Action was something else. Adult education has never been the Catholic style.

Actually, few Catholic parishes are completely devoid of programs about faith aimed at adults. Some have occasional lectures on religious topics, or more organized series during Advent or Lent, or monthly reading and discussion groups. Some have evening Bible study groups similar to those in Protestant congregations. In most cases, these activities engage a very small group of parishioners. In other words, adult religious education is just another parish activity—for those who like that sort of thing, and who mostly happen, by the way, to be older. Others may prefer the bowling team or, to be fairer, the soup kitchen. For Catholics, religious education remains child-centered. The idea that learning, reflecting, discussing is a major pillar of adult discipleship, along with prayer and service, simply hasn't registered.

The bishops, in their document, recognized this. "We are well aware that placing ongoing adult faith formation at the forefront of our catechetical planning and activity will mean real change in emphasis and priorities," they wrote. "We will all need to discover new ways of thinking and acting."

In a fashion unusually concrete for a document like this, the bishops described an essential "infrastructure" of "adult faith formation teams" needed in every parish. In one of the more remarkable understatements ever to appear in an episcopal document, they stated, "We recognize that this plan cannot be implemented all at once. . . . It will take at least one year before local plans can be put into effect."

Needless to say, Catholics who had been urging for years that the church put adults at the center of its catechetical efforts were galvanized.

But are the bishops really committed to the establishment of new positions, the reallocation of resources, and the reorientation of parish energies that their words suggest? According to Edmund F. Gordon, director of the Office of Religious Education for the diocese of Wilmingon, many church offices specializing in adult programs have, if anything, undergone staff reductions rather than expansion in recent years, as the rising costs of employing laypeople rather than priests or sisters have pinched budgets. Why did the bishops so warmly endorse an approach that they appear to be only tentatively supporting in practice?

To Ed Gordon, the answer is obvious: "It's because deep down we know that the old model is not working,"

If the old model was a child-centered, schooling model—Catholic schools for some and 390 K-to-12 classroom hours for others—what is the new, adult-centered model? Is it the same set of clothes but in larger sizes—a schooling model for big people? Proponents of adult faith formation loudly say no.

As soon as they say that, however, they are faced with a major difficulty—rallying the church to something that can appear mysteriously amorphous. What the bishops proposed, basically, was for parish leaders to analyze their local needs and devise programs with a variety of activities likely to engage different individuals and groups.

In the spring of 2002, for example, the adult faith formation committee presented fellow parishioners at Holy Family Parish in Newark, New Jersey, with an array of programs and opportunities that included two weekly evening scripture study groups, one of them especially for women; a gathering every Thursday morning during Lent to discuss the next Sunday's scripture readings; several other weekly Lenten scripture sharing groups that met at different times in parishioners' homes; and two lectures on aspects of Matthew's gospel.

Other events were a lecture explaining the Mass, a five-week discussion series on the Second Vatican Council using a video series originally developed for public broadcasting. The parish DRE led three evening discussions, also using videos, on the theme "Spirituality in Troubled Times." Another evening talk dealt with death and grieving. Several parishioners organized sessions around their own activities—a nurse expert in emergency resuscitation of children; a volunteer in Habitat for Humanity; a parishioner belonging to a national organization of people who have suffered a murder in their families and are seeking healing without vengeance. There was an evening talk on Islam. The program sponsored two field trips, one to the Pope John Paul II Cultural Center in Washington and another to a shrine claiming a relic of the true cross. The parish brochure listing these events also carried a notice of parish library hours and a list of eight retreat centers in the region with their websites.

Altogether, the program covered scripture both in discussion and lecture format (and at different times of the day and evening), Catholic worship, the Second Vatican Council, and practical spirituality. It featured outside speakers, parish staff members, and ordinary parishioners. It addressed personal concerns like bereavement and social issues like homelessness and criminal justice. There were topics and events likely to appeal to more liberal Catholics, and others for more traditional ones.

Parishes have to take into account the kind of differences in knowledge and attitudes among successive generations documented in studies like *Young Adult Catholics.* "You're all too old," Ed Gordon told the adult faith formation teams he is working with in ten parishes. "You've got to find someone under fifty." A survey in the parishes revealed a high demand for programs on "the basics of the faith" as well as scripture study. Adult religious education cannot simply be a hodgepodge; it has to be planned and systematic. But, Gordon insists, it should also be "really nimble in coming up with programs when something happens," expressing disappointment at how few parishes had done anything in response to the sex scandal.

Parishes that do little are, of course, the norm and ones like Holy Family are the exceptions. The bishops' hopelessly optimistic one-year deadline "before local plans can be put into effect" has come and gone. "It's a slow go," admitted Sister Maureen Shaughnessy, a stalwart of adult faith formation efforts who is assistant secretary for catechesis and leadership formation at the U.S. Conference of Catholic Bishops. "There's interest, there's also fear. If we shift the paradigm, what happens? What will happen to the children? Will we abandon them? We won't."

Tom Groome, in fact, insisted on the continuity, the "dialectic," between catechesis at different stages of life. "Adult religious education begins in kindergarten," he said, when children are given "a curiosity, a delight," in learning about their faith that makes them go on. "You can't give kids lousy catechesis and expect them to be interested in it as adults." All these educators warn against compartmentalizing adult faith formation from the life of the parish in general—liturgy, outreach, community service, social justice efforts. "We've got to change the culture of the church," Gordon said. Lay Catholic leaders are wont to complain that the laity's only roles are "to pray, pay, and obey." But Gordon believes that if you ask most adult Catholics what is expected of them, that is exactly what they think: pray, pay, and obey—except, he added, "probably much less of the obeying."

Any understanding of adult religious education that begins to appear coterminous with the whole life of the parish may well prove threatening to pastors. More seriously, such a broad understanding may also be so ambitious that no one can feel accountable for achieving or not achieving objectives more precise than the kind of profound transformation of souls that can be known only to God in his ultimate judgment.

The change in the culture of the church that is called for if faith is to be passed on in a world of educated Catholics would be both enormous and yet subject to measure. It would be the recognition of lifelong religious learning as a mode of piety, a spirituality of study and learning, of "faith seeking understanding." It would have roots in ancient ideals of the contemplative life and the monastic synthesis of prayer, work, and study. It would be informed by the Jewish tradition of Torah study as the birthright and obligation of all who can pursue it.

"FAITH SEEKING UNDERSTANDING" was Anselm of Canterbury's classic definition of theology. Obviously, the relationship between catechetics and theology is an intimate one. It will become more and more so as parish catechetics programs take center stage, as the growing numbers of DREs and catechists are expected to command more theological knowledge, and especially as organized faith formation focuses on parents and other adult parishioners rather than so exclusively on children.

From the Greek *theos*, for "God," and *logos*, for "speech," "word," "reason," or "meaning," theology has come to mean the disciplined discussion or study of the divine mystery. Once it implied a discourse by holy people about the fruits of their own contemplation. In the Middle Ages it became identified, as "queen of the sciences," with a more academic examination of religious questions. In modern times, it no longer reigns but stands alongside other disciplines like anthropology, archeology, biology, and geology. Each one of these historic shifts has been associated with a shift in who theologians are and where, how, and for whom they are doing theology. In recent decades Catholic theology, particularly in the United States, has undergone one of the more radical such shifts in church history.

As I write, I have a photograph in front of me. It shows seventy-two people seated around luncheon tables in a ballrooom at the Commodore Hotel in Manhattan. All seventy-two are men in black suits with clerical collars. This was the founding meeting, June 26, 1946, of the Catholic Theological Society. Here is another image, this one from the society's fiftieth annual meeting, held in June 1995 at the same hotel, now called the Grand Hyatt. About a third of the participants are women and there are almost no clerical collars. Most of the men, whether priests or lay, are wearing standard attire for academic conventions: suits or blazers, ties or sports shirts. The outgoing president, a Jesuit priest, is giving his presidential address, while at the dais sit the incoming vice president, a layman, and the incoming president, a woman, Sister Elizabeth A. Johnson, whose work in feminist theology has garnered major awards.

The contrasting images capture the sea change that five decades have worked on Roman Catholic theology, once the very model of timelessness. Fifty years ago most of the 104 founding members of the Catholic Theological Society were not only priests but also seminary professors. In other words, all unmarried men who felt called to the priesthood, who were ordained after years in seminaries, who had the interest, ability, and determination to pursue further studies, and who became, for the most part, seminary teachers themselves— in short, as one contemporary theologian has noted, "a small pool within a small pool."

By 1995, the society's membership had exceeded fifteen hundred. Priests still probably constituted a majority, but the proportion of laity teaching in colleges and universities was growing rapidly, and one out of every five members was female. Lay men and women had both been admitted to the society in 1965, another one of the many barriers that fell during the Second Vatican Council.

The 1995 meeting displayed much of the awareness of gender

and cultural diversity that has come to mark academic gatherings since the 1960s. Feminist concerns were prominent, and there were sessions on "Black Catholic Theology" and "Hispanic/Latino Theology." This has been equally true of the two annual meetings of the society I have attended since then.

More than adding different people to the mix is involved in this shift from the seminary to the university and, increasingly, from the clergy to laypeople. The priest members of 1946 had all undergone similar spiritual formations in seminaries. They all shared a common theological framework based on modern textbook versions of the medieval achievement of Thomas Aquinas. They largely inhabited an intellectual world of their own, reinforced by the use of Latin and of the technical terminology of neoscholastic theology and philosophy. As teachers and writers their intended audiences were mainly other priests, and the theologian's task was mainly that of clarifying, justifying, explaining, and applying official church pronouncements.

"This system emphasized clarity, certainty, and obedience," wrote Robert J. Egan, a Jesuit who teaches at Gonzaga University in Spokane. "It gave great importance to definitions, distinctions, appeals to authorities, unchanging verbal formulae, passages quoted out of context, and proofs. Even in this system, of course, extraordinary things could happen," he added, "but in many places a tyranny of mediocre minds took over the scene."

Those first meetings of the Catholic Theological Society, held in the years just after World War II, never discussed the Holocaust; and though there were discussions of the use of the atomic bomb and other questions of warfare, they were treated as moral issues and never as radical challenges to faith in a benevolent God. Another glimpse of the older style of theology was caught in a recollection of Brother Luke Salm, for many years the society's secretary. During the 1961 meeting, hotel guests complained of the noise coming from one of the group's suites at three o'clock one morning. The hotel security guard, Brother Luke recalled, found "some of our most distinguished moralists arguing loudly whether it was possible to commit a venial sin in purgatory."

No longer is Catholic theology the work of this isolated seminary world of clerical culture. Laypeople, men and women, single and married, bring different experiences and therefore different questions to their theological reflections. They have studied at all sorts of institutions, including Protestant and predominantly secular ones. So have an increasing number of priests; and indeed, although it is a development that the Vatican has tried to reverse, Catholic seminaries themselves have often opened their classes to lay students of theology—truly, as Egan notes, "an invasion of the ecclesiastical inner sanctum." Whether in Catholic colleges and universities or in the departments of religious studies that have come to exist on many state and secular campuses, most Catholic theologians, including the ordained, now work under normal academic criteria for professional excellence and the reigning standards of academic freedom. They take for granted the ecumenical and interreligious exchanges that are natural in these settings, as well as concerns about tolerance, social justice, and human rights.

All this has loosened the once-tight hold of church authority on Catholic theological scholarship. Theologians are now as likely to be raising questions about official church pronouncements or exploring new ways to understand traditional teachings as they are to be bolstering official doctrine with fresh arguments. Rome and conservative church leaders have accordingly gone into something akin to panic.

Those who welcome the new diversity, opennness, and intellectual standards of Catholic theology in the United States have also sometimes expressed worries. The new campus settings where theologians do their teaching and research are characterized not only by religious diversity but often by a prevailing skepticism that questions the legitimacy of the theological enterprise altogether, none of which does anything to reinforce Catholic identity. Religious faith and, more important, its links with the church are tolerated on condition that they remain personal or private and without any professional significance.

In fact, the transformation of Catholic theology has reached a point where even some moderate liberals worry that doctrine could lose its roots in church tradition. At the 1995 CTSA meeting, Monika K. Hellwig, then a professor at Georgetown University, warned, "The cumulative wisdom of the past is less known," with the consequence that "more and more of us are doing instant theology." Hellwig has since then become the executive director of the Association of Catholic Colleges and Universities, where, ironically, she has felt the brunt of the Vatican's efforts to demand that Catholic theologians obtain an official blessing from local bishops to teach in Catholic institutions.

Egan is another defender of the new diversity and openness in theology and a critic of the required teaching mandate, or *mandatum*. Yet he is also among those willing to recognize that that "something valuable has been endangered in this transition. Theology has tended to become primarily an academic specialization," and the university, despite its hospitality to a range of intellectual currents, has its own narrowness. If priest theologians once wrote for other priest theologians, using dated jargon, academic theologians now tend to write for other academic theologians, using fashionable jargon. What the new university-based Catholic theologians have in common, moreover, is the prolonged, usually rigorous initiation of graduate work, teaching, publishing, and seeking tenure. There are, Egan pointed out, "no requirements involving tact, prayer, spiritual formation, prior philosophical studies, or accumulated pastoral experience." Theology may be—and for many individuals surely remains—an ecclesial, or church-linked, calling; but not necessarily. Spiritually, the new theologians may strive to be exemplars, but it is not required. (One must add that in the days of clerical seminary-based theology spiritual striving may have been expected but was often little evident.)

Catholic Christianity has always been concerned about maintaining orthodoxy—unduly concerned, many would argue. Individual thinkers through the ages have confronted charges of heresy. Since the Second Vatican Council, the fear in Rome has been that not only individual theologians but Catholic theology as a whole would be swept away by new ideas ultimately incompatible with the Catholic tradition. The fear grew intense when an overwhelming majority of moral theologians appeared to question the 1968 reassertion of papal teaching on contraception, and when many of them edged forward into even broader criticism of Catholic sexual teachings, whether on highly technical biomedical matters or on highly visible issues like homosexuality. The alliance of liberation theology with Marxist revolutionary movements in Latin America was another threat, particularly to a pope who had struggled with a Marxist regime in Poland. At a more fundamental level, both liberation theology and feminist theology popularized a hermeneutic of suspicion, the idea that the entire heritage of Catholic Christian teaching had to be scrutinized with an eye to the forms of masculine political and economic power they had historically upheld. In the United States, the clear consensus among theologians favored the ordination of women to the priesthood, and theologians bridled at Rome's attempts to declare the question closed. More recently, the question of Christianity's uniqueness and centrality among world religions has become a flash point for Vatican alarms, although here there appears to be a lot less consensus among theologians.

This is not the place to examine the particulars of these controversies (some are addressed in other chapters) but to examine the problems that the patterns of conflict pose for passing on the faith. Theological controversy is a constant of religious history; in some respects, it is the lifeblood of religious history; but it is not too much to say that the recurring controversies of recent decades have created a condition of low-intensity warfare between church authorities, especially in Rome, and the theological guild. The Vatican's attempts to exercise traditional controls over a drastically altered theological world has more than failed; it has exacerbated the conflict to a dangerous extent.

Some years ago, Cardinal Joseph Ratzinger gave a talk in which he compared theologians to wolves, which many people thought nicely revealed the spirit in which he has carried out his assignment, as head of the Congregation for the Doctrine of the Faith, to stand watch over the theological orthodoxy. But such views are not limited to Rome. In 1997, Cardinal Bernard Law of Boston made one of those statements that helped explain why he had so few friends when he needed them: he denounced the Catholic Theological Society of America as "a wasteland" for its criticism of official church teaching.

The Reverend Avery Dulles, an elder statesman of American Catholic theology who was later to be named a cardinal himself, seconded Law's judgment after reading the proceedings of the society's 1997 convention. His opinion, which even questioned whether the CTSA deserved its label as Catholic, was sharply challenged by officers of the group and other theologians. But no one disputed his conclusion that the gap between the theological community and Catholic authorities revealed "severe fault lines in contemporary American Catholicism."

Is it a healthy state of affairs when leading church officials perceive those trained to explicate the faith as, in fact, prime threats to it? Isn't it somewhat like an airline that suspects its pilots of deliberately trying to crash the planes?

AT THE BOTTOM OF this extraordinary state of affairs is the question of change. As Garry Wills memorably expressed it, the Second Vatican Council "*let out the dirty little secret.* It forced upon Catholics, in the most startling symbolic way, the fact that *the church changes.*" What may have been a secret for ordinary Catholics, theologians had long known and struggled to explain. How could the church come to promulgate beliefs and practices not explicitly stated in scripture or taught in apostolic times while still remaining faithful to what was revealed in Jesus? The question was pressed over the centuries by many reform-minded Christians, most notably by the Protestant Reformers of the sixteenth century, who used the New Testament's vision of church to condemn what they considered later abuses. Many offices of the church—priest, bishop, pope—had not taken the definitive form that the Catholic Church taught until considerable time had passed. Likewise with the Catholic understanding of seven sacraments, and with many complicated teachings on sin, grace, forgiveness, and life after death. Even the great creeds, central to beliefs about Christ and the Trinity in both Eastern and Western Christianity, were not hammered out until the fourth century.

Almost from the start, some Christian thinkers suggested that the church, guided by the Spirit that Jesus had promised his followers, gradually progressed in its understanding of a "deposit of faith" inherited from apostolic days. In the nineteenth century, however, a growing historical consciousness, along with the related popularity of evolutionary theories, led to more precise theories of what John Henry Newman called "the development of doctrine." Newman began *An Essay on the Development of Christian Doctrine* as an Anglican; he completed it as a Roman Catholic. His conversion demonstrated that the case for Catholicism might be bolstered by the idea of development. Development was nonetheless viewed with suspicion and, if not rejected outright as a heretical threat to the church's claim to teaching unchanging truth, then seriously minimized by the dominant school of theology—until, that is (as Wills pointed out), the Council made it undeniable that the church could change in ways that were not merely minor.

Debates about the development of doctrine continue, but about the manner and extent of development and not the fact. Is it a process of relatively seamless unfolding of the church's understanding of the original revelation, each phase of development enlarging or elaborating but not contradicting previous ones? Or is it a much more conflict-ridden process, involving reversals of positions as well as augmentation? The latter seems truer to the historical reality, but theologically it is much more problematic. It raises questions about the guidance of the Spirit during times when the church taught things it later rejected. More pointedly, it raises question about what could possibly be changed in the near or far future. Change, of course, can be for the worse as well as for the better; that was what always drove reformers to demand return to primitive Christianity. The basic challenge, then, is to distinguish between faithful change and unfaithful change or, in the words used by the great ecumenical theologian Yves Congar as the title for a landmark book, between *True and False Reform in the Church*. The related challenge is defining an appropriate role for theology in this process.

In 1999 the Catholic Theological Society made development of doctrine the theme for its annual meeting. The meeting did not dodge hard cases of past teachings that appear to have been reversed or disavowed: the use of coercion to suppress heresy, the official defense of slavery, widespread teachings about Jews and Judaism, the doctrine of "no salvation outside the church," the medieval prohibition of lending money at interest, and many others. Several speakers proposed new theories that might accommodate even these dramatic changes without abandoning the church's claim to be a trustworthy teacher of constant doctrine. Most of the theories seemed to win a moderate interest, none of them a clear acceptance.

As to the appropriate role of theology in doctrinal development, there was at least some consensus about the kind of virtues Catholic theologians needed in addressing the issues it posed: truthfulness, civility, courage, prudence, humility before the tradition, willingness to correct one's colleagues, and a deep-down trust in the church's future. Of course, that hardly settled the matter, since one person's truthfulness is another person's incivility, one person's courage is another's imprudence, and so on. Furthermore, for church authorities, this list of virtues, although welcome, is not enough.

Cardinal Ratzinger and like-minded conservatives in the American hierarchy are too knowledgeable to deny the reality of doctrinal development; they simply want it kept out of sight. The public face of Catholic theology should be one of unity. If Catholic theologians find some teachings ill supported by the current arguments, their obligation is to give the benefit of the doubt to the teachings and seek better arguments to support them. If they still find both arguments and conclusions defective, they should convey their questions and doubts privately to other theologians and church authorities. One can imagine these conservatives might tolerate academic publications raising questions about existing teaching if these publications were sufficiently deferential and obscure to fly below the educated public's radar. The slow, painstaking filtering of valid from invalid change, in other words, must occur in the wings—or at closed rehearsals—until the distant moment when church authorities authorize the appearance of a change onstage.

This view of doctrinal development is logically implied in the stated positions of these conservative church authorities. But none of them, as far as I know, has spelled out this view in so many, or so few, words. Nor can they, really. To explain the process openly, to tell Catholics even in a general way what is going on behind the theological curtain, would be to undercut the whole point. Such an inability to be open leads directly to the kind of habitual duplicity that Garry Wills in another place has labeled "structures of deceit." That is only one of the reasons this strategy is both destructive and doomed to failure. It should not be dismissed, however, without examining the very real conditions to which it responds. When it comes to anything vaguely smacking of controversy or popular interest, theology today operates in a media environment that is strongly biased toward extreme simplification and sharp dichotomies between old and new, up-to-date and out-of-date. One lesson that conservatives can draw from the birth control controversy of the 1960s is that prolonged public discussion can establish expectations, "facts on the ground," that largely foreclose the church's decision. Finally, not only do the media favor novelty, but the academic environment itself offers far more rewards in reputation and professional advancement for propounding new, provocative ideas than for restating or sustaining established ones. It is too easy to consider conservatives merely fearful that church teachings cannot survive on their own merits, as though those merits were to be tested on a level and neutral playing field. In fact they have reason to believe that without exercising some controls over theological speculations, the current environment is biased toward constantly destabilizing church teachings regardless of their merits.

The church, of course, has centuries of experience, a good deal of it unsavory, at trying to institutionalize controls on theological thought. The Index of Forbidden Books, for example, listing books not to be read without special permission, was established in 1557 and given its own papal office in 1571. Censorship of books, the common practice of governments and churches in the early modern period, was maintained by the church right up to the Second Vatican Council. Catholics looked to see whether a religious book had obtained an *Imprimatur* ("Let it be printed") and a *Nihil obstat* ("Nothing stands in the way") from some bishop. Indeed, during the first part of the twentieth century, a papal campaign against a long list of errors grouped under the heresy of "modernism" placed a whole net of restrictions on theologians and theological thought. The fact that the Catholic Theological Society was not founded until 1946 reflected this distrust and the resulting restrictions on theological meetings.

No one can call these controls a success. The massive secularization of Western intellectual life testifies to that, as does the injury to the church's good name and the plummeting of Catholic belief and practice in nations like Italy, Spain, and France. But insofar as such controls were, even in the short run, effective, they rested on certain preconditions. The major institutional linchpin for enforcing these controls was always that theology was dominated by priests. Priests had to seek the *Nihil obstat*, subscribe to various professions of doctrinal conformity, submit to censorship or silencing—or face disciplinary measures. Bishops and ultimately Rome had a material, spiritual, and psychological leverage over the ordained that it could never exercise over the laity. Now that theology is no longer a quasi-monopoly of the clergy, that leverage is gone. Control also rested on a sociological reality: the practical inability of many Catholics, minimally educated as they were, to encounter, grasp, and compare theological ideas. Today many Catholics are well educated and almost bombarded with competing theological notions, whether in scholarly literature or popular media. Finally control rested on two psychological factors: first, the conviction that exploring unauthorized theological theories without permission was a sinful act of some moment, and second, the reflexive reliance on authorized views out of a strong sense of "we" against "them," whether "they" were Protestants, skeptics, atheists, or simply Catholics who had been in some way reproved. Today's church seems well aware of how self-defeating it would be to restrict intellectual exploration under pain of sin. There is a stronger tendency to promote the kind of "we"-versus-"them" mentality that successfully maintains conformity even in the absence of external controls; but to do this wholeheartedly requires a major backtracking on the work of the Second Vatican Council.

In sum, both the hierarchy and Catholic theological scholars must rethink how doctrinal development can proceed with integrity in a radically different environment. Without forgetting that the church and theological truth are ultimately different, there are lessons to be learned from the natural sciences and other professions like law and medicine. How—or whether—the faith is passed on depends on this needed conversation. So far the Vatican's attempts to exercise traditional controls over a drastically altered theological world have more than failed; they have exacerbated the conflict to a dangerous extent. One can see that in two of the areas currently roiling American Catholicism: church teachings on sexual conduct, and the implications of recognizing women's full equality and past subordination.

Chapter Seven

Sex and the Female Church

U NTIL 1960, the most controversial topic confronting
American Catholics was the church's political power. Since
1960 the most controversial topics confronting American
Catholics have been the church's teachings on sex and on women.
The questions about political power came from outside the church;
if anything they united Catholics, who were convinced that they
were good Americans, notwithstanding the pronouncements of Paul
Blanshard or the KKK. The questions about sex and about women
have come from inside the church; they have deeply divided Catholics, who must ask themselves if they are good Catholics, notwithstanding the pronouncements of the pope and other high church
officials.

Neither topic was genuinely addressed by the Second Vatican
Council. The church leaders there—all male and pledged to
celibacy—did devote a chapter of their landmark Pastoral Constitution on the Church in the Modern World to marriage and the family.
Confirming a trend already well under way in Catholic theology,
they emphasized the "unitive" aspect of married sexuality—the fostering of love between spouses—alongside the "procreative" aspect.
Several attempts to reassert the older ranking of procreation as the
primary purpose of sex in marriage, and interpersonal union as sec-

ondary, were voted down. But the pope had already taken the subject of contraception out of the Council's hands and assigned it to his papal commission. The Council document could only indicate that papal action in a footnote while enjoining Catholics to use only the methods of birth regulation not disapproved of "by the teachings of the church"—without saying "at this moment" precisely what those teachings might or might not be.

About women, the Council said even less. When the Council was being planned, the heads of men's orders of priests and brothers were canvassed along with the world's bishops for their ideas. Heads of orders of sisters were not. Nor were any women invited to partici-pate in any capacity during the first session, from October to Decem-ber 1962. Two months into that session, when the liberal Cardinal Leon-Joseph Suenens of Brussels made one of his crucial interven-tions by proposing that a document on the church in the modern world be added to the agenda, he also noted that "half of the church" was missing from the Council's deliberations. A few women were consequently invited to the 1963 session; they could sit in on the bishops' debates in Saint Peter's, and speak but not vote in the com-missions that drafted the documents for the bishops' consideration. Eventually there were twenty-two such women participants, includ-ing one American sister, among the twenty-five hundred bishops and over five hundred (male) Catholic theological experts and observers from other religious groups. Hardly undue representation for "half of the church."

Council documents included a handful of passing references to women. Note was taken of their struggle for equality, their employ-ment outside the home, their necessary role in cultural life, and their place alongside men in carrying out the religious responsibilities of the laity. Discrimination based on sex was included in a list of preju-dices to be overcome. The importance of motherhood was stressed but qualified by the warning that it should not be used in opposition to "the legitimate social progress of women."

Although the Council did not address questions about sexuality or about women directly and at length, it made their emergence unavoidable by its recognition that all the baptized were to be active participants in Catholic life, by its more positive stance toward Protestantism and modernity (contraception had come to be identified with the evils of both), and by its general willingness to reexamine practices, from Latin in the Mass to abstinence from meat on Friday, that had been taken, like opposition to contraception, as badges of Catholic identity. These issues were destined to be addressed in light of the much controverted "spirit" of Vatican II.

THE HAPLESS TALE OF the birth control controversy culminating in *Humanae Vitae* and its emphatic rejection by the Catholic laity has already been recounted. *Humanae Vitae* was issued on July 29, 1968—a time of turmoil around the world. Vietnam had been wracked by some its fiercest fighting. Street battles between demonstrators and police were disrupting the Democratic National Convention in Chicago. Snap elections in France had just put an end to the student uprising in Paris. And a few weeks later, Warsaw Pact forces would invade Czechoslovakia, crushing the lingering freedom of Prague Spring.

"No papal teaching document has ever caused such an earthquake in the church as the encyclical *Humanae Vitae*," wrote the Reverend Bernard Häring, one of Catholicism's foremost moral theologians, shortly afterward. In the United States, a public protest criticizing the encyclical was signed by over six hundred Catholic scholars. A similar statement circulated in Europe. Many of the world's best-known theologians signed one or the other. Polls in country after country showed Catholics overwhelmingly in disagreement with the papal position—and more and more so as time went on. Bishops, sensitive to the revolts brewing within the ranks of both laypeople and clergy—and perhaps sharing some of those doubts themselves—tried to back the pope without slamming the door on those who conscientiously dissented. Whether this made things better or worse is still debated. Certainly the next decade saw the numbers of priests leaving their ministry swell, church attendance drop, and financial contributions decrease.

It is important to recall the precise issue at stake. It did not involve a teaching in scripture or the great creeds, or a belief about God, Jesus, or sacraments. This was not a tenet even about marriage, adultery, or divorce, at least not directly. No one was challenging the church's teaching on marital fidelity: that sexual intimacy belongs within the covenantal relationship of marriage and therefore that premarital and extramarital sexual relations were seriously wrong. No one was challenging the church's teaching on the importance of children: that the love of husband and wife in marriage and their marital sexuality should normally issue in the generation of new life and the care and nurturing of children. No one was challenging the church's teaching on parental responsibility: that married couples had the right, and in some circumstances the obligation, to regulate the size of their families and the spacing of their children. (Since the papacy had previously defended the use of "rhythm," or natural family planning, the debate centered on questions of means, not ends.) No one was challenging the church's teaching on the need for virtue and restraint: that human brokenness makes a force so powerful as sexuality particularly liable to selfishness and harm unless directed by cultural and social constraints and individual habits of care and responsibility.

Directly at issue was one thing only: whether each and every act of marital sexual intercourse must be "open" or "ordained" to the conception of new life, at least in the sense that nothing had been deliberately done to prevent that possibility. The controversial nub of Pope Paul's conclusions are in a few paragraphs among general reflections on marriage, sex, parenthood, and morality. There is an "inseparable connection," the pope declared in those passages, between the reproductive purpose of sexual intercourse and the emotional, physical, and psychological aspects that express a couple's love. Therefore, the argument continued, it was not enough for the marriage as a whole to be open to bringing new life into the world. That had to be true of each sexual act. Deliberately blocking the possibility of procreation violated the act's meaning, a meaning that Pope John Paul II, using a different philosophical vocabulary, has described as "total reciprocal self-giving."

Humanae Vitae, it has been said, is the Vietnam War of the Catholic Church. The comparison makes sense to older Catholics who remember the prolonged, embittering nature of that war in Southeast Asia. But the analogy may go further than that. Vietnam in itself appeared strategically and economically marginal to American interests, but it was elevated to centrality by the domino theory, holding that Communism, if victorious in Vietnam, would engulf one Asian country after another and ultimately tilt the world balance of power against the United States. Even officials who doubted whether the United States should have entered the quagmire of defending a shaky non-Communist regime in Vietnam argued that once America's credibility was at stake, the nation had to see the war through. Similarly, the question of contraception, although in itself marginal among Catholic teachings, was elevated to centrality by a domino theory concerned that all the principles of Catholic sexual morality would collapse, one by one, if change was accepted on this one point. And the church's teaching authority, already committed to condemning contraception, would be dangerously eroded.

Of course, something very much like that did happen—not because the church admitted a change, however, but because it didn't. Just as the interminable warfare in Southeast Asia had precisely the effect on American credibility it was supposed to prevent—draining resources, dividing and demoralizing the nation, and building resistance to overseas interventions—so the papacy's stand on contraception appeared to do much more than leave huge percentages of Catholics unconvinced. It opened up all sorts of questions about other points of sexual morality, about the church's whole approach to morals, and about church authority generally. There is one difference, of course, between the American entanglement in Vietnam and the church's entanglement with birth control: the United States finally got out, while the papacy, under John Paul II, has intensified its commitment right up to the present day.

In 1993, twenty-five years after *Humanae Vitae* was issued, I surveyed some of its long-term effects for the *New York Times*. At that point, eight out of ten Catholics disagreed with the statement "Using artificial means of birth control is wrong"; and nine out of ten said that "someone who practices artificial birth control can still be a good Catholic." Those figures were already steady then and have remained so since. By 1993, it did not seem that for most laypeople the church's position was any longer a matter for serious debate and reflection.

Younger Catholics appeared to take the morality of contraception as much for granted as their grandparents' generation once assumed its immorality. Many I interviewed had never heard of *Humanae Vitae*, let alone grappled with the moral arguments that it reflects. One young graduate of a Catholic college, then planning to pursue graduate studies in theology and eventually devote herself to church work, had just finished two years in a Catholic volunteer program. She had spent much of that time working with teenagers at a government health clinic in Alaska, and providing them with information about birth control. Until reading a newspaper editorial shortly before our conversation, she told me, she had never even seen the name of the papal document condemning contraception. "I'd heard of it and knew the church was against birth control," she said, "although a lot of priests would tell people simply to do what they thought best."

I asked a priest who dealt extensively with young adults how often they had questions about birth control, "In 23 years of talking to people prior to marriage," he said, "the issue of contraception has never come up from them. It is absolutely amazing. Not once." A layman who worked with young adults for Old Saint Patrick's Catholic Church in Chicago said that for them, all that counted about the encyclical was "a public relations image of the church and sexuality that is fairly negative."

"We are now dealing with the children of the people who wrestled with this as young adults in 1968," he said. "That was the first major segment of the Catholic population who were college educated and could engage theologians in real discussions of sexual morality." But after a few years of fierce debate, "it just petered out," and young people "are simply not going to the church" to ask about sexual issues.

ON THE LEVEL OF most individual Catholics, then, *Humanae Vitae* seemed to be a dead letter. And yet the pope's 1968 encyclical and the furor it created was still affecting the church, like a low-grade fever or one of those subterranean coal mine fires, flaring up in nearby areas of morality or even in matters far afield, such as the selection of bishops and ultimately the very nature of church authority. The Reverend Andrew M. Greeley documented what he termed "the catastrophic collapse of the old Catholic sexual ethic," with Catholics rapidly surpassing Protestants in agreeing that premarital sex is "not wrong at all." Greeley attributed sharply falling Mass attendance and financial contributions to unhappiness over the encyclical.

Early in that twenty-fifth anniversary year, the Jesuit theologian Avery Dulles gave a remarkable speech, not on *Humanae Vitae* directly but on the "ripple effect" of the widespread rejection of the papal document "in many other areas of Catholic life." The speech was remarkable because Dulles, as his later elevation to the College of Cardinals showed, was known as a respected, articulate defender of papal positions. It was even more remarkable since it was held at a conference for two hundred bishops sponsored by a conservative church center and aimed at bolstering support for the encyclical.

Dulles averred not to have any problem with *Humanae Vitae*'s doctrine, which "was exactly what I had always believed as a Catholic and what I had been taught in my courses in ethics and moral theology." But "when the emphatic and repeated teaching . . . about key issues of sexual ethics falls on deaf ears and is widely rejected, the church ceases to appear in the world as a sign of the unity God intends for the whole human family," he said. "The more the hierarchy insists on adherence to *Humanae Vitae*, the more alienated the majority of the faithful feel."

The Vatican Council, he continued, "sought to give the laity an active life in the church and in the development of doctrine." But "as long as the overwhelming majority of laypeople are at odds with the hierarchy on the question of birth control, the process of consultation on marriage and family life will be gravely inhibited. The magisterium [authoritative teaching by bishops and the pope] will find itself driven into an isolated clerical world."

"Priests are placed in a difficult position," he said. Most do not agree with the encyclical; those who do fear "antagonizing their hearers and turning them against the whole Catholic system." The consequence is that "lay Catholics receive very little clear guidance on sexual matters from the clergy, who seem to be uncertain and indecisive."

All distinctions about authoritative church teachings get obscured in the battle over birth control, with some theologians dismissing papal authority, others treating it minimally, and "at the opposite extreme," others treating ordinary papal teaching "as though it were, at least in practice, infallible," Dulles said. "In the present polarized situation it is difficult to discuss any issues about the magisterium and dissent in a dispassionate and nonpartisan manner. Everyone is drawn into the battle for or against the encyclical."

The relations between bishops and theologians, cordial at the time of the Council, "have become strained," Dulles said. Bishops eye theologians suspiciously. "Otherwise-qualified theologians who dissent from *Humanae Vitae* find themselves excluded from sensitive teaching positions" and appointments as advisers, while scholars who remain in good standing get "portrayed as sycophantic court theologians."

"Another adverse effect," he said, "has to do with the appointment of bishops." Priests known to be opposed to the encyclical are considered ineligible, narrowing the pool of candidates and producing some appointments of "debatable quality." Because local recommendations are overridden, "Rome is accused of spurning the doctrine of Vatican II" in which the bishop is seen as the servant and representative of the local church.

"Finally, the development of episcopal conferences," he said, "has been stunted by the controversy about birth control." Because Pope Paul VI was disappointed by the "ambivalent responses" of a number of bishops' conferences, the Vatican has downplayed the authority of the conferences and required prior approval of their statements. The dissent from *Humanae Vitae,* he suggested, had become a major obstacle to the "decentralization, participation, and coresponsibility that were foreseen as resulting from the Council."

Dulles urged dissenters to realize that public protests weakened the authority and unity of the church and that pressure in the media was not going to bring about change. "Those who are strongly convinced by the arguments for or against contraception," he added, "should recognize the extreme difficulty of the question and should therefore respect the intelligence and sincerity of those with whom they differ." In what may have been his most surprising recommendation, he said that, while theologians who "aggressively attack" *Humanae Vitae* would seem to disqualify themselves for seminary posts, agreement with the encyclical "should not be made the sole litmus test" for appointment to church offices.

Coming from Dulles, in many respects a very conservative theologian, this testimony about the fallout of the birth control battle is particularly impressive—not only such matters as alienating the majority of the faithful, but also lowering the caliber of bishops; weakening their national conferences; crippling discussion of marriage, family life, and sexual issues generally; isolating church teaching authorities in a clerical culture; surrounding all claims about teaching authority with confusion and suspicion; stigmatizing some of the best theological scholars; and forcing priests to hide their true convictions.

THAT WAS IN 1993. A decade later, the situation has not improved. Catholics are no more persuaded by *Humanae Vitae,* but its serious impact on church life persists. The "deleterious consequences" that Dulles named would be found on many Catholics' lists of factors— whether the erosion of church authority, the quality of episcopal appointments, or the weakening of bishops' conferences—contributing to the sex abuse scandals the church has suffered, yet some Catholic conservatives appear convinced that the revelations about priests sexually molesting minors call for reemphasizing *Humanae Vitae.* Defenders of the encyclical do not deny the unraveling of Catholic confidence in the church's authority and its sexual teachings, but the fault, they believe, is not with the encyclical itself but with (1) the arguments originally made within the papal commission for a change in teaching, (2) the dissenting theologians who continued to make those arguments after the pope had spoken, and (3) the toleration of that dissent by bishops whose own support for the teaching was at most lukewarm. Dissenting theological opinion provided a justification for the moral frailty that leads married Catholics, no less than others, astray.

Dulles's stated concern, too, was with "dissent from the encyclical"; he eschewed any questions about *Humanae Vitae* itself. But he doubted that theologians' dissent had really caused the widespread Catholic rejection of the papal teaching. If anything, the causal relationship was in the other direction, he said: theologians were following "the popular conviction that contraception was tolerable and sometimes necessary." In many places, moreover, his wording did not really specify whether the root of the difficulties was the encyclical or the dissent from the encyclical. The speech caused a good bit of consternation among *Humanae Vitae*'s defenders. Dulles had not included among the deleterious effects of dissent from the encyclical, complained one, "the fact that most Catholic couples are contracepting," putting "the salvation of souls in jeopardy." Even more disturbing was his recommendation that agreement with *Humanae Vitae* should not be a litmus test for appointment to sensitive church posts.

To defenders of the encyclical, standing by what so many considered a relatively minor teaching, despite the risk of massive disaffection and turmoil, was not an act of foolhardiness but bravery. These defenders point to the ravages of the sexual revolution and the ominous shadow of a brave new world of test tube babies, eugenics, and cloning. Pope Paul VI, they claim, was a prophetic voice who had offered a firewall in his insistence that the procreative dimension of sexual intimacy must never, not even in a single act, be separated from committed, uniting love. Separate them, and you open the gates to exploitative sex and manufactured humans.

That moral firewalls are needed would be admitted on either side of this debate. But was the firewall thrown up by *Humanae Vitae* viable? Or was it a defective wall, thrown up in the wrong place?

Those questions raise philosophical and theological issues to begin with. Like much Catholic moral reasoning, the condemnation of any deliberate foiling of what would otherwise be a possibly fertile act of intercourse rests on an interpretation of natural law theory, a philosophical tradition stretching back to the ancients. Theologically the condemnation raises the question of how definitively the church can pronounce on a principle of morality derived philosophically but not found in scripture—and the question of the role of the whole church, the married faithful as well as the celibate clergy, in reaching or ratifying such judgments.

Both sides in the debate accuse the other of some form of dualism, of illegitimately separating the body and the spirit. Critics of the natural law reasoning underlying *Humanae Vitae* protest that it reads moral imperatives in a narrow and static fashion off the biological functions of the sexual organs or the physical structure of sexual intimacy—to the neglect of human intention, disposition, the total well-being of the partners, the totality of marriage, and evolving understandings of the human person and psychology as well as technology. Defenders of the encyclical, citing Paul VI's words on the "inseparable connection" between the reproductive, emotional, and psychological dimensions of sexual intercourse, rejoin that they are the ones insisting that it be viewed in a holistic fashion—and that the critics end up arbitrarily pasting moral meanings on sexual acts without regard to an inherent "language of the body."

There has been no more ardent defender of *Humanae Vitae* than Pope John Paul II. In the decade before his 1978 election to the papacy, the condemnation of contraception appeared to have so little effect on the tide of Catholic opinion and conduct that many people thought that in time the Vatican would quietly abandon its position.

But with John Paul's encouragement, supporters of *Humanae Vitae* rallied. They began publishing fresh philosophical and theological defenses of the encyclical. They have found platforms in new study centers and international conferences financed by conservative Catholic groups like Opus Dei and the Knights of Columbus. They have advocated the litmus test that Dulles counseled against. At one point they argued that the ban on contraception was infallible doctrine, not because Pope Paul had said so but because the ban expressed something universally taught by the church before controversy broke out in the 1960s. This view was rejected by the vast majority of theologians specializing in ethics or in issues of church authority. Nonetheless, rumors circulated that the pope, in one of his anticipated encyclicals on fundamental moral questions, might solemnly declare the ban an infallible dogma that could not be reversed and had to be believed. Rumors also circulated that papal advisers, perhaps including Cardinal Ratzinger, opposed such a momentous step. The solemn declaration never came, although this papacy has employed a novel kind of language of quasi-infallibity that many theologians consider an attempt to claim the same unalterable status for teachings on contraception and other issues without doing so outright.

Supporters of *Humanae Vitae* have also increasingly tied their case to the promotion of natural family planning, the abstention from intercourse during the woman's fertile periods. Although accuracy in identifying those periods has grown markedly since the so-called rhythm method was slighted as "Vatican roulette," the improved method remains debated in medical circles (which are not necessarily free of their own ideological precommitments). Natural family planning, which the pope supports enthusiastically, is now celebrated as a spiritual discipline as much as a practical necessity, and sometimes it appears as though the philosophical condemnation in the encyclical is validated by the physiological, psychological, and spiritual strengths claimed for an alternative birth control method.

Finally, the contraception debate has been affected by the pope's own extensive writings on sexual morality, which have injected a very different set of terms and categories into the discussion, drawn from his personal blending of traditional scholasticism and contemporary phenomenology. The sifting of profound insight from idealized "nonsense on stilts" has only begun, not made any easier by the density and ambiguity of the pope's language.

But however much the discipline of natural family planning, or John Paul's abstract but elevating language about personal embodiment and total self-giving, may enrich Catholicism's approach to sexuality and married love in general, they have fallen far short of any convincing case that the reproductive potential of sexual activity may never—not in any instance—be deliberately obstructed. The new, holistic forms of natural law reasoning and reflections on the "language of the body," the Trinitarian "iconography" of marital sex, or the humanistic personalism of sexual self-mastery may provide important insights into the meaning of human sexuality, the reasons for limiting intercourse to the covenantal relationship of marriage, and the norms that should govern its responsible exercise over the course of married life. To justify an absolute ban on contraception, however, these approaches always seem to be forced and tortured into supporting a foregone conclusion. The final links in the argument always seem to depend on stark assertions (for example, contraception is "hostile" or "degrading" to the spouse; it ruins the "spontaneity and depth" of the experience) or cloudy rhetoric (such as Pope John Paul's) that simply doesn't ring true to the lived experience of too many religiously serious and sensitive people. Blunt questions such as "What does that really mean in the day-to-day life of our marriage and family?" and "How do you know that's true? How do you know it's *always* true?" go unanswered.

Meanwhile, the costs to the church keep piling up. And not only to the church. Defenders of *Humanae Vitae* were not wrong in insisting that birth control, though not one of the great truths of the Godhead and redemption, raised questions of major importance for all of sexual morality and human well-being. The truth is that the ability to control human fertility and to intervene with technology in human reproduction is a development of world-historical dimensions. In other words, it ranks among the great passages in human history: the passage from hunting and gathering to settled agricultural and pastoral societies, for example, or from clans to complex city-based civilizations; the discovery of bronze and iron metallurgy, the invention and perfection of writing and written records; and in the last few centuries, the mechanical harnessing of new energy sources that are the basis for industrialization, urbanization, and now globalization.

These world-historical changes may include developments in warfare, like the invention of wheeled chariots, the use of gunpowder, or the production of nuclear armaments powerful enough to wipe out civilization. Among the world-historical changes are cultural, intellectual, or spiritual passages, like the so-called axial age in the middle centuries of the first millennium before Christ, when spiritual leaders from the Hebrew prophets to the Buddha propounded universalizing systems of ethics and belief; or the new consciousness stemming from the Scientific Revolution in the seventeenth century and its later systematization (Alfred North Whitehead: "The greatest invention of the nineteenth century was the invention of the method of invention"); or the global revolution in consciousness about human rights, national self-determination, and democracy.

Some of these changes are more fundamental and sweeping than others, but to varying degrees they all have reconfigured political and communal ties, family structures, relationships with nature, patterns of leading personality types, codes of virtues and ethics, and, of course, religious systems. Catholicism has been caught out by several of these passages—certainly the Scientific Revolution, the democratic revolution, and the social and economic shift from peasant life in the European countryside to proletarian and middle class life in industrialized cities. Each change took its toll on the church, which usually adjusted belatedly and only after losing both masses of the faithful and many opportunities to shape the emerging realities with its message.

Humanity's new powers of control over fertility and reproduction are just as consequential. They are, of course, part of the larger technological revolution that has brought human life more and more into a humanly created environment and less and less into a directly "natural" one, a process virtually coterminous with humanity itself but accelerating dramatically in the last centuries. I put quotation marks around "natural" because humans too are part of nature; and it is only a convention of speech that makes us refer to an environment as natural that is directly constituted by the raw elements, the uncultivated fields and forests, and the undomesticated creatures, including those microbial ones that so radically affect our health for good or ill, rather than the environments that, by piecemeal adjustment or wholesale design, humans themselves have constructed and maintained. The control of fecundity and changing ideals about family size are not unrelated to the movement from countryside to city, from agriculture to industry, from animal power to coal, oil, and electricity, from population growth held in check by starvation and disease to population growth unleashed by agricultural markets and science, sanitation, and medicine.

LONG BEFORE THE ARRIVAL of the pill, thoughtful men and women recognized that the ability to control fertility, even if imperfectly, and to separate sexuality from reproduction would have profound consequences. Some were enthusiasts of brave new worlds of sexual exploration, trial marriages, free and dissoluble unions, rational and scientific parenthood, and other earnest schemes often giving off a musty odor of the very Victorianism against which they were rebelling. Others were worriers, like Walter Lippmann, who in 1929 declared contraception "an immensely beneficent invention" but acknowledged that the Catholic Church was not wrong in recognizing that "birth control . . . is the most revolutionary practice in the history of sexual morals." Three quarters of a century later, American culture, to say nothing of the situation elsewhere, remains at war with itself in the absence of any cultural consensus on sexual norms. Billions of dollars and immense talent are expended in stirring sexual longings and promoting sexual fantasies. Billions of dollars and immense talent are devoted to repairing the damages of impulsive, irresponsible, or exploitative sexual conduct. Contemporary literature about the sexual revolution portrays a "devaluated world," no less harsh and lacking in lasting joy and trustworthy love than the world Lippmann found in the literature of the twenties. American society is desperately in need of moral analysis beyond the level of bumper stickers, sitcoms, and rock lyrics.

Catholics would like to think that the church could help. Some, of course, believe that it has. They are convinced that the rejection of contraception was a prophetic stance. By declaring that the only method of birth control that did not tear spousal love and procreation asunder was one taking advantage of natural periods of infertility, the church solved the problem at its root. Unfortunately, that position has proven a false defense, philosophically and theologically vulnerable in my view, and certainly unavailing in its effects. Rather than be the prophetic voice that defenders of *Humanae Vitae* imagine, for over thirty years the Catholic Church has been largely missing in action, the result of a self-inflicted wound. What makes sense in its teaching about the inseparable connection between love, marriage, sexual intimacy, and procreation has been pushed beyond the breaking point by decreeing an absolute rule for each and every act of marital sex. Its dogged defense of that position has forced it to minimize the extent to which Christianity has harbored a destructive hostility to the body and physical passion. That minimization, in turn, has hurt the search for a balance that would uphold Catholicism's humanistic celebration of sensual joy and vitality but would also retain the tradition's worldly wisdom about the power of desire, the brokenness of human nature, and the need for an asceticism and spirituality guiding erotic energy for both the married and the unmarried.

What rings true to many Catholic couples is the church's concern about a "contraceptive mentality." Although the phrase has sometimes been used to describe (pejoratively) an emphasis by population and public health planners on contraception as a technological fix to a host of moral and cultural issues, it has been generally used in Catholic discussions to indicate an outlook that views children essentially as a threat to the control and self-fulfillment of adults. This tension between maintaining control and giving life and unconditional love to an independent being is potentially profound. It grows greater as women refuse to identify themselves solely as mothers who must shoulder all the day-to-day responsibilities of child rearing. It has a bearing on the subtle slide between normal parental desire to spare their children, by means of medical interventions, from serious handicaps and the tempting hope of harnessing technology to assure themselves of a "perfect," that is, superior, child. The church's perspective on the limits of human choice and control within a larger understanding of life as a gift speaks to critical new issues of genetic knowledge and the manipulation of early human life.

What does not ring true is the church's jump from this concern about overall attitudes and patterns of conduct to its judgments about particular forms of birth control and its condemnation—as the gravest sort of sin—of contraception in any instance and for any purpose. Burdened by this contradiction of their own experience, a great many Catholic parents for perhaps two generations now have been unable to affirm the church's teaching on sexuality wholeheartedly to their maturing children. The same for catechists, whether in Catholic schools or parish programs, and school counselors. Meanwhile, Catholic moral theologians, similarly unable to affirm a case they find riddled with unwarranted assumptions and leaps in logic, have been sidelined from developing other approaches to sexual morality to fill the void. Discussion has not come to a halt, but like a jam-up on the highway when all the vehicles have to squeeze around a wreck, discussion about sexual morality has slowed to a crawl. In practice, American Catholics have been operating with, at best, a residual sexual ethic of their own, as distinguished from a common American mix of romanticism, individualism, and consequentialism ("something clicked . . . consenting adults . . . don't hurt anybody"), for about thirty years.

CATHOLIC THINKING HAS had little impact, for example, on the dramatic reevaluation of homosexuality, within either the Christian churches or the public at large. That was a question that Catholicism approached with certain advantages. The Hebrew and Christian scriptures had condemned same-sex relations in terms that no one until recently considered at all ambiguous. Historically Catholicism was no less opposed—sometimes lethally so—to homosexuality than were other forms of Christianity. But Catholic moral theology, linked as it had long been to the enumeration of particular sins in the confessional and their categorization as venial or mortal, traditionally focused on specific willed actions more than on states of mind. Sin was what one did, not what one was. (The same tendency had probably contributed to the focus on each instance of sexual intercourse in the case of contraception.) Therefore, to be attracted to the same sex was not in itself sinful but became morally significant when one willed to engage in genitally pleasurable actions or fantasies. Homoerotic attraction of a more sublimated sort was not sinful, nor was unintended pleasurable attraction that was resisted rather than acted upon.

The fact that celibacy was required for ordination to the priesthood in the Latin Rite and for membership in religious orders of both men and women further complicated the church's outlook. Marriage and family were not necessarily the norm for a saintly life; if anything, they were depreciated. At the minimum, there was another model for manliness and femininity. Throughout history, furthermore, the celibate priesthood and life in religious orders almost certainly enlisted disproportionate numbers of those not heterosexually inclined. The clumsy negative formulation is used to avoid reading contemporary psychological categories into the past, and to account for the spectrum of sexual constitutions and for those who may have instinctually shunned marriage and the other sex without consciously recognizing in themselves urges toward conduct the church abhorred. Obviously the psychodynamics of such a situation can be extremely complicated: on the one hand, a sympathy for the plight of the homosexually inclined in a heterosexual society, indeed for the plight of any dissenter from a macho model of sexual roles; on the other hand, a harsh repression of any suspect tendencies felt within oneself or one's associates.

In any case, the distinction between homosexual orientation and acts, along with the consequences of celibacy in Catholic leadership ranks, gave rise to crosscurrents reflected not only in contemporary church documents, which generally reject homosexual activity while insisting on the dignity of homosexuals and pastoral sensitivity for the problems they face, but also in personal attitudes. In my own reporting on these issues, for example, I have never encountered the visceral reaction to homosexuality among Catholic leaders that I have often encountered among evangelicals. Efforts to "convert" gay and lesbian individuals to heterosexuality enjoy little support among Catholics.

Twenty-five years ago the bishops had already declared, "Homosexuals, like everyone else, should not suffer from prejudice against their basic human rights. They have a right to respect, friendship, and justice. They have an active role in the Christian community." But bishops have varied in their responses to proposed legal measures protecting homosexuals from discrimination. Many have opposed such proposals on the grounds that they were aimed at legitimating homosexual conduct, were not needed to deal with justifiable concerns about housing or employment discrimination, gave too much leeway to courts for interpretation, especially in regard to fundamental social institutions like marriage, or threatened the church's freedom to abide by its own religious standards in its own institutions.

But where the church's rights were not threatened, some bishops backed such proposals. Other bishops chose to stay neutral or have worked out compromises, much to the consternation of Catholic conservatives. In several cases, bishops have very visibly refused support for legal initiatives that were viewed as distinctly hostile to homosexuals. In virtually all cases, bishops have strongly denounced violence and discrimination against homosexuals and have tried to distance themselves, not always successfully, from sometime allies with homophobic views.

Similarly, bishops have varied widely in supporting programs of pastoral support for homosexual Catholics and their families, again frequently to the consternation of conservative Catholics, or programs providing ministry to victims of AIDS. Complicating the overall picture have been a series of public and behind-the-scenes Vatican remonstrances against pastoral initiatives that might blur the teaching that deliberate sexual arousal and activity by partners of the same sex, like those of unmarried partners of different sexes, were sinful. In 1986, concerned that the distinction between orientation and acts was leading to an "overly benign interpretation" of homosexuality, a Vatican statement tried to maintain the position that the orientation was not a sin but did constitute "an objective disorder." In 1988, Rome ordered the bishops to modify a statement on AIDS prevention campaigns. Although the bishops had criticized safe-sex campaigns focused on promoting the use of condoms, the statement had accepted that some information about condoms might be included in public health efforts—a position that, to Cardinal Ratzinger in the Vatican and important prelates like Cardinal Law and Cardinal O'Connor in the United States, risked the impression of condoning contraception and sex outside of marriage. Later, Rome warned bishops to dissociate themselves from Catholic gay and lesbian groups or ministries that did not explicitly endorse church teaching on the immorality of homosexual acts.

Partly because of the publicity given Vatican statements, most gay and lesbian advocates have not seen the Catholic Church's position as variegated. Their own position, understandably, has been "for us or against us," and variegated, in any case, is not "for us." "For us" has meant, at a minimum, the equivalence of homosexuality with race, gender, age, religion, and disability as a status protected against discrimination and, more recently, the equivalence of homosexuality with heterosexuality in matters such as adoption, civil and religious marriage, family benefits, inheritance, social behavior, and values instilled in public education. The public discussion is often highly charged, whether the issue at hand is seemingly practical and easily negotiable, like giving gay and lesbian partners next-of-kin rights in medical situations, or fundamental and deeply symbolic, like legalizing gay and lesbian marriage. Most of what passes for factual in these matters is highly politicized. Almost anyone staking out a position either does it from well within the safety of a camp or risks being labeled and stigmatized.

In many respects, the society's anxieties surrounding homosexuality are really only a projection of issues surrounding heterosexuality—once the tight link between sex and procreation is broken. Homosexuality becomes the obvious battleground for addressing questions about nonprocreative heterosexuality. The relatively small gay and lesbian portion of the population bears the brunt of unresolved moral and cultural questions facing the more than 90 percent that is heterosexual. Of course, some gay and lesbian activists and theorists have themselves sometimes seized this assignment, making their own sexuality the launching pad for a deconstruction of traditional committed heterosexual relationships and the model for a better alternative of self-expression and self-exploration.

For the church, then, speaking to questions posed by the movements for gay and lesbian rights and social acceptance is not distinct from the challenge of speaking to questions of heterosexual morality. As long as the church remains entrenched behind its prohibition of all deliberately nonprocreative sex, that certainly provides an unambiguous teaching on all same-sex sexual intimacy: it is sinful. But once that moral Maginot Line collapses or is outflanked by realities it ignores, as has been the case with marital sex between men and women, then the church appears to have little coherent to say about another cultural development with major implications for human dignity and well-being. I believe that, on the contrary, it does have something to say (and to hear also). Some Catholic thinkers have tried to develop answers to the questions posed by gay and lesbian sexuality that do not deny the importance of sexual expression in most healthy lives; that reject the hedonism that has proved destructive and debilitating for many gay and some lesbian people; and that fit homosexuality into patterns of privacy and tolerance but also of social and religious recognition and legal protection generally consistent with the patterns pertinent to heterosexuality, marriage, and child raising.

These thinkers do not agree among themselves; not all their answers will survive scrutiny, maybe none will. At the moment, it is hard to know, since Catholic efforts to rethink sexual morality apart from *Humanae Vitae* operate in a slightly obscure zone of academic theology that may at best influence private pastoral counseling but is carefully fenced off from the church's public speech—in pulpits, religious education, church publications, or official statements. For the moment, it seems, Catholicism's understanding of human nature, of embodiment, of love in its several dimensions, of individual and collective destinies transcending this life must either be mobilized to defend the Maginot Line or be scattered into relative ineffectiveness.

The year 2002 put questions of sexuality and church teaching, which have been reshaping American Catholicism for decades, sometimes visibly, sometimes below the surface, back into the spotlight. Was the sexual abuse of minors by priests rooted in the requirement of celibacy for ordination? Since most of the victims appeared to be boys in their early adolescence, was the problem homosexuality in the priesthood? Were homosexuals being disproportionately drawn to the priesthood, or even coming to dominate it? Or, more specifically, sexually immature or stunted homosexuals? Or sexually immature or stunted heterosexuals? What, in any case, should be done?

One cannot say that this discussion was carried on in a very exacting manner. Maybe it could not have been, given the shocking and sickening conduct at issue. Apart from that, there was only one thing everyone agreed upon—that the church had been living with a serious rift between its officially professed teachings about sex, both heterosexual and homosexual, and the lived reality. *Don't ask, don't tell, don't preach* was one version of the reality. *You pretend to teach, we pretend to obey* was another.

The rift had produced a spider's web of smaller cracks and fissures—dissimulations, denials, evasions, hypocrisies—that threatened the church's integrity. Repairing this rift seemed to be the necessary preliminary step to addressing those other questions. But how could it be repaired? By requiring public affirmation of the church's teaching on sexuality at all levels of Catholic life and without qualification? That was the demand of some leaders and intellectuals. By finding a way to reopen that teaching to examination and to the experience of multitudes of Catholics? That was the demand of others. It is a choice that cannot be continually avoided.

THE RAPIDLY RISING MOVEMENT for the equality of women is also a development of world-historical dimensions, one even greater than the achievement of control over human fertility, on which it is in part based. It is based, in addition, on modern medical advances that have dramatically reduced the rate of maternal deaths in childbirth. It is based on changes in working life that have reduced the importance of physical strength. It is based above all on now universally recognized principles, rooted in Christianity as well as other traditions and belief systems, of human dignity and equality.

One way of thinking about the challenge posed to Catholicism by the women's movement and its ideological or philosophical expression in feminism is to compare it to the liberal and democratic revolutions of the late eighteenth and early nineteenth centuries, which the church, wedded to the Ancien Régime, unhappily refused to countenance for over a century. In fact, feminism ultimately challenges Catholicism even more profoundly at the level of sacred texts and fundamental religious symbols and theology.

All contemporary world religions are patriarchal. They have taken shape in cultures where men held power over women. That power was legitimated by religion. That power was maintained within religious institutions as well as familial, economic, and political ones. The male experience in those patriarchal cultures and the virtues associated with it trumped the experience and associated virtues of women—and were reflected in ideas and images of the divine, in ritual roles, in sacred texts. Patriarchy is not monolithic. Men and women need each other. They even intermarry. Men have mothers, daughters, and sisters. Women have fathers, sons, and brothers. Men and women speak the same languages, have common enemies, share some of the most basic experiences of life—joy, pain, comfort, fear, awe, hunger, infirmity, death—although each of these, in different ways in different cultures, is given its own color and texture depending on whether one is male or female. Women possess power to give and nourish new life that men do not—although that, too, can lead men to fear and control that power as much as to reverence, celebrate, or propitiate it.

Religions are woven of many colors and yarns, and if the dominant pattern can justly be called patriarchal, there are still all sorts of other hues and strands and weaves as well. No one can read the Bible without recognizing how thoroughly patriarchal are both the Hebrew scriptures and the Christian New Testament. Yet no one could start with a one-dimensional theory of patriarchal oppression and hypothesize scriptures like these, with wily matriarchs and flawed patriarchs, with extraordinary heroines, family dramas, sexual politics, female models of holiness, and even feminine personification of the divine.

All this is to say that, over the long run, nothing in Catholic Christianity, like nothing in other forms of Christianity—or in Judaism, Islam, Buddhism, and even Hinduism, superficially the most matriarchal of the great religions—will remain untouched by the passage from a patriarchal era to one of female equality. Compared to other recorded religious transformations, the process will almost surely be accelerated, but it will still be at least a century or so in working itself out unevenly, and no one should be confident about predicting which elements in the great religions will be radically revised, which will be reconfigured, which will remain relatively intact.

There are at least three elements in play. One is feminism, or feminist theory. Another is the world-historical movement for women's equality, which feminism articulates, inspires, defends, and possibly steers in one direction or another, but which is not just a movement of ideas but of massive sociological, economic, demographic, and political forces. A third is the particular set of grievances that move women to protest and to take stock of their larger condition. In the religious case, those grievances have usually involved religious law and authority subordinating women in family matters, and the exclusion of women from ritual roles, institutional leadership, and the opportunity to share in the authoritative interpretation of the tradition.

Challenges to the exclusion and subordination of women in the American Catholic Church have coalesced around two issues: language and ordination. But those two issues cannot be compartmentalized from what feminist theology suggests is potentially a much larger recasting of Catholicism. That is the problem—and the opportunity.

CATHOLIC FEMINIST THEOLOGY, although it can point to forerunners in earlier centuries, is essentially a development of the last four decades. It is, like feminist theory in general, an extraordinarily varied development, ranging from very limited criticism of particular church practices to the most radical questioning of central Christian beliefs. It finds expression in popular writings extolling the spirituality of medieval women mystics or drawing new lessons from scriptural passages involving women that the male-dominated tradition has ignored or deformed. It finds expression in workshops, retreats, summer institutes, and lectures attended for the most part by the many thousands of Catholic women who have always provided the bulk of regular churchgoers, parish volunteers, catechists, teachers, and professional staff in church agencies. It finds perhaps its most impressive expression in biblical research, church history, systematic theology, ethics, and theoretical proposals written primarily for other scholars and feminist theoreticians.

This more intellectual Catholic feminist theology, largely based in the academy, feels itself part of a broad feminist theological project embracing thinkers from other branches of Christianity, from Judaism, and from perspectives that reject Judaism and Christianity in favor of reinvented goddess movements or other forms of women's spirituality. While this broad feminist theological project maintains a great deal of solidarity based on shared experience, it has also been differentiating itself into more and more groups asserting their own distinctive experience: African-American "womanist" theology, Hispanic *mujerista* theology, lesbian variants, and so on.

Within this broad project, Catholic feminist thinkers have been unusually productive and influential. Perhaps the Catholic Church is such a patriarchal stronghold that it has stimulated a vigorous feminist opposition. That, at any rate, is one explanation. More important, I believe, is the role of women's religious orders and the many Catholic women's colleges that they founded and staffed, replete with theology programs.

As far back as 1943, nine years before Pope Pius XII founded an institute in Rome to train women to teach theology, Sister Madeleva Wolff had established a doctoral program in theology for women at the college she headed, Saint Mary's in Notre Dame, Indiana. By no means are all of the outstanding Catholic feminist scholars, writers, and speakers members of religious orders. But Catholic sisters, a large, theologically oriented constituency immersed in church life, provided networks of support for many creators of the new Catholic feminism and a ready pool of consumers for their ideas. This was especially the case because no group in the church experienced patriarchal constraints and authority more severely than religious sisters.

Many orders lived by rules incorporating restraints that had governed the lives of all "respectable" women a century or more in the past, as well as the spiritual authority of male church leaders in the present. The daily schedules of sisters, their clothing, travel, spending money, reading and recreation, family visits, and free time were minutely regulated and usually severely limited. Changes in these matters often had to be approved by male church leaders. This tutelage was in stark contradiction to the relative self-governance enjoyed by many orders of women and to the real authority that sisters exercised in the schools, hospitals, and other charitable institutions they sponsored, although, even there, religious sisters often had to deal with obstreperous or condescending pastors and bishops.

After Vatican II, a movement for reform, already under way in the 1950s, turned into a thoroughgoing reexamination of each order's goals and way of life; and this process, which sometimes created traumatic divisions between innovators and traditionalists and which also encouraged the personal reevaluations leading tens of thousands of women to leave their orders, coincided with the emergence in the United States of the women's movement and its new militant forms of feminism. That movement also coincided with the rapid growth in the number of college-educated Catholic women breaking away from the ethnically defined patterns of marriage and family that had been protracted by the conservative climate of postwar America. The two groups assured that Catholicism would be deeply affected by feminism, but it was the core of sisters (and ex-sisters) who gave Catholic feminism its special flavor.

Catholic feminist theology must not be misunderstood as an enterprise narrowly focused on questions like gender-inclusive or gender-neutral language in scripture translations and liturgical prayers or like ordination of women to the priesthood. Feminist theology encompasses a critique of the patriarchal bias built into all sacred texts and traditional teachings, a struggle to recover women's voices in religious history that have been suppressed or marginalized, and an effort to employ the previously neglected or excluded insights and experiences of women in rethinking the church's whole range of doctrines, symbols, and rituals. That means rethinking ways of interpreting scripture (or even of defining what belongs in scripture), of understanding the Trinity, Jesus' role in redemption, the sacraments, morality, authority in the church, and so on. Catholic feminist theologians have already produced a large body of work of extraordinary quality, and it will be some time before it is sifted through for what is of lasting value for Catholic Christianity. Even now, however, it is safe to say "a great deal." But two complicating factors—Catholic feminism's unreadiness to address questions of boundaries and the movement's distance from many Catholic women—bear on the church's choices in the near future.

Today Catholic feminist theology remains fluid, amorphous, and unfixed. That is significant because it would be disingenuous to ignore the radical nature of some feminist theology and the difficulty of reconciling it with anything remotely continuous with Catholicism and maybe of Christianity, too. Much Catholic feminist thought is relatively uninterested in the whole question of differentiating what is compatible with Catholic Christianity from what is not, and at present underequipped to do so. To many feminists, that question seems at the very least premature, if not a downright preemptive move to quash threatening ideas. Their energy has gone into exposing the feminism-adverse elements in Catholicism, not the Catholicism-adverse elements in feminism. They sense themselves engaged in a common struggle with feminist thinkers and activists of all spiritual stripes, whose work they regularly cite sympathetically and criticize very gently, if at all. The tone of their theological writing is not infrequently apologetic and defensive, as they strive to justify their commitment to Catholic Christianity before an imagined jury of feminists who reject it. Catholic women are pictured as barely hanging on to a faith poisoned by patriarchy. That may very well be these theologians' own case or the case of women like themselves. It may also reflect a fear that to say anything less would remove the pressure for the church to change.

One wonders how many Catholic women or men can be galvanized in the long run by a feminist theology that, despite the unquestionable faith of many of these scholars, so frequently leaves the impression of teetering on the edge of secession. More problematic are the uncertainties created about whether segments of Catholic feminism have already seceded. Women-Church Convergence, for example, was a largely Catholic movement that grew steadily more radical over its first two meetings, in 1983 and 1987. By its third conference, held in 1993 in Albuquerque, New Mexico, Women-Church appeared to have abandoned anything resembling traditional Roman Catholicism except, perhaps, its taste for ritual, now transposed into an inventive New Age key. Over thirty different services were planned for Sunday morning, including goddess worship, a Native American pipe service, Sufi dancing, a Holocaust remembrance, and a Quaker meeting—but no Catholic Mass. A proposal to include one had been rejected by the planners, a coalition of Catholic feminist groups, who instead provided a "Catholic-rooted feminist liturgy."

The conference's literature clearly presented Women-Church as rooted in Christianity but not committed to remaining Christian. The rituals and prayers held in common were "focused on an undefined deity," as Catherine Walsh, a reporter present, put it. "That deity dwells within women, heals and empowers them. There was little talk about Jesus Christ." I interviewed two conference leaders, both prominent in Catholic feminism. One, an activist clearly nervous about Women-Church's image, described the meeting's emphasis on figures like Mary, Jesus' mother, and Mary Magdalene in almost pious terms. Her description fit what feminists in other circumstances have mocked as "Add women and mix." In contrast, the other leader, a theologian, spoke directly of a shift in the locus of salvation, from the male figure on the cross to the women at the foot of the cross and the saving community they formed. "We cannot back away from the relation between the movement and the Catholic or Christian tradition," she told me, but "this weekend we have begged the question of Jesus." Although normally identifying herself as a Catholic, during the conference she drew laughter from participants when she said. "The church I come from—and I emphasize *from*—is the Roman Catholic church."

In my interview, the activist was describing a modest feminist expansion of the familiar Christian story; the theologian was describing a basic rewriting of the story. I recall wondering if I was being treated to the good cop/bad cop routine. I looked from one to the other and pressed them, unsuccessfully, about whether they were really saying the same thing.

These kinds of questions occur not only to male interlopers like myself. In 1993 and on other occasions they have also been raised by a few Catholic feminists, but usually quietly and "within the family." That some Catholic feminist theology might pass well beyond even a renegotiated border of Catholicism is not really surprising, given the circumstances and diversity of the movement and the pressures it feels. Catholic feminists may not want to make that problem their chief priority these days, but others are not unreasonable in being concerned. To treat all such concerns as baseless or even as witch-hunting is disingenuous, and only fuels the suspicion of some conservatives that all Catholic feminist thought is a seamless piece, ultimately inimical to the faith.

The second factor complicating the way Catholic feminist theology affects the church's choices is, for all the talk of women's experience, its distance from a great many Catholic women in the pews. The

Women-Church conference was a striking, almost poignant example. The twenty-five hundred participants were in fact largely white, middle class, and in their fifties and sixties—gray hair predominated. They were also largely Catholic, although when asked about the latter, a conference planner declared, "We refuse to use the terms 'Catholic' and 'non-Catholic' in discussing what kind of conference this is. The word 'Catholic' in this context denotes religious imperialism." Sensitized to complaints about majority hegemony, the planners had structured the gathering not along the lines of religious pluralism but of the ethnic and sexual multiculturalism familiar in academia. In keeping with the "woman's" imagery of sewing and weaving, the conference was organized according to six "threads": Hispanic, Native American, African-American, Asian-American, Euro-American, and lesbian-bisexual. Women were encouraged to bring drums from home, and there was a great deal of pounding and chanting, and fun was had by all. Indeed, many participants had come less for theological content than to experience the Southwest's mix of cultures or reunite with old friends from feminist struggles or church-based efforts to aid the victims of social problems.

During an excruciating closing session, one minority participant after another angrily listed the indignities and injustices she or her group had suffered at the conference. Not all of this was fair. Some smacked of the ritualized assertions of victim status and attacks on the majority that in the sixties became a destructive tool of jousting for power within left-wing groups. But there was a cruel truth in this backlash against the planners' assumption that their refusal of self-definition equaled inclusiveness. As Catherine Walsh later wrote about the gathering, what the planners saw as "investigating, practicing, and evaluating other traditions so that what results is a new synthesis of religious experience," many minority participants saw as "the tendency of the dominant culture to expropriate exotic aspects of their spiritualities." It all came to a head, Walsh continued, "during the final session when a Native American told white women carrying drums, 'Put them down!'"

No doubt the Women-Church gathering was an extreme example. But its allergic reaction to ordinary Catholicism, its fondness for religious smorgasbords, and its attachment to academic political correctness (a shock ran through participants in the 1993 conference when an otherwise applauded minority speaker praised military women who had risked their lives "to free Kuwait"!) taint many other expressions of Catholic feminism just enough to distance them from many Catholic women. This is especially true of those who are not college educated. The education gap is reinforced by a generation gap, a gap widened, it is painful to note, by the strong presence of sisters and former sisters within Catholic feminism.

Even young women sympathetic to the emphasis on God's immanence in feminist theology and not put off by the New Age elements in Catholic feminist practice do not share the intense history of theological battles lived by the Vatican II generation of Catholic women. Nor were they subject to the direct confrontations with church authorities that marked the lives of women religious. If they are married, their views of male-female relations are apt to be different, more shaped by social class, ethnic patterns, and economics than by theology or church authority. If they are employed, as increasingly they are, they encounter both male resistance and receptivity to their skills and hard work, compared to which the situation in the church seems remote and relatively inconsequential. They care about issues bearing on their reproductive lives. They are angered to be told that their daughters cannot be altar servers. But about Jesus' maleness and whether a male savior excludes, they could hardly care less.

These two complications of Catholic feminism—its unreadiness or incapacity to address boundaries and its distance from many Catholic women—hardly mean that the church can afford a complacent attitude in regard to the world-historical movement for women's equality. They do mean that church actions can and should be taken incrementally and with a degree of tentativeness for which

Catholic feminism often displays little patience. On the other hand, actions must be taken. See how this works out in regard to the two concrete issues of language and ordination.

No conflict in American Catholicism today is more unnecessary than the one over gender-neutral language. The issue is not minor. It affects the church's public prayer and scripture translations used in the liturgy, preaching, and hymn lyrics, affects pastoral letters and official texts of all kinds. Social context can turn perfectly acceptable words into affronts as intolerable as the most vulgar and derogatory terms. There is nothing wrong with the word "boy." Used in the segregated South to address an African-American man when "sir" would have been used for a white man, it was as disparaging as "nigger." The insult did not disappear because the user meant no personal harm but was merely conforming to standard usage; the insult was built right into the usage.

The revolution in American race relations has produced other more subtle but no less real changes in language: to speak of someone as a *Negro* writer in the year 2000 rather than a black or African-American writer would carry a different meaning than it would have in 1950. The revolution in women's roles has had comparable effects on language. It is now widely accepted practice to avoid the generic use of "man" and its associated masculine pronouns whenever the alternatives are workable. A host of other words assuming that only men fill certain occupations—"fireman," "policeman," and "businessman," for instance—have given way when alternatives are available, and indeed sometimes the alternatives make more sense, such as "firefighter."

As every writer knows, the matter is not simple. "With a few exceptions (as with *black* and *gay*)," comments the latest edition of *The American Heritage Dictionary* in addressing questions of language and social change, the usage questions raised by the names of ethnic and other groups are socially complicated but linguistically simple. The replacement of one such word by another rarely raises grammatical difficulties or creates ancillary linguistic problems. But gender differences are so extensively and intricately woven into the fabric of the language that efforts to change usage often require a great deal of attentiveness and linguistic ingenuity. So it is not surprising that feminism has had more widespread consequences for questions of usage than any other recent social movement, or that the debate over these issues has been particularly energetic.

Questions of gender and language become thornier still when religion is added to the equation. Now one encounters sacred texts that use terms like "brethren" or traditional translations employing the English language's all-purpose "man" even where the original language uses a word for the generic human different from its word for the male. Now one encounters a commandment against coveting your neighbor's wife that has long been taken to apply equally to your neighbor's husband, although that was not the meaning for the Israelites originally. Should it be translated "spouse"? At the heart of every faith are the names it gives God—names that may be of the greatest significance when part of a ritual formula, such as "I baptize you in the name of the Father and of the Son and of the Holy Spirit."

Catholics, like a number of other religious groups, have distinguished between "horizontal" language, used in prayer, scripture, or hymn lyrics for people, and "vertical" language, used for God. In 1990, the American bishops approved criteria for inclusive language in translations of biblical passages employed in worship. The document recognized increasing sensitivity to exclusive language and the growing sense that words once considered as referring to all humans are increasingly taken as gender-specific and, consequently, exclusive. It also recognized the inaccurate and ungainly results of impromptu efforts to make liturgical language inclusive.

The bishops insisted that biblical translations had to be faithful to the original meaning and to Catholic teachings about God's work in the world and human history. But making liturgical language inclusive where possible was also a legitimate concern. Words like "men," "sons," "brothers," "brethren," "forefathers," and "brotherhood," the bishops say, "today are often understood as referring only to males." Likewise with "he," "his," and "him." "Therefore, these terms should not be used when the reference is meant to be generic," if the truth of scripture can be respected. Where the original languages of scripture uses words denoting human beings rather than males, terms like "person," "people," and "humans" should replace the previous English use of "man." Since many biblical passages already switch inconsistently from "you" singular or plural to "he" or "they," translations can also use "you" or "they" to diminish masculine references.

Adaptation of scriptural texts for public worship is not new, the bishops note; the church has long eliminated verses from psalms "which were judged to be inappropriate in a given culture or liturgical context." In an accompanying set of principles for preparing biblical passages for use in the Mass readings, the bishops specifically call for phrases to be put into the plural or changed from the third person singular to the second person "when it does not affect the meaning"; for the Greek translated "brethren" or "brothers" to be translated "brothers and sisters" whenever scholars feel the context "includes women as well as men"; and for inclusive words to replace exclusive ones whenever "the context includes women as well as men" and "the meaning of the text would not be altered." Inclusive language was not, incidentally, the bishops' only concern. The same guidelines also reaffirm that the blanket expression "the Jews" in the gospel of John should be translated as "the Jewish authorities" or, depending on the context, other appropriate phrases that reduce the danger of fostering anti-Semitic attitudes.

The bishops' stance on inclusive language is obviously a moderate one, with a very cautious approach to vertical language for God.

"Great care should be taken in translations of the names of God and in the use of pronouns referring to God," they write. "While it would be inappropriate to attribute gender to God as such, the revealed word of God consistently uses a masculine reference for God." They do allow "it may sometimes be useful" to repeat the word "God" or "Lord" rather than multiply masculine pronouns. "But care must be taken that the repetition not become tiresome."

The traditional designation of the persons of the Trinity as Father, Son, and Holy Spirit is not to be altered. (Some feminists have proposed substituting formulas like "Creator, Redeemer, and Sanctifier," or "Creator, Liberator, and Advocate.") Old Testament passages that did not refer to divinity for the Israelites but that Christians link to Christ should not lose the masculine references that make that link clear. Even in regard to horizontal language, the bishops want the sex of individuals in narratives or parables retained (not that anyone has proposed a parable of the prodigal daughter, but there are other cases where change might be possible), and while they honor "the perceived need for a more inclusive language," they recognize that there is no mechanical solution that eliminates the need for translators to exercise good sense and good taste. "Such language must not distract hearers from prayer and God's revelation. It must manifest a sense of linguistic refinement. It should not draw attention to itself. . . . The church expects for its translations not only accuracy but facility and beauty of expression."

Translation is, of course, an immensely complex matter—especially when it involves language that carries a lifetime of memories and associations as well as spiritual authority. To avoid masculine pronouns like "he" or "him" by recasting phrases in the plural can dissipate the force of a statement or image into a vague "they." Partisans of different Bible translations, old or new, can volley back and forth almost endlessly instances of odd, clumsy, or downright inaccurate wording. The bishops wisely urge a passage by passage approach to inclusive language rather than a flat rule. Their moderation has not spared them rejection in Rome, however.

IN 2001, WITH *Liturgiam Authenticam,* the Vatican effectively vetoed over a decade of work approved by English-speaking bishops'
conferences around the world on liturgical prayers and texts. Ironically, a major thrust of this work had been to restore a more elevated,
religiously charged language—more traditional and even churchy, if
you will—to the texts that had been hurriedly translated into a
rather prosaic and everyday vernacular following the Council. Conservatives were not satisfied, however, and not all their criticisms of
this or that phrase were off target. But clearly, inclusive language,
which the newly approved texts had adopted along with an otherwise more formal, solemn tone, was an underlying issue. Any concessions to inclusive language are viewed as a beachhead of a
manipulative feminist elite that will ultimately gut the Christian
faith itself.

The conflict is not limited to special sensitivities involved in biblical translation or theologically subtle liturgical formulas. The English translation of the Catechism of the Catholic Church was
delayed for two years because of differences primarily over inclusive
language. An inclusive-language translation, undertaken under the
patronage of Cardinal Bernard Law of Boston, hardly a radical feminist, was junked at the last moment, and a new version produced
from scratch. The opening sentences of the Prologue, following the
subhead "The Life of Man—To Know and Love God," are practically a parody, as ungrammatical and awkward as the horrible
examples of inclusive-language prose frequently skewered: "God,
infinitely perfect and blessed in himself, in a plan of sheer goodness
freely created man to make him share in his own blessed life. For this
reason, at every time and in every place, God draws close to man. He
calls him to seek him, to know him, to love him with all his
strength."

Run through that again, noting what my sixth-grade teacher, Sister Mary Jerome, would have underlined in red as pronouns with

confusing antecedents: "God ... freely created man to make *him* [man] share in *his* [God's] own blessed life. For this reason ... God draws close to man. *He* [God] calls *him* [man] to seek *him* [God], to know *him* [God], to love *him* [God] with all *his* [man's] strength." Obviously, one standard regarding clarity and grace is utilized for judging inclusive language, and another for traditional masculine generics.

It is this kind of flagrant example that grates on the hearing not just of feminist activists but a much wider percentage of Catholic women and Catholics generally. My strong impression is that, by and large, most Catholic women do not feel excluded by the masculine nouns or pronouns for God in Trinitarian formulas or established prayers, and at least some poll data support this impression. Most Catholic women do not want to pray, "Our Father-Mother," however exhilarating some women may find it. They do not want to repeat "God" and "God's" in order to eliminate every "him" and "his" in the Mass prayers, the psalms, or other biblical readings, let alone to eliminate every "Lord," a term some feminist sentries have branded as connoting hierarchy and domination as well as maleness.

I have friends who do all these things, either loudly or quietly, because they have convinced themselves that it is essential to their dignity and the future of women in the church. They have sensitized themselves to hear every "his" as an affront. But they are not representative. For most women, it is the horizontal language that is excluding. No, the word "brothers" does not include them as "brothers and sisters" does; and while I suspect that the abstract "man" is not bothersome to most in traditional translations like "What is man, that thou art mindful of him?" (Psalm 8:5, which most recent translations have stumbled over with "a human being" or "humans"), something is not right about praying in the Nicene Creed that Jesus came down from heaven "for us men and our salvation." (A great many priests simply drop the "men" and stick with "us.") When "man" and "all men" and masculine pronouns are brandished like battle flags, as in the Catechism of the Catholic Church, or when inclusive language can be so easily adopted but isn't, it seems nothing less than a deliberate slap in the face.

This still leaves the important question of naming and imaging God. The bishops' caution is justified, especially given the volatility and fluidity of feminist theology and its distance from many Catholic women. But again incremental steps responding to feminist concerns are in view. One of those concerns was famously expressed by Mary Daly in the slogan "If God is male, the male is God." Daly is, of course, a founding mother of feminist theology, whose trajectory from Catholicism to an aggressive post-Christian stance presents a particular challenge to Catholic feminist theology.

Her slogan suffers from the same weakness as much else in her work. It is theatrical hyperbole and effective provocation. It highlights the reality-shaping power of language and imagery. Unfortunately, taken literally, the slogan collapses. Language does indeed shape the rest of reality, but the rest of reality also reshapes language. As long as males—or kings—hold godlike power, with the blessing of religion, then the metaphor retains its force. Once they lose that kind of nearly absolute power (despite its religious aura), the metaphor also loses its near-literal force. If God is king, the king is God? If God is judge, the judge is God?

Literalism does infect some strands of religious feminism and it influences many who would not avow it but who frequently treat virtually all male imagery as an enemy to be expunged. The opposition to "Lord" is one example; another is the conviction that even "kingdom" must be excised and "rule" or "reign" or even less monarchical images substituted. All revolutions have such aspects. The French Revolution had its phase when the calendar was revised and days and months renamed to propagandize the Revolution's ideals and extinguish France's traditional habits. These scorched-earth policies are bound to fail from grassroots resistance if not from sheer silliness.

If the church wants to remind a world undergoing a basic change in women's roles that God is beyond gender and the divine equally present to women and men, it need not, in fact cannot, simply banish its patriarchal inheritance so much as overcome it. It need not expunge masculine language and imagery for God so much as unmistakably to break their monopoly. As many Catholic feminist thinkers have argued, the key step is not to abolish the masculine language and imagery but to enlarge it very deliberately with feminine language and imagery that can be legitimately retrieved from the admittedly patriarchal sources. Folk Catholicism has done this in its own way with its celebration of Mary the Mother of God over the centuries. Feminist thought has had to grapple with the ambiguities of this celebration: its image of Mary was often one of abnegation; Marian doctrines and devotions have usually had a strong conservative cast; and they have created a barrier to ecumenism. But the feminine image, language, and feeling of Marian celebration, ambiguities and all, can hardly be ignored, given its place in tradition and especially its importance to Latino Catholics.

Much as it runs against the grain of many liberal Catholics (I include myself), a devotional and theological focus on Mary will be an important part of a viable and vital American Catholicism in the next century. Mary, however, will always be properly distinct from the Godhead, and the more directly pertinent resource for breaking the masculine monopoly on God language and imagery is the tradition of Wisdom, the female personification of God's creative presence and activity, found in the Old Testament scriptures and drawn upon by early Christians in their efforts to articulate the divinity of Jesus. This retrieval must be undertaken with a good deal of theological discipline. Already the biblical texts and images of personified Wisdom, *Sophia* in the Greek and a conveniently recognizable woman's name, have been seized upon by some religious feminists to approximate a goddess. Yet it is interesting that the American bishops, in their 1990 statement on inclusive-language translations for worship, singled out the wisdom literature's relevance in a warning that feminine imagery in scripture "should not be obscured or replaced by the use of masculine imagery in English translations," as has often happened.

IN 1965, WHEN THE Vatican Council closed, the idea of female priests was unthinkable to all but the tiniest fraction of American Catholics. Today, over 60 percent favor the idea, and for many of them the church's unwillingness to ordain women priests contradicts its own declared belief in the equality of all and the right of all to full participation in the church's life.

That change in opinion has occurred despite a quarter century of Vatican and papal pronouncements escalating in the apparent finality with which they limited the priesthood to men. Some people have thought the change has occurred not despite but because of the papal insistence. My own impressions support that. Many female friends, acquaintances, and relatives had not only never thought of themselves as potential priests; they had little or no interest in the whole question of ordaining women—until, that is, they felt the sting of Vatican declarations.* Perhaps the first bump in Pope John Paul II's relationship to American Catholicism came during his 1979 trip to the United States when he was welcomed in Washington by Sister Theresa Kane, the elected representative of women's religious orders, with a plea that the church consider including women "in all the sacred ministries." Her remark was applauded. The pope reacted with icy firmness—and made sure, upon returning to Rome, that she was officially rebuked.

No one doubts why, throughout the church's history, women have not been judged eligible for ordination: they were considered constitutionally inferior to men, either ritually impure or morally and psychologically weak, at the very least disqualified for leadership. Those reasons are not sustainable today, and the church has admitted as much. It remains possible that the church has done the right thing for

*After the Vatican issued *Inter Insignores* in 1976, declaring that scripture and tradition barred the ordination of women, one theologian noted that the old slogan *Roma locuta, causa finita*—"Rome has spoken, the matter is settled"—had become *Roma locuta, causa stimulata!*

the wrong reasons, or that the wrong reasons were in reality exaggerated or distorted versions of the right reasons. That, in effect, is part of the church's current position. Women are disqualified specifically from priestly leadership not because they are constitutionally inferior but because they are constitutionally *different.*

That is the linchpin of a three-part argument. First, the church cannot ordain women because its unbroken tradition, which it believes to enjoy the guidance of the Holy Spirit, has extended ordination only to men. Tradition is indeed crucial in Catholic theology, but obviously not everything that the church has done over the long stretch of its history—such as condoning slavery—can be considered to have been guided by the Holy Spirit. Tradition, furthermore, cannot be understood as entirely independent of scripture, which provides a critical norm against which the church must measure its understanding of tradition.

Therefore the argument moves to the second part, the claim that "the will of Christ"—that only men should be ordained—was demonstrated by the gospel record that Jesus called only men as his twelve apostles. Critics question the connection between calling the twelve, who symbolized the twelve tribes of a renewed Israel, and the priesthood, which emerged in a distinct form only gradually over the first centuries. Even more importantly, critics ask whether Jesus' choice of men for these positions of leadership, rather than revealing some essential relationship between priestly leadership and maleness, simply reflected the cultural setting in which he was acting. He had, after all, also only chosen circumcised Palestinian Jews; yet no one reads some unalterable significance about priestly leadership into that. On the contrary, wasn't the nascent Christian movement soon to extend its renewed Israel to uncircumcised gentiles and gentile leadership?

The church's official response has been that we know Jesus' choice was not a cultural limitation, a historical artifact, or even an alterable religious symbol like circumcision. It was indicative of an unalterable, essential relationship because, in a larger theological understanding of Christian priesthood, the priest must act, especially in presiding at the Eucharist, *in persona Christi*—literally, "in the person of Christ"—and that to do so the priest must be male.

This answer, of course, gives rise to fresh questions. What exactly does *in persona Christi* mean? "As a representative of Christ"? "As a representation"? "An image"? "An icon"? Each formulation implies some shift in meaning. Is this way of describing the priest's role singular in the church's tradition, or accompanied by others? Is it a minor theme now enlisted because the arguments from women's inferiority have become an embarrassment? Does the priest at the altar and elsewhere truly act *in persona Christi,* or *in persona ecclesiae* (in the person of the church), or both: *in persona Christi et ecclesiae?* Does the priest act *in persona Christi* because he is acting *in persona ecclesiae,* or does he act *in persona ecclesiae* because he is acting *in persona Christi?*

And what does all this have to do with maleness? As one defender of the church's position has stated, "It is far from obvious today that to act in persona Christi requires some gender qualification." The church has spoken of the necessity for a "natural resemblance" between Christ and the priest, an explanation that struck many as either vague (height? hirsuteness? pitch of voice? Semitic features?) or euphemistic. Does a chubby, bald, blue-eyed, red-faced, bibulous, weak-willed, and irritable seventy-year-old man display more of such a "natural resemblance" than a fit, dark-haired, brown-eyed, olive-skinned, strong-minded, eloquent, and compassionate woman of thirty-five? If so, it may be crude but unavoidable to ask, isn't "natural resemblance" just a euphemistic way of saying "possessing a penis"? No wonder that this phrase "natural resemblance" has faded from the argument.

Instead the church has explained the necessary link between Christ, priestly leadership, and maleness in terms of the Bible's gender-based spousal imagery describing the church as bride and Christ as bridegroom. In this explication of the role of priest, acting in the name of Christ is given priority over acting in the name of the church. But even the emphasis on this one set of spousal symbols does not settle the matter of maleness. Men are subsumed under the symbol of the church as bride; why cannot women likewise take the role of the symbolic bridegroom, Christ? Again, the church has an answer. It does not turn on superficial physical resemblance or attributes but on the more fundamental nature of masculinity and femininity, which rests on bodily realities, yes, but with thoroughgoing psychological and spiritual dimensions. This is the famous (or infamous) principle of male-female "complementarity." By nature, humans are equal but they are also deeply gendered. God created humans male and female; and both, in their difference as well as in their similarity, reflect God's image. Humans are born male and female, in families of male and female. Given the different roles of men and women in human reproduction and nurturance, evolution has favored different traits as predominant in males and females.

In this vision of complementarity, as expounded by its defenders, the structuring of human experience by the categories of male and female, although expressed quite variously in different times and places, is inevitable: it is grounded in the body, biology, and family— across cultures and history. Relative to each other, the masculine is initiating and active; the feminine, receptive and passive or (in a concession to contemporary views) "actively" passive. In the marriage between God and Israel, between Christ and the church, the masculine is the most appropriate symbol of initiating divine love and the feminine of responding people and church. The sex that has the symbolic charge of masculinity, not because of genitals but because of a much deeper structuring of embodied human experience, is the one that appropriately acts *in persona Christi.*

EVERY STEP OF THIS argument has been contested, defended, elaborated, reviewed, rebutted, and restated in countless historical studies and theological polemics. The nonspecialist—overwhelmed, frustrated, or just skeptical about obscure references and subtle distinctions—may be tempted to dismiss the whole debate. In fact it has shed light on important questions not only about priesthood but about the Eucharist and other sacraments, interpreting biblical symbols and metaphors, and the very nature of the church.

At the same time, one has to ask why the church's position has proved so unconvincing to masses of American Catholics? Admittedly, only a few have been exposed to the details of the case; that is the way with theology. But most have encountered its conclusions along with the drift of the supporting argument, solemnly declared by the highest authority in support of a familiar practice and in opposition to a rather dramatic change. Yet neither these authoritative pronouncements nor an instinctual conservatism in religious matters have prevented a rapid swing in Catholic opinion.

One reason, of course, is that older Catholics have grown accustomed to the idea of changes in practices that they never expected would be altered—Mass in Latin, no meat on Friday, no handling of the consecrated host—and younger Catholics have never been inculcated with the idea of a church beyond change. Another reason may be the practical concern about a growing priest shortage, although ordaining married men would seem like a solution at hand requiring a much less drastic break with Catholic tradition. But obviously the issue of women's equality looms large. Catholics are simply less and less able to accept the church's insistence that its refusal to ordain women is completely consistent with its teachings on the equality of men and women and on the calling of all the baptized to full, active participation in the church.

What the world-historical movement for women's equality has done, along with the Vatican Council's recognition of the "priesthood" of all the baptized, is to shift the burden of proof. The emergence of female leaders in all areas of life has transformed the question for average Catholics from "Why women priests?" to "Why *not* women priests?" Even the best-made arguments will not get a hearing if they appear self-serving, overly subtle, and blind to patriarchal biases riddling Christian tradition.

The question of ordination, church authorities have repeatedly declared, is not a question of power but of faithfulness to God's will; indeed, they have frequently chastised feminists for supposedly being unduly focused on power. Yet ordination remains, for the most part, the key to decision-making power in the church. Where women hold decision-making positions, they almost always do so at the will of ordained men and often only because ordained men are in short supply. As long as this is the case, even the best case for ordaining only men will look self-serving.

Likewise, under current circumstances, complex theological reasoning about biblical imagery or *in persona Christi* is doomed to read like elaborate rationalization for the status quo. Years ago I came across (and alas, did not save) a satiric brochure produced by a British group supporting women's ordination. It was titled something like *Why Men Should Be Ordained to the Priesthood*. It was written on the premise that men were barred from ordination; and as I recall, it gravely tried to rebut all the obvious indications of male unfitness (notorious insensitivity, aggressiveness, promiscuity, bad biblical precedents, historic failures of male leadership, and so on). It wittily demonstrated how the debate could be turned on its head once a different status quo and starting point were assumed.

Indeed, the biblical imagery and symbolism cited to support a males-only priesthood have a fluid and multivalent character. Exactly how they are interpreted and deployed, whether they are taken literally or figuratively, can seem dictated by the present practice and by social attitudes that undergo change. When official statements say that the faithful must be able to perceive the priest as a sign of Christ "with ease" or that that such an image of Christ "would be difficult to see" if the priest were not male, they have to be recognized as judgments about a particular cultural moment rather than an unchanging reality. Were the church to have ordained women priests long ago, it is hard to imagine that it would not be living comfortably with the very same imagery, symbols, and assumptions about men and women—adjusted, of course, but no less compelling.

One can easily imagine the arguments that might then be made.

Complementarity of the sexes, for example, might be said to *require* both men and women as priests rather than limit priesthood to one sex. The spousal imagery of church as bride and Christ as bridegroom, it might then be noted, should provide for women alongside men on the bridegroom (Christ/priest) half of the symbol no less than it recognizes men alongside women on the bride (church) half of the symbol.

Instead of delineating male-female difference, spousal imagery might simply stress an intimacy, union, and interdependence in divine-human love that would be incongruous with excluding one sex from priesthood. Were women priests already the reality, wouldn't the church be citing other scriptural references as keys to understanding priesthood, spousal imagery, or representation of Christ: the role of the Blessed Virgin, the role of the women in accompanying Jesus in death and as first witnesses to his resurrection, the role of other women in the early church?

Finally, until opponents of ordaining women really appear to have grasped how deeply patriarchal assumptions are imbedded in inherited institutions and in Christianity itself and how much modernity has altered traditional constraints on women's lives, Catholics will remain unimpressed by the church's case. Catholic feminists may be overly quick to reject all notions of male-female complementarity out of hand, flying in the face of a good bit of evolutionary theory, biology, psychology, primatology, and anthropology. But given the abuses of complementarity as a way of legitimating female subjection, there is every reason to be suspicious of any such notion unless it arrives accompanied by a full awareness of its sorry history and a convincing strategy for not repeating it.

IN REGARD TO WOMEN, Catholicism is at a very strange juncture. Although only a small fraction of Catholic women are interested in the priesthood personally, ordination has become a key symbol of the church's attitude toward women. For Catholicism in the United

States, Europe, and a swelling proportion of formerly traditional populations elsewhere, the restriction of Catholic priesthood (and leadership) to men will become increasingly anomalous.

At the same time, to ordain women would be a major departure for a church that takes faithfulness to tradition with the utmost seriousness. Continuity with the apostolic age guards against conformity with our own. Not only that. The papacy has weighed in heavily against ordaining women. Pope John Paul II, as though determined to tie the hands of his successors or of a future council, has stopped just short of declaring the issue irreformable. Whatever questions may be raised about this exercise of authority, it cannot be taken lightly.

Is this the familiar meeting of irresistible force and immovable object? There are three possible outcomes: Women will be ordained, or the church will render its teaching convincing, or Catholic commitment to equality and justice for half the human race will be in doubt.

Ultimately I believe women will be ordained. The arguments against it strike me as wanting. If the ordination of women occurs in conjunction with the massive entry of women into leadership positions in specific cultures, I believe that in those cultures women priests will appear so natural and in continuity with Catholic tradition that people will quickly wonder what all the fuss was about.

That is also the judgment of many thoughtful Catholics. Yet given the weight of tradition and authority on the other side, we should be willing to proceed step by step, testing whether the church's position on ordination can be rendered convincingly consistent with its teaching on women's equality and on the full participation of all the baptized in the life of the church.

What does testing the church's position imply? Obviously it means setting aside any idea that the ordination of women is a question beyond theological exploration. To forbid discussion of a church practice is a virtual admission that it cannot withstand scrutiny. More substantively, as I have already suggested, testing the position means seeing whether it is supported by clear arguments that do not beg the question or rely on the status quo for their persuasiveness. It also means relying only on biblical interpretations and notions of complementarity that show themselves disinfected of patriarchal assumptions and immunized against abuses. The premise "equal but different" has too much bad history to expect anything less.

Finally, it means showing that even without ordination to the priesthood women can be given central public roles and decision-making positions in the church. If they cannot, the church's limitation of priesthood to men will not escape the judgment that, despite all the protests to the contrary, the restriction is merely a way of preserving a bastion of male power. There are three clear ways in which women can be give this kind of role and authority: by extending their presence in administrative, theological, and liturgical positions; by ordaining them deacons; and by increasing decision making by the laity generally, both women and men.

Currently women do serve as diocesan chancellors, marriage tribunal members, seminary professors, parish administrators where priests are unavailable, and especially directors of religious education. Women have visible liturgical roles as lectors, Eucharistic ministers, and cantors. Much more can be done along these lines. And the positions women now occupy must be given greater permanence and symbolic recognition, indicating that they are not there simply as a man's deputy or because no priest is available. Invidious distinctions should be removed from church law—for example, the provision allowing both men and women to serve as lectors at Mass but only men to be formally "installed" as such.

A further possibility, much discussed, is the ordination of women not to the priesthood but to the permanent diaconate. That would allow women to proclaim the gospel and preach at Mass as well as witness marriages, baptize, perform funeral and burial rites (although not funeral Masses) and other services like distribution of ashes on Ash Wednesday. They could counsel, catechize, and oversee charitable works. As clergy, they would be attached to a bishop and could form their own councils or join with those of the priests. As individuals they could participate in parish, diocesan, and even national decision making on questions of teaching and practice considered the province of clergy, not laity. With less of a jolt to current procedures and concepts, outstanding deacons, and women in particular, could be named cardinals, serving as papal electors and advisers.

Women deacons—or deaconesses—are found in the New Testament and functioned into the fourth century or so in the Western church and even longer in the East. Their exact role and the nature of their ordination is surrounded by historical debate. Their role, which often pertained specifically to other women in the church, was surely different than it would be today; yet their ordination rites were quite parallel to those of male deacons, who have been acknowledged as members of the clergy. The precedent for ordaining women deacons to a position in the clergy like that of today's permanent deacons seems more than ample, if the church had the will. The case has become all the stronger as the debate about ordaining men or women to the priesthood has come to center, not on older assumptions of female inferiority, but on the priest's Eucharistic role and, secondarily, his role in the remission of sins, neither of which is at issue for deacons.

Women's participation in the public life and decision making of the church also depends on the scope of such participation by all laypeople, men and women. In daily life, laypeople *are* the face and hands of the church understood as the people of God. Within the institution as well, from the national conference of bishops to local diocesan and parish staffs, laypeople, many of them women, serve as experts and managers. Participation in decision making is very real wherever bishops are dependent on the expertise, dedication, and numbers that only laypeople have, although these laypeople usually remain answerable to a layer of priests at the very top; and the bishops (and Rome) always retain the final word. Participation is much more iffy on all the councils where laypeople serve not as experts but as *representatives;* all these bodies remain advisory and can be ignored or treated perfunctorily by the clergy. It will take considerably more evolution of lay roles in church decision making to convince Catholics that women are truly represented there, despite being barred from priesthood.

It is not impossible, however. And if the current demand for priestly ordination arises primarily from the concern that without such ordination women remain excluded from real decision-making power and from real opportunities to exercise their spiritual gifts in the church, then finding other ways to extend that power and those opportunities—increasing women's numbers in visible administrative, educational, and liturgical offices; opening (or reopening) the diaconate to them; and turning over significant decision making to laity of both sexes—should answer the demand. With women preaching and prominent in sacramental roles outside of the Eucharist, with women shaping administrative decisions and seminary education, with women among the cardinals heading Vatican offices and electing popes, Catholics might well conclude that reserving the priesthood to males was only a symbolic division of labor, resonant perhaps with some deep-seated psychic way of structuring experience, rather than a gender-based hierarchy of power. Liberated not only from the repudiated belief in women's inferiority but from any suspicion of rationalizing a male monopoly of ecclesiastical governance, the tradition might possibly be reaffirmed as consistent with the church's and the culture's commitment to women's equality. This may not be the outcome that seems most likely, or most logical, to me; but the life of the church is something organic that must be tested in practice—"By their fruits you shall know them"—and not only by logic and likelihood.

ROME, UNFORTUNATELY, HAS been moving in the opposite direction. One exception was the papal decree allowing females to become altar servers assisting the priest during Mass and other ceremonies, and even this decree was so fiercely opposed by some traditionalists that it still left bishops and pastors the option of permitting males alone. Otherwise, Vatican instructions have warned against many developments that promise to give women liturgical prominence and access to decision making at the risk of diminishing the distinction between priest and laity generally, and the Vatican has specifically dismissed possibilities like restoring the female diaconate. Conservative Catholics in the United States have strongly supported these measures.

The reasons for this resistance are not mysterious. To many current church leaders, expanding women's roles is the very step that could make ordaining women to the priesthood more thinkable—and not ordaining them less tolerable. These officials and their supporters know that serving Mass has been the experience that led many a boy to consider the priesthood and will likely spark the same idea in girls. They know the risk involved in seeing women not only read from the pulpit, distribute Communion, and handle the altar vessels, as is currently done, but also preach at Mass, officiate at marriages, and bury the dead, as deacons do. These officials and their supporters worry about the effect of laywomen being prominently recognized as sharing in the church's decision making. Won't all this simply accustom Catholics to the idea of women serving as priests on the altar and in the deliberations of the church?

Of course, these worried church leaders are right. But their worry reveals a circularity in their position. On the one hand, they insist that maleness is essential to the Christ-priest connection because the symbol must be seen "with ease" and "would be difficult to see" if the priest were female, while the male priest is a "natural sign . . . imprinted on the human psychology." On the other hand, they fear that with a little acclimatization, Catholics may all too easily see the image of Christ in a woman priest—and therefore must be kept from anything approaching that. How can they have it both ways? Either they have little confidence in their own argument about what is "imprinted" and what is easy or difficult to see or they have little confidence that Catholics' perceptions and psychology are not now so thoroughly corrupted that they can no longer register what is "natural" or obvious.

If the church's case against ordaining women to the priesthood is valid, it should withstand the test of Catholics' becoming familiar with women ordained to the diaconate and women holding positions of real decision-making power. Those are conditions that could possibly demonstrate the church's tradition of an all-male priesthood to be compatible with women's equality and full participation in the church. And if the demonstration still falls short, the church would have at least tested its tradition and prepared itself, theologically and psychologically, to take the logical step and ordain women.

AT PRESENT, THE CATHOLIC Church's official stances on sexual morality and on the role of women constitute a form of Catholic fundamentalism. Fundamentalism is a modern phenomenon. It is a defensive reaction to threatening change. It reflects the fear—and by no means a groundless one—that a whole tradition might be swept away or drastically denatured unless protected by an unambiguous line or a nonnegotiable principle. When major segments of American Protestantism recoiled from the threat of liberal theology and evolutionary science, that line and that principle centered on the literal reading of an authoritative scripture. Any departure from a literal understanding of, say, the six days of creation threatened to open the floodgates to all kinds of biblical reinterpretation. The Catholic Church has tried to do something similar. One might argue that the condemnation of contraception rests on a rather literal reading of the functions of sexual organs and sexual intimacy. But more important, the insistence that the procreative possibilities of sexual intercourse may never be deliberately impeded is viewed as the crucial barrier against a massive abandonment of Catholicism's sexual wisdom. Likewise, by refusing concessions to gender-neutral language, to ordaining women even as deacons, or to admitting them into real decision-making offices, church leaders believe they are protecting

Catholicism against a full-scale examination and critique of its patriarchal dimensions.

Unfortunately, the bright lines and absolute principles of fundamentalist reaction seldom prove to be as unambiguous or immutable as hoped. Maintaining these defenses always consumes tremendous amounts of spiritual energy, intellectual credibility, and institutional authority, inevitably diverted from engaging rather than staving off new ideas and historical shifts. And yet these defenses prove to be brittle and inflexible bulwarks that eventually collapse before the pressures of change or are outflanked by them. The field is then open for precisely those massive losses that fundamentalism most feared. For Catholicism, that is what has already happened in regard to sex, and is on the verge of happening in regard to women.

Chapter Eight

＋————————————————————＋

At the Helm

T HE leadership throughout American Catholicism is changing. Nothing can stop that. Leadership by priests and nuns
is giving way to leadership by laypeople. Leadership by
Catholics formed in the very different, tightly bounded, highly defined Catholicism that flourished before Vatican II is giving way to
leadership formed in the vibrant, open, rapidly changing, and often
unstable Catholicism introduced by the Council. The negotiation of
these intersecting transitions—and their long-range consequences
for the twenty-first century—is what the next decade or two of
American Catholicism is all about.

Yet there is one peculiarity about this change of leadership—
bishops. The very top level of American Catholic leadership, the
level with major responsibility for negotiating the transformation
now under way, is relatively removed from it. When many organizations change leadership at the top, one can expect that change to be
reflected through the ranks. In other cases, when change takes place
at the grass roots or in middle management, it soon works its way, often with pushing and shoving, to the top.

The Catholic Church is different. Bishops are appointed by Rome,
and at present with a very free hand. They can be unrepresentative
of broad changes taking place among the nation's faithful and even

among its clergy. Bishops are also appointed to serve until they are seventy-five, which can introduce a serious lag between changes in the church generally and changes in the hierarchy. Finally, the power of bishops to shape even the middle-level leadership below them has remained nearly absolute in principle but has become constricted in practice. Their power to name pastors, for example, is total; yet they must recruit pastors from the shrinking pool of ordained celibates. As the number of priests and nuns decreases, and as more and more responsibilities fall to lay men and women working for parishes or other Catholic institutions, ambiguities about the relationship of the bishops to this growing lay category of Catholic leadership have become pressing.

The year 2002 was not a good one for Catholic bishops in the United States. January began with charges that Cardinal Bernard Law of Boston had failed to take actions to protect children and teenagers from sexually predatory priests. After the deaths of Cardinal Bernardin in 1996 and Cardinal O'Connor in 2000—and probably even earlier—Law had become the most powerful figure in the American hierarchy, able to have his auxiliary bishops named heads of dioceses throughout the country and frequently serving as the conduit of Vatican orders for the American hierarchy. Throughout 2002 similar charges were being made against bishops in every region of the country, until it seemed as if the entire hierarchy were implicated in a pattern of neglect, complicity, secrecy, and callousness. By June, when the bishops met in Dallas to approve a stringent common policy for dealing with priests who abused minors, Catholics were seething at their leaders and ready to see any number of them replaced. Bishop Wilton D. Gregory of Belleville, Illinois, the elected president of the United States Conference of Catholic Bishops, spoke repeatedly in his presidential address of "failures in our leadership," bluntly employing the language Catholics use in confessing their sins.

The Dallas meeting did not put to rest complaints about episcopal leadership. Although Gregory and many bishops acknowledged the hierarchy's responsibility for the sex abuse scandal, they had neither the authority to compel any resignations—only Rome could do that—nor the will to publicly demand them. So now they were seen as picking on accused priests, some long-ago offenders, while saving their own skins.

By November, when the bishops gathered again, this time in Washington, they had engaged in a complicated dance with Vatican officials over revising their Dallas policy. The revised version appeared to mollify complaints from priests without substantially weakening the policy, although proof of that would come only as the policy went into actual operation. It did not, however, do much to restore the bishops' image, who were now seen as rushing to put the whole sex scandal behind them and return to business as usual. Cardinal Law's reappearance in a prominent role didn't help.

No doubt resignations, Cardinal Law's in particular, would have been cathartic, as in fact his proved to be in December 2002. Less clear is whether resignations would have illuminated the nature of the bishops' failure of leadership. The dynamics of litigation and dramatization by the news media cast that failure largely in very personal terms: heartless bishops had fully recognized the dangers that certain priests posed to youngsters but let those priests carry on unchecked, either to protect the church's reputation or to shield fellow members of the clergy, because these bishops had no respect for complainants, or no concern for victims, or no willingness to entangle themselves in personal or legal conflicts. Some cases pretty clearly fit this pattern. Indeed, several bishops were guilty of sexual molestation themselves.

But most of the failures of leadership were less personal, more systemic, and more indicative of the bishops' leadership problems in general.

There was a failure of comprehension and empathy. During the decade before 1985, when awareness of the extent and seriousness of sexual crimes against minors was growing in American society—a development related both to the surge in sexual candor and to feminism—the bishops stayed locked in psychologically naïve ideas about the predators, the crimes, and the realities of treatment. They managed to remain untouched by new ideas and by the pain of victims and their families.

There was a failure of decisiveness. Between 1985 and 1993, the bishops were confronted with the reality of the sex abuse problem and began to take action locally and nationally. Measured against the inaction of past years, this was progress. Measured against the appalling nature of the abuse—its destructive effect on individual lives, families, parishes, the priesthood, and the whole fabric of trust in the church—this movement by the bishops remained disgracefully slow.

There was a failure of focus. These were years when Rome was pressing for the removal of Father Charles Curran from the Catholic University of America theology faculty for his criticism of official church teaching on contraception and other sexual issues; when the Vatican tried to strip Seattle's maverick archbishop, Raymond Hunthausen, of his powers; when Cardinal Ratzinger forced the American bishops to draw back from their statement on combatting AIDS. Dealing with sexual abuse, in short, was anything but high among Vatican priorities. The American hierarchy was only a little better. There was resistance to open discussion at bishops' meetings, resistance to gathering full data, resistance to any national policy that might impinge on the prerogatives of bishops in their own dioceses.

There was a failure of persistence and follow-through. In June 1992, the bishops had approved five broad guidelines for dioceses to take in dealing with abuse cases—but stopped short of fleshing out the details or trying to make the guidelines mandatory. One year later, the bishops established a special Ad Hoc Committee on Sexual Abuse with a broad mandate to investigate all aspects of the problem and make recommendations to the bishops. Stunned by local scandals, individual bishops like Cardinal Bernardin in Chicago and Archbishop John Roach in St. Paul–Minneapolis established offices to review old and new allegations with the help of experts and laypeople—and other dioceses adopted similar procedures. But collectively the hierarchy still balked at considering a mandatory national policy, collecting accurate data about the cases and their disposition, or embarking on major new research.

There was a failure of openness. The nature of this failure is obscured by terms such as "cover-up," "gag orders," and even "hush money" that have become standard usage in reports of the scandal. Certainly the church did its best to cover up sexual abuse before the mid-eighties, and it quite often had the cooperation of civil authorities, even families of victims and victims themselves. Covering up shameful sexual conduct had long been a social norm, almost always reinforced by organized religion, and the Catholic Church was slower than many other groups to change its ways.

In the last ten to fifteen years, instances of deliberately circumventing established practices—disregarding reporting laws, for instance, or prevailing on families or police to keep something off the books—became rarer. But the problem of lack of openness did not go away. The new failure was in not aggressively informing Catholics and the public of wrongdoing even when neither the law nor habit nor the average parishioner in the pews was really demanding this information. Priests with credible complaints on their records from decades earlier were usually eased out of active ministry with as little fuss as possible. Bishops could take comfort that sealing settlements and damping down publicity conformed to standard legal practice, moved things along smoothly, and frequently met the needs of the known victims—but not, of course, unknown ones.

Although many diocesan newspapers matter-of-factly reported accusations of current misdeeds, arrests, or trials, few bishops worried about the fact that such spot news items (in papers read by only a fraction of the Catholic population) did little to make sure parishioners knew the full sex abuse story in their own diocese or in the whole country. And why publicly tabulate the sums spent on dealing with clergy sex abuse cases, as long as almost no one was asking? One of the Five Principles endorsed in 1992 was that "within the confines of respect for privacy of the individuals involved," dioceses should "deal as openly as possible with the members of the community." At best, bishops took this as a commitment not to conceal information that would normally be available. Hardly any saw it as a call to provide, proactively, information that would normally not be available. For bishops, the default position was decision making behind closed doors by a small, mostly clerical circle. This was not a departure from the normal; it *was* the normal.

Finally, *there was a failure of explanation.* Bishops were caught off guard by the blizzard of Boston stories in 2002. Within a short time, it was clear that the scandal, even if limited to Boston, would have national consequences, and in fact would not be limited to Boston. By and large, the bishops hunkered down and limited themselves to no doubt heartfelt but very general expressions of sorrow over the crimes committed. There were many efforts to reassure, but few concerted efforts to explain—to inform people proactively of precisely what the church had done and not done, the good and the bad, the old and the new. Where facts were available, they should have been at hand. Where facts were not known, there should have been an emergency rush to discover them or set in place independent inquiries in which people could have confidence. Bishops should have had their communications directors calling the media, not waiting for the media to call (or worse, avoiding the media's calls). The point would not have been damage control (except insofar as truth is damage control) or making the church look good. It would have been to give people, Catholics first of all, what they were owed—an accounting. Instead, on a national level and in too many dioceses locally, for most of three months there was silence or faltering, minimal response. Throughout 2002, the bishops struggled to convince the faithful that they had put in place a nearly foolproof system for preventing a scandal like this from reoccurring, but they had not offered any satisfactory explanation of why this one happened in the first place. Perhaps they had lost the possibility of doing so in those first three months.

THE SEX ABUSE SCANDAL can illuminate the general problems of episcopal leadership, but only if one can get away from the now popular idea of bishops as heedless villains. Of course there are exceptions, but mediocrity, not malevolence, is the more typical episcopal infirmity. And even that needs qualification. Individually, bishops oversee their own dioceses; collectively, they give a national direction to the church. Bishops who are good at the former may be poor at the latter, and vice versa.

It may also be helpful to distinguish between leadership and management. Bishops manage the equivalent of sizable corporations, some manage the equivalent of giant corporations—except that, while not ignoring the bottom line that governs corporations, bishops must operate by quite different and much more complicated standards, and with a completely different understanding of "output" and "product," in allocating resources and handling personnel. Bishops who may be perfectly competent at such management, in the sense of keeping parishes, schools, and a whole range of ministries operating—sometimes a daunting task in the face of financial strains and personnel shortages—may fail at leadership, either locally or nationally, in the sense of foreseeing new challenges and mobilizing energy, creativity, and resources to meet them. Of course the distinction has its limits. Management cannot be successful and ignore the changing environment; leadership cannot ignore the everyday, on-the-ground problems of existing operations.

The sex abuse scandal illustrates all these aspects. Certainly, before 1985 and for years afterward in some dioceses, there was a shocking management failure to respond to allegations and remove priests at the local level. After 1985, there was a failure at the national level to act swiftly and decisively in instituting a mandatory national policy. At both local and national levels, even after many dioceses put in place much more effective policies for rooting out abusers in the early 1990s, there was a failure, first of imagination and then of will, to inform Catholics aggressively about past abuse and current settlements—and to be prepared with the facts that could have countered the charges of hiding wrongdoing.

Yet making the sex abuse scandal the framework for viewing every challenge of leadership the bishops face is a mistake. The bishops have not always failed as leaders, nor have all their failures been so needless and resounding. (Nor could one probably get a consensus on what were failures and what were successes.) Each issue, furthermore, has its own special characteristics. Articulating church positions on public issues demands different skills from assuring the quality of worship or catechetical formation. Issues of sexuality or of women's role in the church pose challenges of yet another nature since they touch on matters held by the whole church and therefore of special concern to Rome.

What virtually all of them require is a willingness to acknowledge problems candidly and to eschew prefabricated responses. Bishops need a rich understanding of revelation and tradition and of church history. They need an imaginative and empathetic grasp of why people of goodwill, and fellow Catholics not least, disagree on important matters. They need to be decisive when necessary but also to admit and live with ambiguities. All this demands, as foundation, considerable intellectual and spiritual depth.

No one has ever explicitly opposed such traits in the selection of bishops—with the possible exception of candor. For a long time, however, American bishops seemed to be chosen on the basis of their administrative abilities and their connections in Rome. From 1973 to 1980, when Archbishop Jean Jadot was the apostolic delegate representing the Vatican in the United States—and therefore the key official for recommending new appointments—what was most highly valued was a pastoral outlook. Under John Paul II, Jadot fell from favor and was rather unceremoniously kicked upstairs and out—first back to a Vatican post and then, without the usual honor of being named a cardinal, into retirement in Belgium. The so-called Jadot bishops, who were essential to the initiatives that the bishops' conference took in the 1980s, the pastoral letters on nuclear weaponry and on economic justice, were succeeded by a different sort. Theological skills were now emphasized, but only if they were devoted to upholding papal positions, particularly on *Humanae Vitae*, priestly celibacy, and women's ordination. Charismatic personality, administrative experience, and concern for the poor were all valued, but they could be trumped by one thing above all: readiness to follow Vatican orders.

The result, by and large, has been paralysis. Year after year, the bishops have crept forward, making a little progress on this or that issue with a carefully framed statement or a modest initiative—all the while glancing over their shoulders to see what Rome thinks and drawing back at each frown of disapproval. On issues of social justice and international peacekeeping, the bishops can be confident enough of a Vatican green light that they mainly hash out the liberal-conservative differences among themselves. On other big questions, from the Catholic identity of health care or higher education, liturgical language and participation, divorce and remarriage, sexual morality, the role of women and the laity generally in ministry, the bishops mainly stand and wait for cues.

NO LONG-TERM DEVELOPMENT poses a greater test of the bishops' leadership, or better illustrates their paralysis, than the shrinking number of priests. From the second century on, bishops have exercised ultimate institutional leadership in the Catholic Church, with the bishop of Rome increasingly acknowledged as preeminent among them. For most Catholics, however, the pivotal leader has been the priest. Priests have been the key figures in the ecology of Catholic life. No wonder that few developments in contemporary Catholicism have stimulated so much study and debate—and unfortunately so little practical action—as the growing shortage of priests.

"The Roman Catholic church faces a staggering loss of diocesan priests in the United States as it moves into the 21st century. There is little chance of reversing this trend in the lifetime of the current generation of churchgoers." Those statements opened the most detailed demographic study of the American Catholic priesthood, *Full Pews and Empty Altars,* by Richard A. Schoenherr and Lawrence A. Young, published in 1993. Noting the simultaneous decline in active priests and increase in the Catholic population, the authors state that "these are astonishing figures and citing them produces an array of reactions. For some, the response is anger and denial. For others, it's grief and despair. And for still others, it's hope for a better church with more lay participation. When social scientists look at the trends they recognize an organizational crisis of immense proportions," indeed, "one of the most pervasive changes in the Catholic ministry since the Reformation."

Counting priests turns out to be not as simple as it seems. Which ones are counted as active, which as retired? Are records accurate, despite reassignments between dioceses or even countries? Such uncertainties produce slightly different figures but the same direction: down.

By one reckoning, in 1950, there was one priest for every 652 American Catholics. In 2000, there was one for every 1,257 Catholics. The number of men being ordained each year has declined from almost 1,000 in 1965 to under 800 in 1975 to fewer than 550 in 1985 and 1995, dipping below 500 in 2000. While the Catholic population has been growing by 8–12 percent every ten years, the number of diocesan priests has been dropping by about 13 percent each decade, and the number of priests in religious orders by about 20 percent. For every 100 priests who die, only 35 new ones are being ordained— and, with an already aging priest population, a lot will be dying in the next five to ten years.

These trends have been long in the making, but the full impact has been much delayed. Large parishes in East Coast cities, for example, have often boasted three or four resident priests. When that number falls from four to three or two, the change may not be obvious. When there is only one priest left, the conflicting demands— five or more Masses on weekends, daily Mass, weddings, funerals, baptisms, marriage preparations, religious instruction, meetings of all kinds, administrative tasks, and civic responsibilities—become overwhelming. That is the reality in the great majority of U.S. parishes. Indeed, 16 percent have no resident priest. Of smaller parishes, those with fewer than 450 registered parishioners (still larger than most Protestant congregations), more than a quarter are without a resident priest. Nearly six out of ten priests serve alone in their parishes, which often adds loneliness to the burden of overwork.

As the number of priests has dropped, their average age has risen. Nearly 25 percent of diocesan priests are over 65, almost 60 percent over 55, while only 5 percent are under 35. The full impact of this aging promises to be sudden. A priest's working effectiveness may not noticeably decline between ages 45 and 60; in some respects, it may increase. Obviously, there is an upper limit, and the American priesthood is approaching it when one contemplates priests 65 years of age or older serving alone as pastors of large parishes or circuit riding between several smaller ones. In addition, the graying of the priesthood is a handicap in the crucial area of drawing young adults to the church. It renders it all the less likely that young men will identify themselves with a priestly calling.

Considerable energy has been expended in trying to deny or minimize these developments. Some commentators have suggested that these figures are less grim than they appear. They point to much bleaker ratios of priests to people in other parts of the world or even in earlier periods of American Catholicism—that is, things could be worse. One scholar combines this view with the observation that, given decline in Catholic church attendance and other sacramental participation, the ratio of priests to *active* Catholics has really not worsened. While this is true, it offers faint consolation. Indeed, it opens up a bizarre line of thought: the problem of a priest shortage could be solved if only sufficient numbers of Catholics grow disenchanted enough to stop attending church.

A more direct and less perverse approach to the shrinkage of priestly ranks is the hope of reversing it. Are priests simply no longer broaching the possibility of a priestly calling with young prospects? Many bishops are urging unrelenting efforts at personal recruiting and take pride in mentioning the topic themselves at every confirmation, commencement, parish visit, and conversation with altar boys. Those arguing that the decline in numbers can be reversed take heart from the growing numbers of priests in other parts of the world, without registering the fact that most of this is merely the effect of growing Catholic populations, and indeed often disguises an increasingly unfavorable priest-Catholic ratio. Optimists also point to a few generally conservative dioceses and seminaries with full complements of candidates for ordination. Similar conservatism defines religious orders like the newly founded Legionaries of Christ that appear to be overflowing with seminarians. In this view, the key to increasing the numbers of priests is to recruit enthusiastically and to offer an elevated, disciplined model of priestly identity, sharply defined in everything from dress to spirituality and unmistakably distinct from the laity's.

These claims deserve careful investigation. Highly conservative reputations have turned some seminaries into magnets for young men who shun their own dioceses' seminaries, judging the theology unorthodox or the spiritual formation lax. Some conservative candidates have been rejected—rightly or wrongly—from other seminaries. All sorts of disputes rage about the character of different seminaries and their standards for attracting or rebuffing young men—about liberal dogmatism, conservative rigidity, or the toleration of gay seminarians and subcultures. The first question, however, is simply numerical. Are the seminaries with full enrollments really attracting a higher proportion of young men to the priesthood? Or are they merely concentrating certain types of young Catholic males from far and wide in a handful of places, so that if these seminaries were more widely replicated, their enrollments would not be? And if what draws young men to the priesthood is the promise of a clear and unambiguous priestly role, is that good, or bad?

Obviously, questions of quantity are not separated from questions of quality. Decades ago, young men ordained to the priesthood emerged from a large pool of potential candidates. Including every altar boy as part of that pool may be a bit fanciful, but it was hard to spend many mornings assisting the priest at Mass—especially before the hormonal distractions of adolescence kicked in—without sometimes imagining oneself in that sacred role. From that population of altar boys and other devout youngsters, many dioceses once enrolled numerous teenagers in junior seminaries—high schools with extra doses of religious formation (and Latin) for those aspiring to the priesthood. A much diminished number, along with some fresh applicants, would go on to seminary proper, progressing through college and graduate level studies in theology, philosophy, and other pastoral studies, and undergoing a rigorously supervised life of spiritual exercises. All along the way, individuals dropped out of their own accord or were culled out as unsuited by seminary officials.

From all those who entered the large end of this funnel, only a few emerged to be ordained. It was a kind of Darwinian survival of the fittest, and yet (as in Darwinism itself) "fittest" did not necessarily mean anything beyond "fittest to survive." A certain threshold of intelligence and studiousness was normally necessary to meet the academic demands, along with a genuine degree of piety and devotion to survive the spiritual rigors. Whether the system also "selected" young men for ordination because of qualities like creativity, inquisitiveness, and initiative (rather than conformity, dependability, deference, and docility) or whether candidates survived despite the former qualities rather than because of them is another matter.

That selectivity is a thing of the past. Junior seminaries were almost all closed in the years after the Council; seminary educators came to doubt the wisdom of placing adolescents on a separate track toward the priesthood before they had the maturity and experience to make that kind of choice. Post-high-school applications to seminaries plummeted in the 1960s. Today, the average seminarian is in his thirties; he will be ordained at thirty-six. And he has emerged from a much smaller pool of potential candidates.*

Priests have probably always been as prone to generational conflicts as other people. Today the suspicions between the recently ordained and their elders seem unusually intense. To grossly oversimplify the tensions, a generation for which Vatican II was the formative influence confronts a generation for which the papacy and person of John Paul II are decisive. The Vatican II generation, in this case, embraces both those well formed in their faith before the Council and reoriented by its changes and those entering the seminary as much as fifteen to twenty years after the Council closed. The John Paul II generation is limited largely to priests ordained in the 1990s. In reality, attitudes within each generation stretch out along a broad spectrum, and the contrast may be mainly between the leading minorities in each generation. But there is no doubt that a shift—think of it as a shift in the center of gravity—has taken place.

It seems clear that the newly ordained priests are generally more conservative, expressing significantly higher agreement with contested church teachings like requiring celibacy for ordination or restricting the priesthood to males. A larger proportion than a few decades ago insist on strict adherence to hierarchical, especially papal, authority in teaching and liturgical practices, express enthusiasm for non-liturgical Eucharistic and Marian devotions, and believe that priests should be clearly understood as set apart from the laity. Dean Hoge, in a study of younger priests, writes, "A portion of Catholic seminarians today are firm in their loyalty to Pope John Paul II, their adherence to all church teachings about sexual morality and contraception, and their preference for tradition and formality in ritual and priestly roles. They feel comfortable wearing cassocks in public, un-

---

*Amid all the attention directed to the priest shortage, no one has thought about the ex-seminarian shortage. For every seminarian eventually ordained, the seminaries exposed a great many other young men to a more than average amount of theological and spiritual training. Efficiency experts might consider that a waste of resources. In fact, many former seminarians brought that extra degree of religious fervor and theological literacy to small roles in parishes or large ones in Catholic organizations.

like the vast majority of priests two or three decades ago." An outspoken few barely consider their elders to be truly Catholic. A young
priest who described his seminary as "really opposed to Catholicism"
is typical of this militant minority. He recalled having to constantly
put up with professors teaching "dissent," but at least he wasn't alone.
"We were the first orthodox class," he explained. "We loved the Pope,
we prayed our rosaries. . . . We wanted John Paul canonized while he
is still alive."

Is this priest an extreme example? Discussion of differences between Vatican II and John Paul II priests is plagued by caricatures on
all sides. Young, self-consciously conservative priests dismiss older
ones as having substituted social change for sanctification and cultural fashions for faith. Older priests describe younger ones as less interested in either social change or sanctification than in fussing about
their clerical wardrobes and other priestly prerogatives. Those who
welcome the turn toward traditionalism portray it in terms of spiritual sacrifice and heroism. Those who oppose it portray it in terms of
psychological insecurity and a consequent grasping at office and authority. Everyone has a distressing anecdote. No one can really know
whether the recent changes represent a moderate swing of an always
adjusting pendulum or a drastic repudiation of the recent past, especially as young priests are seasoned by their experiences in parishes.

What is reliably known is that the new priests, like new recruits to
Protestant ministry, take up their vocation later in life than their
predecessors and, by many reports, are less academically qualified.
Younger priests have entered the seminary after finding secular life
and first careers wanting. Is this a welcome indication of greater maturity and spiritual hunger or, on the contrary, a worrying indication
of a retreat to security after failure in the wider world? The turn to
the priesthood has often followed an intense religious experience or
awakening, of actual conversion to Catholicism for a few, of recon-
version from a lapsed or somewhat indifferent faith for most. Where
their elder colleagues commonly moved with minimal breaks from
Catholic families and Catholic schooling to seminary to ordination,

the younger group more typically enters seminary either after a period of disconnection from the church or, even though many were
raised in devout families, with the religious illiteracy widespread in
their generation. A highly structured, systematic, traditional Catholicism that seminarians two decades earlier found it exciting to
question, and sometimes to shed, is often a fresh discovery to the new
recruits and an essential source of identity, which they prize and re-
sent seeing challenged.

John Paul II priests also seem to focus strongly on those activities
that are distinctively priestly—administering the sacraments, leading devotions, giving spiritual counsel, preaching—and much less on
the organizational and administrative tasks common to leadership
generally. Do these priests understand ministry as an individual effort that is "theirs" to dispense, or as a community effort that they
lead? Is their task primarily to bring priestly ministry themselves to
people in need, or to build up a ministering community? Do they
tend to be solo "doers," rather than "animators" of others' gifts?
This is of particular concern as the thinning ranks of priests make
parishes increasingly dependent on effective collaboration with lay
staff and volunteers. Young priests appear to welcome collaboration
in principle but may lack skills or harbor attitudes so that it becomes
difficult in practice.

That collaboration is part of the larger relationship of the priest to
the laity. Currently the John Paul II priests and the laity stand far
apart in their views on church authority, sexual morality, women's
roles, divorce and remarriage, liturgical obligations, and many other
topics. Most younger priests want to be both pastorally sensitive and
pastorally effective without trimming their doctrinal positions.
Whether they have the intellectual resources to make those positions
persuasive or perhaps to reconsider them is an open question.

Also in this context of a potential mismatch between priests and
laity, questions have arisen about a growing proportion of seminarians and priests who are homosexual. In 1987, the Reverend Richard
P. McBrien, a theologian of moderately liberal views but of excep-

tional candor, pleaded that these questions "be articulated and addressed" rather than left "to gossip, to unexamined, closed-door decisions, or to policy by default." Among the questions was whether gay candidates for the priesthood had such a dominant presence in many seminaries as to discourage those heterosexual candidates who were not already deterred by celibacy. McBrien's liberal credentials did not spare him accusations of gay bashing, despite his insistence, then and later, that he was not questioning the character and ministry of individual gay priests but rather the pastoral consequences of an overall pattern created by the celibacy rule and seminary culture in tandem.

McBrien had, in fact, bravely opened up a topic that was awkward to discuss but that exploded when the victims of the sexual molestation that came to light in 2002 turned out to have overwhelmingly been boys or male adolescents. Homosexuality within the priesthood has been difficult to discuss, because the subject is riddled with guesswork and shadowed both by prejudice and the fear of feeding prejudice. If it was always allowed that there were proportionately more homosexual men in the priesthood than in the general population (the latter percentage a matter of debate itself), the percentages tossed around went from 10 percent to over 50.

By now the consensus is that, at least among recent priests and seminarians, the higher range is more likely. But how different is the recent situation from decades or centuries past? How many seminarians and priests remain uncertain or unresolved, perhaps willingly so, about their sexual orientation? Did that change as society increasingly accepted homosexuality over the last several decades or as sexuality became openly discussed in seminaries? Is it changing again as candidates for the priesthood reflect a more traditional piety and affirm traditional moral strictures? Given the reality that some priests, like some married people, violate their vows of celibacy at one time or another, is this any more or less likely to be true of gay priests? Are those who seek sex with underage youths more likely to be gay? What about the perception of many priests that a distinct gay subculture, involving shared interests and sensibilities regardless of sexual activity, operates in the priesthood? Is that accurate? Is it significant? And once again, is the perception or the reality all that different than in the past? Most of these questions remain without answers. As for comparisons between past and present, it is certain that the gay candidates for the priesthood who declare they are determined to live celibately have been more welcome in seminaries during the past several decades. But it is doubtful that the priesthood is actually attracting more gay men, rather than attracting fewer heterosexual men because of the church's more positive attitude toward marriage and sexual intimacy within marriage, registered in Vatican II's Pastoral Constitution on the Church in the Modern World and discussed below. More than anything else, that more positive attitude toward an alternative state of life for heterosexual men has changed the sexual "ecology" in seminaries.

The known facts about priests who have preyed sexually on minors contradict both those who wish to dismiss homosexuality as a pertinent issue and those who blame recent, more tolerant attitudes toward homosexuality or post–Vatican II criticism of the church's sexual teachings. The vast majority of cases now coming to light did involve minor boys, and most of them in their adolescent rather than prepubescent years. At the same time, a great number of offenders, including many of the most notorious ones, did their seminary studies and were ordained when attitudes toward homosexuality were fiercely condemnatory and church sexual teachings firmly upheld. Many of these predators appeared able to rationalize or compartmentalize their compulsive behavior while apparently maintaining otherwise orthodox beliefs.

Worried about reports that some American seminaries were nests of sexual activity and that the number of sexually active gay priests was growing, the Vatican has struggled to heighten the scrutiny of gay candidates for the priesthood without quite denying the basic Catholic teaching that celibacy is the critical test and not sexual orientation. In the wake of the sex abuse revelations, more such rumblings were heard from Rome. The pope's press secretary, a layman who is smart enough to know better, advanced the theologically preposterous claim that homosexuals could not be validly ordained— which would also make sacraments they had administered, like Eucharist or absolution or, in the case of a bishop, the ordination of other priests all invalid. Ultimately, a document did appear from one Vatican office warning against ordaining anyone with a homosexual orientation, and therefore accepting them in a seminary, but leaving enough leeway that church officials could probably still ignore the declaration in the case of individuals committed to celibacy and psychologically prepared to observe it. The Vatican, it seemed, wanted to discourage gay candidates for the priesthood without, perhaps, creating too much of a fuss or disallowing completely young men adamantly affirming that "homosexual acts are intrinsically disordered" and that homosexual orientation, although not itself a sin, "must be seen as an objective disorder."

This policy seems based on the premise that the priestly promise of celibacy is being deliberately shrugged off by gay seminarians and taken lightly by seminary officials. That may indeed have been the case in some seminaries years ago, although to what extent cannot be easily unscrambled from mostly anonymous stories. Some people claim it is still the case here or there, and how can one absolutely prove otherwise? Most informed observers, however, tell a much different story. Such aberrations are exceptions, they say, and the more general problem is much more complicated psychologically.

Although questions of sexual orientation are now frequently surfaced in seminary training, they still often remain clouded by layers of denial and uncertainty, posing the danger, according to many observers, of belated and compulsive acting out. It is feared that the Vatican's policy, which reflects a deep suspicion of modern psychology, seems likely to add more deception (and self-deception) to a situation where honest examination and discussion are already seriously inhibited.

THE NUMBERS OF PRIESTS in religious orders have been dropping
even faster than those of diocesan priests. Currently they constitute
about one-third of the nation's priests. A little more than one-third of
that third serve in parishes; the rest serve in high schools, colleges
and universities, monasteries, chaplaincies, hospitals, missions, religious publishing, and a variety of other ministries. Younger priests in
orders appear to be somewhat more conservative than their predecessors but more liberal than their diocesan counterparts. Again, the
exceptions as regards both growth and outlook are a few extremely
conservative orders. By and large, religious orders face the same
questions as the diocesan clergy: about generational differences
within their own ranks, a possible gap between younger priests and
the laity, and conflicts caused by either openly avowed or cloaked homosexual orientation.

Two other leadership groups have suffered the most drastic de-
clines in numbers.

Religious brothers—men vowed to living celibate lives in community—include major orders such as the Christian Brothers and
the Marianists, specializing in education, and the Alexian Brothers,
specializing in medical care, as well as nonordained men who are
vowed members of orders that include priests. From over 12,000 in
1965, their numbers fell to under 6,000 by 2000.

More dramatic was the exodus of women from convents, from
180,000 religious sisters in 1965 to 81,000 by 2000 and 75,000 by
2002. The loss was accompanied by a dispersal of sisters from assignments concentrated in their own schools and hospitals to a much
wider variety of ministries in the church. Sisters brought new energies to parish work, prison chaplaincies, community organizing,
poverty projects, battered women's shelters, spirituality centers, and
scores of other undertakings, all compensating somewhat for the
massive impact of their declining numbers on many Catholic institutions. Why did so many women so rapidly leave their religious or-

ders? Although many eventually married, the desire for marriage does not seem to have weighed so heavily in their immediate motivation as it did for priests.

After the Council, women's orders were reassessing their missions and rules of life at the same time as the women's movement was transforming social attitudes and practices. Existing disciplines and loyalties could not easily survive two such simultaneous and interacting upheavals. More significant than the religious orders' loss of members has been their inability to attract new ones. Many orders of sisters are now primarily devoted to caring for their own elderly, and smaller orders will soon go out of existence. Some orders are experimenting with looser forms of affiliation, encompassing married women or single women who do not take vows or live in community, or who take vows that commit them for a limited number of years. Reversal of the recent decline is out of the question.

In fact, it is a major premise of this book that without drastic changes in ordained or vowed life, none of these trends, whether for diocesan priests, priests in religious orders, nuns, or brothers, will be reversed. Recruit as energetically as possible, define the priesthood or religious life in whatever unambiguous, privileged, or heroic terms one chooses, and still the most that can be expected is a leveling off of the declining numbers, primarily of priests and men's religious orders, but with no possibility of catching up with the Catholic population growth or restoring the old near monopoly on leadership.

THE REASONS ARE PROFOUND. They are primarily religious, not sociological or cultural. They are the church's own teachings. Contemporary Catholicism has affirmed the goodness of the world and the goodness of the body, the call to holiness in everyday, secular activities, and the call to holiness in marriage and family—and no one is inclined to retract this.

These are not new teachings. They are rooted in the fundamental beliefs in God's creation and incarnation. But they have been given a new emphasis in grassroots Catholicism, previously dominated by a spirituality of escape from the world and from the flesh. What is involved is a new configuration of enduring beliefs, not the simple supplanting of one by the other. The themes of a broken world and a broken human nature, of the need for redemption, sacrifice, and judgment, have not disappeared. They have been reconfigured with elements of a Catholic humanism that are also not new but were only fragmentarily present in the popular otherworldly faith of most Catholics.

Talk of a new configuration and a Catholic humanism sounds abstract—until it turns to sex. The history of Christian attitudes toward the body, sexuality, marriage, and celibacy is enormously complicated and easily oversimplified. The church has defended the body and sexuality against dualistic heresies that assumed a radical struggle between good and evil in which good was identified with the spirit or soul and evil with the flesh or body. Marriage has been blessed and celebrated as a sacrament. Catholicism has frequently incorporated erotic imagery and pre-Christian fertility rites with a minimum of embarrassment. At the same time, there has been a strong suspicion of the body and sexuality (and women) running throughout Christian history, sometimes rising to a pitched hostility and aversion. Until modern times, most moral theologians held that it was at least venially sinful for married couples to engage in even procreative intercourse primarily for pleasure, although most married Catholics may have remained blissfully unaware or negligent of this teaching.

Celibacy has its own complicated history of theological justification, overlapping with this suspicion but not identical to it. Celibacy has been understood as preparation for the imminent coming of Jesus; as a sign of a heavenly kingdom ("For in the resurrection they neither marry nor are given in marriage, but are like angels in heaven": Matthew 22:30; Mark 12:25; Luke 20:35) and a witness to a transcendent reality beyond all earthly attachments; as a form of heroic sacrifice continuing the work of the martyrs; as a prolongation of cultic purification; as a condition for the formation of monastic and apostolic communities; as a safeguard against familial expropriation of church resources; as an indication of radical commitment to Jesus; and as a practical measure of availability for service.

Some of these purposes are deeply rooted in Catholic theology and the human psyche. Celibacy, I believe, will continue to have an important place within Catholic life. But the popular perception of celibacy not only as a condition of priesthood but as a positive, attractive feature of it had much to do with the antiworld, anti-body, anti-sexuality spirituality and a two-class understanding of holiness that rested, at least for ordinary Catholics, on the downgrading of sexuality and marriage.

Marriage, sex, and family were the lot of the religiously average—the spiritual C students—who, if they should rise above their ordinariness, would do so by some heroic sacrifice on behalf of their faith and not through their married life (unless perhaps it entailed some great tribulation) and certainly not through their sexual intimacy. Of course, there were a few contrary signals, but even when the Catholic culture, otherwise replete with celebrations of virgins, martyrs, missionaries, and founders of religious orders, honored outstanding Catholic families, an inevitable highlight was how many priests and nuns they had produced.

That is what has changed. Contemporary culture looks askance at celibacy, much as the church once looked askance at sexuality, but that is not so different from fifty or a hundred years ago. What is different is that the church has come to recognize marriage and sexuality as paths to holiness no less authentic, demanding, and rewarding than that of the ordained or vowed celibate—not just as a principle tucked away in theology texts, but in the religious instruction and culture of ordinary Catholics.

The change took time. Its progress was signaled by the emergence in interwar Europe of personalist theologies of marriage that emphasized the personal intimacy and relationship of spouses as a path to holiness and not only their fulfillment of obligations as parents, and by the success of the Christian Family Movement and Cana Conferences in 1950s America. One could probably trace the change in high school textbooks and pamphlet advice dealing with sex, marriage, and vocation. The change culminated in the Council's declaration on marriage and family—and in John Paul II's paeans to sexuality as a reflection of divine love.

Celibacy is not unnatural, but it is exceptional. The church has all the theological and spiritual resources necessary to maintain celibacy as a distinctive symbolic and practical calling—but an exceptional one. It can continue to be the chosen witness of some individuals and above all the mark of communities of men and of women whose lives of prayer, service, or struggle for justice constitute something like utopian experiments, outposts reminding us that God's reign exceeds all normal ties and expectations. But the status that celibacy once enjoyed as *the* model of holiness, to be routinely required of every parish priest and Eucharistic minister, is simply incompatible with the church's currently affirmed Catholic humanism. If the church wants to restore celibacy to that former status, there is really only one practical way to do it: demote marriage to the second-class standing it once had. Despite a few halfhearted attempts in this direction, no one, from parents to pastors to pope, wants to do this. The church has made a choice. Now it must figure out how to live with the consequences, namely a permanently smaller percentage of celibate priests and members of religious orders.

THE CHURCH'S FUTURE CANNOT be understood apart from the astonishing emergence of a new category of Catholic leadership that has already quietly transformed much of church life.

Before the 1960s, priests staffed parishes. Sisters ran the schools. Laypeople were volunteers, except perhaps for the rectory cook, the parish janitor, and the part-time organist or choir director. Today there are over thirty thousand lay parish ministers paid for at least twenty hours a week, working in over 60 percent of the nation's parishes. Seventy percent work full-time. They are running religious education programs, parish liturgy and music, youth ministry, home care for the sick and elderly, community and social justice programs, prayer and Bible study groups, marriage preparation and family support services, and a myriad of other pastoral activities. Some have specialized fields, like the directors of religious education or liturgists. Some are general parish ministers whose work, with the exception of administering the sacraments, covers almost the full range of responsibilities traditionally carried out by priests. Some are pastoral coordinators who oversee parishes that no longer have a resident pastor.

In the five years after 1992 alone, the ranks of this new category of church leader increased by 35 percent. By 1997 the numbers of these lay ministers in the parishes had surpassed the number of parish priests. Almost three quarters of these ministers view themselves as engaged in a life's work. Half feel they have received a call from God, and at least another quarter appear to be motivated more by some concept of religious service other than personal fulfillment.

New circumstances, new religious needs, and new spiritual energies have fused into an extraordinary innovation in American Catholic life. Some observers see this development as akin to the emergence in the twelfth and thirteenth centuries of new kinds of religious orders more appropriate than the old rural monasticism to Europe's nascent culture of town and city; or akin to the explosion of women's religious orders and Catholic workers' movements that responded to the conditions created by industrialization, urbanization, and immigration in the nineteenth century; or akin to the institutional creativity that forged the pennies, talents, and dedication of Catholic immigrants into the network of schools, hospitals, orphanages, and social agencies discussed in Chapter Four.

Two decades ago, a majority of lay ministers doing pastoral work were sisters. Although sisters are technically lay because they are not ordained, and though they often sought these positions on their own rather than being assigned by their orders, the distinctly lay character of the new leadership may have been initially obscured. Sisters, after all, do occupy a special, in-between status as vowed members of religious orders. Today over 70 percent of these parish ministers are fully lay, many of them married; and because the sisters active in parish work are aging and not being replaced by new members in their orders, the percentage of unambiguously lay ministers will increase. The married have lives centered in family: anxious spouses, after-school play groups, difficult teenagers, recitals, report cards, mortgages, and college tuitions. Many of the unmarried are normally intent on dating and courtship. All remain free to "take and leave their positions, as one would a job." And at least up to the present, they "are freely hired and fired by pastors without respect for their continuing in any role in ministry."

The feminine character of this development is clear. More than 80 percent of the lay parish ministers are women. Questions and tensions about women's roles in the church are clearly not going to subside. In addition, parish ministries, regardless of who carries them out, are increasingly activities—education, caregiving, nurture, and support—often associated with women in our culture. Understanding and empathy count more than authority; and a relational style of working is increasingly a hallmark of parish staffs, adopted by priests and other males.

Because centralization of power has long appeared to be a dominant trend in the Catholic Church, certainly during the papacy of John Paul II, perhaps the most surprising aspect of the emerging lay parish ministry is the major growth in local power it represents. Bishops have traditionally controlled who exercised ministry in parishes. Directly or through appointees, bishops decided who would pursue seminary studies and be ordained. Bishops decided who would be assigned to which parishes and eventually promoted to become pastors. Bishops ultimately determined diocesan practices for limiting assignments and making new ones. Lay parish ministers, by contrast, have almost always been hired and fired by the pastor, who often chooses them from active parishioners and increasingly involves the parish council or the current staff members in these decisions. In effect, oversight of what now constitutes the majority of the nation's pastoral leaders has shifted from bishop to pastor and from diocese to parish.

THE EMERGENCE OF AN unprecedented type of parish ministers poses questions about recruitment, screening, training, and credentials; practical questions, of the sort surrounding all employment, about job security, wages, and benefits; and also religious questions, particular to ministry, about personal faith and relationship to the larger church and its structures of authority. Recruitment, screening, and all the practical matters of employment fell at first largely into the hands of the pastor and the local parish. In the five years between 1992 and 1997, diocesan involvement in these areas expanded enormously, doubling in the area of recruitment but growing three- to eightfold in areas such as screening, evaluation, salary guidelines, and continuing education. Pastors can increasingly avail themselves of job registries or listings, diocesan standards, screening procedures, model contracts, and other devices that move the process beyond their own contacts and proclivities. Training and certification programs have grown up under the auspices of diocesan offices and Catholic colleges and universities.

The lore of American Catholicism is rife with images of authoritarian, misogynist pastors ensconced in their rectories and marinated in a narrow clerical culture—not the stuff of collaborative ministry with laypeople, most of them women. Yet the transfer of many pastoral responsibilities to lay parish ministers has been achieved with far less conflict than might have been predicted. Personal conflicts or change of pastor rank surprisingly low among lay ministers' reasons for leaving their posts, The desire for new challenges or new opportunities to grow in their work rank higher, as do changes in their personal lives (for example, a family relocation necessitated by a spouse's job) not related to their work. Job satisfaction generally is remarkably high, even with salaries that inevitably remain well below what people at these educational levels could earn in secular work.

The harmony shouldn't be exaggerated. Lay parish ministers report considerable stress and tension in their work, and pastors' view of the collaborative effort appears to be a good bit more upbeat than the staff's. The practical problems of sufficient wages and security have not gone away. A good many pastors look to minimize parish obligations by hiring people who are not the main or only source of their households' income and whose health insurance is covered by some other source. While in reality a change of pastors does not usually result in the large-scale turnover in staff that one might expect, lay ministers feel vulnerable and anxious about this possibility. When turnover does occur, given that lay ministers are often parishioners and have had long tenure, the reverberations in the parish can be painful.

Concerns that John Paul II priests will prove less attuned to collaboration and working with women are untested. Two additional flash points may be the centrist-to-liberal outlook of many lay parish ministers and the fact that many may be older and more experienced than their newer pastors, who because of the priest shortage are actually being appointed to head parishes at younger ages. So far, however, anyone familiar with the daily conflicts occurring in almost all workplaces or anyone conversant with the low-intensity warfare between pastors and their assistants, fellow priests all, that once characterized rectory life and was rendered so unsparingly in the fiction of J. F. Powers (and sentimentally in *Going My Way*) can only marvel at the first decades of lay parish ministry.

The gravest problems may arise not from the presence of lay ministers but from their absence. Since these laypeople are paid, poor parishes, whether rural or inner-city, often cannot avail themselves of this new pastoral help. And less than 5 percent of the lay parish ministers are Hispanic; well under 2 percent are African-American; and other minority groups like Asians, Pacific Islanders, and Native

Americans have less than 1 percent. The only mitigating fact is that this underrepresentation is at least better than among the priests.

SUCH INNOVATIONS ALWAYS shake existing church structures, raise misgiving, and force adjustments. Medieval popes and bishops battled with Franciscans and Dominicans over how upstart orders of preachers and mendicants could best fit into the church's lines of authority and understanding of spiritual life. Nineteenth-century mother superiors had to cross words, if not swords, with bishops who thought a sister's place was strictly in the convent.

The emergence of lay parish ministers has led to fears of "clericalizing" the laity, a dismissive term that covers three distinct worries. Two concern the impact of the growing role of laypeople in formal church ministries on other lay Catholics. It is feared that this type of church leader might not only depreciate the work of the volunteers who always carry out most parish functions, but even convey the impression that responsibility for the parish's activities and mission rests with a new caste of experts, professionals, or specialists. Second, it is feared that highly visible lay leadership in parish life might mislead the laity into thinking that they are called primarily to churchy activities rather than living out the gospel in their families, jobs, and civic obligations.

The chief studies of the new ministry take both worries seriously, emphasizing the essential role of parish activists and declaring the fear of downplaying "lay mission in the world" to be "not entirely misplaced." The evidence suggests that lay parish ministers do not supplant parish volunteers but recruit, support, and train far more of them. And rather than diverting laypeople from taking their faith out of the church and into the world, lay ministers, although still falling short of what is desirable, seem to help parishioners do it.

Another fear is that lay parish ministers will blur the distinction between the ordained and the nonordained and infringe on matters reserved to priests. That was clearly the thrust of a major 1997 Vatican document. Some of its concerns were elementary and noncontroversial. But stipulations that laypeople not use titles such as "chaplain" (which many nuns and some laypeople use in hospitals and prisons) or "moderator" or "coordinator" revealed that maintaining a moat around the priesthood was more important than positively welcoming a new form of Catholic ministry and trying to integrate it into the framework of church life.

That integration is unlikely unless one recognizes that lay parish ministers are not just substitutes or emergency fill-ins, a second-string variation on the clergy or those in vows. Nor is lay parish ministry a new profession defined by credentials and skills, despite offering some professionally determined technical competence in fields like catechetics, liturgy, or youth ministry, and despite the emergence of professional organizations (National Association of Parish Catechetical Directors, National Federation for Catholic Youth Ministry, National Association of Pastoral Musicians, and so forth). Lay parish ministers are chosen and valued for spiritual strengths and pastoral sensitivities as well as for specialized skills. Lay ministry of this sort must be recognized as something new, distinct, and not to be squeezed into a preexisting category—and for which, therefore, the church must make some new provision, as it did for the emerging nonmonastic religious orders in the Middle Ages.

At the moment, lay ministers and bishops appear to be circling each other warily. Each sees advantages to operating as free agents, striking bargains in a market for pastoral skills, however much that slights the theological meaning and personal religious commitment involved in these ministries. With Rome suspicious of any innovation, no matter how hopeful, that might detract from its determination to prop up a familiar but expiring model of priesthood, isn't it most prudent to let things develop in an ad hoc way?

For the moment, perhaps. But besides establishing diocesan guidelines and continuing education programs, should bishops begin commissioning and installing these lay ministers and symbolically including them among those gathered around the bishop in the cathedral at key liturgical events? Should bishops take a more proactive role in the recruitment, training, and distribution of such lay ministers, to assure, for example, that minority groups and poorer parishes benefit from this development? Monsignor Philip Murnion, who has traced the growth of these forms of lay ministry more closely than anyone else, alludes to the bishop who periodically meets with his *ministerium,* an assembly embracing all the ordained and the nonordained who exercise formal ministry in the church's name. He also alludes to *Ministeria Quaedam,* a document issued in 1972 by Pope Paul VI that envisions a formal recognition, although one other than ordination, for newly emergent kinds of ministry. Some such development is necessary, Murnion suggests, to "provide standards and stability in ministry," creating, for example, bonds of accountability and responsibility between the parish ministers and the local bishops, not as extensive as those between priests and bishop, to be sure, but having something of that nature.

In some respects, the future of lay parish ministry is assured. Catholics are willing. The church needs them. The parish of 2025 will employ them. What remains to be determined is who will be drawn to these positions and how they will be trained, appointed, promoted, retained, and supported in their work and their personal spiritual growth. With sufficient neglect and discouragement, of course, their numbers could level off (replicating the problem of selectivity now affecting the priesthood), turnover could increase, those with greatest potential for leadership could be driven away, or the polarization that has injured other aspects of Catholic life could settle in here, too. At the very least, one hopes for local church policies that rather than impeding the growth of lay parish ministry will energetically encourage it and incorporate it, theologically and organizationally, into the church's recognized leadership.

AMERICAN CATHOLICISM NEEDS more priests than it is getting. But if the number of priests per thousand Catholics is looking bleak, the number of ministers, counting the nonordained along with the ordained, looks much better, though far from satisfactory. The number of priests is not the primary issue. Leadership is, and a certain kind of leadership: American Catholicism needs priest leaders for a church of lay leaders.

Without effective priestly leadership, parishes can survive, but it is unlikely that they will remain vital. Sitting in on meetings of directors of religious education, I have heard groans and seen knowing glances exchanged when someone mentions a nonsupportive pastor or one who is running on empty theologically or perhaps even psychologically. One can do only so much when there is a void at the center of parish leadership.

There will always be vastly different ways of being a priest. A man whose manner is unprepossessing may galvanize loyalty and change lives; a charismatic personality may turn out, over time, to be a facade. But the priests of the future, beyond the holiness that all Christians strive for, will need three things. First, they will need a theological capacity to render the sacraments, the Word of God, and the joys and sufferings of everyday life meaningful. They will have to do this in their preaching, in their public prayer and responsibility for the liturgy, in their concern with catechesis and sacramental preparation; and they will have to do this across ethnic lines and increasingly to a well-educated, socially assimilated Catholic population. Second, priests will need a capacity to animate and guide others in leadership roles. They may well deputize others to take care of the strictly administrative worries about boilers and bookkeeping that priests so often complain about, but they will have to be able to organize and inspire people, to identify and reinforce the gifts of staff and parishioners, and to sustain them spiritually.

Third, priests will have to become accountable. Revelations about priests' sexual misdeeds and bishops' failures to act decisively against offenders stimulated a great deal of talk about "accountability" and "checks and balances" in the church—formal mechanisms giving representatives of the laity and clergy a significant role in making or reviewing decisions now reserved to the bishop and his appointees. Such mechanisms are badly needed to provide safeguards against abuses. But a wider sense of accountability is needed to ensure a priestly leadership striving to achieve and maintain excellence and not simply to avoid gross lapses.

The current situation has been described bluntly by the Reverend George E. Crespin, a pastor in Berkeley, California, and former chancellor and vicar for priests of the Oakland diocese: "For all practical purposes, priests are accountable to no one if they so choose, whether in the area of their personal lives or their pastoral ministry. . . . Only if a priest is seriously involved in some kind of questionable or scandalous activity is he called to account." Ordination, in effect, becomes a lifetime license to preach, preside, instruct, counsel, and run parishes—perhaps superbly, perhaps indifferently, perhaps terribly—with little likelihood of any regular measurement of performance and ultimately answerable only to one's own perceptions and standards, which may be acute and demanding, or not.

The remedy is not some clerical version of the mania for testing and ranking now dominating public education. Nor is it "the heavy-handed, authoritarian style that existed in some dioceses in previous generations," says Father Crespin. "That was fear, not accountability." He sees accountability operating in the mode of spiritual direction. One can imagine a variety of forms, in fact. Priests already belonging to spiritual support groups could develop procedures for reviewing one another's parish leadership. Pastors could employ both face-to-face discussion and unsigned surveys to obtain feedback about different aspects of parish life and their own leadership. Dioceses should develop reviews of parishes and pastoral leadership by outside committees of clergy and laity along the lines of the procedures used in academic accreditation. Lay representatives should serve on the personnel committees that in most dioceses play an important role in advising bishops about new assignments for priests. Participation in serious continuing education should not be voluntary for priests, as it commonly is, but required as in a number of professions. Bishops and, in larger dioceses, the vicars for different areas should be in continuing communication with their priests about parish and personal challenges. The point of all this should not be to grade or rank priests but to identify strengths and shortcomings and offer advice and assistance so that strengths can be magnified and shortcomings not become lifelong handicaps. Now and then, however, it might be salutary if a priest were unceremoniously yanked from all active service not for misconduct but for falling below a minimum standard of performance—lackadaisical liturgical leadership, boring and unprepared preaching, staff disarray, no community involvement, and such. It would signal that the church is serious about the quality of its priestly leadership.

IN THE QUEST FOR the priestly leadership Catholicism needs, the church faces three alternatives. Its current choice is to refuse rethinking the rule of celibacy and to reemphasize differences in responsibilities and way of life between priesthood and laypeople that had been diminished in light of Vatican II's theology of the baptismal vocation of all. Only a well-defined priesthood will draw young men; only a heroic way of life, as defined by celibacy, will draw outstanding young men—so goes the theory, sometimes invoking Paul's admonition "If the trumpet give an uncertain sound, who shall prepare himself to the battle?" (1 Corinthians 14:8).

It is true that a completely amorphous priesthood is unlikely to attract many takers and that the heroic demand of celibacy has frequently lent the priesthood a powerful distinction and authority. But the drawbacks to this theory have to be entered into the equation. A prepackaged, sharply defined status in the world can also substitute for genuine lack of definition in the work itself, and it can appeal to the insecure, unfocused, or less talented individual unable to define or earn his own distinctive place in the world. Celibacy has indeed appealed to the spiritually heroic—but also to the sexually confused. Celibacy has reduced—and as long the church does not reverse its theological stance toward marriage and presence in the world, celibacy will continue to reduce—the pool of candidates for the priesthood to a point where selectivity on any other grounds becomes difficult. How rigorous can seminaries today be in requiring good evidence that candidates possess the intellectual aptitude and leadership skills to preach, preside, and animate the average Catholic parish of over twenty-five hundred parishioners who are increasingly either middle class or professional, on the one hand, or ethnic and immigrant, on the other? Finally, the heightening of clergy-laity distinctions does little to promise a cadre of priests either interested in or capable of effectively animating lay leadership—a lay leadership, recall, emerging not only to fill gaps created by fewer priests and nuns but, quite independent of that need, reflecting a new and irreversible sense of the laity's place in the church.

A real-world scenario illustrates the problem: Consider a lone pastor in a not untypical city parish with three thousand or more registered members. The parish also has a married permanent deacon who, when free on evenings and weekends from his employment as a bank manager, can conduct marriage preparations, witness marriages, baptize infants, and preach a homily at Mass. There is a full-time laywoman pastoral associate available to prepare couples for marriage, lead prayers at wakes and gravesides for deceased parishioners, bring Communion to the seriously ill at home or in the hospital, and meet with the Latino and Vietnamese who gather weekly for prayer and planning parish activities. Finally there is a director of religious education, also a woman, who runs the extensive catechetical program for children and teenagers, including preparation for First Communion and confirmation, and who is trying to develop a menu of events for adult education. Although these other ministers may well possess skills and experience the pastor may not have—for example, as married people, the deacon and pastoral associate can speak to engaged couples from personal knowledge—many parishioners are disappointed and resentful. They feel that anything but a priest present in the pulpit on Sunday, or at their mother's wake, their daughter's wedding, their grandson's baptism, their devotional group's planning session, or the adult Bible study is second best.

Does the pastor himself think of them or treat them as second best? Does he respect their expertise and encourage their ideas and initiatives, or always manage to remind them that he is in charge? Are they colleagues, or employees? Would he want to spend any leisure time with them or their families? If a thirty-year-old seminarian comes to the parish for field training, does the pastor make it clear that the young man is expected to learn from these parish ministers? Apart from these personal interactions, what does he convey to the parish about these ministers? Does he reinforce the presumption of second best by emphasizing his own distinctive role and keeping them in the background? Or does he counter that presumption by associating them with his own leadership, making them prominent in parish worship, often naming and thanking them publicly? The strategy of separation and distinctiveness, aimed at bolstering vocations to the priesthood, will be tested in circumstances like these.

THE SECOND AND THIRD alternatives for assuring priestly leadership are incompatible with the first but compatible with each other. The second, of course, is removing the requirement of celibacy for ordination to the priesthood and opening the way for the ordination of women to the diaconate and possibly, if experience and theological reflection so indicate, to the priesthood. With the pool of candidates accordingly enlarged, the highest standards of intellectual preparation, personal integrity, sacrificial service, spiritual practice, and collaborative leadership could and should be enforced. The average age of priests could be lowered. The underrepresentation of ethnic groups like Latinos and African-Americans could be repaired. The goal would be quality, not quantity. The priesthood should be distinguished—an elite, if you will, but an elite of learning, service, spiritual wisdom, and charity rather than simply of sexual sacrifice.

At this moment, the papacy is adamantly opposed to a married priesthood. American Catholics (and other nationalities as well) should prepare for an eventual change of heart by devising concrete plans. Task forces of knowledgeable, serious Catholics (they would probably have to be laity) should be producing dispassionate studies of the advantages and problems associated with a married clergy, drawing on the experience of Eastern Rite Catholics, Orthodox, Anglicans, Lutherans, and other Christian bodies.

Of even greater importance—because it seems to paralyze the Catholic imagination—planners should address the challenging problem of a transition: How could a priesthood not restricted to the celibate be established with as little theological, psychological, and financial disruption as possible? What limited experiments might come first, involving, for example, exceptions from existing canon law for certain priestless regions or ministries? How would seminary education, field training in parishes, living arrangements, and acclimatization of the laity be handled—again, with an eye always to raising, not lowering, standards and expectations? Here, planners might draw on the experience of married clergymen who are converts from other denominations, who have been ordained Catholic priests, and who currently serve in Catholic dioceses.

The third alternative involves further rethinking of priesthood and its current forms in church life and law. This alternative could be pursued in conjunction with the passage to a married priesthood or in conjunction with the maintenance of a celibate clergy for the foreseeable future. A variety of ideas might be considered theologically and tested practically for maintaining continuity with the historical priesthood but adapting it to new circumstances.

Could diocesan priests be ordained with a promise to celibacy for a limited number of years, after which they would be free to marry but continue to function as deacons? Could a mature, natural leader, married or celibate, of a small or isolated parish be ordained with abbreviated training but with faculties (official authorization to minister) only to preside at the weekly Eucharist in that parish, while priestly duties requiring more extended education (hearing confessions, preparing people personally or hiring staff to prepare people for other sacraments) were reserved to a full-time priest overseeing several parishes?

Effective, thoughtful, biblically informed preaching is desperately needed in Catholic worship, but it requires time for study, reflection, and preparation that a reduced number of priests can scarcely spare. Could a ministry of lay preaching be developed, with demanding standards of natural abilities and concentrated training in scripture and speaking? (Most parishes now include a fair-sized pool of highly educated and thoughtful people for whom effective public speaking as teachers, lawyers, public officials, and so on is a professional responsibility; it is not unusual for some of them even to have pursued theological study on their own.) With one or two lay preachers to assist him (or her), the lone pastor of a parish might have to prepare and preach only every second or third week, while retaining oversight over the preaching of others.

I can hear the chorus of theological objections to each of these ideas, as would doubtless be raised to many others, all of which seem to split off certain activities that have historically been attached to priesthood. I leave the debate to others, merely pointing out that the assignment of liturgical and decision-making responsibilities, particularly in the early centuries, evolved and shifted between bishops, priests, deacons, and laypeople. Furthermore, the church has officially and semiofficially recognized a variety of ministries over its long history, including vowed but nonordained life in religious orders; the so-called minor orders of acolyte, lector, porter, exorcist, and subdeacon; and service in various brotherhoods and communal movements of women and men.

In some respects, proposals of the sort I have mentioned tend to make priests more like bishops, exercising oversight over a number of authorized and institutionalized ministries, whether these are understood as delegated from above or arising from the priesthood of all the baptized. Bishops, in turn, become more like bishops of bishops. The rather protean office of deacon, created in apostolic times to meet particular needs, adapted to a wide range of ministries in the early centuries, and renewed by Vatican II, is a resource to incorporate the leadership potential of men and women into the traditional framework of church offices and authority.

WHICH OF THESE STRATEGIES will the American bishops choose for remedying the growing shortage of priests and the disappearance of many women religious? How will the bishops respond to the surge of lay men and especially women into parish ministry? Can the bishops mobilize Catholics' creativity, energy, and resources to develop effective catechetics programs, reverse the drastic decline of young adults into religious illiteracy and detachment from church life, and make intellectual engagement with the faith a lifelong activity? Can the bishops address the questions, objections, and outright incredulity that the church's sexual teachings provoke among many Catholics? Can the bishops help steer Catholicism through the world-historical transformation of women's roles in childbearing, the family, work, and public life? Will the bishops help, or hinder, Catholic higher education, health care, and social services in retaining both a meaningful religious identity and an influential place in a pluralist culture?

Setting out a list of questions does not enkindle optimism. To lead rather than react, the bishops will have to change their style, stop their subservience, and reform the way they are selected.

I pretend to no inside knowledge about bishops. Although almost all have treated me well as I followed their doings, as a class they are not given to inviting reporters into their confidence. I have come to know a few in more than a passing way, almost all of them intelligent, compassionate, genuinely good, and terribly overburdened men. Others, whom I have observed from a distance, display the most complex of personalities—or none at all.

Obviously bishops, like priests, come in many models. Collectively, however, they hew to a certain style. There is much to be said for it.

They are careful to a fault about what they say and do, and how they come to say and do it. They prize consensus and abhor public discord. They usually do and say nothing officially that has not run a gauntlet of committee discussion, drafting, redrafting, and approval. The intricate exercises in line-by-line revising and amending documents that occupy much of their semiannual meetings can give the impression of terminal pedantry and legalese. Aren't religious leaders supposed to be charismatic and prophetic? Watching the governing bodies of several other religious groups take positions with little consultation, or with theological abandon, or after hopelessly entangled and poorly focused debate has made me appreciate the Catholic bishops' meticulous approach.

What has been sacrificed, however, is the kind of honest debate and respectful but frank disagreement that brings pressing issues to the forefront and opens them to analysis. Occasionally, at the bishops' meetings, amid the fine-tuning of positions already thoroughly blended in committee, a proposed change will signal a significant disagreement. The conference president may extend time for more of the brief interventions that bishops typically make; but the feeling is that the time for real argument has already passed, the relevant committees have already taken into account this disagreement (which should not be described too bluntly in any case), and bishops are now speaking more for the record than to persuade.

This style is not limited to the bishops' meetings. The bishops dread public confrontations, even polite ones; indeed, since their etiquette rejects confrontations altogether, there can be no such thing as a polite one. (This was one reason Cardinal Bernardin was so pained by Cardinal Law's 1996 attack on the Common Ground Initiative, although there was nothing particularly polite about Law's harsh and immediate criticism in any case.) Consequently, any bishop first seizing media attention with a controversial statement, as Cardinal John O'Connor of New York was wont to do or as some bishops have done on the abortion issue, is likely to go unchallenged or at most encounter muted demurrers. When several bishops questioned the good faith of the lay group Voice of the Faithful and barred it from meeting in church facilities, other bishops, who favored outreach to this and other groups arising in response to the sex abuse revelations, stayed quiet. The church's public profile is apt to be determined, people have said, by the loudest common denominator.

Closely allied to this style of suppressing differences is the bishops' habit of subservience. Why are American bishops so consistently spineless in their dealings with Rome? Why are they so pliable before the nation's handful of cardinals? Before Vatican II, figures such as New York's Cardinal Francis Spellman were personifications of a Rome-centered view of church authority, but they also had a keen sense of their own authority. When a Vatican official attacked a professor at the New York archdiocesan seminary, Spellman named the man a monsignor. When the Jesuit theologian John Courtney Murray was barred from publishing his important views on religious liberty, Spellman took him along to the second session of the Council as a personal adviser. With a few notable exceptions, today's bishops seem to cringe and backtrack at every sign of Vatican displeasure and to tolerate Vatican procrastination or reversals that appear plainly insulting. These are men who call themselves successors of the apostles and essentially hold lifetime tenure. Do they fear being excluded from the club of other bishops? Do they fear the low-level harassment that Vatican offices can conduct? It is hard to believe that so many of them are itching for bigger and better dioceses and fear spoiling their chances.

Selection is obviously a key factor. Complicated, somewhat arcane procedures govern the selection of new bishops or the appointment of a bishop to a new diocese. They involve collecting the names of likely candidates from regional groups of bishops, gathering information on these candidates through confidential questionnaires and consultation, the listing of top candidates by the papal nuncio (ambassador) in Washington, and further rounds of consultation with the American bishops' conference and sources knowledgeable about the diocese involved.

Crucial power rests, first, with the papal nuncio, who forwards three names to Rome along with an extensive report, documentation, and his recommendation; second, with the Congregation for Bishops, a hardworking Vatican office that synthesizes the nuncio's material and eventually conducts a vote among a group of cardinals resident both in Rome and elsewhere; third, with certain American cardinals—most notably Cardinal Law in recent years—who are kingmakers and whose backing weighs heavily with the nuncio and the Vatican (after Cardinal O'Connor's death in 2000, Cardinal Law became the one American member of the Congregation for Bishops still resident in the United States); and finally with the pope himself. Although the American bishops' conference has a standing Committee on Selection of Bishops, consultation with it or even with the conference's officers, let alone with priests or laypeople in a diocese awaiting a bishop, is negligible.

This is a process that must be opened up. Maximal proposals include election of bishops by diocesan councils of priests and laity. Minimal proposals include reestablishing a genuine consultative role for the bishops' conference and its elected officers. There are a lot of possibilities in between. Although election of leaders, including the pope as well as bishops, abbots, and superiors of religious orders, is well established in Catholic history, the idea of electing bishops renders most conservatives and virtually all the hierarchy and Vatican officialdom apoplectic. They consider that freeing the choice of bishops from pressures exerted by governments and placing it in the hands of the pope has been one of the most important achievements of the church over the last two centuries. And they are right.

Perhaps this should not rule out elections of bishops in countries with a solid tradition of separation of church and state, but the church has to establish procedures with an eye to many parts of the globe. Enthusiasts for electing bishops might look, in addition, at the experience of religious groups that elect their bishops or other leaders. The results are not the nightmare the Vatican dreads, but not so inspiring either. Catholics—bishops, priests, and laity—would do well to press for intermediate improvements. Since the Second Vatican Council, canon lawyers, both individually and in the Canon Law Society of America, have circulated proposals for reform. Generally these proposals involve opening up the pipeline providing names and documentation to Rome. Standing diocesan committees for the selection of bishops, with lay representation; the diocesan priests' councils; and various groups of bishops, regionally and through the national conference, would participate in producing a shortlist of candidates, from which Rome, at least under normal circumstances, would make a choice. Bishops might have to be chosen from priests or bishops already serving in that province or in the larger region—a brake on a powerful cardinal's ability to place "his" bishops all around the country. The ultimate goal would be to make sure that priests whose very talents—intellect, enterprise, invention, and candor—might make them threatening to the status quo remain in consideration; to keep the kingmakers from unduly shaping the hierarchy; and to make the hierarchy reflective of the American faithful as well as the instrument of unity with tradition, the universal church, and the pope.

WITH FRESH THEOLOGICAL understanding, the offices of bishop and priest may change over time, but they remain defining marks of Catholicism. They will not be replaced by lay leadership. Lay leadership is the future of the church, nonetheless. Laypeople are taking charge of the church's vast network of institutions and activities. They are coming to constitute the bulk of theologians, church historians, perhaps even canon lawyers. They staff Catholic schools and pass on the faith in catechetics and adult education programs, prepare people for the sacraments, hold key posts in parishes and increasingly dioceses, too. American Catholicism's public presence in politics, economic life, and culture will be the task of political leaders, thinkers, and activists, civil servants, executives, financiers, labor leaders, scholars, writers, artists, and performers. Bishops and priests have largely lost whatever limited sway they ever had in the United States over Catholic voters, politicians, and pundits, let alone over Catholic participation in intellectual life, the fine arts, or popular entertainment.

Two newly emerging categories of Catholic lay leadership have been described. Lay professionals in Catholic higher education, health care, and social service agencies face the challenge of preserving and renewing, in a pluralist context, the distinct Catholic identity of their institutions, a task once accomplished by religious orders and diocesan clergy. Lay ecclesiastical ministers are creating a new category of parish and diocesan leadership. But there is another, older category of Catholic lay leadership. Call them the influentials—people who can exercise influence because of their ideas, skills, drive, devotion, charisma, connections, articulateness, or just plain money.

Most such individuals have always wielded that influence, presumably shaped in some measure by their Catholicism, in their secular fields of activity, while limiting their explicitly religious involvement to their personal observance, their parishes, and perhaps one of two favored causes or charities. A certain proportion of these people have always involved themselves more extensively in internal church affairs as thinkers, writers, artists, organizers, or donors. Traditionally they applied their talents or their money to projects or institutions directed by bishops, clergy, or religious orders.

Before Vatican II, it was liberal laypeople who typically founded and led a variety of movements, organizations, magazines, and publishing houses that basically operated independently of the bishops or orders but often with the help of activist priests and the blessing of sympathetic church officials. The aim was either to reform some aspect of church life, like liturgy or religious art, or to apply church teachings in areas like labor relations or racial justice, where an institutional presence seemed lacking. Prime examples were *Commonweal,* "a review of public affairs, religion, literature, and the arts," founded by laypeople in 1924; the Catholic Worker movement, founded by Dorothy Day and Peter Maurin in 1935; and Sheed & Ward, a British lay-owned publisher whose American branch brought the latest European theology to American Catholics in the 1940s and 1950s.

In the postconciliar period, conservative laity have been at least as energetic in creating new organizations, publications, and institutions—even colleges and universities—to counter what they consider liberal or radical dissent. Yet most Catholic lay influentials seem increasingly disinclined to entangle themselves with these matters. Perhaps they are discouraged by the polarized atmosphere or the shadows of scandal, or perhaps they are simply reflecting their assimilation into mainstream America and their consequent loss of intense Catholic identity. Whatever the reason, during a critical passage, when the bishops and the clergy appear either weak or paralyzed, the involvement or indifference of this kind of lay leadership could make a critical difference.

Finding a Future

THIS BOOK BEGAN WITH the funeral in 1996 of Cardinal Joseph Bernardin. It is being finished a few months after Cardinal Bernard Law felt compelled to resign from office. As of now, a very different kind of grief hangs over the Catholic Church in the United States. How long will it be, I wonder, before the death of a powerful American archbishop can again call forth the kind of outpouring I witnessed seven years ago in Chicago?

From start to finish, this book has been about leadership, the leadership of a church that, locally and nationally, is a massive part of the nation's institutional, moral, and intellectual infrastructure. At one level, I have argued, a great deal of that leadership is changing—willy-nilly. At another level, negotiating that transition in leadership is something that itself requires leadership.

How should such leadership be exercised? Where will it come from?

THE COMMON GROUND INITIATIVE was a characteristic Bernardin venture in leadership. So was the consistent ethic of life. So were the open hearings, the consultations with military and political experts, in and out of government, and the subsequent public debates of successive drafts that marked the writing of the bishops' 1983 pastoral letter on nuclear defense policy. Bernardin believed in collegial decision-making and in strengthening the bishops' conference. He believed in consultation. He believed in mediating different points of view.

As the 1980s passed into the 1990s, that manner of leadership was steadily pushed aside, put on the defensive, confined to matters of secondary importance. The fear that it might be revived may best explain why Bernardin, in his final months, came under attack from the very cardinal whose own style of leadership has now cast a shadow over the entire hierarchy.

The fear, it seems, has not disappeared. It has resurfaced in the backwash of the sex abuse scandal. The poisonous root of the scandal, it is declared, is the "culture of dissent," primarily, that is, the rejection by many laypeople, clergy, and theologians of *Humanae Vitae*. The remedy is certainly not consultation and dialogue, therefore, but the reassertion of authority, especially papal authority, and the rooting out of church roles of all who do not quite publicly and unquestioningly identify themselves with it.

This vision of exercising leadership talks of "purification," but what it seems to mean is "purge." It exploits a vastly simplified and distorted account of the sex abuse scandal. Its proponents are apparently given no pause by the fact that the church leader to whose attack on the Common Ground Initiative many of them once rallied oversaw the most spectacular of scandals, while the church leader who proposed the Initiative pioneered a critical change in the way church authorities handled these crimes.

Through this book, quite apart from the specific proposals argued in various chapters, I have implied that the leadership American Catholicism needs now is quite different. It should have two characteristics. It must be determined to break out of the trench warfare that has constricted discussion within American Catholicism since the Second Vatican Council. It must balance a concern for theological underpinnings with close attention to the practical pastoral realities of animating vital worship, passing on the faith, and fostering Catholic identity.

FOR ALMOST FORTY YEARS, debates among American Catholics have been framed in terms set by the Second Vatican Council and the divisions that emerged during its historic four sessions, held each fall from 1962 to 1965. How could it be otherwise? The council was a landmark event in church history. The issues it examined were fundamental, and much that it called for has yet to be achieved. The conciliar debates are not a closed chapter.

At the same time, the framework of the conciliar and immediate postconciliar conflicts has become constricting. Too much that has happened since then is ignored or minimized if it does not fit this framework or if it imperils the hardened lines of the contending camps. Occasionally, one finds Catholic leaders or thinkers who pass from one of these camps to another. But rarely does one hear liberals or conservatives acknowledge that forty years of postconciliar experience have convinced them that the opposing perspective may have turned out to be right about some, although not all, things, or that there are matters falling entirely outside their points of contention.

Reinforcing that division are two lessons supposedly derived from religious history. One compares the experience of the declining mainline Protestant churches in the United States to that of their growing evangelical Protestant counterparts. Religious groups that flourish, the lesson goes, are ones that foster distinctive identities, maintain recognizable boundaries, and make significant demands on adherents.

The other lesson is derived from the rather longer perspective of European history. Religious groups that want to flourish over time must acknowledge and engage great transmutations in civilization's history like the Scientific Revolution, industrialization, and mass migration from rural to urban life, the movement in support of human rights and democratic government, and national self-determination.

Catholics on the liberal or radical end of the spectrum of church opinion have often stayed blithely indifferent to the first lesson. They have been reluctant to measure their program of doctrinal revision and democratic governance in the church against the liberal Protestant experience. They are given no pause by the fact that the ordination of married men and of women; the acceptance of contraception, abortion, and remarriage after divorce; inclusivity in membership; latitude in theological doctrine; and general alignment with liberal social and political concerns—all aspects of contemporary mainline Protestantism that many proponents of an egalitarian and democratic Catholicism would like to emulate—have proved no antidote to decline in these Protestant church bodies.

More conservative Catholics are equally unready to admit that the historical lesson is not so clear: Not only are some growing, conservative churches marked by considerable lay participation and decision making and by a focus far more on powerful religious experience than orthodox religious doctrine, but also, over time, even those groups have modified their identities, boundaries, and demands in keeping with changing conditions and perceptions. Today's burgeoning evangelicals and overflowing megachurches are not yesterday's fundamentalists. They are no longer preaching against dancing, gambling, drinking alcohol, doing business on Sunday, women working outside the home, and even divorce.

Nor do these Catholic conservatives grapple with the second lesson. They brush aside the numerical losses and moral compromises that arose from Catholicism's nineteenth-century crusade against modernity. They belatedly grant the validity for civic existence of liberal and democratic values, once denounced by popes, while denying these values any serious place within the life of the church.

The kind of leadership Catholicism in the United States needs now will hold to these lessons as caveats but reject them as iron laws. It will press liberals to take seriously conservative anxieties about the loss of Catholic identity, some of the tendencies of academic theology, and the shortcomings of liturgical and catechetical renewal. It will press conservatives to treat world-historical shifts in attitudes toward sexuality and the equality of women as more than afflictions to be resisted or minor change requiring only cosmetic adjustments.

It will criss-cross the party lines that have hardened since Vatican II and mix and match ideas from each party's agenda.

"WE SHOULD TEST ALL proposals for their pastoral realism and potential impact on living individuals as well as for their theological truth. Pastoral effectiveness is a responsibility of leadership."

Working on this book repeatedly reminded me of the value of that admonition from the inaugural statement of the Common Ground Initiative. Too many debates about American Catholicism are "over-theologized," at least if theology is identified with reasoning about relatively abstract propositions rather than reflection grounded in the actual practices of a believing and worshiping community, both in the present and through time.

In examining worship, I noted the dearth of empirical studies and the importance of what in athletics is called "execution," what musicians or dancers would call performance, what Cardinal Daneels of Brussels has called craftsmanship. In discussing catechetics, I noted the increasingly sophisticated but underutilized efforts at assessment and the enormous practical problems of simply spending sufficient time with young people. Yet in both areas the amount of energy expended on assuring the theological orthodoxy of texts—whether the translations of prayers, the lyrics of hymns, or the lessons in textbooks—is wildly disproportionate to the energy directed toward studying and solving practical pastoral challenges.

The kind of leadership needed to steer the American Catholic church through its current changes must reemphasize practical skills, pastoral results, empirical measures, organizational effectiveness. The Catholic identity of church-related institutions cannot be assured by any piling up of Vatican instructions, mission statements, norms, quotas, or juridical ties—apart from the persistent exercise of leadership by people (increasingly laypeople) who are both committed and skillful. The fidelity of Catholic academic theology cannot be assured by official mandates, oaths, job pressures, and censorship

but by genuine conversation between church authorities and scholars. Claims about gender and language, or gender and the imagery
for God, Christ, and the church must be tested not only by theoretical
argument but by real-world knowledge of how words, metaphors,
and symbols operate among the faithful. Debates about celibacy or
discussions of alternative procedures for selecting bishops must give
serious attention to the practical experience, both good and bad, of
fellow Christians, whether Protestant, Eastern Orthodox, or from the
non-Latin rites of the Catholic Church.

WHICH BRINGS ME TO the final question of where this leadership
might come from. In 1992, after eight years of drafting and redrafting a pastoral letter on issues of concern to Catholic women, the national conference of bishops buried their own effort. It was a
revealing moment. The bishops had been able, in 1983 and 1986, to
produce pastoral letters on the morality of the nation's nuclear defense strategy and on the justice of the nation's economy. Not without
difficulty, of course, not without heated controversy, as befit issues of
such importance to the country, but the bishops had succeeded,
nonetheless. When it came to a topic of similar importance for the internal life of American Catholicism, however, the bishops recoiled. To
be sure, they were buffeted by criticism from both Catholic feminists
and conservative groups of Catholic women. Much more important,
they worked under constant hostile scrutiny and pressure from Rome,
dead set not only against anything that could be seen as a step toward
ordaining women but anything that could be seen as a concession to
feminism. The opposition was echoed in the changing ranks of the
American episcopacy, and the result was theological gridlock.

It was a pattern. Over the last decades, bishops varied widely, as
they always have, in the kind of leadership they exercised in their
own dioceses. Nationally, they plugged away at a long list of pastoral
challenges, from new translations for the liturgy to new plans for
Hispanic or African-American or young adult ministry. But on too

many big questions, as the sex abuse scandal made so painfully clear, collectively they stalled and individually they were silent. Will the hierarchy now be jolted out of that stalemate? Or will the bishops be driven even deeper into it?

The prospects, for the time being, do not look good. The end of any papacy tends to be a time for standing pat. The end of this papacy may be a time for last-minute efforts to reinforce its ecclesiastical conservatism. And the long-run prospects are not encouraging either. Tomorrow's bishops will be chosen from today's young priests, and today's young priests are a smaller pool, increasingly conservative, less inclined to conceive and favor new initiatives, indeed less temperamentally inclined toward church leadership than face-to-face priestly roles.

Leadership in Catholicism, despite appearances, has never been restricted to the bishops. Often enough, bishops find themselves responding to the initiatives of other Catholic leaders. The climate of the times suggests that Catholics, ordained and lay, will have to exercise responsibility for the vigor of Catholicism within their own sector of activity.

Laity at the parish and diocesan level must avail themselves of all the advisory councils now called for—and invent new mechanisms for informal or formal accountability. Catholic politicians have to do more than endorse or fend off the positions taken by the hierarchy; they must articulate theologically informed positions of their own, linking moral principles with factual assessments and prudential judgments. Catholic educators, health care administrators, and social service leaders cannot leave it to others, bishops included, to define and assure the Catholic identity of their institutions.

The liturgical and catechetical establishments and the guild of academic theologians, which have often generally assumed the defense of innovation while leaving the task of protecting continuity to the hierarchy, will have to broaden their own sense of responsibility for the whole Catholic tradition. Catholic donors are going to have to fund independent centers of serious Catholic thinking and scholarship, alongside traditional Catholic philanthropies. Finally, Catholic intellectuals who have come into their own in specialized fields of research, public policy, communications, or the arts must bring not only opinions but well-founded reflection back to their church and faith.

THESE FINAL PAGES ARE being written on March 25, the Solemnity of the Annunciation, a feast day that the church naturally places exactly nine months before Christmas. The archangel Gabriel appeared to Mary, who consented to be the mother of the Redeemer. Perhaps because of the simplicity of the two figures, perhaps because of the opportunity the winged visitor has given to the artistic imagination, no other biblical scene, not even Nativities and Crucifixions, I hazard to say, has produced more wonderful art. Poets, too, from Hildegard of Bingen to William Butler Yeats and W. H. Auden, have tried to capture the instant.

Yet the whole drama is condensed into the three biblical statements and responses, each followed by a Hail Mary, that constitute the Angelus, the beautiful medieval prayer that Catholics once paused to say when the church bells rang out at dawn, noon, and dusk: "The angel of the Lord declared unto Mary, *and she conceived of the Holy Spirit.*" "Behold the handmaid of the Lord, *be it done unto me according thy word.*" "And the Word was made flesh, *and dwelt among us.*"

To Protestant eyes, Catholic devotion to the Blessed Virgin had often seemed to rival faith in Jesus and to elevate her into a quasidivinity. To counter that impression, the Second Vatican Council, in a strongly contested decision, chose to incorporate its teachings on Mary not in a separate document but in its Dogmatic Constitution on the Church. The Council wanted to place that devotion firmly within its vision of the church: Mary, who "stands out among the poor and humble," is the first among disciples, model of holiness, mother of the church as well as of Christ.

She is, the bishops of the Council said, "the image and beginning of the church as it is to be perfected in the world to come." She is, on earth now, "a sign of certain hope and comfort to the pilgrim People of God." Hope, comfort, pilgrimage. They are the notes on which to end.

Notes

PAGE

xiii Besides my own observations and those of Dan Dorfman, a reporter for the *Times* in Chicago, I have depended on descriptions of the mourning, funeral cortege, and burial of Cardinal Bernardin appearing in the *Chicago Tribune* and *Chicago Sun-Times* and carried on local television.

xiv The press conference is described in Eugene Kennedy, *My Brother Joseph* (St. Martin's Press, 1997), 152–53.

INTRODUCTION

2 Poll data on Mass attendance and figures saying faith is very and fairly important can be found in George Gallup Jr. and D. Michael Lindsay, *Surveying the Religious Landscape* (Morehouse Publications, 1999), 14–15, and in Bryan T. Froehle and Mary L. Gautier, *Catholicism USA* (Orbis, 2000), 22–24. The impact of the sex scandal, as measured by Gallup, was reported in David Gibson, "Scandal Hits Catholic Church in the Pews," Religion News Service, Dec. 20, 2002.

3 Jesus' phrase "I shall give you living water" is inscribed in all thirty-eight languages on a fountain in the plaza of the new Los Angeles cathedral. I encountered the bilingual phone message in the Holland, Michigan, parish some years ago, and a recent call there confirmed that the monthly Vietnamese Mass continues.

3 For the history of Catholicism in the colonies and since, see James Hennesey, S.J., *American Catholics* (Oxford, 1981); Jay P. Dolan, *The American Catholic Experience* (Doubleday, 1985) and *In Search of an American Catholicism* (Oxford, 2002); and Charles R. Morris, *American Catholic* (Times Books, 1997). There is a discussion of Catholic growth and the statistical record in Roger Finke and Rodney Stark, *The Churching of America, 1776–1990* (Rutgers University Press, 1992), 110–15. Figures for the church in 1976 are from *The Official Catholic Directory* (P. J. Kenedy & Sons, 1976). The annual editions of the directory are the source of many statistics and statistical comparisons throughout this book.

9 There is a vast literature on the rise and decline of different religious groups in the United States, which overlaps with the vast literature debating the causes

and course of secularization. The most discussed challenge to the modernization thesis was Dean Kelley's *Why Conservative Churches Are Growing* (Harper and Row, 1972), which has been supported by sociologists of religion favoring concepts like religious competition, costs, markets, and market shares, adapted from economics. Finke and Stark, in *The Churching of America* and other works, are representative of this school, which is sometimes stronger on iconoclasm than detail or nuance.

1. THE BATTLE FOR COMMON GROUND

17 Cardinal Joseph Bernardin and Archbishop Oscar H. Lipscomb, *Catholic Common Ground Initiative* (Crossroad, 1997), contains all the initiative's foundational documents and an introduction by Monsignor Philip J. Murnion explaining the genesis of the effort and the response to it. Hoping that the word "initiative" in the title might emphasize the openness of the effort to many participants and points of view, Cardinal Bernardin had quickly renamed what was first announced as the Common Ground Project. Other information about the Common Ground Initiative comes from my wife's participation, my own attendance at Common Ground meetings, and conversations with Monsignor Murnion and the other original and later participants.

20 Andrew M. Greeley, *White Smoke* (Forge, 1996), and Malachi Martin, *Windswept House* (Doubleday, 1996). I wrote about the two papal potboilers in the *New York Times,* June 15, 1996.

24 The account of the cardinals' attack on the Common Ground Initiative is based on published reports and personal interviews.

27 I reported Archbishop Quinn's speech in the *New York Times,* "Archbishop Seeks Reform in the Papacy," June 30, 1996; it was later developed into a book, *The Reform of the Papacy: The Costly Call to Christian Unity* (Crossroad, 1999).

29 Figures for the Catholic population and the number of parishes, priests, ordinations, sisters, and brothers: "The Catholic Church in the United States at a Glance," distributed by the Department of Communications of the U.S. Conference of Catholic Bishops, adapted from a table prepared by the Center for Applied Research in the Apostolate (CARA) at Georgetown University, using information from various editions of *The Official Catholic Directory* and the Vatican's Statistical Yearbook. Figures for 1965 Mass attendance from Andrew M. Greeley, *Religious Change in America* (Harvard, 1989), 42–46; and for 2002 from a year 2000 finding from the CARA Catholic poll, reported in Bryan T. Froehle and Mary L. Gautier, *Catholicism USA,* 24. The estimates of reception of Communion are widespread, coming from those who deplore the change as well as applaud it. Estimates about financial contributions from Dean R. Hoge et al., *Money Matters* (Westminster John Knox, 1996), 12, 20–23, and passim; also Joseph Claude Harris, *The Cost of Catholic Parishes and Schools* (Sheed & Ward,

1996), and Greeley, *Religious Change,* 67–75. Figures on elementary schools, colleges, and universities, and their students, and on health care institutions and numbers treated, and on converts, from *The Official Catholic Directory 1965* and *2002.* Number of full-time lay "ecclesial ministers" from Philip J. Murnion and David DeLambo, *Pairishes and Parish Ministers* (National Pastoral Life Center, 1999), 4, 22. Ages of diocesan priests from Richard A. Schoenherr and Lawrence A. Young, *Full Pews and Empty Altars* (University of Wisconsin, 1993), 28–33, and Froehle and Gautier, *Catholicism USA,* 112.

2. THE SCANDAL

40 *Boston Globe* figures are from several databases. The number of stories carried by major news media before the June meeting is based on an analysis done by RF Binder Partners for the bishops' Committee on Communications.

41 Poll data reported by David Gibson, "Scandal Hits Catholic Church in the Pews," Religion News Service, Dec. 20, 2002, and also by Kevin Eckstrom in the Religion News Service digest for June 25.

42 Stephen J. Rossetti, "The Catholic Church and Child Sexual Abuse," *America,* April 22, 2002, 14.

43 *National Catholic Reporter,* Feb. 7, 2003, 21.

44 Peter Steinfels, "The Church Faces the Trespasses of Priests," *New York Times,* June 27, 1993.

45 Laurie Goodstein, "Trail of Pain in Church Crisis Leads to Nearly Every Diocese," *New York Times,* Jan. 12, 2003.

45 The "sustained crisis" quote is in my July 27, 1993, article.

47 The Gauthé story was first reported at length by Jason Berry and forms the basis for the gripping first part of his *Lead Us Not into Temptation: Catholic Priests and the Sexual Abuse of Children* (Doubleday, 1992). His reporting on sex abuse by priests in the *National Catholic Reporter* was recognized with an award from the Catholic Press Association in 1986.

47 Peter Steinfels, "Inquiry in Chicago Breaks Silence on Sex Abuse by Catholic Priests, *New York Times,* Feb. 24, 1992; "New Panel in Chicago to Study Sexual Abuse of Children by Priests," *New York Times,* June 16, 1992; "Church Panel to Investigate Sexual Abuse in Chicago," *New York Times,* Sept. 22, 1992. Philip Jenkins, *Pedophiles and Priests* (Oxford, 1996), presents very helpful chronologies of both the events and the coverage. His book's thesis about the extent to which the earlier sex abuse scandal was "socially constructed" is controversial, but the book is full of valuable information and insights, especially when read along with an account like Berry's.

48 The Five Principles were long posted on the bishops conference website and have been widely distributed.

50 Interview with Bishop Kinney, June 14, 2003, and subsequent phone conversations.

53 *Crisis* magazine survey, question 24.

57 New York legislation: Shaila K. Dewan, "Clerics' Sex Reporting Bill Proves Un-
    expectedly Complicated," *New York Times,* June 28, 2002.

57 On tracking convicted offenders: William K. Rashbaum, "A Closer Eye on the
    Worst Offenders," *New York Times,* Jan. 28, 2003; Linda Greenhouse, "States'
    Listings of Sex Offenders Raise a Tangle of Legal Issues," *New York Times,* Nov.
    4, 2002; and many other articles.

58 Adam Liptak, "Judges Seek to Ban Secret Settlements in South Carolina," *New
    York Times,* Sept. 2, 2002.

59 Joseph Zwilling, paper prepared for a meeting of the advisory Communications
    Committee of the U.S. Conference of Catholic Bishops, Jan. 14, 2003. I partici-
    pated in this meeting, as did Bill Mitchell, the online editor for the Poynter Insti-
    tute for media studies in Saint Petersburg, Florida, who had overseen the
    institute's daily posting of articles on the sex abuse scandal.

63 Loyal defenders: George Weigel, *The Courage to Be Catholic* (Basic Books, 2002),
    117–46. Weigel was biting in his comments on the Vatican's lack of understand-
    ing and general incompetence (the pope always excepted) during a panel discus-
    sion in which I participated at the Ethics and Public Policy Center, Washington,
    D.C., May 30, 2002.

3. THE CHURCH AND SOCIETY

69 Renee K. Gadoua, "Poll Suggests Bishops May Still Have Influence on the
    Laity," Religion News Service, Dec. 16, 2002, reported on a LeMoyne College/
    Zogby poll of Catholics released on Dec. 11, 2002.

69 For the encounter between Catholicism and the United States, besides the histo-
    rians mentioned previously, see Philip Gleason, *Keeping the Faith: American
    Catholicism Past and Present* (Notre Dame, 1987), and "American Catholics and
    Liberalism, 1789–1960," in R. Bruce Douglass and David Hollenbach, eds.,
    Catholicism and Liberalism (Cambridge, 1994), 45–75; David O'Brien, *Public
    Catholicism* (Macmillan, 1989); and of course, John Courtney Murray, *We Hold
    These Truths: Catholic Reflections on the American Proposition* (Sheed & Ward,
    1960). In Morris's *American Catholic,* the chapter "The Whore of Babylon
    Learns How to Vote" describes the violent side of the encounter. Philip Ham-
    burger, *Separation of Church and State* (Harvard, 2002), reveals the importance
    of anti-Catholicism in America's understanding of religious freedom, and John
    T. McGreevy, *Catholicism and American Freedom* (W. W. Norton, 2003), shows
    the complexity of the relationship between American Catholicism and liberal
    impulses. McGreevy deals with the slavery debate there as well as in an earlier
    paper, written for the American Catholics in the Public Square project, found on
    its website, catholicsinpublicsquare.org, and to be included in a forthcoming
    volume.

70 Charles Morris on "prickly apartness" and all-enveloping cocoon: *American Catholic*, vii; on the Washington monument, 55, 62–63; on Academy Awards, 196–200.

72 McGreevy reports the favorable responses to Blanshard in *Catholicism and American Freedom*, 167–68, and discusses Blanshard's influence on the court, 184–86.

77 Opposition by O'Connell and other Catholic leaders to child labor laws: Hennesey, *American Catholics*, 233.

78 William B. Prendergast, *The Catholic Voter in American Politics* (Georgetown, 1999), is a Republican analyst's account of the loosening of Catholic Democratic ties in presidential politics. In many articles, Andrew Greeley has insisted that Catholics' Democratic loyalties endure. See the CARA study for the American Catholics in the Public Square project and the papers by E. J. Dionne, Steven Wagner, David C. Leege, Kate O'Beirne, and William Bole on catholicsinpublicsquare. org (and in a forthcoming book). The 2000 election exit polls are from Voter News Service and can be found on beliefnet.com. The differences between more observant, less observant, and Hispanic Catholics are from University of Akron Survey Research Center, *The Third National Survey of Religion and Politics*, summarized by John C. Green, James L. Guth, Lyman A. Kellstedt, Corwin E. Smidt, "How the Faithful Voted: Religion and the 2000 Presidential Election," *Center Conversations* (Ethics and Public Policy Center), March 2001, 11–12. John C. Green of the University of Akron provided me with figures that were not broken out in the original report.

79 William Bole, "Communitarian Lite," *Commonweal*, Sept. 11, 2002, 12–16, and the CARA studies for the American Catholics in the Public Square project.

85 Joseph Cardinal Bernardin, *A Moral Vision for America*, edited by John P. Langan, S.J. (Georgetown, 1998), 12, 14, 45.

87 O'Connor quoted in Nat Hentoff, *John Cardinal O'Connor* (Scribner's, 1988), 77–78.

87 Cuomo and his son: Morris, *American Catholic*, 424–25.

88 Cuomo's Notre Dame address can be found in Patricia Beattie Jung and Thomas A. Shannon, eds., *Abortion & Catholicism: The American Debate* (Crossroad, 1988), 202–16; it is excerpted in Steven M. Avella and Elizabeth McKeown, eds., *Public Voices: Catholics in the American Context* (Orbis, 1999), 371–75.

89 O'Connor, Malone, and Hyde and reported in Hentoff, *John Cardinal O'Connor*, 78–83.

89 Bernardin speeches in *A Moral Vision for America*; quote on 91.

91 On revision of the Democratic abortion plank: Prendergast, *The Catholic Voter*, 195–96.

92 Stephen L. Carter, *The Culture of Disbelief* (Basic Books, 1993), 56, 58.

95 Administrative Board of the U.S. Catholic Bishops, "Faithful Citizenship: Civic Responsibility for a New Millennium" (United States Catholic Conference, 1999).

99 Dionne's views are summarized in Bole, "Communitarian Lite"; Dionne's fuller argument is at catholicsinpublicsquare.org and in a forthcoming volume. The churchgoing Catholics and Republican "moral restoration" argument is repre-

sented on that website by Steven Wagner and by Catholic advisers to the White
House like Robert P. George of Princeton and Deal Hudson of *Crisis* magazine.
David Leege's view are found on catholicsinpublicsquare.org, and also in David
C. Leege, Kenneth D. Wald, Brian S. Krueger, and Paul D. Mueller, *The Politics
of Cultural Differences* (Princeton, 2002), 192–93.

101   Novak's letters: "Moral Clarity in the Nuclear Age," *National Review*, Apr. 1,
       1983, and *Toward the Future: Catholic Social Thought and the U.S. Economy* (Lay
       Commission on Catholic Social Thought and the U.S. Economy, 1984).

4. CATHOLIC INSTITUTIONS AND CATHOLIC IDENTITY

103   Our Lady of Victory and similar establishments are described in John T. Mc-
       Greevy, *Parish Boundaries* (University of Chicago Press, 1996), 14–15.

104   Rich descriptions of this array of Catholic institutions can be found in Charles R.
       Morris, *American Catholic*, and especially Jay P. Dolan, *The American Catholic
       Experience*.

104   The structure of the church and statistics regarding its institutions and activities
       are summarized in "The Catholic Church in the United States at a Glance," a
       "backgrounder" issued by the Department of Communications of the U.S. Con-
       ference of Catholic Bishops, 2002. The basic source for much of this data is the
       annual *Official Catholic Directory* (P. J. Kenedy & Sons). Information here is also
       found in annual reports of the Catholic Health Association and of Catholic Char-
       ities USA; in Bryan T. Froehle and Mary L. Gautier, *Catholicism USA*; and in
       Clarke E. Cochran, "Catholic Health Care and the Challenge of Civil Society," a
       paper prepared for the Feb. 22–24, 2002, Commonweal Colloquium, part of the
       American Catholics in the Public Square research project (catholicsinpublic-
       square.org and forthcoming volume). Helpful clarification of the terminology of
       religious "orders," "institutes," "congregations," etc., can be found in Froehle
       and Gautier, *Catholicism USA*, 125–26. See also "Religious Orders and Congre-
       gations" and related entries in the very useful *HarperCollins Encyclopedia of
       Catholicism*, edited by Richard P. McBrien (HarperCollins, 1995). Recent edi-
       tions of *The Official Catholic Directory* have listed over 125 religious institutes
       of men and over four hundred religious institutes of women in the United
       States. A few, like the Society of Jesus (Jesuits) and the Sisters of Mercy, have
       thousands of members; other orders range in size from several hundred down to
       several dozen or even fewer.

114   The history of Catholic health care is recounted in Christopher J. Kauffman,
       *Ministry & Meaning: A Religious History of Catholic Health Care in the United
       States* (Crossroad, 1995), and in Suzy Farren, *A Call to Care: The Women Who
       Built Catholic Healthcare in America* (Catholic Health Association, 1996). Kauff-
       man, 25–26, mentions Florence Nightingale's suspicions and the Sisters of
       Mercy; elsewhere he reports on Nightingale's religiosity positively.

116   Sisters of Charity in Baltimore: Kauffman, *Ministry & Meaning*, 33–49.

116   Debate over garb: ibid., 181–84. Controversy also arose over summer school ses-

sions in medical practice for sisters, because the sisters would be taught by non-Catholics, mix with laity, and live outside their regular convent routines (ibid., 172–75).

117 Kauffman, ibid., 168 ff., deals with Flexner and the founding of the Catholic Hospital Association, which renamed itself the Catholic Health Association in 1979. The organization's history is the spine of the rest of his book.

117 Two heart attacks: Cochran, "Catholic Health Care," citing Guenter B. Risse, *Mending Bodies, Saving Souls: A History of Hospitals* (Oxford University Press, 1999), chap. 10.

118 The mergers and affiliations are traced on these organizations' websites.

118 Transcripts of the Malibu discussion are on catholicsinpublicsquare.org. The Cochran paper was posted there and will be published in a forthcoming volume.

120 Ann Neale, "Catholic Identity: Realized in Conversation," *Health Progress*, Mar.–Apr. 1997. This article and many issues of *Health Progress*, published by the Catholic Health Association, can be found on its website, www.chausa.org.

122 Materials from the Catholic Health Association: Rabbi Milton L. Kroopnick's testimony is in *A Shared Statement of Identity for the Catholic Health Ministry* (2001), 6–7. Under the general title *Living Our Promises, Acting on Faith*, three reports from the "benchmarking" and "best practices" project were published by the association in 2000 (baseline data and observations) and 2001 (employee satisfaction with their role in decision making and data and observations from nursing facilities).

123 On mergers, abortion, sterilization, and pro-choice campaigns, see Francis J. Butler, "Will Charity Laws Close Catholic Hospitals?" *America*, Oct. 29, 2001, 12–15. Women's Law Center website and other references. "The Freedom to Serve in a Pluralistic Society," statement by the Catholic Health Association.

124 The Vatican and sterilization: Keven D. O'Rourke, Thomas Kopfensteiner, and Ron Hamel, "A Brief History: A Summary of the Development of the Ethical and Religious Directives for Catholic Health Care Services," *Health Progress*, Nov.–Dec. 2001.

132 238 schools: "Catholic Church . . . at a Glance" and *The Official Catholic Directory*.

132 Enrollment and percentage: See the sources in the previous note and *Digest of Education Statistics, 2001*, http://nces.ed.gov/pubs2002/digest2001/ch3.asp.

133 Peter Steinfels, "Catholic Colleges Chart Paths Still Catholic and Yet Diverse," *New York Times*, May 1, 1991.

135 The history of critiques of Catholic intellectual life are related in Charles R. Morris, *American Catholic*; and Jay P. Dolan, *The American Catholic Experience* (Doubleday, 1985), and *In Search of an American Catholicism* (Oxford, 2002); and elsewhere. Key statements were John Tracy Ellis, "American Catholics and the Intellectual Life," *Thought*, autumn 1955, 353–86, and Thomas F. O'Dea, *American Catholic Dilemma: An Inquiry into Intellectual Life* (Sheed & Ward, 1958), but a vast literature—especially in Catholic periodicals like *America* and *Commonweal*, as well as in books like Daniel Callahan, *The Mind of the Catholic Layman* (Charles Scribner's Sons, 1963)—surrounded them. Philip Gleason,

Keeping the Faith: American Catholicism Past and Present (Notre Dame, 1987) gives a historian's perspective. Gleason's *Contending with Modernity: Catholic Higher Education in the Twentieth Century* (Oxford, 1995) is the definitive history.

143 Besides the activities mentioned, a stream of excellent books, to which I am indebted, took up the topic of Catholic identity. Some have already been mentioned. George M. Marsden, *The Soul of the American University: From Protestant Establishment to Established Nonbelief* (Oxford, 1994), told the story of the secularization of the nation's major universities, in a way that reinforced Catholics' doubts about their own immunity. Theodore M. Hesburgh, C.S.C., ed., *The Challenge and Promise of a Catholic University* (University of Notre Dame Press, 1994), and John P. Langan, S.J., ed., *Catholic Universities in Church and Society* (Georgetown University Press, 1993), were important collections of essays. David J. O'Brien, *From the Heart of the American Church* (Orbis, 1994), and Michael J. Buckley, S.J., *The Catholic University as Promise and Project* (Georgetown University Press, 1998), were analyses by a historian and theologian, respectively. Alice Gallin, O.S.U., a historian, former college president, and for many years director of the Association of Catholic Colleges and Universities, wrote *Independence and a New Partnership in Catholic Higher Education* (Notre Dame, 1996) and *Negotiating Identity* (Notre Dame, 2000), dealing with the transition to lay governance and the debate over *Ex Corde Ecclesiae*. The 1990s began in the shadow of the removal of the Reverend Charles E. Curran from the theology faculty at Catholic University; the consequent questions of Vatican pressure, religious authority, and academic freedom were examined in Larry Witham, *Curran vs. Catholic University* (Eddington Rand, 1991), and Charles E. Curran, *Catholic Higher Education, Theology, and Academic Freedom* (Notre Dame, 1990). James Tunstead Burtchaell, *The Dying of the Light* (William B. Eerdmans, 1998), is an extensively researched, influential, and cutting account of "the disengagement of colleges and universities from their Christian churches."

144 Alice Gallin, "Making Colleges Catholic: Bishops & Academics Reach Common Ground," *Commonweal*, Mar. 28, 1997, 14–17, described these earlier rounds of discussion between Vatican officials, Catholic educators, and bishops.

144 Rome's determination: Peter Steinfels, "A Journalist's View: Does Rome Have the Best Answer?" (in a special supplement, "Keeping Colleges Catholic: What's at Stake?"), *Commonweal*, Apr. 9, 1999, 14–17.

147 Alasdair MacIntyre, *Three Rival Versions of Moral Enquiry* (Notre Dame, 1990), cited by David B. Burrell, C.S.C., "A Catholic University," in Hesburgh, ed., *Challenge and Promise*, 37–39.

147 George Dennis O'Brien, *The Idea of a Catholic University* (University of Chicago, 2002), analyzes the presuppositions of the dominant research university.

149 Andrew M. Greeley, "A Sociologist's View: What Catholics Do Well," in *Commonweal*, Apr. 9, 1999, 26–30.

150 O'Brien, *Idea of a Catholic University*.

151 Sullivan and Flynt are real, not hypothetical, episodes.

152 Absentee landlordism: Melanie M. Morey and Dennis H. Holtschneider, "Keeping the Faith on Campus," *Commonweal,* Apr. 20, 2001, 20–23.

152 George M. Marsden, "What Can Catholic Universities Learn from Protestant Examples?" in Hesburgh, ed., *Challenge and Promise,* 193.

5. AROUND THE ALTAR

165 Church attendance: Bryan T. Froehle and Mary L. Gautier, *Catholicism USA,* 22–24.

165 Kathleen Hughes, *Saying Amen: A Mystagogy of the Sacraments* (Liturgy Training Publications), xiv.

166 "Source and summit of the Christian life": Dogmatic Constitution on the Church (*Lumen Gentium*) 11; Catechism of the Catholic Church 1324–27. See also the Constitution on the Sacred Liturgy (*Sacrosanctum Concilium*) 10, pertaining to the liturgy in general.

167 Children of Mass attenders: James D. Davidson et al., *The Search for Common Ground* (Our Sunday Visitor, 1997), 98.

170 "Aim . . . full, conscious, and active participation": Constitution on the Sacred Liturgy 13.

172 Andrew M. Greeley, *The Catholic Myth* (Charles Scribner's Sons, 1990), 5, 21, 133, reports 87 percent of Catholics approving of the English liturgy, as measured by the National Opinion Research Center's polls. Greeley reported this earlier, in *The American Catholic* (Basic Books, 1977), 130, and elsewhere.

172 Kenneth Untener, "Is the Church in Decline?" *Church,* summer 99, 5.

172 The pope's only mention of sin is relegated to a brief footnote quoting the catechism; see *Dies Domini* (1998), 47 and n. 83.

172 Andrew M. Greeley, *Religious Change in America* (Harvard University Press, 1989) devotes chap. 4 to church attendance, much of it to the Catholic decline (44–56). He has written on this elsewhere, in both more popular and more technical terms. See, for example, the books noted above and his *American Catholics Since the Council* (Thomas More Press, 1985), 71–79.

173 Tridentine Mass advocates: William D. Dinges, " 'We Are What You Were': Roman Catholic Traditionalism in America," in Mary Jo Weaver and R. Scott Appleby, eds., *Being Right: Conservative Catholics in America* (Indiana University Press, 1995), 242. Fewer than 200 churches or chapels offering "episcopally approved traditional Latin Masses" in the U.S., many only once a month, were listed on an updated website in April 2003. See www.ecclesiadei.org/direct00.htm.

174 Sheila Durkin Dierks, *WomenEucharist* (WovenWord Press, 1997), catches this mood.

175 Thomas Day, *Why Catholics Can't Sing* (Crossroad, 1990), 35–36 and passim.

178 Rembert G. Weakland, "Liturgy and Common Ground," *America,* Feb. 20, 1999, 7–11.

178 Hughes, *Saying Amen,* xii, xiii.

182 Paul Wilkes, *Boston Globe,* Dec. 19, 1999.

183 Lawrence J. Madden, S.J., *The Awakening Church: 25 Years of Liturgical Renewal* (Liturgical Press, 1992). Interview with Father Madden, Feb. 23, 2000.

187 Rembert G. Weakland, "Off Key and off the Mark," *Commonweal,* Jan. 25, 1991, 65–67, and later in *America,* Feb. 20, 1999, 7–11.

194 Roper Center poll for *Catholic World Report,* reported in March 1997 issue; also www.cnnews.com/Browse/1997/02/4353.htm.

197 Ibid.

198 Godfried Cardinal Danneels, "Liturgy Thirty Years After the Council: High Point or Recession?" in Eleanor Bernstein, C.S.J., and Martin F. Connell, eds., *Traditions & Transitions* (Liturgy Training Publications, 1998), 17.

198 Interview with Bishop Kenneth Untener, Apr. 15, 2000; Ken Untener, *Preaching Better* (Paulist, 1999), 1–5.

201 Many possibilities: "Gather Faithfully Together," a pastoral letter by Cardinal Roger Mahony, became the basis for a major educational effort in the Los Angeles archdiocese, as well as a video and discussion guide. The cardinal's letter was attacked as heretical by Mother Angelica, who heads the Eternal Word Television Network (EWTN).

201 Lori Carrell, *The Great American Sermon Survey* (Mainstay Church Resources, 2000).

6. PASSING ON THE FAITH

205 Negative judgments in Dean R. Hoge, William D. Dinges, Mary Johnson, S.N. de N., and Juan L. Gonzales Jr., *Young Adult Catholics* (University of Notre Dame Press, 2001), 135.

205 On "core" teachings: ibid., 64, 200–205, 220–21, 226, 254–55 (on "traditional doctrine scale"). See also William V. D'Antonio, James D. Davidson, Dean R. Hoge, and Katherine Meyer, *American Catholics: Gender, Generation, and Commitment* (AltaMira Press, 2001), 46–50, 137–38. James D. Davidson, Andrea S. Williams, Richard A. Lamanna, Jan Stenftenagel, Kathleen Maas Weigert, William J. Whalen, and Patricia Wittberg, S.C., in *The Search for Common Ground* (Our Sunday Visitor, 1997), stress the agreement among all Catholics, including younger ones, about "pan-Vatican II beliefs" like the incarnation and the resurrection, but they combine them with more specifically preconciliar items to create a "traditional beliefs and practices index," which does show strong generational decline. Andrew Greeley has stated that there are no data suggesting that post–Vatican II Catholics are "any less loyal, any less committed, any less devout than their predecessors"—see *The Catholic Myth,* 257—although here and elsewhere he does not mention belief and generally emphasizes sensibility, devotion, and attachment.

206 Change in terminology: Gabriel Moran, "Religious Education After Vatican II," in David Efroymson and John Raines, eds., *Open Catholicism* (Liturgical Press, 1997), 149.

207 "Formation and transformation" is one of many formulas about faith and catechesis in the thought of Thomas H. Groome and like-minded catechetical leaders that emphasize totality. Referring to paragraphs in the Vatican's 1997
General Directory for Catechesis, Groome writes, "Faith is a way of believing, a
way of worshipping, and a way of living (*credendi, orandi, vivendi* #122); it is
cognitive, affective, and behavioral (#35); it engages people's minds, emotions,
and wills; it is to permeate how we make meaning out of life, the quality of all
our relationships, and the ethic by which we live (#16)." See Thomas H.
Groome, "Claiming and Breaking Ground: The General Directory for Catechesis," in Thomas H. Groome and Michael J. Corso, eds., *Empowering Catechetical
Leaders* (National Catholic Educational Association, 1999), 239.

208 Hoge et al., eds., *Young Adult Catholics,* 44–46; for sampling, see 39–42 , 58, and
243–47.

209 Sobering note: ibid., 221–28.

210 "Implications": ibid., 228. "A flashing yellow light": interview with William D.
Dinges.

211 On Catholic schools: Timothy Walch, *Parish School* (Crossroad Herder, 1996), 54.

212 Decline of sisters, brothers, and priests: James Youniss, introduction, to James
Youniss and John J. Convey, eds., *Catholic Schools at the Crossroads* (Teachers
College Press, 2000), 2. Percentage now lay: "Fact Sheet," National Catholic Ed-
ucational Association, 2002.

212 Decline in enrollment: Youniss and Convey, *Catholic Schools.*

213 Minority and non-Catholic enrollment: NCEA "Fact Sheet."

214 Percentage of students: James Youniss, John J. Convey, and Jeffrey A. McLellan,
eds., *The Catholic Character of Catholic Schools* (University of Notre Dame
Press, 2000), 5.

215 Percentage of lay principals: Kathleen Carr, C.S.J., "Leadership Given to the Religious Mission of Catholic Schools," in ibid., 62.

216 Principals' attitudes: Carr, "Leadership," 62–81, especially 69–72, 77.

216 "Cataclysmic shift": Paul W. Galetto, O.S.A., *Building the Foundations of Faith*
(National Catholic Educational Association, 1996), 32.

217 Lay teachers of religion: Paul Galetto, O.S.A., "Religious Knowledge and Belief
of Lay Religion Teachers in Catholic Elementary Schools," in Youniss et al.,
Catholic Character, 124–41; for recommendations, Carr, "Leadership," 72–75,
and Galetto, *Building the Foundations,* 105–7.

219 Debate over Catholic schools: Walch, *Parish School,* 169–87. "stink bomb": 177.

221 Parishes with schools, budgets, and expenditures are examined by Joseph Claude
Harris, "A Plan to Pay for Catholic Schools," in Regina Haney and Joseph
O'Keefe, S.J., eds., *Creatively Financing and Resourcing Catholic Schools* (National
Catholic Educational Association, 1999), 49–71, and in "The Funding Dilemma
Facing Catholic Elementary and Secondary Schools," in Youniss and Convey,
eds., *Catholic Schools,* 55–71.

221 Supreme Court ruling: *Zelman* v. *Simmon-Harris,* June 27, 2002.

222 A small sampling of perspectives can be found in the concluding chapter, by
Maureen Hallinan, in Youniss and Convey, *Catholic Schools,* 201–20; in the chap-

ters by Harris cited above; and in Jerome Porah, "Not Just Religious Formation," in Youniss et al., *Catholic Character*, 219–39.

224   On Barron's "beige Catholicism": Andrew M. Greeley, "A Cloak of Many Colors," *Commonweal*, Nov. 9, 1999, 10.

225   CCD: "Confraternity of Christian Doctrine," in Richard P. McBrien, ed., *HarperCollins Encyclopedia of Catholicism* (HarperCollins, 1995).

226   Percentages in catechetics programs and in schools: Bryan T. Froehle and Mary L. Gautier, *Catholicism USA*, 76.

227   Andrew D. Thompson, *That They May Know You* (National Catholic Educational Association, 1982), and John J. Convey and Andrew D. Thompson, *Weaving Christ's Seamless Garment* (National Catholic Educational Association, 1999).

227   "Nonsense and rubbish": Alfred McBride, O. Praem., *NCEA Religious Education Forum Newsletter*, June 1978, quoted in Michael J. Wrenn, *Catechisms and Controversies* (Ignatius Press, 1991), 135–37.

228   Percentage of unenrolled: Froehle and Gautier, *Catholicism USA*, 76.

229   Criticism: See Wrenn, *Catechisms*, for example, or most recently Eamonn Keane, *A Generation Betrayed* (Hatherleigh Press, 2002); a profile of Catholics United for the Faith, which has generated much of this criticism, by one of its leaders, James A. Sullivan, appears in Mary Jo Weaver and R. Scott Appleby, *Being Right*, 107–37.

229   Fundamental terms: "Appendix A: Catholic Faith Literacy," *NCEA ACRE Interpretation Manual* (National Catholic Education Association, 2001), 37.

230   Interviews with Groome and Corso.

231   Parents born after 1960: Froehle and Gautier, *Catholicism USA*, 78–79, from a CARA poll conducted in 2000.

232   Thomas P. Walters, "Catholic Literacy: A Modest Proposal," *Living Light*, Winter 1999, 64–66. The distinction between initiation and schooling is credited to Didier Piveteau, "School, Society and Catechesis," in Dermot Lane, ed., *Religious Education and the Future* (Paulist Press, 1986), 21. Walters has also advanced his ideas in "Religious Education Update: The Opening of the American Mind," *Living Light*, Summer 1989, 208–20.

234   Family-based programs: Judith Dunlap has written on family-based catechesis for *Church* magazine and elsewhere. With Mary Wlodarski, she has written *God Is Calling* (St. Anthony Messenger Press), a series of textbooks for family-based catechesis. I interviewed both authors in February 2001.

234   Intensive camps and other alternatives: At the national convocation of the National Association of Parish Catechetical Directors (NCPD), Leisa Anslinger described such a program at Immaculate Heart of Mary parish in the Cincinnati diocese. The April 3, 2002, workshop, conducted with Diana Dudoit Raiche of the NCEA staff, dealt with using the NCEA assessment instruments.

234   On retreats: Hoge et al., *Young Adult Catholics*, 141–42.

235   Qualities needed by DREs are examined in several chapters in Groome and Corso, eds., *Empowering Catechetical Leaders*.

235 350,000: The Vatican Statistical Yearbook, cited in *CARA Report*, summer 2002, says 365,592.

236 Parishes with DREs and salaries: "Diocesan Directors Assess Catechetical Ministry," *CARA Report*, fall 1999, 3, and "National Profile of Catechetical Ministry," *CARA Special Report*, Nov. 2000. Although these reports appear to be based on the same survey, the *Special Report* seems to indicate a higher percentage of full-time DREs, estimating that 23 percent of DREs are part-time and only about 15 percent are volunteers.

237 Budgets: *CARA Special Report;* but especially Thomas P. Walters and Rita Tyson Walters, *Catechetical Leaders: A Statistical Profile* (National Catholic Educational Association, 1998), 22. See also Harris, "The Funding Dilemma," in Youniss and Convey, eds., *Catholic Schools*, 68.

237 Statement of the U.S. Catholic bishops: "Our Hearts Were Burning Within Us: A Pastoral Plan for Adult Faith Formation in the United States" (United States Catholic Conference, 1999), 4, 34–52, 59.

238 Interviews and e-mail exchanges with Edmund F. Gordon, Sister Maureen Shaughnessy, and Thomas H. Groome; Holy Family Parish website and e-mail with Frank Strawser.

242 "A small pool,": Robert J. Egan, S.J., "Who's Doing Catholic Theology?" *Commonweal*, Mar. 13, 1992, 14. I have leaned heavily on this article, sometimes paraphrasing it, as well as on my own report (which it undoubtedly influenced) on the 1995 Catholic Theological Society meeting, "50 Years of Catholic Talk: New Faces and New Ideas," *New York Times,* June 20, 1995.

243 Egan, "Who's Doing Catholic Theology?" 15.

243 First meetings: observations of Sister Elizabeth A. Johnson, the society's newly elected president in 1995, who had organized that year's meeting on the theme of "Evil and Hope." Brother Luke Salm's recollections: also at the 1995 meeting.

244 "Inner sanctum": Egan, "Who's Doing Catholic Theology?" 14.

245 "Something valuable has been endangered" ibid.

247 Avery Dulles, Mary Ann Donovan, and Peter Steinfels, "How Catholic Is the CTSA? Three Views," *Commonweal*, Mar. 27, 1998, 14. Dulles quotes Law's denunciation, 13.

247 Garry Wills, *Bare Ruined Choirs* (Doubleday, 1972), 21.

249 The book by Congar, whose work had an enormous influence on the Council, was published in French in 1950—and then ordered by the Vatican to be withdrawn.

250 *Structures of Deceit* is the subtitle of Garry Wills, *Papal Sin* (Doubleday, 2002); see 7–9.

7. SEX AND THE FEMALE CHURCH

253 The Council and sex: *Gaudium et Spes* (Constitution on the Church in the Modern World) 48; Thomas Davey, O.P., "Marriage and Sexuality," in Adrian Hastings, ed., *Modern Catholicism: Vatican II and After* (Oxford, 1991), 267.

254 The Council and women: *Gaudium et Spes* 9, 29, 52, 60; Rosemary Radford Ruether, "The Place of Women in the Church," in Hastings, ed., *Modern Catholicism,* 260–61.

255 Bernard Häring, "The Encyclical Crisis," *Commonweal,* Sept. 6, 1968, 588.

256 Directly at issue: *Humanae Vitae* 11, 12.

258 Peter Steinfels, "Vatican Watershed—A Special Report: Papal Birth-Control Letter Retains Its Grip," *New York Times,* Aug. 1, 1993.

259 Greeley quoted ibid. Greeley has argued for the widespread repercussions of the encyclical—on Mass attendance, contributions, and church authority—in many places.

259 Avery Dulles, S.J., " 'Humanae Vitae' and the Crisis of Dissent," *Origins,* Apr. 22, 1993, 774–77.

262 "Souls in jeopardy": Janet E. Smith, "A Stalled and Stale Debate," *Catholic World Report,* Nov. 1993, 58.

264 On infallibility, see John C. Ford, S.J., Germain Grisez, Joseph Boyle, John Finnis, William E. May, *The Teaching of Humanae Vitae: A Defense* (Ignatius Press, 1988); Ford and Grisez press the case for infallibility, 117–219.

266 Alfred North Whitehead, *Science and the Modern World* (1925; reprint, Free Press, 1967), 96.

268 Walter Lippmann, *A Preface to Morals* (1929; reprint, Transaction Publishers, 1989); see the chapter "Love in the Great Society"; quotations from 307, 291.

268 Missing in action: Abundant evidence can be found in Andrew M. Greeley, *The Catholic Myth,* chap. 5, "Sex and Family," 91–105.

271 National Conference of Catholic Bishops, "To Live in Christ Jesus."

272 Congregation for the Doctrine of the Faith, "Pastoral Care of Homosexual Persons," *Origins,* Nov. 13, 1986.

272 Rome on AIDS prevention campaign: I followed this clash in the *New York Times:* "Catholic Bishops Refuse to Rescind AIDS Policy," Mar. 26, 1988; "Catholic Bishops Vote to Retain Controversial Statement on AIDS," June 28, 1988; "Bishops Shift Earlier Stance on AIDS," Oct. 13, 1989; "Bishops' AIDS Policy Urges Abstinence," Nov. 11, 1989.

273 Dissociation with gay and lesbian groups: Congregation for the Doctrine of the Faith, "Responding to Legislative Proposals on Discrimination Against Homosexuals," *Origins,* Aug. 6, 1992.

279 Sister Madeleva Wolff: Regina A. Coll, "Women in the Church," in Richard P. McBrien, ed., *The HarperCollins Encyclopedia of Catholicism* (HarperCollins, 1995), 1332–33.

280 The scope of Catholic feminist theology is exemplified by Catherine Mowry LaCugna, ed., *Freeing Theology: The Essentials of Theology in Feminist Perspective* (HarperCollins, 1993), and Anne E. Carr, *Transforming Grace* (Continuum, 1988). See also Mary Jo Weaver, *New Catholic Women* (Indiana University Press, 1986, 1995).

281 Peter Steinfels, "Women's Group Recasts Religion in Its Own Image," *New York Times,* Apr. 21, 1993, and "As Catholic Feminists Meet, Some Question Their

Faith," *New York Times,* Apr. 16, 1993; Catherine Walsh, "Bang the Drum—Not," *Commonweal,* June 4, 1993, 6–7. Walsh, an editor, reporter, and columnist for several Catholic magazines in the 1980s and 1990s, helped report this conference for the *New York Times.* Rosemary Radford Ruether, who helped inspire and guide the Women-Church movement, has a factual history of it in Mary Jo Weaver, ed., *What's Left? Liberal American Catholics* (Indiana University Press, 1999), 46–64.

285 Geoffrey Nunberg, "Usage in *The American Heritage Dictionary,*" in *The American Heritage Dictionary of the English Language,* 4th ed. (Houghton Mifflin, 2000), xxix.

286 National Conference of Catholic Bishops, "Criteria for the Evaluation of Inclusive Language Translations of Scriptural Texts Proposed for Liturgical Use." The bishops also approved "Principles for Preparing Pericopes from the New American Bible for Use in the Second Edition of the Lectionary for Mass."

289 Catechism of the Catholic Church 1.

290 Some poll data: Roper Center poll by *Catholic World Report,* March 1997.

291 Daly's work has been very shrewdly analyzed as a species of guerrilla theater by Weaver, *New Catholic Women,* 174–77, 253 n. 97.

292 In an introduction to a new edition of *Transforming Grace,* xv, Anne E. Carr has an eloquent paragraph on "the singular importance" of Mary in popular Catholicism. She concludes, "I believe we can trust the instinct of faith that for centuries has turned to Mary in her many embodiments even as we may be critical of aberrations and extremes in some devotions to her."

292 Wisdom: See Elizabeth A. Johnson, *She Who Is: The Mystery of God in Feminist Theological Discourse* (Crossroad, 1992), and the same author's "Redeeming the Name of Christ," in LaCugna, *Freeing Theology,* 115–37.

293 Over 60 percent: in William V. D'Antonio, James D. Davidson, Dean R. Hoge, and Katherine Meyer, *American Catholics: Gender, Generation, and Commitment* (AltaMira Press, 2001), 109.

293 *Roma locuta:* Leonard Swidler, quoted in Weaver, *New Catholic Women,* 115.

293 Old reasons not sustainable: *Inter Insigniores* ("Declaration on the Question of the Admission of Women to Ministerial Priesthood") 1.

295 "Far from obvious": Benedict Ashley, O.P., *Justice in the Church: Gender and Participation* (Catholic University of America Press, 1999), 89.

299 Spousal imagery opposed to exclusion: Susan A. Ross, *Extravagant Affections: A Feminist Sacramental Theology* (Continuum, 1998), 102–15.

299 Spousal imagery, intimacy, and interdependence: Ibid.

301 The question of deacons is fully explored in Phyllis Zagano, *Holy Saturday: An Argument for the Restoration of the Female Diaconate in the Catholic Church* (Crossroad, 2000). John Wijngaards, *No Women in Holy Orders? The Women Deacons of the Early Church* (Canterbury Press, 2002), appeared too late to be consulted.

303 Altar servers: The pope's ruling was made public in April 1994.

8. AT THE HELM

313 Management: Thomas J. Reese, *Archbishop* (Harper & Row, 1989), is essential for understanding the nuts and bolts of all bishops' activities.

314 Jadot's role: ibid., 41–47. Reese does not want to overdo the difference between "Jadot bishops" and others, perhaps for diplomatic reasons. Charles Morris, *American Catholic*, 485, comments on how widely the notion is used. Bishop Untener was the last Jadot appointment and laughingly calls himself the "reductio ad absurdum" of the "Jadot bishops."

316 Richard A. Schoenherr and Lawrence A. Young, *Full Pews and Empty Altars* (University of Wisconsin Press, 1993), xvii–xviii.

316 Ratio of priests: Dean R. Hoge, *The First Five Years of the Priesthood* (Liturgical Press, 2002), 2.

316 Ordinations: ibid. and "The Catholic Church in the United States at a Glance," a "backgrounder" prepared by the Department of Communications, U.S. Conference of Catholic Bishops (2002), 4. Also see Bryan T. Froehle and Mary L. Gautier, *Catholicism USA*, 117.

316 Growing population and dying priests: Hoge, *First Five Years*, 2.

317 No resident priest or serving alone: *CARA Report*, Spring 2002, 12.

317 Average age: Froehle and Gautier, *Catholicism USA*, 112–13.

317 One scholar: D. Paul Sullins, "Empty Pews and Empty Altars," *America*, May 13, 2002, 12–15.

318 Overflowing with seminarians: David Yamane, introduction to Richard A. Schoenherr, *Goodbye Father: The Celibate Male Priesthood and the Future of the Catholic Church*, edited by David Yamane (Oxford, 2002), xvii.

318 A recent round of such disputes was provoked by the lurid tales showing "how liberals brought corruption into the Catholic Church," in Michael S. Rose, *Goodbye, Good Men* (Regnery, 2002).

320 Newly ordained priests: Hoge, *First Five Years*, 5.

321 First orthodox class: ibid., 56–57.

322 Richard P. McBrien, "Homosexuality & the Priesthood," *Commonweal*, June 19, 1987, 380–83.

323 Percentage of homosexual priests: McBrien lists *Newsweek*, the *Atlantic Monthly*, and the *National Catholic Reporter* among publications speculating on the topic. See, most recently, Donald Cozzens, *The Changing Face of the Priesthood* (Liturgical Press, 2000), which renewed the discussion.

324 Laurie Goodstein, "Trail of Pain in Church Crisis Leads to Nearly Every Diocese," *New York Times*, Jan. 12, 2003, is one of the sources suggesting that the evidence does not fall neatly on either side in this debate.

324 Vatican worries and policies about gay candidates can be found in the articles in *America*, Dec. 16, 2002. The quotes are from "Pastoral Care of Homosexual Persons," issued by the Congregation for the Doctrine of the Faith in 1986.

326 Numbers for religious priests, brothers, and sisters: "The Catholic Church . . . at a Glance," 4.

331 Numbers and motivations of lay ministers: Philip J. Murnion, *New Parish Ministers* (National Pastoral Life Center, 1992), v; Philip J. Murnion and David DeLambo, *Parishes and Parish Ministers: A Study of Parish Lay Ministry* (National Pastoral Life Center, 1999), iii–iv, 39–40.

331 "Underneath the statistics," Murnion and DeLambo write, "something quite profound is happening" (*Parishes and Parish Ministers,* 69). Murnion, a New York priest-sociologist, founded the National Pastoral Life Center in 1983 to support parishes with research, analysis, publications, workshops, training courses, social action programs, and other activities. With DeLambo and others, including the researchers at CARA, he has produced the most thorough studies and analyses of lay parish ministries.

332 The quotes are from Murnion, *New Parish Ministers,* 11; I have broken up a passage and inserted some qualifying phrases because of trends reported by Murnion and DeLambo in *Parishes and Parish Ministers.*

333 My points are all drawn from Murnion and DeLambo, *Parishes and Parish Ministers,* supplemented by several interviews with Monsignor Murnion.

336 "Instruction on Certain Questions Regarding the Collaboration of the Non-Ordained Faithful in the Sacred Ministry of Priests." This document was issued by no less than eight Vatican offices, a sure sign of its importance.

339 Crespin: Hoge, *First Five Years,* 109.

341 This scenario was stimulated by some of the exercises set out in the fourth part of Cardinal Roger Mahony's pastoral letter on ministry, written in consultation with Los Angeles's priests, *As I Have Done for You* (Liturgy Training Publications, 2000), 29–36; also found in *Origins,* May 4, 2000, 750–52.

347 The selection of bishops is described probably as knowledgeably as any outsider could by Reese in his first chapter of *Archbishop.*

Index